Alan Ellman's

THE BLUE COLLAR INVESTOR

Complete Encyclopedia For Covered Call Writing

Volume 2

A compilation of ninety-six journal articles and one hundred fifty-seven color charts and graphs published since the original version was produced

By Alan Ellman: The Blue Collar Investor

Complete Encyclopedia For Covered Call Writing
Volume 2

10 9 8 7 6 5 4 3 2 1

First Printing: August 2015

ISBN: 978-1-942634-21-8 (paperback)

Printed in the United States of America

Published by Digital Publishing of Florida, Inc.

www.digitaldata-corp.com

My Philosophy of Books

"When I read a finance book I hope to glean two or three new ideas that will enhance my investment success. When I write a finance book my objective is to provide many dozens of ideas to help improve the reader's financial IQ and ensuing success. Only you can decide if I have achieved my goal"

Alan Ellman, on behalf of

Blue Collar Investors all over the world

Dedication

I dedicate this book to my grandsons, Seneca and Jordan, who have added a wonderful dimension to my life I never dreamed possible. A special thank you also to *Thomas the Train*.

Table of Contents

Acknowledgments

When the manager of a baseball team wins the World Series or has any degree of success he is immediately categorized as a great manager. But let's face it, without his team, his coaches, his ownership and a myriad of other support staff, he would simply be just another guy with the love and passion of a great sport.

I, too, have been blessed with an outstanding foundation of support personnel:

My beautiful wife, Linda, my Mom Minnie, my children Jared, Craig, David, Hannah and Aubrey, and my grandchildren, Seneca and Jordan...my A Team.

Barry Bergman is the BCI Director of Research who is responsible for publication of our incredible Premium Stock Reports and also manages our mentoring program.

Adele Bergman has been a valuable member of our BCI team with her assistance during live seminars.

Barbara Karnes is a true genius in so many areas and handles our social media programs and is always there for me when I need guidance.

Darius Wright is our lead "tech guy" who works his magic with video and online graphics and he is there for me in areas when my tech skills fall short.

Gabriel Klavun is our programmer who manages and upgrades the BCI web site and always figures out ways to get us going when the internet lets us down.

Adam Rauch manages our large email database and generates our weekly newsletter to our growing membership. He is always reliable and never missed a mailing.

You, our members: You put BCI on the map. Without our members I would simply be a man with a few ideas and a dream. Because of you that fantasy became a reality.

Thanks to one and all for allowing me to experience the time of my life. I am truly humbled.

Introduction

Education is power. That's the premise of the Blue Collar Investor. When the *Complete Encyclopedia for Covered Call Writing* was published at the end of 2011 and immediately became the best-selling book on this great strategy I realized that eventually there would be a Volume 2. It took me four years to gather the information for the original version and I projected four years down the road and realized that more information would become available, more examples could be provided to clarify certain issues and BCI members would make me aware of tangential topics of interest. I also write weekly newsletter articles for the BCI site as well as for other US and international financial venues. It didn't take a stroke of genius to craft a plan that would allow me to provide new and enhanced information and keep it within the framework of the *Complete Encyclopedia for Covered Call Writing*, a format you have embraced more than I could ever have imagined.

Here was my plan of action: Each time I wrote an article on a particular topic, I placed that material in the appropriate corresponding chapter of the original publication. So, if an article was related to technical analysis, it was placed in Chapter 4- Technical Analysis. If it was related to calculations, it was entered into Chapter 6- Calculations and so on. The result has been ninety-six articles with one hundred fifty-seven color charts and graphs. As I type this introduction, I already have several more articles published that will be placed into Volume 3, a publication for some future date.

This book should be treated as an adjunct to the original. After reading and mastering each chapter in the original *Complete Encyclopedia* (guess it wasn't "complete" after all!) the reader can then read the corresponding chapter in Volume 2. Why not know more than everybody else? Why should the learning process ever end?

This has been, and continues to be, an enlightening situation for me as well. When you suggest a topic to me, it's time to go to work and research the subject. Sure I know much of what is asked, but not everything. So I am focused in on learning just as you are.

I hope you enjoy and benefit from this book. Without your feedback, many of the topics covered would not be included in this publication so you have as much to do about this book as I have (but don't consider yourself my partner…not happening!).

Wishing you a profitable and enjoyable financial future.

Alan

THE BLUE COLLAR INVESTOR

Chapter 1

An Introduction and Preview Examples of Covered Call Writing

Chapter outline

1. Real Life Covered Call Trade with PRLB

Real Life Covered Call Trade with PRLB

Part of our covered call writing education involves looking back on both successful and unsuccessful trades and learning from them. Here is one such example which will highlight a trade I made over a two-month time frame, September and October, 2013, which resulted in a rewarding conclusion.

Proto Labs Inc. Com (NYSE: PRLB) was a stock on our Premium Watch List with outstanding fundamentals and technicals. I sold multiple contracts on this security, but will use one hundred shares and one contract to simplify the math.

The overall trade:

- 9/23/2013: Buy 100 x PRLB at $78.10
- 9/23/2013: Sold 1 x October $80.00 call at $3.30 for an initial one-month return of 4.2%
- 10/8/2013: Buy-to-close the $80.00 call at $0.45 (slightly higher than our 10% guideline…that's why I call it a guideline!)

- 10/14/2013: Sell-to-open the $80.00 call at $1.40 (hitting a double exit strategy) for an additional $95.00 credit per contract ($140.00 – $45.00)
- 10/18/2013: Allow assignment as the stock is trading above $80.00 and there was an upcoming earnings report on 10/31/2013
- 10/19/2013: Shares are sold for $80.00 for an additional profit of $190.00 per contract (purchased at $78.10)
- Total profit = $330.00 + $95.00 + $190.00 = $615.00 per contract = 7.9%, one-month return

Let's take a look at a one-year chart in Figure 1 which included this trade:

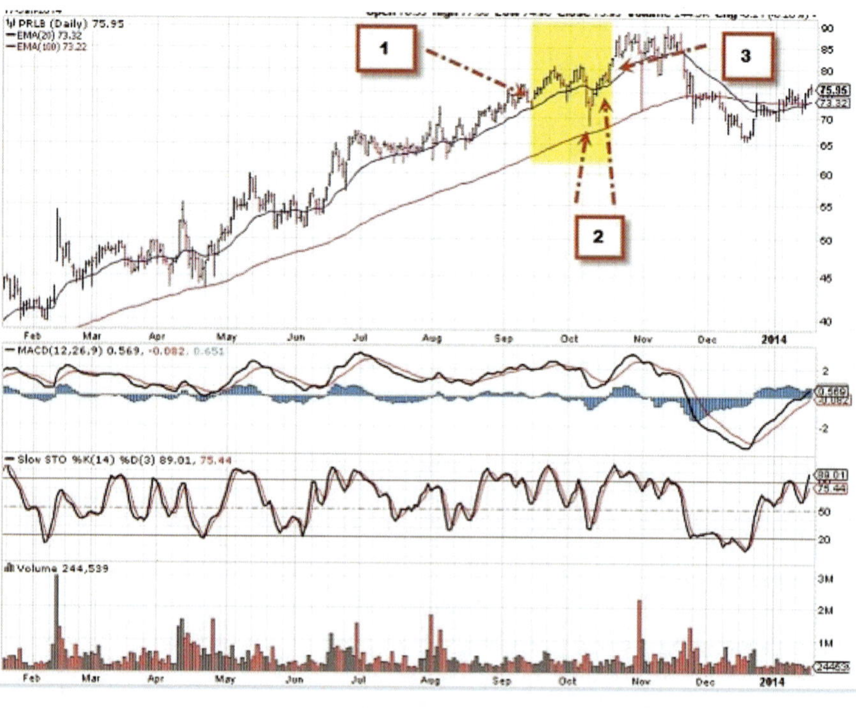

Figure 1- PRLB: One-Year Chart

Please note:

1: Entered trade

2: Hit a double as share price declined and then recovered

3: Allowed assignment as share price was in-the-money at expiration

Let's now take a closer look at the one-month chart shown in Figure 2:

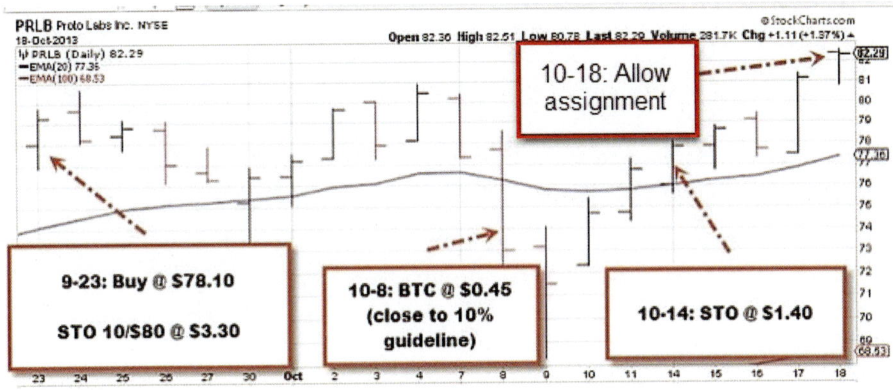

Figure 2- PRLB: One-Month Chart

Summary

Here is a summary of the BCI principles, rules and guidelines used in this successful trade:

- Stock selection using fundamental and technical analysis as well as common sense principles
- Option selection based on market assessment, chart technicals and risk tolerance
- Exit strategy execution using the 20%/10% guidelines
- Expiration Friday decision based on earnings report rule (one of our common sense principles)

Chapter 2

Option Basics

Chapter outline

1. Am I Losing Money when Option Value Increases after Entering a Covered Call Position?
2. Early Exercise: I Don't Want to Sell my AAPL Shares
3. How to Maximize Covered Call Writing Returns by Understanding Time Value and Theta
4. The "Mark" vs. "Marking the Close"
5. "Moneyness" of Call and Put Options: Understanding Strike Prices
6. Profit and Loss Graphs for Covered Call Writing
7. Selling Deep Out-Of-The Money Covered Call Options
8. Weekly Stock Options for Covered Call Writing: Pros and Cons
9. Weekly Options: Standard and Expanded Expirations
10. When and Why will my In-The-Money Strike be Exercised?
11. When Strike Prices Disappear: Contract Adjustments

Am I Losing Money when Option Value Increases after Entering a Covered Call Position?

The risk in covered call writing is in the stock purchased not in the option sold. Sound familiar? It's in all my books and DVD Programs and mentioned in my seminars and webinars. Yet it appears that when we look at our brokerage statements this concept is not true. That is because we see a minus sign after having sold the option and the number adjacent to that minus sign gets larger and larger if the value of the option increases. That leads some investors to believe that if option value increases, there are terrible losses about to be realized…not true.

To explain, let's have a look at Halliburton Company (NYSE: HAL) where the following covered call position was established:

- Buy at $62.00
- Sell the $62.50 call at $1.25
- A 2% initial return is generated
- The price of HAL begins rising after the covered call position is executed

Next, let's have a look at the price action of this option as share price rises (Figure 3):

Figure 3- Chart of the $62.50 Call Option for HAL

As the price of HAL rises to $64.38, the option value moves above $2.00…are we now losing $0.75 per share or $75.00 per contract?

Before we answer that question, let's view the price chart for HAL (Figure 4) which is fueling the rise in option value:

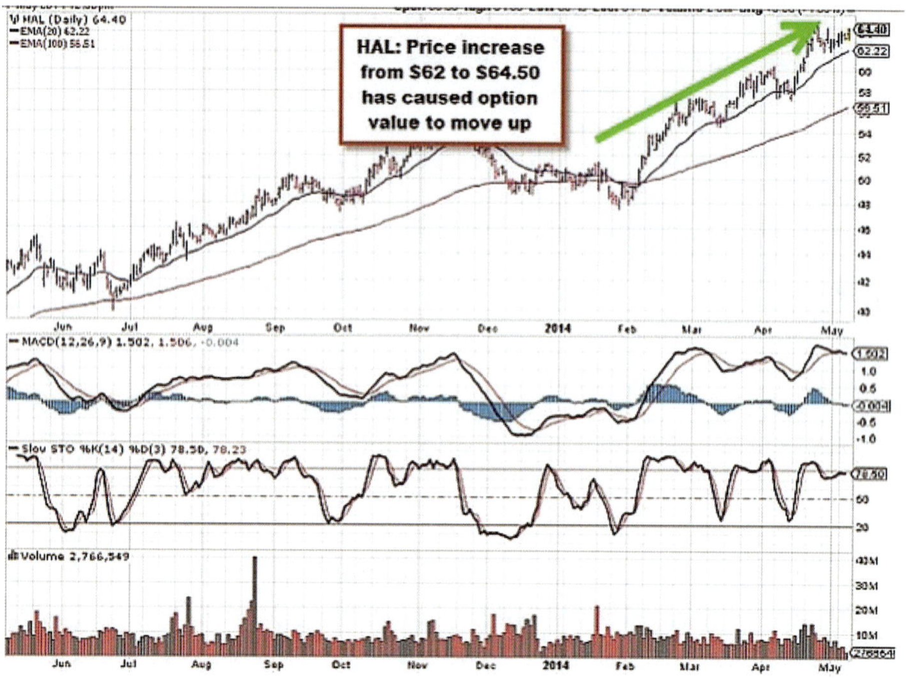

Figure 4- Price Chart for HAL

We have learned from studying the *Greeks* that an option value will change by its delta for every $1.00 increase or decrease in share value. We also know that as a strike moves deeper in-the-money (as this option is doing) the delta moves higher or closer to "1". In this case, the option is nearly $2.00 in-the-money, so the intrinsic value alone is close to $2.00. Therefore, *theta* (time value erosion) is having a lesser impact on option value than is delta.

Are we now losing money on the option side?

NO we are not. The minus signs or brackets displayed in our broker statements are there for accounting reasons and mean that we have an "open" position which in order to close would leave us in a net debit position (a loss). However, the choice to close the position is totally ours to make and will not be executed unless it is in our best interest to do so. For example, we may close the short position if rolling the option on or near expiration Friday which will result in a net credit that meets our goal. Another example where we may close our short position at a higher price than entered is when we execute the mid-contract unwind exit strategy (pages 264 – 271 of the *Complete Encyclopedia* Vol I...). These two scenarios are favorable trades that generate additional cash flow into our portfolios.

Finally, we can take no action at all. If the price of the stock is above the strike and it doesn't make financial sense to close the short position, we allow assignment which means that we have maximized our trade. We received the initial option premium plus any share appreciation from purchase price to the strike and our shares are sold for the price we agreed to sell them for when the trade was initiated. The cash is then used to establish a new covered call position the following contract month. Once the position is closed, the negative (brackets) signs will disappear in our brokerage statements and our option gains will be realized.

Summary

Rising option value is a positive for us despite the negative appearance on our brokerage statements. Our main concern is when share value declines and in that case losses may occur.

Early Exercise: I Don't Want to Sell my AAPL Shares

Covered call writing obligates us to sell our shares to the option buyer at any time up to 4 PM ET on expiration Friday should the buyer choose to exercise those options. That is the definition of *American Style* options, the type we are dealing with when selling options against stocks and exchange-traded funds or ETFs. The buyer is in control unless we buy back the options. Now, we may not want our shares sold and there is so much we can do to prevent exercise from occurring but it is one of the risks we are exposed to as covered call writers. For those of us trading in sheltered accounts, exercise risk is miniscule. For investors trading in non-sheltered accounts there may be tax consequences. It is important to understand all the pros and cons of any investment strategy we are using and to discuss tax issues with our tax advisors.

On February 7th, 2014, Alex wrote to me about the following trade he executed (I will reduce to one-contract statistics):

The trade:

- Buy 100 x AAPL at $502.00 (before the stock split seven-for-one)
- Sell 1 x February $510.00 call
- Stock price currently at $520.00

Alex felt that early exercise was imminent and wanted to *roll up* to retain his shares. His other concern was that because AAPL was experiencing volatility, it would result in a lot of "buying and selling" during the current contract.

Let's, for a moment, change hats and take the position of the option buyer who holds a call contract giving him (her) the right but not the obligation to purchase AAPL at $510.00. At the time, AAPL was trading at $519.68.

Credit for early exercise:

- Buy AAPL at $510.00 per share
- Sell AAPL at $519.68 per share

- Credit calculates to $9.68 per share

Credit for selling the option:

Figure 5 shows the options chain at the time I am writing this article:

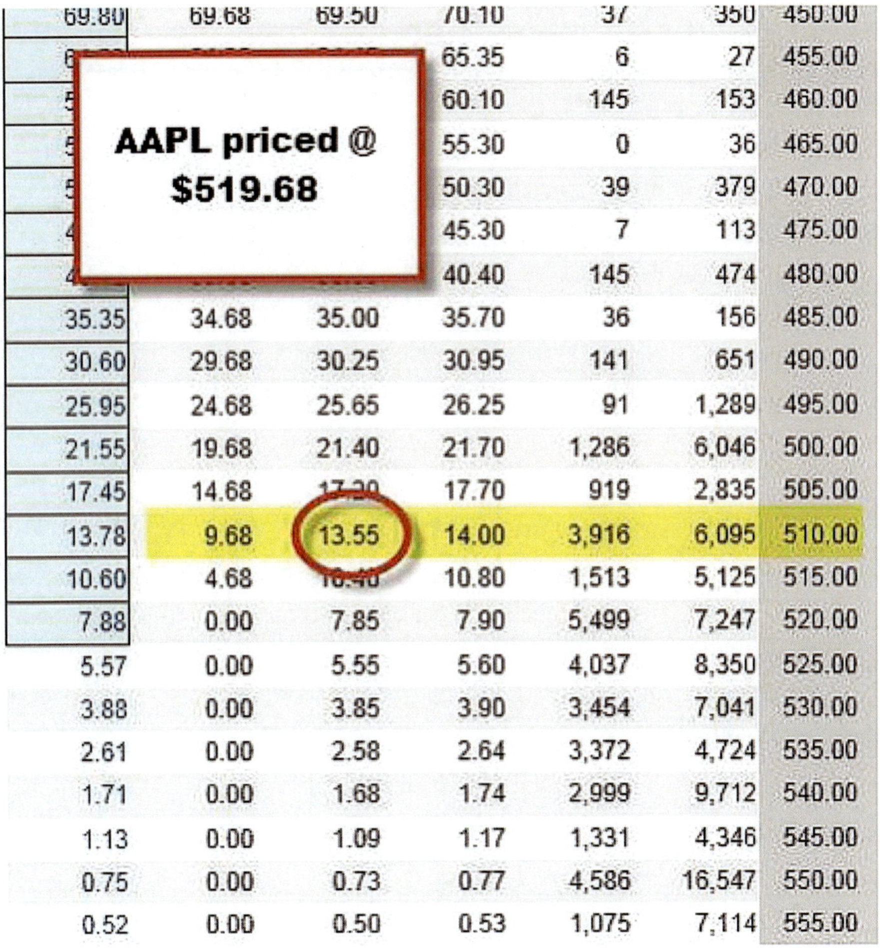

69.80	69.68	69.50	70.10	37	350	450.00
[illegible]	[illegible]	[illegible]	65.35	6	27	455.00
[illegible]	[illegible]	[illegible]	60.10	145	153	460.00
[illegible]	[illegible]	[illegible]	55.30	0	36	465.00
[illegible]	[illegible]	[illegible]	50.30	39	379	470.00
[illegible]	[illegible]	[illegible]	45.30	7	113	475.00
[illegible]	[illegible]	[illegible]	40.40	145	474	480.00
35.35	34.68	35.00	35.70	36	156	485.00
30.60	29.68	30.25	30.95	141	651	490.00
25.95	24.68	25.65	26.25	91	1,289	495.00
21.55	19.68	21.40	21.70	1,286	6,046	500.00
17.45	14.68	17.20	17.70	919	2,835	505.00
13.78	9.68	13.55	14.00	3,916	6,095	510.00
10.60	4.68	10.40	10.80	1,513	5,125	515.00
7.88	0.00	7.85	7.90	5,499	7,247	520.00
5.57	0.00	5.55	5.60	4,037	8,350	525.00
3.88	0.00	3.85	3.90	3,454	7,041	530.00
2.61	0.00	2.58	2.64	3,372	4,724	535.00
1.71	0.00	1.68	1.74	2,999	9,712	540.00
1.13	0.00	1.09	1.17	1,331	4,346	545.00
0.75	0.00	0.73	0.77	4,586	16,547	550.00
0.52	0.00	0.50	0.53	1,075	7,114	555.00

Figure 5- AAPL Options Chain as of 2/7/2014

The published bid is $13.55 per share, $387.00 per contract more than taking the route of early exercise ($13.55 - $9.68). Any educated options buyer would not take the route of early exercise.

The key point to takeaway is that **early exercise captures intrinsic value only, whereas selling the option captures both intrinsic value and time value**.

Aside from the option buyer doing the wrong thing, there is one exception to this rule. When there is a dividend distribution, it may make sense for the option holder to exercise early. **If the dividend about to be distributed is greater than the time value remaining on the option premium it is more likely that early exercise will occur…but not guaranteed**. When this does occur, it will take place the day before the *ex-dividend date* (date you must own the shares to benefit from the dividend distribution). To avoid this small chance of early exercise we must check this ex-date and buy back (or roll) the option prior to the ex-date. I checked the ex-date when Alex wrote me and, as it turned out, it was on February 6th, the day prior to his email so this was a non-factor.

Summary:

Early exercise is very rare but possible. The main reason it will occur is investor error or dividend distribution. Understanding the relationship between option time value and dividend amount along with checking the ex-dates will generally allow us to avoid early exercise. Although small, the risk will always exist for early exercise.

How to Maximize Covered Call Writing Returns by Understanding Time Value and Theta

Mastering the concepts of the time value of our option premiums and how theta impacts our option profits will help elevate our returns to the highest possible levels. Let's first define these terms:

Definitions

Time value: The portion of the option premium that is attributable to the amount of time remaining until expiration as well as the volatility of the underlying security. It is the amount above any intrinsic value (intrinsic value is the amount the strike price is in-the-money).

Theta: An estimate of how much the theoretical value of an option will decline with the passage of one calendar day.

Roll of the Greeks

As option sellers, we capture the entire premium once the trade is executed. The option buyers now own a decaying asset that is losing time value every day. Once again, the cash generated from the sale of the call options we sell is in our account and the amount we capture cannot be diminished. Another point to remember is that the initial profits generated from the sale of the call options is measured in time value only, not intrinsic value if we sold in-the-money strikes. Therefore, if we bought a stock for $32.00 and sold the $30.00 call for $3.00, of that $3.00, $2.00 is intrinsic value (NOT profit) and $1.00 is time value, our initial profit.

Since our motivation is to generate monthly cash flow in a low-risk fashion, let's focus in on maximizing time value by avoiding the impact of theta. One of the characteristics we need to be aware of is that time value erosion (theta) is logarithmic in nature NOT linear especially for near-the-money strikes. This means that the time value component of our one-month option premium starts to erode slowly at first and then more rapidly as we approach expiration Friday as shown in Figure 6:

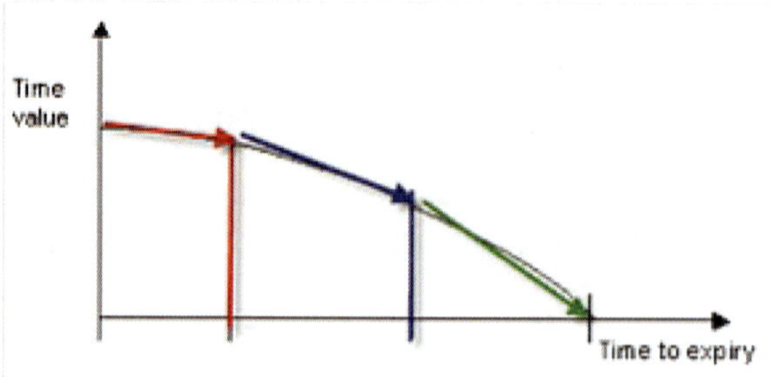

Figure 6- Theta: Time Value Erosion of our Option Premiums

Taking advantage of theta

Sell the options early in the one-month contract: By doing this we will be avoiding the impact of the logarithmic nature of the time value erosion of our options which start declining in value slowly but then "fall off a cliff" later in the contract.

Weeklys vs. Monthlys: There are pros and cons to both but from the perspective of time value and theta let's view the one-week (Figure 7) and four-week (Figure 8) options chains for HAL captured in the first trading week of August, 2014:

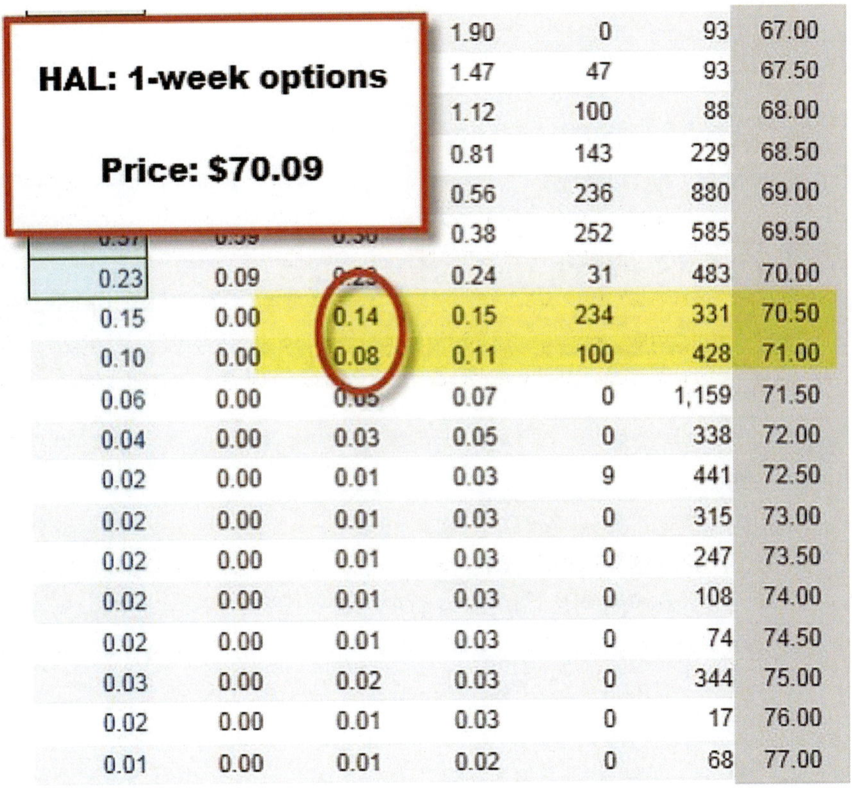

[illegible]	[illegible]	[illegible]	1.90	0	93	67.00
[illegible]	[illegible]	[illegible]	1.47	47	93	67.50
[illegible]	[illegible]	[illegible]	1.12	100	88	68.00
[illegible]	[illegible]	[illegible]	0.81	143	229	68.50
[illegible]	[illegible]	[illegible]	0.56	236	880	69.00
[illegible]	[illegible]	[illegible]	0.38	252	585	69.50
0.23	0.09	[illegible]	0.24	31	483	70.00
0.15	0.00	0.14	0.15	234	331	70.50
0.10	0.00	0.08	0.11	100	428	71.00
0.06	0.00	[illegible]	0.07	0	1,159	71.50
0.04	0.00	0.03	0.05	0	338	72.00
0.02	0.00	0.01	0.03	9	441	72.50
0.02	0.00	0.01	0.03	0	315	73.00
0.02	0.00	0.01	0.03	0	247	73.50
0.02	0.00	0.01	0.03	0	108	74.00
0.02	0.00	0.01	0.03	0	74	74.50
0.03	0.00	0.02	0.03	0	344	75.00
0.02	0.00	0.01	0.03	0	17	76.00
0.01	0.00	0.01	0.02	0	68	77.00

Figure 7 - HAL: One-Week Options Chain

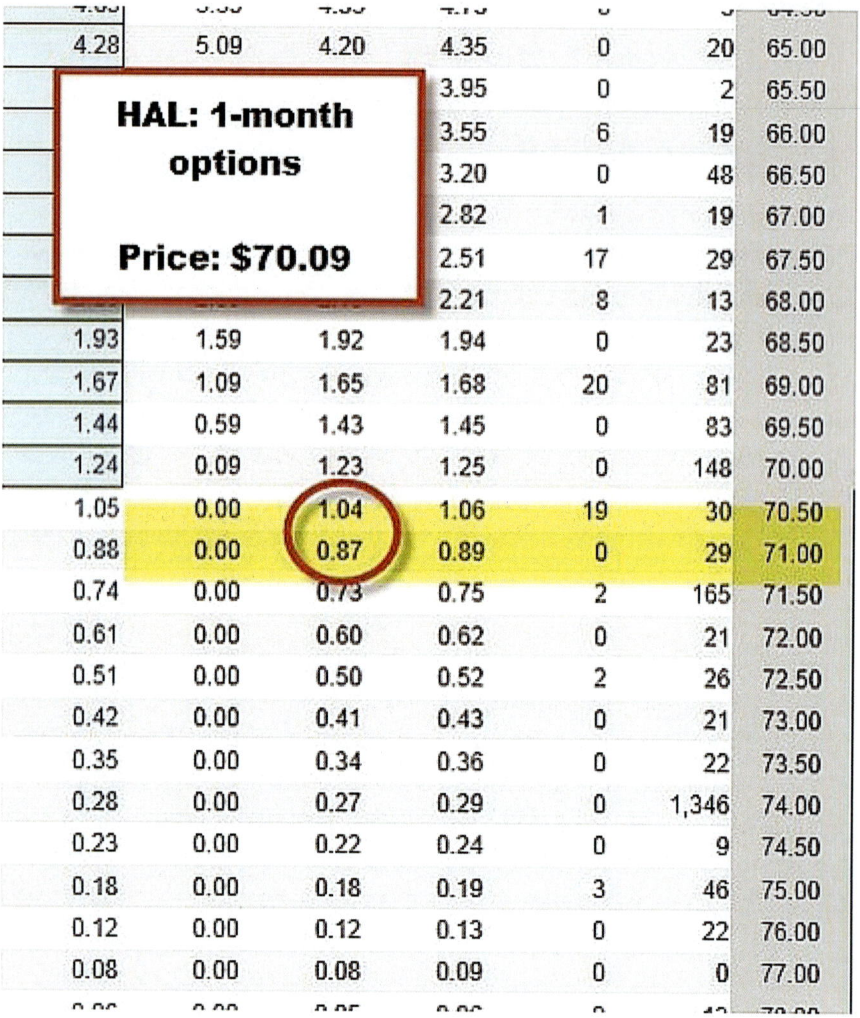

4.28	5.09	4.20	4.35	0	20	65.00
			3.95	0	2	65.50
			3.55	6	19	66.00
			3.20	0	48	66.50
			2.82	1	19	67.00
			2.51	17	29	67.50
			2.21	8	13	68.00
1.93	1.59	1.92	1.94	0	23	68.50
1.67	1.09	1.65	1.68	20	81	69.00
1.44	0.59	1.43	1.45	0	83	69.50
1.24	0.09	1.23	1.25	0	148	70.00
1.05	0.00	1.04	1.06	19	30	70.50
0.88	0.00	0.87	0.89	0	29	71.00
0.74	0.00	0.73	0.75	2	165	71.50
0.61	0.00	0.60	0.62	0	21	72.00
0.51	0.00	0.50	0.52	2	26	72.50
0.42	0.00	0.41	0.43	0	21	73.00
0.35	0.00	0.34	0.36	0	22	73.50
0.28	0.00	0.27	0.29	0	1,346	74.00
0.23	0.00	0.22	0.24	0	9	74.50
0.18	0.00	0.18	0.19	3	46	75.00
0.12	0.00	0.12	0.13	0	22	76.00
0.08	0.00	0.08	0.09	0	0	77.00

Figure 8 - HAL: Four-Week (One-Month) Options Chain

If time value were linear (straight line) then we would expect the option value of the one-week options to be 25% the value of the four-week option values but that is not the case:

$70.50 call: $0.14/$1.04 equals 13.5%

$71.00 call: $0.08/$0.87 equals 9.2%

Now <u>there are exceptions to these general rules</u> when the market is anticipating a more volatile movement in share price in the near-term due to some upcoming event or due to general market volatility. However, understanding how theta impacts time value in most cases is an important concept to master in order to achieve the highest possible covered call writing returns.

Conclusion

Understanding the concept of how theta impacts the time value of our option premiums teaches us to *enter one-month contracts early in the contract* and explains one of the possible advantages of Monthlys over Weeklys (there are pros and cons to Weeklys but that's a topic for another day). Please note that *when the market is anticipating more near-term volatility in a security, selling weeklys may result in higher annualized returns.*

The "Mark" vs. "Marking the Close"

Education is what makes covered call writers in the BCI community an elite group of retail investors. In 2014, I produced an *Ask Alan* video titled *What Role does the Mark Play in our Covered Call Writing Decisions?* A few members inquired if the mark was related to a term they had heard named *marking the close*. This article will define the terms, explain the differences and show some examples.

The Mark

Let's start with the more recognizable term, the *mark*: This is the mid-point between the *bid-ask spread*. If the *"bid"* is $3.00 and the *"ask"* is $3.40, the mark is $3.20. In our covered call writing strategy we use the mark as a guideline for *playing (negotiating) the bid-ask spread*. Let's view a real-life example: Figure 9 is the options chain for PRLB:

PRLB: $64.65

Calls						Aug 13
Last	Intrinsic Value	Bid	Ask	Vol	Open Interest	**Strike**
34.65				0	0	30.00
29.70				0	0	35.00
24.75				0	0	40.00
19.95				0	0	45.00
15.40	14.69	15.20	15.60	0	5	50.00
11.20	9.69	11.00	11.40	0	3	55.00
7.70	4.69	7.60	7.80	0	24	60.00
4.85	0.00	4.70	5.00	4	121	65.00
2.85	0.00	2.75	2.95	7	124	70.00
1.52	0.00	1.45	1.60	0	33	75.00
0.77	0.00	0.70	0.85	0	11	80.00
0.38	0.00	0.30	0.45	0	1	85.00
0.20	0.00	0.15	0.25	0	0	90.00

Figure 9- PRLB Options Chain

For the $65.00 call options, the bid-ask spread is $0.30 and the mark is at $4.85. When placing our *limit order* to sell our covered call options, we slightly favor the market maker and may place a limit order slightly below the mark, say at $4.80. If executed, this puts $10.00 per contract of additional cash into our pockets over the published bid of $4.70. Agreed this is not a windfall but it does add up over the years and is money better in our pockets than in those of the gazillionnaire market-makers. More information on playing the bid-ask spread can be found on pages 223 – 227 in Volume 1 of the *Complete Encyclopedia for Covered Call Writing*.

Marking the close

This is an illegal act, usually by fund managers, of buying a large number of shares of a specific security at the end of a quarter at a much higher price than the current market value. This will drive up the value of the stock and make the fund look more successful in the eyes of its investors. This is also known as *portfolio pumping*. The *Wall Street Journal* did a study that found that on the last trading day of a quarter there was a substantial number of stocks that beat the market by more than 5% and then trailed it by more than 3% the next trading day. This stat showed up 23% more on the final day of a quarter than any other trading day in a quarter. Figure 10 displays a real-life example with Iridex Corp. (NASDAQ: IRIX) during the last trading day of the second quarter, 2012:

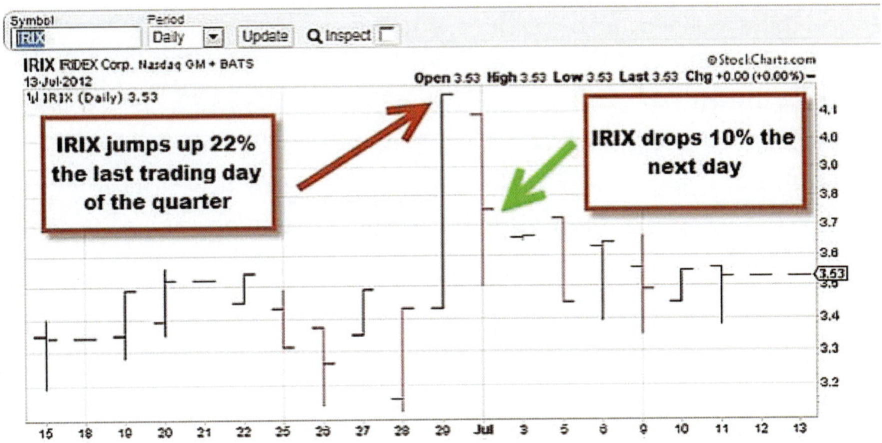

Figure 10- Marking the Close with IRIX

IRIX didn't break through the $4.00 level until October, 2012. The SEC and FINRA are well aware of this practice but it is very difficult to measure and even harder to prove.

Conclusion

The *mark* and *marking the close* are two completely different concepts. We use the mark as a guide for retail investors to negotiate a better bid price when selling covered call and put options. Some fund managers illegally mark the close to make their holdings appear more successful to their investors. That being said, most fund managers are ethical players who abide by the rules.

"Moneyness" of Call and Put Options: Understanding Strike Prices

Strike price selection is an essential aspect of options trading basics and options calculations. There are three types of strike prices for both put and call options: *in-the-money*, *at-the-money* (and the closely related *near-the-money*) and *out-of-the-money*. *Moneyness* tells option holders whether exercising will lead to a profit. Moneyness looks at the value of an option if you were to exercise it right now (from the perspective of an option holder). A loss would signify the option is out-of-the-money, while a gain would mean that it's in-the-money. At-the-money means that you will break even upon exercise. In this article, I will show examples of the three types of strikes and the moneyness of each as they relate to put and call options.

Hypothetical example

Let's assume the price of a stock is $22.50. Here's the easy part first: The $22.50 strike price would be **at-the-money** for both puts and calls. If the option holder (buyer) exercised the option and bought or sold the stock for $22.50, it would represent a breakeven situation compared to the current market value of $22.50.

Next, we will evaluate the $20.00 strike price. For call options this strike price is **in-the-money** because if the call was exercised, the call buyer would then buy the shares at $20.00 and can sell those shares at market for $22.50, generating a profit of $2.50 per share. The amount that the strike price is in-the-money is known as *intrinsic value*. For put options, however, the $20 strike is **out-of-the-money** because the holder has the right to sell the shares for $20.00, below market value.

Looking at the $25.00 strike price, the call holder has the right to buy the shares for $25.00, well above market value and therefore with no inherent or intrinsic value. For call options this strike is out-of-the-money. For put options, however, the $25.00 strike is in-the-money because the holder of the put has the right to sell his shares for $25.00, well above market value of $22.50. This option then has $2.50 of intrinsic value. **The moneyness of in-the-money and out-of-the-money strikes is inversely related for calls and puts**. A reliable way to determine the moneyness of an option is to ask this question: If I am the holder of the option, am I better off exercising the option or buying or selling the stock at market. If you are better off exercising then the strike price is in-the-money and has intrinsic or inherent value..

Example of calculating moneyness for call options using the Ellman Calculator *(get a free copy using the "free resources" link at the top black bar of the Blue Collar web pages: www.thebluecollarinvestor.com)*

RETURN ON OPTION (ROO) CALCULATOR - MULTIPLE STOCKS

Stock Name or Symbol	Stock $/sh	Option $/sh	Strike $	Expires	Intrinsic	Upside	Breakeven	ROO	Up Potential	Down Protect
BCI	$22.50	$3.00	$20.00	09/20/14	$ 2.50	$ -	$ 19.50	2.5%	0.0%	11.1%
BCI	$22.50	$ 2.00	$ 22.50	09/20/14	$ -	$ -	$ 20.50	8.9%	0.0%	0.0%
BCI	$22.50	$1.00	$25.00	09/20/14	$ -	$ 2.50	$ 21.50	4.4%	11.1%	0.0%

Call Moneyness:

$20 strike: ITM
$22.50 strike: ATM
$25 strike: OTM

Figure 11- Call Options-Calculating Moneyness

Each strike has its benefits:

- $20.00 in-the-money: Offers 11.1% protection of the initial option profit (ROO or 2.5%). I favor these in bear or volatile markets

- $22.50 at-the-money: Offers the highest initial returns (ROO or 8.9%) but no upside potential or downside protection of the ROO
- $25.00 out-of-the-money: Offers a nice initial return (4.4%) and the potential for another 11.1% if share value appreciates to the $25.00 strike

Example of calculating <u>moneyness for put options</u>

THE BCI P-C-P SYSTEM CALCULATOR (ver.1.0)

SELLING CASH SECURED PUT (CSP) LEG...

TRADE DATE (mm/dd/yyyy)	08/28/14	08/28/14	08/28/14
STOCK SYMBOL	BCI	BCI	BCI
CURRENT PRICE ($xxx.xx)	$22.50	$22.50	$22.50
EXPIRATION DATE (mm/dd/yyyy)	09/20/14	09/20/14	09/20/14
PUT STRIKE ($xxx.xx)	$20.00	$22.50	$25.00
PUT PREMIUM ($xxx.xx)	$1.00	$2.00	$3.00
RETURN ON PUT OPTION (ROO %) IF UNEXERCISED	5.26%	9.76%	13.64%
STOCK COST BASIS (IF EXERCISED) / BREAK-EVEN ($)	$19.00	$20.50	$22.00
% PURCHASE DISCOUNT IF EXERCISED (%)	15.56%	8.89%	2.22%
CASH REQUIRED PER CONTRACT ($)	$1,900.00	$2,050.00	$2,200.00
NUMBER OF DAYS IN THE TRADE	23	23	23
ANN. RETURN ON OPTION (ROO) IF UNEXERCISED (%)	83.52%	154.83%	216.40%

<u>Put Moneyness</u>

$20: OTM
$22.50: ATM
$25: ITM

Figure 12- Calculating Moneyness for Put Options

Each strike has its benefits:

- $20.00 out-of-the-money: Excellent initial return (5.26%) if unexercised and opportunity to purchase at a 15.56% discount from current market value if exercised

- $22.50 at-the-money: Generates a higher initial return (9.76%) than the $20.00 put and an opportunity to purchase the stock at an 8.89% discount from current market value if exercised
- $25.00 in-the-money: Offers the highest initial return if unexercised (13.64%) and an opportunity to buy the stock at a 2.22% discount from current market value if exercised

Summary

The moneyness of in-the-money and out-of-the-money strikes are inversely related for calls and puts. Each strike offers certain advantages that should be taken advantage of depending on market conditions, chart technicals, strategy goals and personal risk tolerance.

Profit and Loss Graphs for Covered Call Writing

Covered call writing, like most investment strategies, has a certain risk/reward profile relating to potential profits and losses. A *profit and loss graph* is a graphical representation of the potential outcomes of this or other strategies. Let's first have a look at a generic profit and loss graph shown in Figure 13:

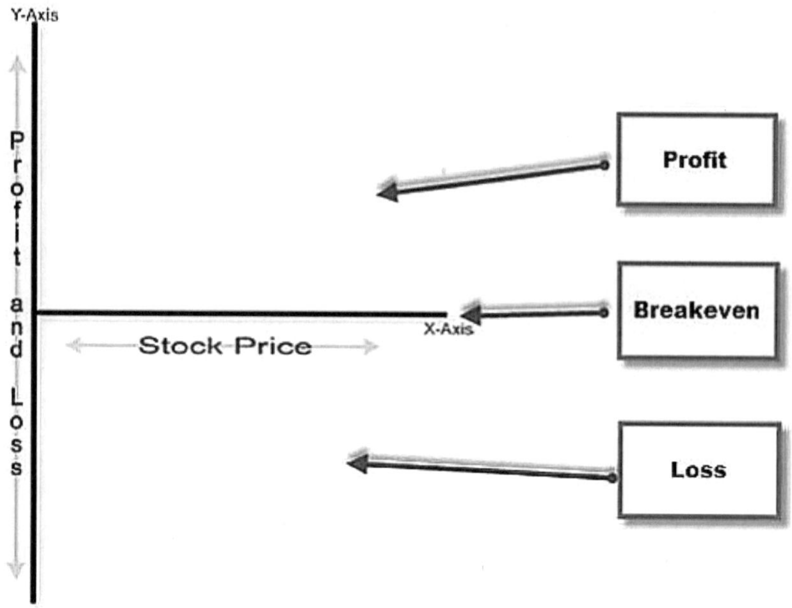

Figure 13- Components of a Profit and Loss Graph

Components of a profit and loss graph

- Vertical axis represents the amount of profit or loss
- Horizontal axis ($0) represents the *breakeven point*
- Above the horizontal is profit
- Below the horizontal is loss

Example of a profit and loss graph for covered call writing

In this hypothetical we will buy a stock at $50.00 and sell the $50.00 call option for $1.00, generating $100.00 per contract (less commissions). This would represent a 2% return ($100.00/$5000.00). Here is the graphic shown in Figure 14:

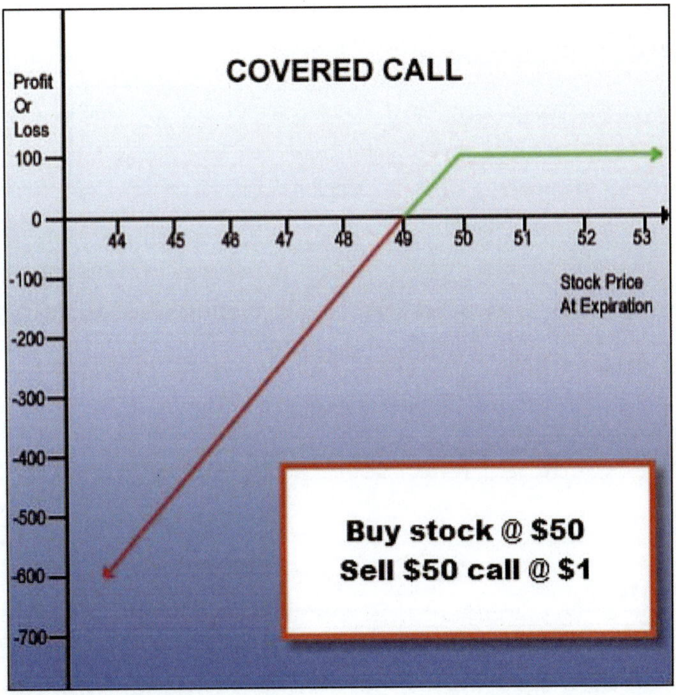

Figure 14- Profit and Loss Graph for Covered Call Writing for a $50.00 Stock and a $1.00 Call Option

Pros and cons demonstrated

Every strategy has its advantages and disadvantages and the profit and loss graph gives us an outstanding depiction of those pros and cons for covered call writing:

- We immediately have an initial gain of $100.00 upon entering our position
- We have a guaranteed profit as long as share price remains above $49.00
- We have downside protection of our investment
- Our profit potential is limited by the strike price ($50.00)
- ***Loss potential is the stock price minus the option premium, $49.00 per share in this case

Loss potential for covered call writing as shown by the profit and loss graph

When viewing the profit and loss graph for covered call writing a new or uninformed investor may reject the strategy because the upside is limited but the downside appears unlimited. This conclusion assumes that the investor will take no action if the trade turns against him. This is a strategy that should never be employed unless an appropriate arsenal of exit strategies is in place for all possible scenarios. This will include share price depreciation, share price appreciation, dividend distributions, avoiding assignment and contract adjustments. Position management is one of the three essential skills required when selling call and put options.

Conclusion

A profit and loss graph for covered call writing will show the advantages and disadvantages of this strategy and particularly highlight the need for preparation and execution of exit strategy opportunities when indicated. Mastering position management will mitigate the potential losses and elevate our profits to the highest possible levels.

Selling Deep Out-Of–The-Money Covered Call Options

Strike price selection is a critical concept needed to master covered call writing. Selling in-the-money strikes is the most conservative approach to this strategy and selling out-of-the-money strikes is the most bullish. We use the latter when the overall market is bullish and chart technicals are bullish and confirming. Once we have decided that a bullish approach is indicated the next decision is how far out-of-the-money should we go when selecting our call strike prices.

Let's first review the pros and cons of a deep out-of-the-money call vs. an out-of-the-money call with a lower strike price:

Advantages of deeper out-of-the-money calls

- More room for share appreciation
- Less likely to be assigned
- The *net effective sale price* (NESP: call strike price + call premium) is higher

Disadvantages of deeper out-of-the-money calls

Lower call premiums

Lower final returns if share price remains static

If we decide to sell deep out-of-the-money strikes we must be bullish on the overall market and the stock itself. The way to determine how far out-of-the-money to go is to first set our investment goals for the month. My personal goal in normal market conditions for a one-month initial return is two to four percent for stocks and one to two percent for exchange-traded funds. Of course, each investor can tweak these guidelines based on their personal risk tolerance. The deeper out-of-the-money we go, the closer to the two percent figure we get (and then below) and the further from the four percent stat. Let's take a look at a real-life example (Figure 15) using one of the stocks on our *Premium Stock List*: YNDX:

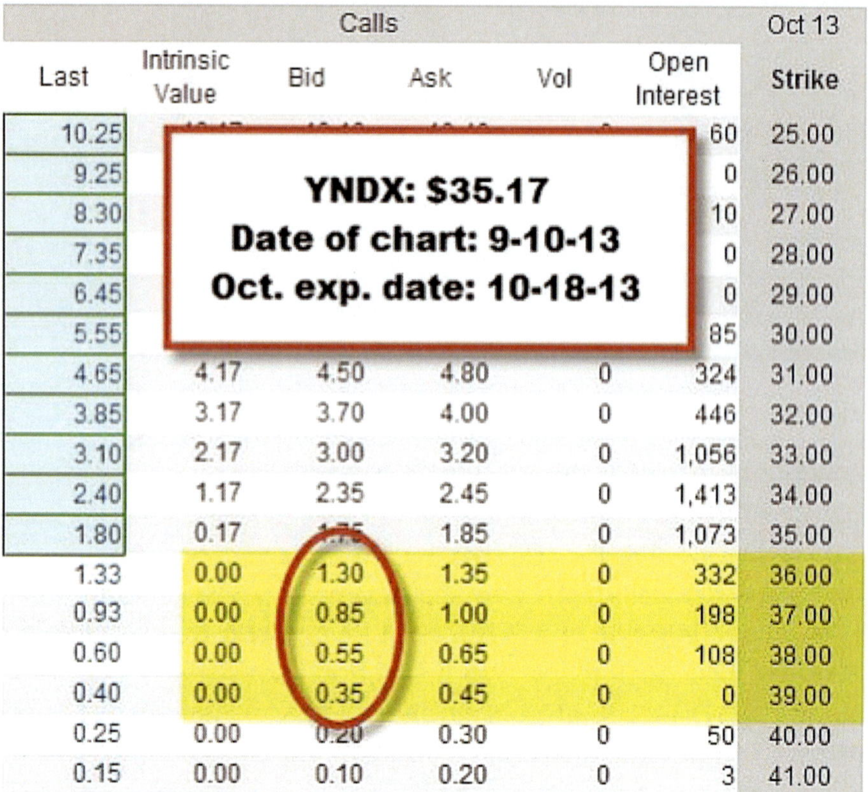

Calls						Oct 13
Last	Intrinsic Value	Bid	Ask	Vol	Open Interest	Strike
10.25					60	25.00
9.25					0	26.00
8.30					10	27.00
7.35					0	28.00
6.45					0	29.00
5.55					85	30.00
4.65	4.17	4.50	4.80	0	324	31.00
3.85	3.17	3.70	4.00	0	446	32.00
3.10	2.17	3.00	3.20	0	1,056	33.00
2.40	1.17	2.35	2.45	0	1,413	34.00
1.80	0.17	1.75	1.85	0	1,073	35.00
1.33	0.00	1.30	1.35	0	332	36.00
0.93	0.00	0.85	1.00	0	198	37.00
0.60	0.00	0.55	0.65	0	108	38.00
0.40	0.00	0.35	0.45	0	0	39.00
0.25	0.00	0.20	0.30	0	50	40.00
0.15	0.00	0.10	0.20	0	3	41.00

Figure 15 - Options Chain for YNDX

Please note the following:

- On 9/10/2013 YNDX was trading at $35.17
- We will look at the October 18th expiration, five weeks away
- We will evaluate four out-of-the-money strikes: $36.00, $37.00, $38.00 and $39.00
- Bid prices range from $1.30 down to $0.35

Next we will enter the options chain information into the "multiple tab" of the Ellman Calculator as shown in Figure 16:

RETURN ON OPTION (ROO) CALCULATOR - MULTIPLE STOCKS

Stock Name or Symbol	Stock $/sh	Option $/sh	Strike $	Expires	Intrisic	Upside	Breakeven	ROO	Up Potential	Down Protect
YNDX	$35.17	$1.30	$ 36.00		$ -	$ 0.83	$ 33.87	3.7%	2.4%	0.0%
YNDX	$35.17	$0.85	$37.00		$ -	$ 1.83	$ 34.32	2.4%	5.2%	0.0%
YNDX	$35.17	$ 0.55	38		$ -	$ 2.83	$ 34.62	1.6%	8.0%	0.0%
YNDX	$35.17	$0.35	$39.00		$ -	$ 3.83	$ 34.82	1.0%	10.9%	0.0%

Figure 16- Ellman Calculator: Multiple Tab for YNDX

The two strikes that meet our criteria of a two to four percent initial return (ROO column) are the $36.00 (3.7%) and $37.00 (2.4%) strikes. The $38.00 strike just misses at 1.6% but can be used at the investor's discretion. The same holds for the $39.00 (1%) strike. The maximum returns for the two strikes that do meet our initial criteria are 6.1% for the $36.00 strike and 7.6% for the $37.00 strike (when adding in upside potential or price appreciation to the strike price). The ultimate decision rests with the individual investor. For me, I would opt for the $37.00 strike in a bull market environment and be happy with a 2.4%, five-week return and thrilled with a 7.6% five-week return. As always, we must follow our exit strategy guidelines once these positions are entered.

Conclusion

Deep out-of-the-money strikes can be used in a bull market environment with strong chart technicals. The higher the strike selected, the lower the initial return but the higher the maximum return possibility (net effective sale price). Strike selection should be based on sound fundamental, technical and common sense principles along with our personal risk tolerance comfort level.

Weekly Stock Options for Covered Call Writing: Pros and Cons

Weekly options (*Weeklys*) are becoming an attractive choice for many covered call writers. These are options that expire every week rather than the more conventional monthly options which expire on the third Friday of the month at 4 PM ET. **Weeklys are listed each week except that no new Weeklys are listed that would expire during the expiration week for standard options** (the third Friday of each month), nor would they be listed if they would expire on the same date as a Quarterly option on the same underlying security. Other than SPX Weeklys (S&P 500 as the underlying index which are AM settled), closing times for Weekly options match the closing times for standard, non-Weeklys on the same underlying stock or exchange-traded fund (4 PM ET or PM settled).

On Nov 15, 2013, U.S. options exchanges expanded the listing of weekly contracts from one expiration week to five straight weeks for a group of the most-actively traded options on stocks and exchange-traded funds. These security options are part of the ***expanded** Weekly options program* compared to the original *standard Weekly options program*. Most securities that appear on the BCI Premium Stock and ETF Reports are part of the expanded program. Both of our premium reports (stock and ETF) highlight which securities have Weekly options associated with them.

Figure 17 shows a partial list of exchange-traded funds (ETFs) with Weeklys as well as their participation in the standard and expanded programs:

Ticker	New?	Name (* Indicates weekly also trades on C2)	Product Typ	List Date	Standard Weekly	Expanded Weekly
OEX		S&P 100 Index (American style)	Index, pm-settled, cash	20140619		
XEO		S&P 100 Index (European style)	Index, pm-settled, cash	20140619		
SPX**		S&P 500 Index	Index, pm-settled, cash	20140619		
DJX		Dow Jones Industrial Average	Index, am-settled, cash	20140619	X	
NDX		Nasdaq-100 Index	Index, am-settled, cash	20140619	X	X
RUT		Russell 2000 Index	Index, am-settled, cash	20140619	X	X
AGQ		ProShares Ultra Silver	ETF	20140619	X	X
DIA		SPDR Dow Jones Ind Av ETF Trust *	ETF	20140619	X	X
DUST		Daily Gold Miners Bear 3x Shares	ETF	20140619	X	X
DXJ		Wisdom JPN Hedged EQ Fund	ETF	20140619	X	X
EEM		iShares MSCI Emerging Markets Index*	ETF	20140619	X	X
EFA		iShares MSCI EAFE Index Fund *	ETF	20140619	X	X
EPI		Wisdom Tree India Earnings Fund	ETF	20140619	X	X
EWJ		iShares MSCI Japan Index Fund *	ETF	20140619	X	
EWW		iShares MSCI Mexico Capped ETF*	ETF	20140619	X	X
EWZ		iShares MSCI Brazil Capped ETF*	ETF	20140619	X	X
FAS		Direxionshares Daily Financial Bull 3X Shares *	ETF	20140619	X	X
FAZ		Direxionshares Daily Financial Bear 3X Shares *	ETF	20140619	X	X
FXE		Currency Shares Euro Trust *	ETF	20140619	X	X
FXI		Ishares FTSE/Xinhua China Index Fund *	ETF	20140619	X	X
FXY		Currency Shares Japanese Yen Trust	ETF	20140619	X	X
GDXJ		Market Vectors Junior Gold Miners ETF	ETF	20140619	X	X

Figure 17- ETFs with Weeklys

Note that EWJ (highlighted in the yellow row) is part of the standard Weekly program but not part of the expanded Weekly program.

Advantages of Weeklys

- Annualized returns can be higher in some cases
- Can avoid exposure over weekends
- Can generate greater premium as earnings report

dates are approached and trade up to the week before earnings and again after earnings is reported

Disadvantages of Weeklys

- The pool of stocks with Weeklys is much smaller than those with Monthlys
- Management is much more time-consuming as "rolling" possibilities come up every week
- Less time for exit strategy execution ("hitting a double", "mid-contract unwind" etc.)
- **Quadruple the number and amount of commissions**
- Lower option liquidity
- Wider bid-ask spreads leading to less favorable price executions

There are many ways to make money in the stock market and using Weeklys may be appropriate for some investors. My personal preference is still Monthlys but encourage those interested in Weeklys to paper-trade with them to see which time frame leads to the greatest success.

Weekly Options: Standard and Expanded Expirations

Selling one-month options is a core principle in the BCI methodology for covered call writing. As interest in stock options has been growing significantly so have the number and type of options products available. It's all about supply and demand. Over the past several years we have seen the number of securities associated with options grow dramatically as well as the development of new products such as *Weeklys* and *Mini Options*. In this article I will focus on Weeklys, options with weekly expirations.

Weeklys are options that provide expirations every week. *Standard Weeklys* are listed on Thursdays and expire on the following Friday. A weekly is not listed if it expires on the third Friday of the month, the date that monthly options expire. Most recently, a new program of Weeklys has been initiated, called *expanded Weeklys*, where trading is permitted in up to five consecutive weekly option expirations for stocks, ETFs, ETNs (exchange-traded notes) and indexes. In Figure 18, we see a screenshot of weekly expirations available for both standard and expanded Weekly programs:

Standard Weeklys Available Expirations:	6/5/15	6/12/15			
Expanded Weeklys Available Expirations:	6/5/15	6/12/15	6/26/15	7/2/15	7/10/15

Figure 18- Standard and Expanded Weekly Options

As of 6/4/2015:

- Standard Weeklys available (top row): 6/5/2015 (about to expire) and 6/12/2015
- Expanded Weeklys available (second row): 6/5/2015, 6/12/2015,6/26/2015,7/2/2015,and7/10/2015

As of December, 2013, the BCI team expanded the *Premium Watch Lists* to include those stocks that have passed our rigorous fundamental, technical and common sense screens that also have Weeklys available. This information is located mid-report in the *running list* as shown in Figure 19:

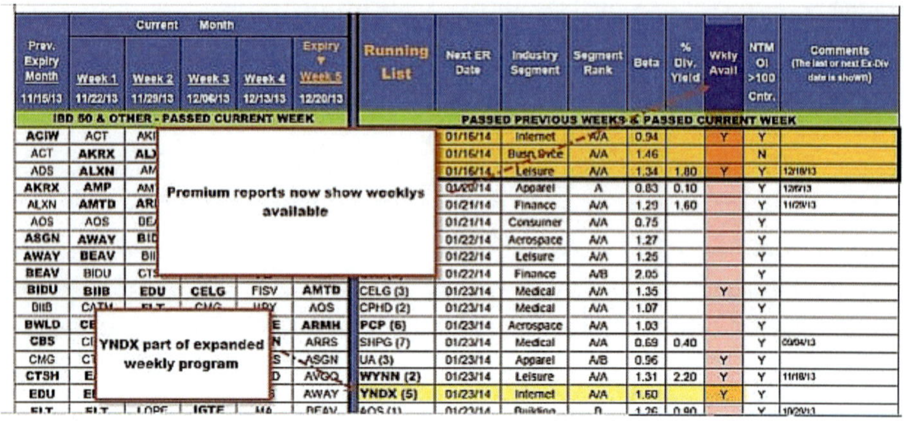

Prev. Expiry Month 11/15/13	Current Month Week 1 11/22/13	Week 2 11/29/13	Week 3 12/06/13	Week 4 12/13/13	Expiry Week 5 12/20/13	Running List	Next ER Date	Industry Segment	Segment Rank	Beta	% Div. Yield	Wkly Avail	NTM OI >100 Cntr.	Comments (The last or next Ex-Div date is shown)
IBD 50 & OTHER - PASSED CURRENT WEEK						PASSED PREVIOUS WEEKS & PASSED CURRENT WEEK								
ACIW	ACT						01/16/14	Internet	A/A	0.94		Y	Y	
ACT	AKRX						01/16/14	Busn Svce	A/A	1.46			N	
ADS	ALXN						01/16/14	Leisure	A/A	1.34	1.80	Y	Y	12/18/13
AKRX	AMP						01/20/14	Apparel	A	0.83	0.10		Y	12/6/13
ALXN	AMTD						01/21/14	Finance	A/A	1.29	1.60		Y	11/29/13
AOS	AOS						01/21/14	Consumer	A/A	0.75			Y	
ASGN	AWAY						01/22/14	Aerospace	A/A	1.27			Y	
AWAY	BEAV						01/22/14	Leisure	A/A	1.25			Y	
BEAV	BIDU						01/22/14	Finance	A/B	2.05			Y	
BIDU	BIIB	EDU	CELG	FISV	AMTD	CELG (3)	01/23/14	Medical	A/A	1.35		Y	Y	
BIIB					AOS	CPHD (2)	01/23/14	Medical	A/A	1.07			Y	
BWLD					ARMH	PCP (6)	01/23/14	Aerospace	A/A	1.03			Y	
CBS					ARRS	SHPG (7)	01/23/14	Medical	A/A	0.69	0.40		Y	09/04/13
CMG					ASGN	UA (3)	01/23/14	Apparel	A/B	0.96		Y	Y	
CTSH					AVGO	WYNN (2)	01/23/14	Leisure	A/A	1.31	2.20	Y	Y	11/18/13
EDU					AWAY	YNDX (5)	01/23/14	Internet	A/A	1.60		Y	Y	

Figure 19- Weeklys and the Blue Collar Premium Watch List

The column highlighted in pink lists the stocks in our report that also have Weeklys associated with them (a "Y" indicates yes for weeklys). I highlighted YNDX in the yellow row. Let's have a look at the January, 2014 options chain for YNDX demonstrated in Figure 20:

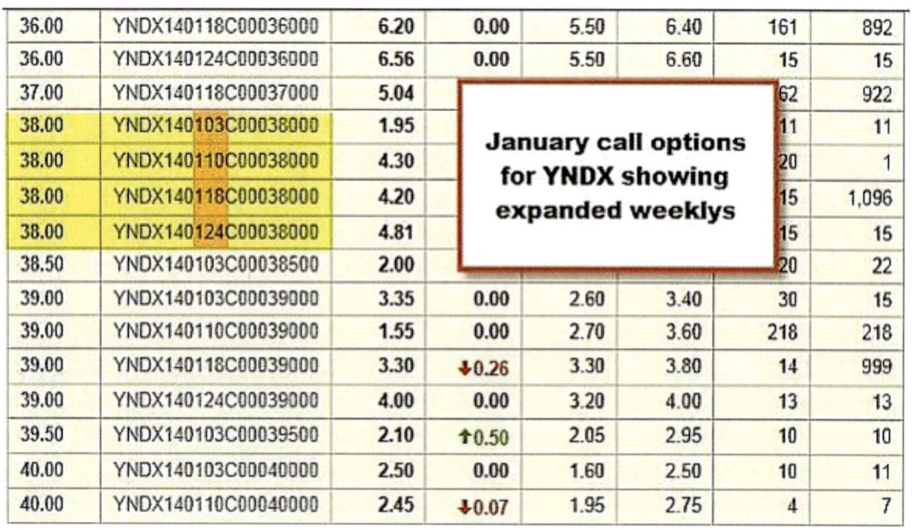

36.00	YNDX140118C00036000	6.20	0.00	5.50	6.40	161	892
36.00	YNDX140124C00036000	6.56	0.00	5.50	6.60	15	15
37.00	YNDX140118C00037000	5.04				62	922
38.00	YNDX140103C00038000	1.95				11	11
38.00	YNDX140110C00038000	4.30				20	1
38.00	YNDX140118C00038000	4.20				15	1,096
38.00	YNDX140124C00038000	4.81				15	15
38.50	YNDX140103C00038500	2.00				20	22
39.00	YNDX140103C00039000	3.35	0.00	2.60	3.40	30	15
39.00	YNDX140110C00039000	1.55	0.00	2.70	3.60	218	218
39.00	YNDX140118C00039000	3.30	↓0.26	3.30	3.80	14	999
39.00	YNDX140124C00039000	4.00	0.00	3.20	4.00	13	13
39.50	YNDX140103C00039500	2.10	↑0.50	2.05	2.95	10	10
40.00	YNDX140103C00040000	2.50	0.00	1.60	2.50	10	11
40.00	YNDX140110C00040000	2.45	↓0.07	1.95	2.75	4	7

Figure 20- YNDX: January Options Chain

In the yellow field you will note four $38.00 strike prices. In the brown column one can see four distinct expirations: January 3rd, 10th, 18th (monthly) and 24th. YNDX was one of fifteen stocks with Weeklys in our Premium Watch List that week. In our weekly ETF Report, an additional nine securities also had Weeklys associated with them that week for a total of twenty-four securities with Weeklys. Of the fifteen stocks in the report dated 12/20/2013, fourteen were part of the Expanded Weekly Program. Only *LVS* was part of the Standard Weekly Program.

Conclusion:

Options are in great demand and so the number and type of products available are expanding as well. Our focus is mainly on Monthly options but Weeklys will also have a place in the portfolio of many Blue Collar Investors. It is critical to stay educated as to the opportunities available to us as shown in this article.

When and Why will my In-The-Money Strike be Exercised?

Covered call writers receive option premiums for undertaking the obligation to sell our shares to the option holder should that holder decide to exercise that right. Understanding when and why exercise will take place is critical to the implementation of appropriate exit strategies and therefore maximizing our option and stock profits.

Let's first look at our covered call trade from the perspective of the option buyer. As the holder of the call option, the buyer's goal is to make the most money possible. This can be accomplished by exercising the option and buying the stock below market (when the strike price is in-the-money) or by selling the option prior to expiration. If the strike price is in-the-money will the options be exercised early (prior to 4 PM ET on expiration Friday), will they be exercised after expiration Friday or will they never be exercised? To get an understanding of how this works we must first look at the premium of the call option and the equation that defines what the premium consists of:

Option premium = Intrinsic Value + Time Value

The *intrinsic value* is the amount that the option strike price is in-the-money and time value is the amount above the intrinsic value. If the option buyer exercises the option, the intrinsic value is captured but the time value is forfeited. This means that it is highly unlikely that the option will be exercised early. A rare exception to this rule is when a dividend is about to be distributed prior to expiration (it is actually the ex-dividend date that must take place prior to expiration) and when that **dividend amount is greater than the time value remaining on the premium**. Let's look at a real-life example to make all this come alive:

On August 24th, 2013 I published an article on this site showing a trade I made using KORS as my underlying. KORS was purchased for $72.36 and slightly out-of-the-money $72.50 calls were sold. As of September 1st, the share price rose to $74.09, leaving the $72.50 calls now in-the-money. The question now is will early exercise occur resulting in the sale of my shares? To get an answer, we look to a current options chain shown in Figure 21:

Calls						Sep 13
Last	Intrinsic Value	Bid	Ask	Vol	Open Interest	Strike
31.25	31.59	30.90	31.60	0	0	42.50
28.80	29.09	28.40	29.20	0	0	45.00
26.40	26.59	26.00	26.80	0	0	47.50
23.70	24.09	23.20	24.20	0	3,132	50.00
21.20	21.59	20.70	21.70	0	0	52.50
18.80	19.09	18.40	19.20	0	123	55.00
16.20	16.59	15.70	16.70	0	2	57.50
13.80	14.09	13.40	14.20	0	417	60.00
11.25	11.59	10.80	11.70	22	440	62.50
8.85	9.09	8.40	9.30	11	592	65.00
6.80	6.59	6.60	7.00	41	667	67.50
4.75	4.09	4.70	4.80	57	1,449	70.00
2.98	1.59	2.95	3.00	366	9,193	72.50
1.62	0.00	1.60	1.65	3,044	17,175	75.00
0.73					874	77.50
0.28					687	80.00
0.10					0	82.50
0.08					232	85.00
0.05					1	90.00
0.05					0	95.00

KORS: $74.09
3-weeks to Expiration
Friday (9/20/13)

Figure 21- KORS Options Chain as of 9/1/2013

Amount option holder will receive if early exercise is invoked and shares are sold:

Amount generated equals $74.09 – $72.50 = $1.59 or $159.00 per contract

Amount option holder will receive if option is sold rather than exercised:

Amount generated = $2.95 or $295.00 per contract

The breakdown of the option premium is as follows:

$2.95 = $1.59 (intrinsic value) + $1.36 (time value)

It is apparent that if the holder chooses the path of early exercise, time value will be lost and that makes no financial sense. Now if there is an ex-dividend date prior to expiration Friday resulting in an amount greater than $1.36, early exercise would be much more likely but not guaranteed (many retail investors do not know about dividends and ex-dates as they relate to the time value of an option premium).

Are we assured that early exercise will not occur if there is no dividend to consider?

NO. Some investors want to own the stock and will exercise (rarely) even if selling the option and then buying the stock at market price will make more sense. We cannot account for other investors making poor financial decisions. These investors should sell the option and then buy the shares at market thereby capturing the time value that early exercise would deprive them of. In these unusual instances of early exercise, The *Options Clearing Corporation (OCC)* randomly assigns exercise notices to brokerage firms, which then assigns these notices to their customers (could be you or me!). Our covered call writing decisions should not be based on rare and unusual circumstances but rather on the most likely scenario which is that our in-the-money strikes will not be exercised (barring a dividend issue) prior to 4 PM ET on expiration Friday. Therefore, if we wanted to hold onto our shares, we would need to buy back or *roll an in-the-money option* prior to expiration.

Conclusion

To determine the likelihood of early exercise we need to look at the option premium of an in-the-money strike. Early exercise will result in loss of time value for the option holder and therefore makes no financial sense. Early assignment is possible when there is a dividend distribution or when the holder incorrectly decides to exercise early and the assignment randomly finds its way into our account.

When Strike Prices Disappear: Contract Adjustments

Stock options are contracts with terms that can change prior to expiration. Mergers, acquisitions, special dividends and *stock splits* are some of the events that may necessitate the change in terms. In early September, 2013 New Orient Edu&Tech (EDU) had been on the Blue Collar Premium Watch List. In the middle of September, I received several emails from members wondering what happened to the strike prices they sold. Several members had sold the $21.00 call options and wanted to buy them back prior to expiration but they no longer existed...they were gone!

EDU had issued a *one-time special cash dividend* of $0.35 per share with an ex-dividend date (date you must own the shares in order to capture that dividend) of September 4th and payable on October 7th. Figure 22 shows the information gleaned from the CBOE web site (www.cboe.com):

Contract Adjustment for the Special cash Dividend

Pursuant to OCC rules (Article VI, Section 11 and 11A), all outstanding EDU option series will be adjusted to reflect this special cash dividend on the ex-distribution date, at 8:30 A.M. Chicago time. **On Wednesday, September 4, 2013, each EDU series shall be adjusted by decreasing the strike price by $0.35, the amount of the cash dividend.** The option symbol for the adjusted contracts will remain the same. Premiums and strike-price amounts for the adjusted EDU options

Figure 22- EDU: Contract Adjustment

The dividend would be earned by all who held ownership in the shares on September 4, 2013. Whenever a dividend is distributed the price of the stock will decrease by the amount of that dividend because the company will have that much less cash and therefore would be worth less. In order to make buyers and sellers of calls and puts "whole" after the price change, adjustments are made in the contract terms. In this case the strike prices were adjusted down by the dividend amount as shown in Figure 23:

Adjusted Option Symbols

On Wednesday, September 4, 2013, trading in EDU series will be on an adjusted basis. At 8:30 A.M., Chicago time, an opening rotation will be effected with the following adjustments:

EXISTING SERIES					ADJUSTED SERIES*			
EDU	15.00	2013-09-21	C/P	=>	EDU	14.65	2013-09-21	C/P
EDU	16.00	2013-09-21	C/P	=>	EDU	15.65	2013-09-21	C/P
EDU	17.00	2013-09-21	C/P	=>	EDU	16.65	2013-09-21	C/P
EDU	18.00	2013-09-21	C/P	=>	EDU	17.65	2013-09-21	C/P
EDU	19.00	2013-09-21	C/P	=>	EDU	18.65	2013-09-21	C/P
EDU	20.00	2013-09-21	C/P	=>	EDU	19.65	2013-09-21	C/P
EDU	21.00	2013-09-21	C/P	=>	EDU	20.65	2013-09-21	C/P
EDU	22.00	2013-09-21	C/P	=>	EDU	21.65	2013-09-21	C/P
EDU	23.00	2013-09-21	C/P	=>	EDU	22.65	2013-09-21	C/P
EDU	24.00	2013-09-21	C/P	=>	EDU	23.65	2013-09-21	C/P

Figure 23- EDU: Strike Price Changes

The row highlighted in yellow shows the change in the $21.00 strike price to $20.65. As covered call writers, although the price of our shares will technically decline in value, we will capture the dividend on October 7th to make us "whole"

To retain ownership of the shares and to roll the option, a covered call writer would then buy back the $20.65 strike and re-sell that or another option strike price the next month. Figure 24 shows the short-term price dip at the time of the ex-dividend date and the performance of this equity since that time:

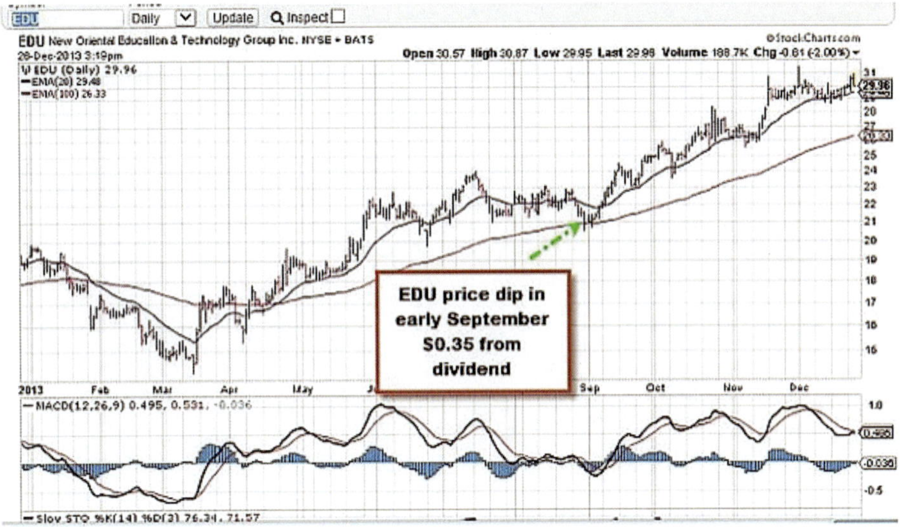

Figure 24- EDU Price Chart Showing Price Dip near the Time of the Ex-Date

The price dip was partially due to the special dividend.

Conclusion

When we see that a strike price that we had previously sold no longer exists, it is usually due to a corporate event that caused the Options Clearing Corporation (OCC) to change the terms of that option contract. The changes are established to make investors on both sides of that trade "whole" The best action to take is to call your broker or check the CBOE site or a similar one to learn the new parameters of the contract.

Chapter 3

Fundamental Analysis

Chapter outline

1. Overview of Fundamental Analysis
2. Using Fundamental Analysis to Screen for Option-Selling Stocks

Overview of Fundamental Analysis

Fundamental analysis is a method of evaluating a company's stock by examining its *financial statements* (including measures such as earnings, sales and debt), and also involves analyzing industry conditions and the overall economy. The most important part of fundamental analysis, however, involves evaluating those financial statements of a company, which are the medium by which a company publically discloses information concerning its financial performance.

Why is fundamental analysis important? Put simply, fundamental analysis is the foundation of solid investing. It gives us a look at a company's DNA, or the overall health of a company. For our wealth-building portfolio, we only want to invest in the stocks of financially sound companies – ones that will continue to grow, earn money, and profit over time. Fundamental analysis helps us find those companies, or in other words, helps us determine which companies have strong fundamentals (are financially healthy), and which ones have weak fundamentals (unlikely to be favored by institutional investors). Similarly, fundamental analysis also helps us gain a better understanding of whether the price of the stock is undervalued (a good buy) or overvalued (a rip-off) at the current market price. Below are just a few of the important questions fundamental analysis seeks to answer:

- Has the company been making profits consistently, and have those profits been growing or declining over time?
- Is the company holding its own relative to its competition?
- Is company in an industry that is growing or declining in importance to the overall economy?
- Can the company pay its bills?
- Is management trying to "cook the books"?

Does a company's fundamental soundness (or lack thereof) affect stock price? Absolutely. The stock prices of companies with strong fundamentals tend to go up over time, while fundamentally weak companies typically see their stock prices fall. Not surprisingly, institutional investors (mutual funds, hedge funds, banks and insurance companies), or the "big boys" as I sometimes call them, also favor fundamentally sound companies. We want to own or leverage stocks that the institutional investors favor because their buying power is the primary fuel for a major increase in the price of a stock. Put differently, institutional investors usually buy stock in large quantities given their vast financial resources, and when they do, supply and demand dictates the price of the stock they are buying will experience a nice increase. If we own a stock that becomes extremely popular with institutional investors, there's a good chance we will see a nice spike in its price. Likewise, when institutional investors start selling a stock that we own, it's usually a bad sign of things to come. When selling options, our goal is to leverage companies more likely to increase in value.

Now that we have a general understanding of fundamental

analysis, let's briefly discuss how the rest of this article will play out. First, we're going to review the major financial statements, which are the primary sources of information institutional investors use to fundamentally evaluate companies. For purposes of our wealth-building portfolio, *it is not essential to master the specific contents of these financial statements but a general overview is definitely useful.* Next, we will learn how to use ratio valuation to compare and select stocks. Ratio valuation uses information from a company's financial statements to form mathematical ratios that provide statistics that give us a quick way to get an idea of whether a stock is undervalued or overvalued. The BCI screening process discussed in Volume 1 of the *Complete Encyclopedia for Covered Call Writing* uses many of these ratios to create a watch list of the greatest performing stocks in the greatest performing industries. First we will discuss the major financial statements and then the most important ratio valuations.

The Major Financial Statements

There are three major financial statements: (1) the Balance Sheet; (2) the Income Statement; and (3) the Statement of Cash Flows. All three statements can be found in the 10-Q and 10-K reports discussed below.

Balance Sheet

The balance sheet represents a record of a company's assets, liabilities and equity at a particular point in time. It basically shows that a company has to pay for all the things it has (assets) by either borrowing money (liabilities) or raising money from shareholders by selling stock (shareholders' equity). In other words, the balance sheet is a "snapshot" of a company's net worth *on a specified date*. Balance sheets must follow the following formula:

$$Assets = Liabilities + Shareholder\ Equity$$

Assets represent the resources that the business owns or controls at a given point in time, and include items such as cash, inventory, machinery and buildings. Liabilities represent debt, and include items such as accounts payable and wages payable. Equity represents the total value of money that the owners (including shareholders) have contributed to the business, including retained earnings (the profit made in previous years). The SEC requires public companies to publicly file earnings reports *quarterly* (on a form called a 10-Q) and *annually* (on a form called a 10-K), as will be discussed shortly.

Income Statement

The income statement, also known as a "profit and loss statement," measures a company's performance over a specific time frame. It presents information about sales, expenses and profit generated from the company's operations *over a given period*.

Statement of Cash Flows

The statement of cash flows represents a record of a company's cash inflows and outflows *over a period of time*. Typically, a statement of cash flows focuses on the following cash-related activities:

- Operating Cash Flow (OCF): Cash generated from day-to-day business operations
- Cash from investing (CFI): Cash used for investing in assets, as well as the proceeds from the sale of other businesses, equipment or long-term assets
- Cash from financing (CFF): Cash paid or received from the issuing and borrowing of funds

10-K and 10-Q

In the United States, the Securities and Exchange Commission (SEC) requires all companies that are publicly traded on a national securities exchange to submit periodic filings detailing their financial activities, including the financial statements mentioned above. The 10-K and 10-Q are two of the most well-known filings, and can be found on the SEC's website: www.sec.gov/edgar.shtml. However, these filings can usually be found in a more reader-friendly format on the website of the particular company you are researching (check the "investor relations" link).

The 10-K is an *annual* filing that discloses a business's performance over the course of the fiscal year. A company's financial statements for the recent year (balance sheets, income statement and statement of cash flows) can be found in the 10-K, and the SEC requires these financial statements to be audited by an independent accountant before the 10-K is filed (the auditor's report is a key part of the 10-K). In addition to the financial statements for the most recent year, the 10-K also provides information relating to a company's historical financial data, along with information describing the operations of the business, including the number of employees, biographies of managerial personnel and future plans for growth, among others.

Businesses also release something called an "annual report," which some people also refer to as the 10-K. The annual report is essentially the 10-K professionally packaged. It includes much, but not all, of the same information that can be found on the 10-K.

The 10-Q filing is a smaller version of the 10-K. The10-Q reports a company's performance *after each fiscal quarter*. Each year, three 10-Q filings are released, one for each of the first three quarters. There is no 10-Q for the fourth quarter because the 10-K filing is released during that time. Unlike the 10-K filing, the SEC does not require10-Q filings to be audited.

Ratio Valuation

Ratio valuation uses *figures from the financial statements* to form financial ratios or mathematical calculations that help us gain an idea of a company's valuation (undervalued, overvalued, etc.) and financial performance. Using ratio valuation is a key component in selecting the best stocks for our wealth-building portfolios.

So what does ratio valuation actually do, and how can it help us? Let's start with a basic, non-investment related analogy to get our feet wet with this concept. If two NFL quarterbacks both threw fifteen touchdowns last year, who's the better quarterback?

Knowing that statistic only, which quarterback would you rather have on your fantasy football team? Not sure? Me neither. What if I told you quarterback A threw fifteen interceptions last year, but quarterback B only threw five interceptions? Which quarterback would you rather have on our fantasy football team now? Seems to me B is now looking a lot better than A. What if B had a completion percentage of 60% while A had one of 45%? B is definitely looking more and more like our man! That's ratio valuation in a nutshell - by comparing *multiple* data points, individual statistics become much more meaningful.

Let's walk through one more example before we delve into the second set of rules for our wealth-building portfolio. Assume you are trying to decide whether to invest in Company A or Company B. You know that both companies had earnings (profits) of $1 million in 2014. Which company is the better investment? Tough to tell- we need more information. Now assume that in 2013, Company A had earnings totaling $500,000.00, while Company B had $2 million in earnings. Given this new information, Company A now appears to be the better investment choice because it saw its earnings *increased* one hundred percent from 2013 through 2014, whereas Company B's earnings *decreased* by fifty percent over the same time period. Applying additional valuation ratios may either confirm or contradict this initial sentiment. However, the important takeaway here is that, just as in the NFL example, utilizing ratios (in this case, growth rate) provided additional perspective on two companies that initially did not appear to be distinguishable from each other.

Ratios will give more meaning and perspective to data points in the financial statements. Below is a brief discussion of some of the most well-known valuation ratios which can be used in our stock selection process. Most of these ratios can be found in the "key statistics" link on the www.finance.yahoo site. However, there is no need to look these up individually as they are part of our previously-described stock screening process (in the original *Complete Encyclopedia for Covered Call Writing*). Specific *requirements are based on the generally accepted statistics representing sound financial or healthy corporate finances.*

Price to Earnings Ratio (P/E Ratio)

Years ago, investors, stockbrokers and financial advisors wanted to know the "P/E" of an equity (stock) before making a buy-decision. Back then, if someone recommended that you buy a particular stock, your first question likely would have been "What's the stock's P/E?"

The P/E ratio is a valuation ratio that compares the price of a stock to the per share earnings, and tells you how much you are paying for the current price of a stock for each dollar of a company's earnings (profit). For example, if you buy a stock with a P/E ratio of 10, that means you are willing to pay $10.00 for each dollar of the company's profit, or ten times the earnings for one share of stock. A different way of looking at it is that it will take ten years of the company's earnings at the current rate to add up to your original purchase price. *Investors use P/E ratios to assess whether a stock is overvalued, undervalued, or priced just right. Those that rely on this valuation ratio generally view a stock with a low P/E ratio as cheap (i.e. a "good buy") and expect its price to eventually rise, and view stocks with high P/E ratios as overvalued and more risky*. To ascertain whether a stock's P/E ratio is "low" or "high," investors compare the stock's current P/E ratio to its own past P/E ratio(s) and the P/E ratios of other companies in the same industry. Some also compare this ratio to the PE over the overall market or the S&P 500.

To calculate the P/E ratio of a particular stock, simply divide the current price of one share of stock (also known as Price per Share) by its annual Earnings per Share:

P/E Ratio = Price per Share/Earnings per Share (EPS)

If the *previous* four quarters of earnings are used for this calculation, you have calculated the stock's *trailing P/E*. If the expected earnings (analyst consensus) for the next four quarters are used, you have calculated the stock's *forward P/E*. Longer average time frames can also be used to calculate PE ratios. For example, if a stock is priced at $30.00 per share and its anticipated earnings over the next five years averages out to $2.00 per share, it's forward PE ratio is 15 ($30.00/$2.00).

The problem I noticed when I started evaluating P/E ratios was that many of the companies with *high* P/Es back in the early 1990s were the ones that performed the *best*. Investors who automatically dismissed companies with high PE ratios would have missed out on a myriad of investment opportunities if they didn't also factor in earnings growth. These were the growth companies. Institutional investors were willing to pay *more* for these companies, driving up prices due to *expectations* that earnings would increase. Peter Lynch, one of the most successful and well-known investors of all time, addressed this issue in his book *One up on Wall Street* by stating "the P/E ratio of any company that's fairly priced will equal its *growth rate*." He added, "Every stock price carries with it a built-in growth assumption." In other words, if the P/E ratio equals a stock's growth rate, the stock is fairly priced *no matter what* the P/E is. Therefore, *evaluating a PE ratio with respect to its growth is a more useful tool than using the PE ratio by itself*. For example, if Company A is projected to have two times the earnings growth as Company B, investors will be willing to pay more for Company A. Thus, a P/E of 15 may be fairly priced for Company B, and a P/E of 30 may be fairly priced for Company A. Dividing by growth projections will put these two companies on a level playing field. Enter the *PEG ratio*.

Price/Earnings to Growth (PEG) Ratio

The PEG ratio is valuation ratio that is also used to determine the value of a stock (e.g. overpriced, underpriced, etc.) while accounting for the company's earnings growth. In other words, the PEG ratio (unlike the P/E ratio) accounts for how much the company will earn next year compared with what it earned this year. The PEG ratio is calculated as follows:

PEG = PE Ratio/Annual EPS Growth

The PEG ratio, like the P/E ratio, can be trailing or projected, and EPS growth can represent expected growth over the next year, or over the next five years. Like P/E ratios, a lower PEG ratio is also considered "better" (cheaper), and a higher PEG is generally considered "worse" (expensive). *A stock that is reasonably priced will have its PEG equal to 1 or lower*. The PEG ratio is not an exact, scientific number because it is based on *expected* growth. However, to completely ignore the PEG Ratio because it is subject to the limitations of projecting future events (expected growth) is *too conservative* a strategy for us – it would likely result in missed buying opportunities, especially for growth companies. Remember, we are willing to take "reasonable" risks, and relying on a company's expected growth (and consequently, the PEG ratio itself), in conjunction with our other fundamental and technical screens, is a reasonable risk for our investment purposes. Generally**, we like to see a PEG ratio under 2 and closer to 1.**

Back to our football analogy. If two running backs both gained one thousand yards last year, but running back A has shown declining stats the past few years, while running back B has boasted accelerating stats, wouldn't we be willing to pay B more than A? That's our football PEG ratio!

Return On Equity (ROE)

ROE is the amount of a company's net income returned as a percentage of shareholder equity. It measures a corporation's profitability relative to the profitability of other companies in the same industry by revealing how much profit a company generates with the money shareholders have invested (investor equity). The higher a company's ROE, the more that company creates for its shareholders, and the better return they can expect on their investment. ROE is calculated as follows:

Return on Equity = Net Income/Shareholder's Equity

Let's evaluate two hypothetical, high-end jewelry stores located in our local mall (Store A and Store B). Both stores generated $5 million in profits (net income or earnings) last year. However, Store A generated its profits with $20 million in shareholder equity (from shares sold), while Store B needed $50 million in investor equity to obtain the same result. Using the ROE formula provided above, Store A boasted an ROE of 25% ($5million/$20 million), while Store B's ROE was only10% ($5 million/$50 million). Store A therefore, was more efficient and profitable than Store B because it created more profit for each of its shareholders.

A company's ROE is often compared to that of other companies in the same industry, whereas EPS (see below) and P/E ratios are better used as a barometer of whether the shares themselves are over or undervalued.

We like to see our stocks with ROEs of 15% or higher. This is generally considered a financially healthy statistic. Other ratio requirements are also set because they meet the generally accepted "healthy financially" standards of analysts.

Earnings Per Share (EPS)

EPS is the portion of a company's profit allocated to each outstanding share of common stock, and serves as a measure of a company's profitability:

EPS = [Net Income – Dividends on Preferred Stock] / Average Outstanding Shares

Let's look at two carpet companies. In 2012, Company A generated an annual profit of $1 million, while Company B generated twice that amount, or a $2 million annual profit in the same year. Company B, at least initially, looks like the better company/stock. Assume further that in 2012, both companies distributed $200,000.00 in dividends to its shareholders. However, Company A has 100,000 shares outstanding, while Company B has 300,000 shares outstanding. Let's do some quick math:

- EPS (Company A) = $1,000,000.00 – 200,000.00/100,000.00 = $8.00 per share
- EPS (Company B) = $2,000,000.00 – $200,000.00/300,000.00 = $6.00 per share

For this ratio, Company A is the winner.

We prefer our stocks to have positive EPS growth during the past five years and projected EPS growth of 10% or greater over the next five years. This demonstrates past EPS strength and analyst consensus for future EPS success.

Sales Growth

Sales growth represents the rate at which a company can, or has, achieved growth by increasing output and enhancing sales. A generally accepted yardstick for financially sound companies is a sales growth rate of 10% or better. **We like to see our shares to have achieved a positive sales growth over the past 5 years**.

Price to Book (P/B Ratio)

This ratio compares the price of a stock to the value of the company assuming the company is broken up and sold today. This ratio is calculated by dividing the current closing price of the stock by the book value (total value of the company's assets that shareholders would receive if a company were liquidated) per share for the most recent quarter:

P/B Ratio = Stock Price/ Total Assets – Intangible assets *and Liabilities*

Assume one of our local jewelry stores has a book value of $2 million, with 200,000 shares outstanding and a current share price of $30.00. We would calculate the P/B ratio as follows:

- Book value = $2,000,000.00/200,000 = $10.00 per share
- The P/B ratio = $30.00/$10.00 = 3

A generally accepted P/B for healthy companies is "4" or lower. **We therefore prefer our securities to have P/B Ratios of "4" or less**.

It is not essential for you memorize all these stats because in our BCI methodology, I have simplified the process with the series of screens we run our candidates through. This is detailed in Volume 1. Of course, BCI Premium Members, receive the watch list of screened stocks and ETFs on a weekly basis and can therefore concentrate on trade execution and management as the BCI team will do all the screening for you.

Using Fundamental Analysis to Screen for Option-Selling Stocks

Fundamental analysis, technical analysis and common sense principles make up the three-pronged screening system used in the BCI methodology for locating option selling stocks. We start with the *IBD 50* and move to the other screens from there but I always encourage the use of additional resources to locate elite candidates to serve as the underlying securities. Over the years, the BCI team has identified a database of over three thousand stocks that have been, at one time, excellent option-selling securities. Each week, we screen that database along with the *IBD 50* for our Premium Members. In this article, I will demonstrate one way to form your own database of fundamentally sound stocks which are then ready to continue through our technical and common sense screens.

(Premium members need not go through this process as we do it for you).

Fundamental analysis is all about earnings and revenues growth and the associated ratios gleaned from corporate financial statements (see Chapter 3 in the *Complete Encyclopedia for Covered Call Writing as well as the previous article*). An excellent free site to generate this information is: www.finviz.com

In Figure 25, there is a screenshot of fundamental screens that generated forty five candidates. Adjustments in the screening criteria can be made to be more difficult or less challenging to pass:

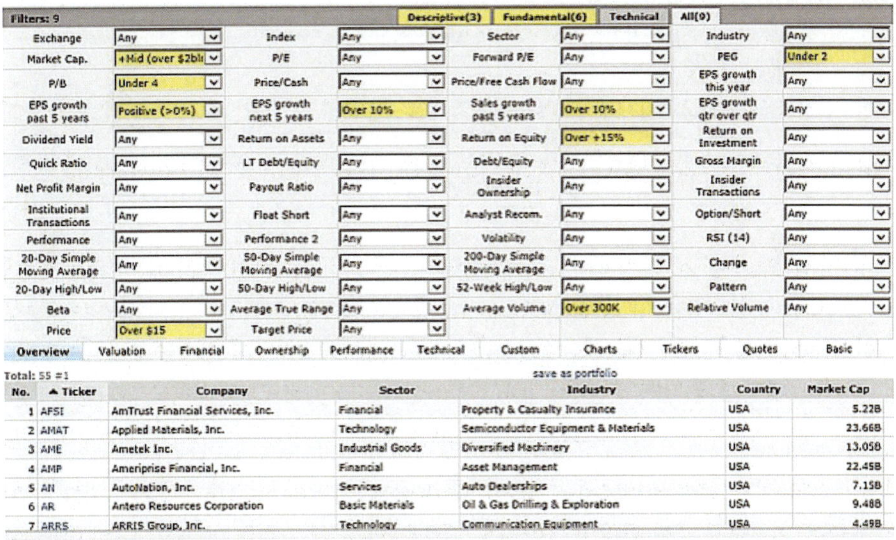

Filters: 9 — Descriptive(3) | Fundamental(6) | Technical | All(9)

Exchange	Any	Index	Any	Sector	Any	Industry	Any
Market Cap.	+Mid (over $2bln	P/E	Any	Forward P/E	Any	PEG	Under 2
P/B	Under 4	Price/Cash	Any	Price/Free Cash Flow	Any	EPS growth this year	Any
EPS growth past 5 years	Positive (>0%)	EPS growth next 5 years	Over 10%	Sales growth past 5 years	Over 10%	EPS growth qtr over qtr	Any
Dividend Yield	Any	Return on Assets	Any	Return on Equity	Over +15%	Return on Investment	Any
Quick Ratio	Any	LT Debt/Equity	Any	Debt/Equity	Any	Gross Margin	Any
Net Profit Margin	Any	Payout Ratio	Any	Insider Ownership	Any	Insider Transactions	Any
Institutional Transactions	Any	Float Short	Any	Analyst Recom.	Any	Option/Short	Any
Performance	Any	Performance 2	Any	Volatility	Any	RSI (14)	Any
20-Day Simple Moving Average	Any	50-Day Simple Moving Average	Any	200-Day Simple Moving Average	Any	Change	Any
20-Day High/Low	Any	50-Day High/Low	Any	52-Week High/Low	Any	Pattern	Any
Beta	Any	Average True Range	Any	Average Volume	Over 300K	Relative Volume	Any
Price	Over $15	Target Price	Any				

Overview | Valuation | Financial | Ownership | Performance | Technical | Custom | Charts | Tickers | Quotes | Basic

Total: 55 #1 — save as portfolio

No.	▲ Ticker	Company	Sector	Industry	Country	Market Cap
1	AFSI	AmTrust Financial Services, Inc.	Financial	Property & Casualty Insurance	USA	5.22B
2	AMAT	Applied Materials, Inc.	Technology	Semiconductor Equipment & Materials	USA	23.66B
3	AME	Ametek Inc.	Industrial Goods	Diversified Machinery	USA	13.05B
4	AMP	Ameriprise Financial, Inc.	Financial	Asset Management	USA	22.45B
5	AN	AutoNation, Inc.	Services	Auto Dealerships	USA	7.15B
6	AR	Antero Resources Corporation	Basic Materials	Oil & Gas Drilling & Exploration	USA	9.48B
7	ARRS	ARRIS Group, Inc.	Technology	Communication Equipment	USA	4.49B

Figure 25- FINVIZ Screen for Fundamental Analysis

In this screen, I set up three descriptive criteria and six fundamental requirements highlighted in the "yellow cells" as an example:

Descriptive screens (avoid thinly-traded and penny stocks)

- Market cap: mid-cap and larger
- Price: over $15.00
- Average volume: over 300k shares/day

Fundamental screens

- Price/Book ratio: under 4 (closer to "3")
- Earnings/share growth past five years: positive
- Earnings/share growth projected over next five years: over 10%
- Sales growth the past five years: over 10%
- Return on equity: over 15%
- PEG ratio: under 2

The criteria set up in this screen can be adjusted but I've shown several elite requirements from a fundamental perspective and it generated forty five candidates, some of which are shown in Figure 25 at the bottom of the screen shot. The next step would be to add in the fifty stocks from the *IBD 50* (minus those that have no options) and move on to the technical and common sense screens. Ultimately, we will create a watch list of high-quality candidates for our option-selling strategies.

The screen shots below demonstrate the screening process used to craft our premium reports and a sample of a partial Premium Watch List developed from the process:

Symbol	Company Name	Weekly Rank or Other Source	Price	Opts Avail (Y/N)	Report Same Store Sales (Y/N)	Pass Fund'l And Tech'l Screens (Y/N)	Avg. Vol.: >250K Sh/Day (Y/N)	Pass Risk vs. Reward (Rank 5 or Higher)	Chart: PRICE BAR above 20 EMA above 100 EMA (Y/N/@)	Tech Ind. OK: MACD & Stoch. (Y/N/?)	Earn. Report In This Option Month (Y/N)
Passed All Screens - ELIGIBLE CANDIDATES											
AAP	Advance Auto Parts	26	154.18	Y	N	Y	Y	7	Y	Y	N
AMAT	Applied Materials Inc	Other	25.04	Y	N	Y	Y	9	Y	Y	N
AMBA	Ambarella Inc	49	54.69	Y	N	Y	Y	5	Y	Y	N
ARMK	Aramark	Other	30.13	Y	N	Y	Y	8	Y	Y	N
AVGO	Avago Technologies	Other	103.99	Y	N	Y	Y	9	Y	Y	N
BIIB	Biogen Idec Inc	46	340.87	Y	N	Y	Y	7	Y	Y	N
CAVM	Cavium Inc	16	58.77	Y	N	Y	Y	8	Y	Y	N
DLTR	Dollar Tree Inc	Other	68.41	Y	N	Y	Y	9	Y	Y	N
EA	Electronic Arts Inc	Other	46.66	Y	N	Y	Y	7	Y	Y	N
EXR	Extra Space Storage	Other	59.44	Y	N	Y	Y	9	Y	Y	N
FFIV	F 5 Networks Inc	24	133.26	Y	N	Y	Y	9	Y	Y	N
FL	Foot Locker Inc	Other	56.70	Y	N	Y	Y	10	Y	Y	N
IDTI	Integrated Device Tech	Other	19.90	Y	N	Y	Y	7	Y	Y	N
JAZZ	Jazz Pharma	15	178.36	Y	N	Y	Y	6	Y	Y	N
MANH	Manhattan Associates	12	42.38	Y	N	Y	Y	7	Y	Y	N
MPWR	Monolithic Power Systems	33	49.67	Y	N	Y	Y	7	Y	Y	N
MSCC	Microsemi Corp	Other	29.01	Y	N	Y	Y	7	Y	Y	N
MYL	Mylan Inc	Other	58.41	Y	N	Y	Y	6	Y	Y	N
NCLH	Norwegian Cruise Lne	Other	45.48	Y	N	Y	Y	7	Y	Y	N
NVDA	Nvidia Corp	Other	21.07	Y	N	Y	Y	10	Y	Y	N
PANW	Palo Alto Networks	Other	118.88	Y	N	Y	Y	5	Y	Y	N
PKG	Packaging Cp Of Amer	30	78.01	Y	N	Y	Y	9	Y	Y	N

Figure 26- Premium Report Screening Process (blue row at top)

Running List	Price	# Wks On Run List	Next ER Date	Industry Segment	Segment Rank	Beta	% Div. Yield	Wkly Avail	NTM OI >100 Cntr.	Comments (The last or next Ex-Div date is shown)
PASSED PREVIOUS WEEKS & PASSED CURRENT WEEK										
NKE	99.33	2	12/18/14	Apparel	A/A	1.13	1.10	Y	Y	12/11/14
GPN	84.56	8	01/07/15	Finance	A/A	1.09	0.10		N	11/12/14
OZRK	37.18	6	01/13/15	Banks	B/B	1.20	1.30		Y	10/15/14
TSM	22.74	7	01/15/15	Chips	A/B	0.83	1.80		Y	07/14/14
MANH	42.38	9	01/20/15	Software	A/A	1.33			Y	
FFIV	133.26	6	01/21/15	Internet	A/A	1.32		Y	N	
NXPI	77.23	6	01/21/15	Chips	A/A	1.85			Y	
ORLY	187.94	3	01/21/15	Retail	B/C	1.00			Y	
ABC	92.21	5	01/22/15	Medical	B/B	0.84	1.30		Y	11/13/14
N	107.11	5	01/22/15	Software	A/A	1.90			N	
OTEX	59.49	5	01/22/15	Software	A/A	0.16	1.20		Y	11/19/14
SWFT	28.66	3	01/22/15	Transport	A/A	1.58			Y	
MSCC	29.01	1	01/22/15	Chips	A	1.57			N	

Figure 27- BCI Premium Watch List ("running list")

Conclusion

In the BCI methodology we begin the screening process for option-selling candidates using fundamental analysis. This is done for BCI Premium Members on a weekly basis and can be accomplished without membership with such free sites as *www.finviz.com*.

Chapter 4

Technical Analysis

Chapter outline

1. Combining Technical Analysis and Market Assessment to Determine Strike Selection
2. Technical Analysis and Covered Call Decisions: Looking Back on KORS
3. Technical Analysis: An Example of a Complete Technical Breakdown

Combining Technical Analysis and Market Assessment to Determine Strike Selection

Mastering stock and strike price selection are key components of successful covered call writing. There is no one factor that will dictate our choices but rather a mosaic of bits of information that will lead us to the best selections. In this article, I will discuss two of those critical components: technical analysis of the underlying security and overall market assessment. Let's start with viewing the chart (Figure 28) of Continental Res, Inc. or CLR from our Premium Watch List dated 4/4/2014:

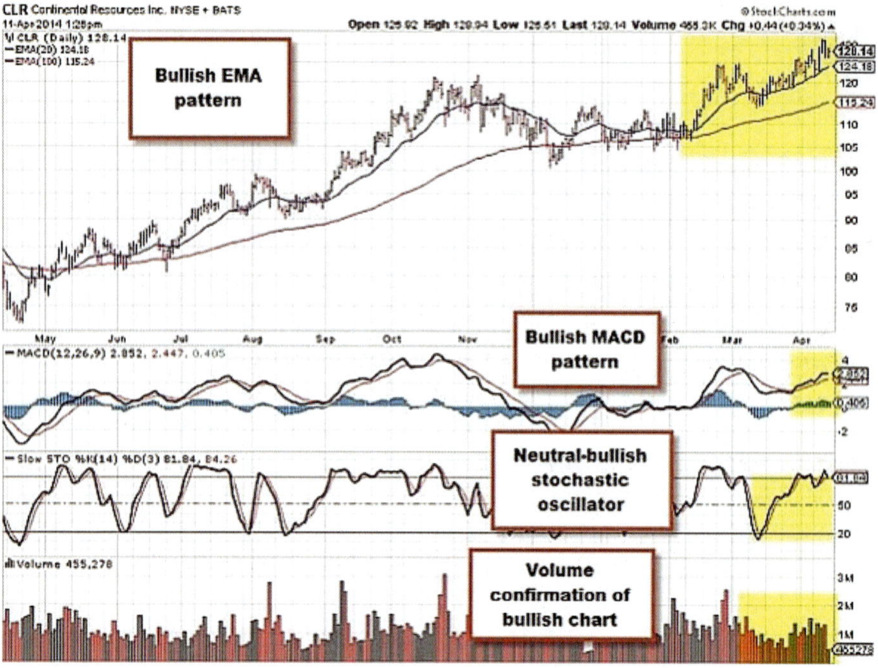

Figure 28- CLR- Bullish Chart Pattern

At this point, we have an elite performer both fundamentally and technically and one would be leaning to selling one of the bullish out-of-the-money strikes. But first, let's have a look at the chart of the S&P 500 and VIX (CBOE Volatility Index or investor fear gauge) in Figure 29 to evaluate our overall market assessment:

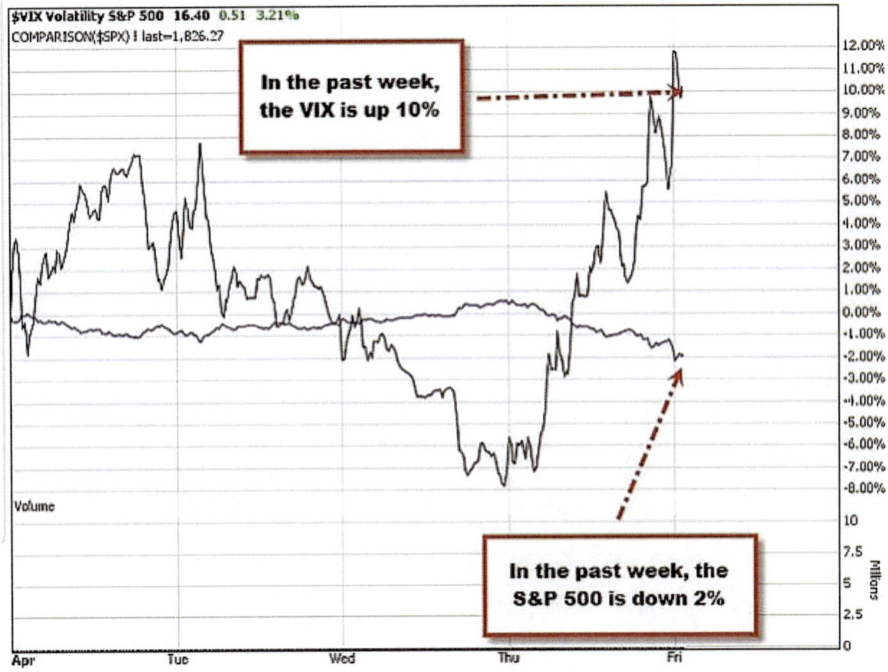

Figure 29- VIX Rising and S&P 500 Declining

S&P 500 versus the VIX

Note that in the past one week, the market volatility has increased significantly (10%) while the value of the S&P 500 has declined by 2%. For many investors, this red flag guides us from bullish out-of-the-money strikes to the more conservative in-the-money strikes giving us a bit of a cushion when it comes to capital preservation. Next, let's view the options chain for CLR at the time I produced the above screenshots:

CLR: $128.02

		Calls				May 14
		Bid	Ask	Vol	Open Interest	Strike
		42.00	43.60	0	0	85.00
		37.10	39.20	0	0	90.00
32.90	33.02	32.00	33.80	0	0	95.00
28.05	28.02	27.00	29.10	0	2	100.00
23.35	23.02	22.10	24.60	0	10	105.00
18.65	18.02	17.20	20.10	0	5	110.00
14.50	13.02	13.00	16.00	0	29	115.00
10.65	8.02	9.60	11.70	0	21	120.00
7.30	3.02	7.10	7.50	0	120	125.00
4.60	0.00	4.40	4.80	189	409	130.00
2.75	0.00	2.65	2.85	0	111	135.00
1.48	0.00	[illegible]	1.65	0	84	140.00
0.75	0.00	0.60	0.90	0	25	145.00
0.40	0.00	0.25	0.55	0	0	150.00
0.17	0.00	0.05	0.30	0	1	155.00

Figure 30- CLR- Options Chain

With CLR trading at $128.02, we will evaluate the in-the-money $125.00 strike and out-of-the-money $130.00 and $135.00 strikes feeding the stats into the multiple tab of the Ellman Calculator as shown in Figure 31:

	A	B	C	D	E	F	G	H	I	J	K	L	M
3	Stock Name or Symbo	Stock $/sh	Option $/sh	Strike $	Expires	Intrisic	Upside	Breakeven		ROO	Up Potential	Down Protect	
4													
5	CLR	$ 128.02	$ 7.10	$ 125.00	05/17/14	$ 3.02	$ -	$ 120.92		3.3%	0.0%	2.4%	
6	CLR	$ 128.02	$ 4.40	$ 130.00	05/17/14	$ -	$ 1.98	$ 123.62		3.4%	1.5%	0.0%	
7	CLR	$ 128.02	$ 2.65	$ 135.00	05/17/14	$ -	$ 6.98	$ 125.37		2.1%	5.5%	0.0%	
8													
9													
0													
1													
2													
3													

Figure 31- Calculations for CLR

The out-of-the-money $130.00 and $135.00 strikes create the potential for returns of 4.9% and 7.6%, respectively (adding up return on option plus upside potential). Neither offers downside protection of the time value (different from breakeven). The in-the-money $125.00 strike generates a nice 3.3%, five-week return (time value only) with downside protection of 2.4%. This means that we are guaranteed a 3.3%, five-week return as long as our shares do not depreciate in value by more than 2.4% by expiration. I call this downside protection (of the initial time value profit), an insurance policy that is paid for by the option buyer, not by us.

Conclusion

Many factors are considered when selecting underlying securities and strike prices for covered call writing. Taking the most bullish positions (out-of-the-money strikes) are most appropriate when both chart technicals are bullish and confirming as well as the overall market assessment also being bullish. If either component is compromised, selling in-the-money strikes will afford us downside protection and provide a cushion for capital preservation.

Technical Analysis and Covered Call Decisions: Looking Back on KORS

Technical analysis is an integral part of our covered call writing decisions for both stock and option selections. It also impacts our exit strategy decisions. KORS has been a favorite of Blue Collar Investors for quite some time as a frequent member of our Premium Watch List. For the week of September 16th through the 20th in 2013, KORS was 'bumped" from our Premium Watch List because of weakening technicals and BCI members were wondering whether to roll the option on expiration Friday. In Figure 32, I present a look at the predominantly bearish price chart that week:

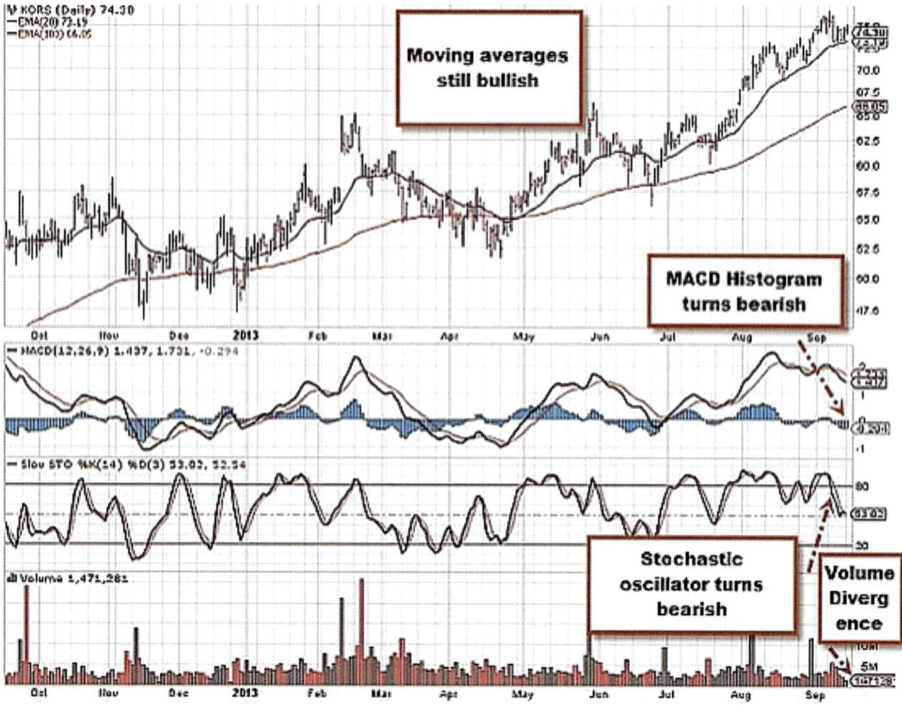

Figure 32- Technical Analysis of KORS for Covered Call Writing

Since the price of this equity had been rising, most of our members were faced with the decision to either roll the option or allow assignment. The earnings were not due out until November 5th. One of our BCI guidelines is to roll out rather than out-and-up if technicals are mixed. Figure 33 is a screenshot of an options chain I captured when KORS was trading at $74.30 and considering rolling out to the $72.50 strike:

Last	Intrinsic Value	Bid	Ask	Vol	Open Interest	Strike
3.55	3.30	3.30	3.80	0	0	71.00
3.12	2.80	2.95	3.30	0	0	71.50
2.70	2.30	2.60	2.80	0	11	72.00
2.25	1.80	2.15	2.35	0	8,703	72.50
1.90	1.30	1.80	2.00	0	25	73.00
1.60	0.80	1.55	1.65	0	35	73.50
1.30	0.30	1.25	1.35	0	42	74.00
1.02	0.00	0.95	1.10	0	45	74.50
[illegible]	[illegible]	0.75	0.85	0	17,378	75.00
[illegible]	[illegible]	0.40	0.50	0	80	76.00
[illegible]	[illegible]	0.15	0.25	0	1,475	77.50
[illegible]	[illegible]	0.05	0.15	0	20	79.00
[illegible]	[illegible]	0.05	0.10	0	941	80.00
[illegible]	[illegible]	N/A	0.10	0	0	81.00
0.05	0.00	0.05	0.05	0	11	82.50
0.05	0.00	0.05	0.05	0	232	85.00
0.05	0.00	N/A	0.05	0	1	90.00
0.05	0.00	N/A	0.05	0	0	95.00

KORS: $74.30

Spreads for Sat Sep 21 01:00:00 PDT 2013 Options: Bull Call Spreads | Bull

Calls						Oct 13
Last	Intrinsic Value	Bid	Ask	Vol	Open Interest	Strike
23.80	24.30	22.80	24.80	0	0	50.00
19.85	19.30	19.10	20.60	0	0	55.00
14.55	14.30	14.40	14.70	0	58	60.00
12.45	11.80	11.80	13.10	0	2	62.50
9.90	9.30	9.50	10.30	0	1	65.00
7.50	6.80	7.30	7.70	0	101	67.50
5.45	4.30	5.30	5.60	0	162	70.00
3.70	1.80	3.60	3.80	0	854	72.50
2.38	0.00	2.30	2.45	0	1,986	75.00
1.38	0.00	1.30	1.45	0	1,587	77.50
0.75	0.00	0.70	0.80	0	305	80.00
0.38	0.00	0.30	0.45	0	267	82.50

Figure 33- KORS Options Chain as of 9/17/2013

When feeding this information into the Ellman Calculator, we determine that rolling out would generate a 1.7%, one-month return

(21% annualized) with 2.4% protection of that profit. If those stats meet your goals, rolling out should be considered.

Next, in Figure 34, let's take a look at a chart from that date moving forward:

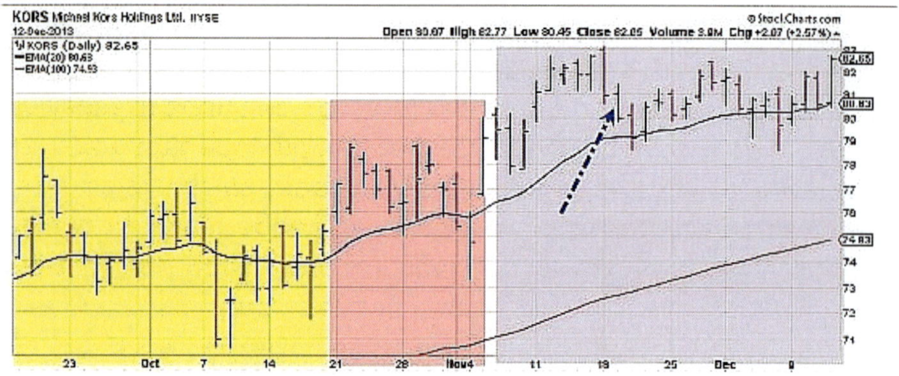

Figure 34- KORS Price Chart after 9/17/2013

- Yellow field: After rolling out, price holds in the mid-$70s and the 1.7%, one-month return is realized
- Pink field: Because earnings was due on November 5th, we would allow assignment and have our shares sold at $72.50
- Purple field: After a positive earnings surprise on November 5th, the chart technicals improved and a more bullish position could be taken (new contract starts at the blue arrow) as the stock price moved from the high $70s to the low $80s

Technicals are important but not our only consideration. We also view our overall market assessment and personal risk tolerance to make our final covered call writing decisions.

Summary

Technical analysis plays a vital role in our covered call writing decisions. We are more inclined to take a bullish stance when technicals are all confirming and bullish and a conservative approach when the technicals are mixed. There are no guarantees that this approach will work every time but it will absolutely throw the odds dramatically in our favor.

Technical Analysis: An Example of a Complete Technical Breakdown

Technical analysis or fundamental analysis...which should we favor in the stock selection process for covered call writing? Many sophisticated investors can make an impressive argument for one or the other. I say why not use both? As most of you know, in the BCI methodology we use three types of stock screens: fundamental analysis, technical analysis and common sense principles (like avoiding earnings reports). Most would agree that institutional investors (mutual funds, hedge funds, banks and insurance companies) have a major impact on the price of our shares. These players love companies that produce strong earnings and revenues. They scrutinize the three major financial statements of these corporations before taking a position in a stock. In my view, since fundamentals are important to these impact players, it should also be important to us. So our first series of screens are fundamental in nature. Common sense principles are just as critical as the other two screens and are detailed in my books (including Chapter 8 of this book) and DVDs.

That leaves technical analysis, the subject of this article. If a company is fundamentally sound, why bother? The reason has to do with the myriad of other factors that can impact share price in between financial statement reporting. Global issues, political factors, economic reports, psychological issues and corporate news to name a few. Technical analysis will alert us to changes in market analysis of a particular equity. A company can be fundamentally sound but technically collapsing.

Enter Sodastream International Ltd. – (NASDAQ: SODA). This company was previously on the Blue Collar Premium Watch List and once responsible for some pretty terrific returns for many of us. At the end of June, 2013, SODA was removed from our "running list" because of a complete technical breakdown. It wasn't fundamental-related because the earnings report was not due out until July 31st. It appears that the collapse and subsequent share depreciation was related to corporate news and perhaps some market psychology (fear based on rumors). There was an analyst downgrade and rumors regarding a potential acquisition by Coca Cola. Remember, the fundamentals of this company were still strong. Let's look at the technical chart in Figure 35, using the parameters detailed in my

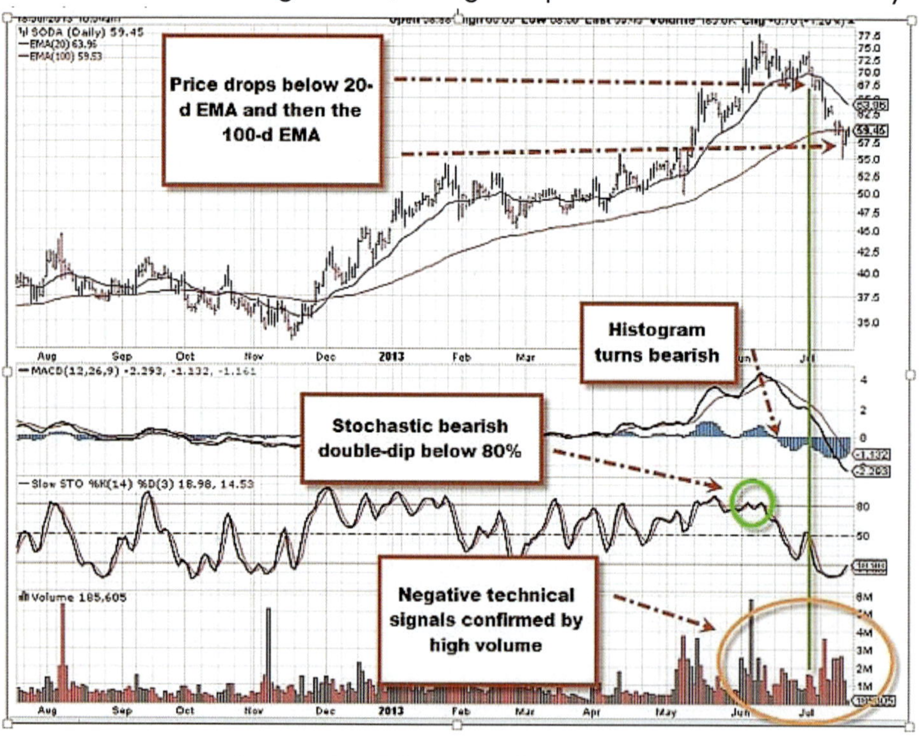

Figure 35- SODA as of 7/18/2013

Note the following technical events:

- The vertical green line shows the price breaking below the support of the 20-d exponential moving average in very early July, a bearish flag
- The price breaks through support of both the 20-d exponential moving average and then the 100-d exponential moving average as shown by the top two broken red arrows
- The MACD Histogram turned bearish in mid-June (broken red arrow in middle of chart) predicting a possible price trend reversal
- The stochastic oscillator showed a double-dip below 80% (green circle) in mid-June also a bearish technical signal and prior to the actual price decline
- All these bearish signals took place on high volume, confirming these red flags

How do we manage a covered call position when there is a complete technical breakdown?

The first step to take is to follow the 20%/10% guideline as set up in the BCI methodology. Curling up into the fetal position and feeling sorry for ourselves is <u>not</u> one of our choices! Following this guideline is easy and can be automatic if we set up limit orders to close our short option positions. Next we research the cause of the collapse. An excellent site I use for researching stock news is:

<u>*www.finviz.com*</u>

Most of the time, when there is a total technical breakdown we are going to close our entire position…buy back the short option and sell the long stock. Then we immediately put this cash to work in a completely new covered call position. I call this "converting dead money to cash profits"

What if the collapse was due to a market over-reaction?

We must still take action to protect our hard-earned money. As they say, "You can't fight city hall" Once again, we buy back the option and, at least, roll down to generate some additional downside protection for our investment. If the price continues to decline, sell the stock or roll down again but don't freeze and take no action. *A complete technical breakdown in conjunction with negative news is too serious a circumstance for us to freeze and take no action.* We all work very hard for our money and should protect it in every way possible.

Technical analysis and the Premium Report:

A stock that is experiencing a complete technical breakdown will be removed from the Premium Watch List ("running list") as was SODA. The BCI team does a complete technical analysis on all covered call candidates after 4 PM ET every Friday and the report shows those stocks that passed all technical screens and those with "mixed technicals" as shown in Figure 36:

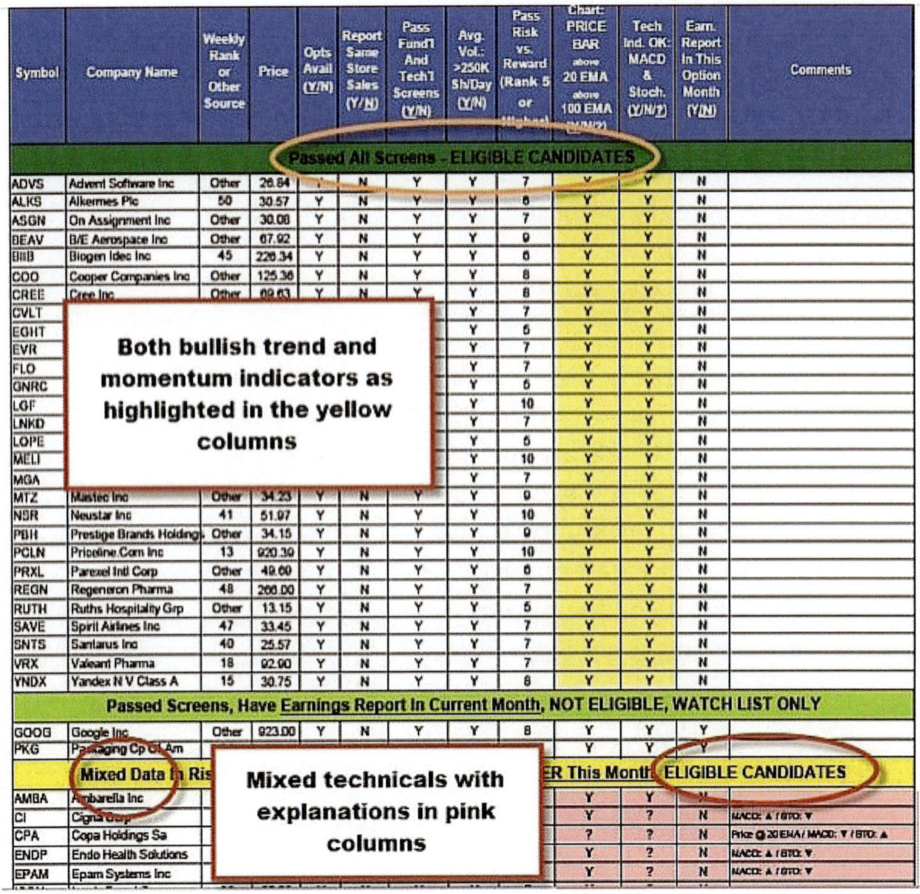

Figure 36- Technical Analysis and the BCI Premium Watch List

Conclusion:

A complete technical breakdown, especially in conjunction with negative corporate news, is a serious matter that requires us to be proactive in our position management trade executions. At the very least, rolling down after share depreciation is required. Frequently, unwinding the entire position and using the cash to establish a new position is most appropriate.

Chapter 5

Portfolio Management

Chapter outline

1. Using Online Stock Screeners

Using Online Stock Screeners

I am a big believer in setting ourselves up for success. This is accomplished through education, motivation, commitment and *organization*. In committing to this book, you have already demonstrated your motivation and pledge towards educating yourself about stock and option investing. However, without organization, not only will the learning process become more difficult, but the implementation process – the part where you actually start buying and selling stocks and options - will become much more tedious and perhaps unmanageable. With more than eight thousand stocks and exchange-traded funds (ETFs) that trade on U.S. Exchanges, it is imperative to develop a manageable watch list of stocks and ETFs from which we will make our selections. For covered call writing and selling cash-secured puts, the best screening methodology is described in chapters 3, 4 and 8 of both *Encyclopedias* or can be provided to you as a BCI Premium Member. For purposes of a more general portfolio or for those who are not Premium Members, this list can be generated by an online screener (like *www.FINVIZ.com* or one similar). As we create a watch list of the greatest performing stocks in the greatest performing industries, it becomes essential to set up organized lists of accurate information. Enter *portfolio management*.

We already know that a portfolio is a collection of financial assets such as stocks, bonds, and cash. *Portfolio management* is simply the art and science of making decisions about this investment mix, including decisions related to asset allocation, matching investment objectives to goals, entry and exit strategies and balancing risk versus returns. For purposes of our wealth-building plan, these organized lists will include:

- Stocks and ETFs on our watch list, which essentially will be stocks that have passed all of our screens but have not yet made it into our portfolio (FINVIZ screener or a similar one)
- Stocks actually selected from the watch list and purchased for our option-selling portfolio (on our brokerage statements or created by us on a spreadsheet)
- Profit/loss statements (provided by your brokerage company or our own spreadsheet)

Having these organized lists will allow us to do the following in a time efficient and accurate manner:

- Select the most appropriate stocks for our portfolios or as underlying securities for call and put-selling
- Prepare for potential exit strategy executions (buying back an option and/or selling an underperforming stock)
- Select replacement stocks when an underperformer is sold

Creating a Watch List for Your Wealth-Building Portfolio

Figure 37 demonstrates an organized list of stocks (ticker symbols) and their current prices, generated from the FINVIZ screener. This site also has a feature where you can save a list of the stocks in your portfolio or on the watch list. Later in this chapter, we will discuss how to calculate the number of shares to purchase or option contracts to sell for our wealth-building portfolio based on the current market value of each stock in your portfolio:

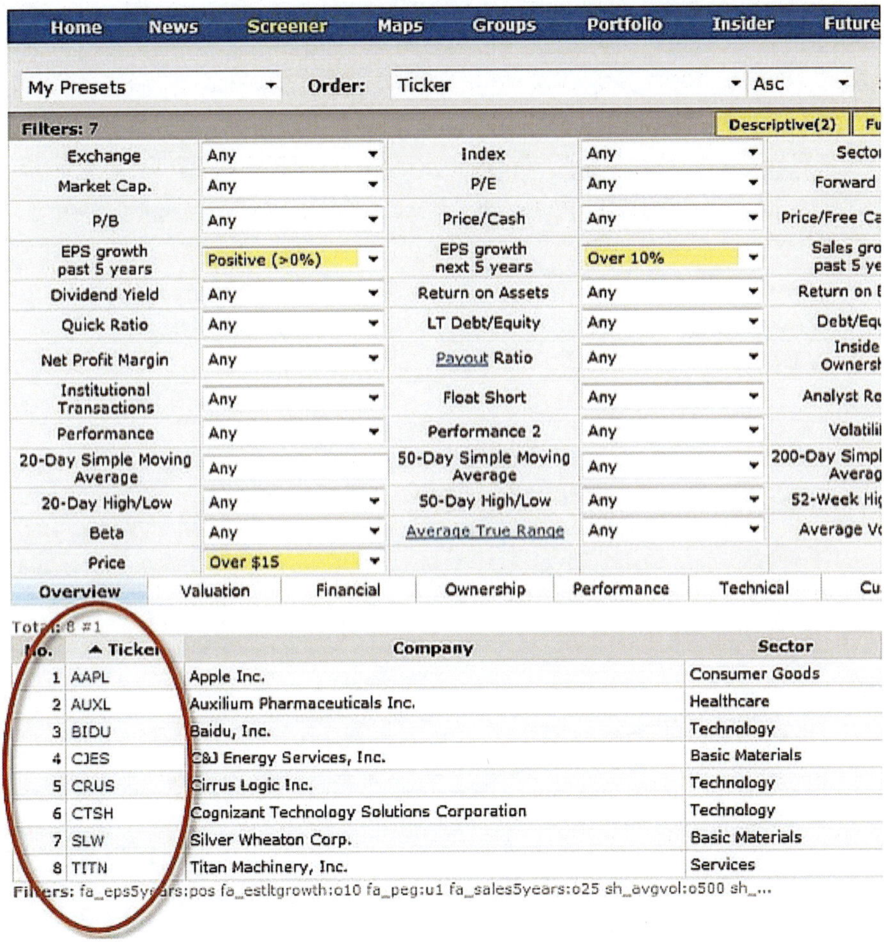

Figure 37 - Sample Watch List of Stocks from the FINVIZ Screener

The drop down arrows shown on the top half of this screenshot will permit the investor to incorporate the minimum fundamental, technical and descriptive requirements that will meet our strict standards.

Sample Brokerage Statement - Holdings Section (Figure 38)

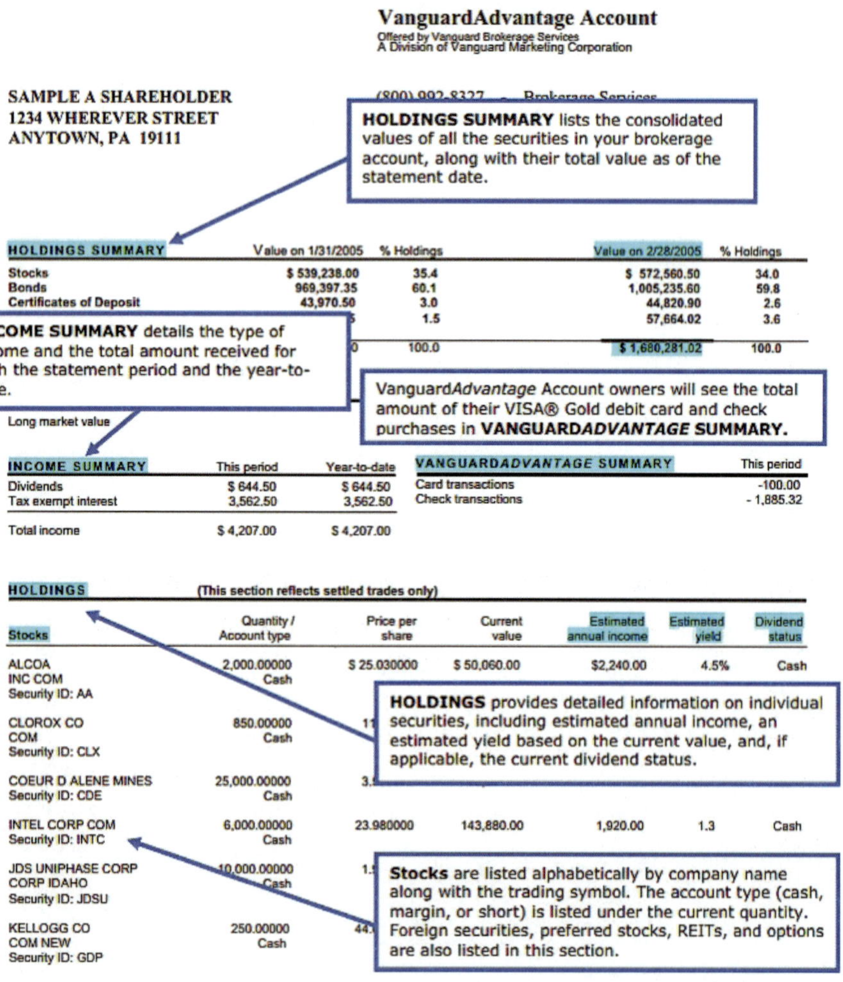

Figure 38- Sample List of Portfolio Holdings

Brokerage statements give a lot more information than what is shown in Figure 38 (such as security values, interest and dividends and much more), and it is important to review the account summaries periodically to determine how your positions are performing.

Diversification

Diversification is a risk management technique that mixes a wide variety of investments in a portfolio. The rationale behind this strategy is that a portfolio of non-correlated investments will, on average, yield higher returns and present a lower risk than any one individual investment within that portfolio. **For our wealth-building portfolios, we must be diversified in the following three areas**:

- Stock
- Industry or sector (sectors provide broader diversification than industries)
- Cash allocation

I believe that no one stock or industry should represent more than 20% of our total stock portfolios. **Therefore, to be adequately diversified we must invest in *at least* five different stocks in five different industries or sectors with similar cash allocation (discussed shortly)**. In our wealth-building portfolio, this can be accomplished with broad-market exchange-traded funds (which give us automatic diversification) or individual stocks depending on the cash available in the portfolio and your personal risk tolerance.

Asset Allocation

Asset allocation aims to balance risk and reward by dividing a portfolio's assets according to an individual's goals, risk tolerance and investment horizon. Each of the three main asset classes - stocks, fixed-income (bonds) and cash and equivalents – have different levels of risk and return, and so each asset class will behave differently over time. Asset allocation is one of the most important decisions that investors make. Here is an example of how we can divide all of the assets (not just the stock portion) in our wealth-building portfolio among the different asset classes:

- Stocks/Mutual funds
- Bonds
- Real estate (your home is a real estate investment)
- Bank savings accounts

As an example, outside of your personal residence, you may allocate your total portfolio as follows (just an example that may be appropriate for a young adult):

- Stocks: 80%
- Bonds: 10%
- Cash equivalents (savings): 10%

As you get older and closer to achieving your wealth-building plan you should start to consider a heavier presence in bonds and fixed income securities and perhaps this will be the topic for another book. *This book focuses on the stock and option portion of your portfolio, however it is important over the long haul not to neglect the other asset classes.*

Common Sense Principles (review from Volume 1)

Thus far we have factored in fundamentals, technical indicators, and organized lists. This is the foundation for our stock selection process. There are, however, five more critical considerations we must consider when making our final decisions, which I call "common sense principles." Our five commons sense principles are as follows:

1. *Minimum Trading Volume (common sense principle 1)*

   Since some stocks with very low daily trading volume can be easily manipulated and may also have wide bid-ask spreads (buy/sell quotes), our common sense rule is to **never buy a stock with an average daily trading volume lower than 250,000 shares per day**.

2. *Stock and Industry Diversification (common sense principle 2)*

   Investing a high percentage of your cash into one stock or industry is risky if that security or group falls out of favor with the institutional investors. By diversifying, as much as possible, with non-correlated underlying securities, we will be reducing this risk. The common sense rule is **to invest in a minimum of five different stocks in five different industries or sectors where no one security or group will represent more than 20% of your portfolio**. A way of circumventing this issue is to invest in exchange-traded funds.

3. *Cash Allocation (common sense principle 3)*

   In addition to stock and industry diversification, we must also **allocate a similar amount of cash to each segment of our portfolios.** For example, if we have five stocks in our portfolio, it wouldn't make sense to have one hundred shares of a $15.00 stock, and one hundred shares of a $150.00 stock.

To carefully balance our portfolios by cash, we will take the following steps:

- Determine how many stocks will fit our portfolio needs. A $50,000.00 portfolio will typically be best suited for about five stocks, allocating about $10,000.00 per security
- Divide the current price per share into the amount allocated per stock and round off to the nearest one hundred since each option contract consists of one hundred underlying securities

Figure 39 demonstrates how this cash allocation breaks down for a hypothetical $50,000.00 portfolio:

STOCK	PRICE	# Shares/$10k
A	$10	1000
B	$20	500
C	$30	333
D	$50	200
E	$100	100

Figure 39 - Cash Allocation at about $10,000.00 per Stock

In Figure 39, Stock "C" would be rounded down to 300 shares and therefore three contracts.

4. Avoid earnings reports (common sense principle 4)

5. Avoid the "banned stocks" (common sense principle 5). These are the stocks that report monthly same store retail sales as well as airline stocks that report monthly "capacity reports"

Portfolio Rebalancing

Once a year, we should look at our long-term holdings to make sure they are properly balanced, as shown in Figure 39. With covered call writing and selling cash-secured puts our portfolios are being updated and rebalanced on a monthly basis. But what about long-term holdings? If any of our positions have dramatically risen in price, it may have a dominant impact on our stock portfolio if the price declines. Rebalancing is usually done at the end of the calendar year and involves buying or selling assets in our portfolio to maintain our original desired level of asset allocation. Those with larger portfolios may want to rebalance more than once a year. For example, if at the end of the year, *stock A* represents 30% of our portfolio and *stock B* represents 10% of our portfolio, we may want to sell some shares of stock A and purchase some shares of stock B so they both then represent 20% of our overall stock portfolio.

***Information in this article included concepts that mainly apply to option-selling but additional information was discussed that applies to longer-term holdings as well.

Chapter 6

Calculations

Chapter outline

1. Achieving the Highest Covered Call Writing Returns using the Blackjack Analogy
2. Calculating Future Returns using Delta
3. Calculating Protective Puts: The Collar Strategy
4. Calculating Two-Month Returns when Rolling Out and Up
5. Covered Call Writing with a Twist: Selling Two Calls per One Hundred Shares
6. Ellman Calculator: Enhancements made in the 2014 Version
7. Exit Strategy Calculations vs. Final Calculations
8. Generating Profit when Share Price Declines 10% in Two Months
9. How Much did that Stock Cost Us?/ How Much did we Receive when we Sold it?/When Options are Exercised
10. Option Premiums: How Intrinsic Value Protects Time Value
11. Selecting a Specific Strike Price for our Covered Call Positions

12. Show or Fill Rule/ How to Negotiate Better Option Prices
13. Stock Exchanges: The New Way to Calculate Trading Volume

Achieving the Highest Covered Call Writing Returns using the Blackjack Analogy

Covered call writers and all investors using stock option strategies have one thing in common: we all want to achieve the highest possible returns within the framework of our own personal risk tolerance. The focus of *The Blue Collar Investor* is to provide the education and to share ideas that will help achieve these goals. Education is power and that is our starting point but where do we go from there? In this article, I will focus on the thought process that can be used to become an elite covered call writer and how it reminds me of the casino game of blackjack.

Recently, Mark T. wrote to me with a valid question: "If I achieve a 2% return on the sale of my option and one of my trades turns against me, I will end up with less than a 2% return…should my initial goal be higher than 2% to end up with that final goal?" So the question becomes how can we generate an initial return and protect and manage our positions such that it will coincide with our final returns or at least as close as possible. The answer lies in throwing the odds in our favor in ways that few covered call writers ever think of. Let's turn to blackjack first just for the fun of it. I am no expert in this card game but when I do play, I have all the charts memorized. That tells me that given my two cards and dealers one up card, what the computers project is the best play…take a card, stand pat, split or double down. If we have a two-card total of 11 and the dealer is sitting with a 6, we double down (double our bet) and take advantage of a favorable situation where we can increase our returns. If we are sitting with a 6 against a dealer's ace, we take a card hoping to improve a losing situation. Each situation is handled on its own merit as we strive to move the odds in our favor and, much like covered call writing, it all starts with education. The major difference between these two strategies is that covered call writers will make money in the long run and most blackjack players will lose money. The main point here is that Blue Collar Investors must take advantage of all aspects of our BCI methodology to throw the odds in our favor to the highest degree and that is what will make us elite covered call writers.

The three required skills that will give us opportunities to generate the highest possible returns are:

- Stock selection
- Option selection
- Position management

By selecting the best performing underlying securities from fundamental, technical and common sense perspectives, we begin the process of throwing the odds in our favor. Option selection is based on overall market assessment, personal risk tolerance and chart technicals. Let's look at a real-life example for KORS, a stock on our Premium Watch List at the time I am penning this article. With KORS trading at $95.56, Figure 40 shows the options chain for March, 2014, a five-week return:

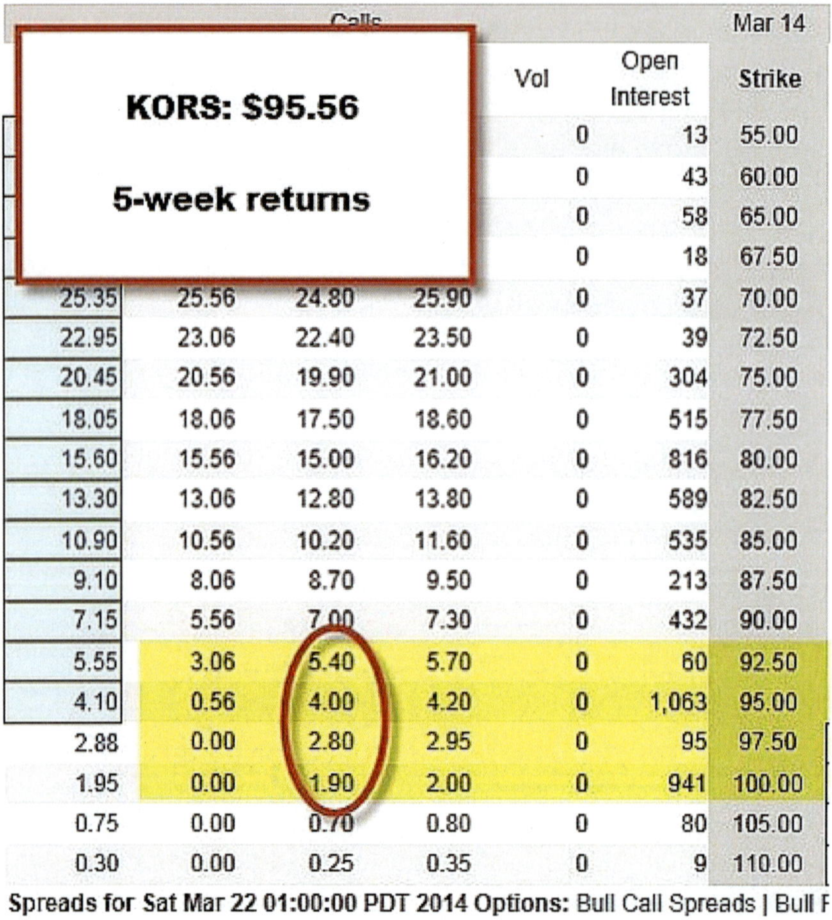

Calls						Mar 14
				Vol	Open Interest	Strike
				0	13	55.00
				0	43	60.00
				0	58	65.00
				0	18	67.50
25.35	25.56	24.80	25.90	0	37	70.00
22.95	23.06	22.40	23.50	0	39	72.50
20.45	20.56	19.90	21.00	0	304	75.00
18.05	18.06	17.50	18.60	0	515	77.50
15.60	15.56	15.00	16.20	0	816	80.00
13.30	13.06	12.80	13.80	0	589	82.50
10.90	10.56	10.20	11.60	0	535	85.00
9.10	8.06	8.70	9.50	0	213	87.50
7.15	5.56	7.00	7.30	0	432	90.00
5.55	3.06	5.40	5.70	0	60	92.50
4.10	0.56	4.00	4.20	0	1,063	95.00
2.88	0.00	2.80	2.95	0	95	97.50
1.95	0.00	1.90	2.00	0	941	100.00
0.75	0.00	0.70	0.80	0	80	105.00
0.30	0.00	0.25	0.35	0	9	110.00

Spreads for Sat Mar 22 01:00:00 PDT 2014 Options: Bull Call Spreads | Bull F

Figure 40- KORS Options Chain for March, 2014 Expiration

We will evaluate the in-the-money $92.50 and $95.00 strikes as well as the out-of-the-money $97.50 and $100.00 strikes as we feed these stats into the "multiple tab" of the Ellman Calculator (get a free copy in the "free resources" link at the top black bar of thebluecollarinvestor.com web site):

RETURN ON OPTION (ROO) CALCULATOR - MULTIPLE STOCKS

Stock Name or Symbol	Stock $/sh	Option $/sh	Strike $	Expires	Intrisic	Upside	Breakeven	ROO	Up Potential	Down Protect
KORS	$95.56	$5.40	$ 92.50	03/21/14	$ 3.06	$ -	$ 90.16	2.5%	0.0%	3.2%
KORS	$95.56	$4.00	$95.00	03/21/14	$ 0.56	$ -	$ 91.56	3.6%	0.0%	0.6%
KORS	$95.56	$ 2.80	$97.50	03/21/14	$ -	$ 1.94	$ 92.76	2.9%	2.0%	0.0%
KORS	$95.56	$1.90	$100.00	03/21/14	$ -	$ 4.44	$ 93.66	2.0%	4.6%	0.0%

5-week returns for KORS

Figure 41- The Ellman Calculator: Calculations for KORS

Now it's time to throw the odds in our favor. In a bull market environment with chart technicals favorable, we are sitting with an 11 against the dealer's 6. Time for an out-of-the-money strike. These strikes ($97.50 and $100.00) will generate excellent initial returns (2.9% and 2% in yellow field) but also give us the opportunities for additional income streams from share appreciation (2% and 4.6% more in pink field). This is like doubling down in blackjack or taking advantage of a favorable situation to elevate our returns.

In a bear market environment or with chart technicals mixed, we need an insurance policy to protect our capital. We are sitting with a 6 against the dealer's ace. We throw the odds in our favor by selling an in-the-money strike ($92.50 or $95.00), both of which return decent initial option profits (2.5% and 3.6% in yellow field) and one (the $92.50 strike in brown field) offers decent protection of that option profit (3.2%). So what we have accomplished here is to generate some protection against a potential losing trade and to enhance profit potential for winning trades and this will allow us to achieve our goals in normal market conditions.

We are not finished yet because we haven't started to execute our exit strategy opportunities. Some ("hitting a double", the "mid-contract unwind") will allow us to generate a second income stream in the same month with the same cash and others (like rolling down or closing the entire position) will allow us to mitigate losses. These strategies are discussed in detail with examples in Volume I of the *Complete Encyclopedia* and in my DVD Programs as well as later in this book in Chapter10.

Throwing the odds in our favor and taking advantage of opportunities are factors that distinguish Blue Collar Investors from all the others. When we're sitting with a 16 against the dealer's ace we do not sit there like a deer in headlights with sweat pouring down our foreheads...we take a card. There may not be a great play all the time but there is always a best play and it's all about throwing the odds in our favor like nobody's business (an expression my mother uses).

Calculating Future Returns using Delta

Understanding option calculations is an integral part of the BCI methodology. Using the Ellman Calculators (Basic and Elite versions) will facilitate the process but knowing the "how" and "why" of these numbers will make us all better investors.

This article was inspired by Peter, one of our members. He was concerned about the potential drop in share price of a covered call trade he was in and wanted to calculate future returns based on the current delta of the option. Before I set up the trade for you let's define *delta*:

The amount an option value will change for every $1.00 change in share price. Delta values run from 0 to 1 for call options and the greater the chance that the strike will end up in-the-money, the higher the delta (the closer it is to 1).

Here is Peter's trade from several months ago so I will use our generic BCI as the stock and one contract for simpler math:

- Buy 100 x BCI at $62.46
- Sell 1 x $55.00 call at $9.75
- Current share price is $60.06
- Current "ask" for the $55.00 call is $9.85 (cost to buy back the option)

- Delta for the $55.00 call is 0.68 (moves $0.68 for every $1.00 move in share price)

Peter's initial returns using the multiple tab of The Ellman Calculator (Figure 42):

Stock Name or Symbo	Stock $/sh	Option $/sh	Strike $	Expires	Intrisic	Upside	Breakeven	ROO	Up Potential	Down Protect
BCI	$ 62.46	$ 9.75	$ 55.00	06/20/14	$ 7.46	$ -	$ 52.71	4.2%	0.0%	11.9%

Figure 42- Calculating Initial Returns using the Ellman Calculator

We see an impressive one-month return of 4.2% (time value only) and protection <u>of that profit</u> of an also impressive 11.9%. These high numbers are indicative of a volatile underlying security.

Calculating future returns using delta

Peter was wondering where his position would be if share price dropped by $2.00 in the next week. Let's calculate using delta with the understanding that there are other factors that will influence option premium like time value erosion (Theta) and changes in implied volatility of the underlying security (Vega). So all other factors remaining about the same, the delta of 0.68 will cause option value to decrease by $1.36 (2 x $0.68) when share value drops to $58.06 ($2.00 lower than current market value). That means the cost to close ("ask") will be $8.49 ($9.85 – $1.36). Okay everybody, take off your shoes and socks and let's calculate this hypothetical circumstance:

- Share loss would be $4.40 ($62.46 – $58.06)
- Option credit would be $1.26 ($9.75 – 8.49)
- Net debit would be $3.14 per share or $314.00 per contract ($440.00 – $126.00)

The takeaway here is that if Peter closes his entire position given this hypothetical scenario, he would lose $314.00 per contract. So where would he be if he didn't close?

To close or not to close

Unless some egregious news has come out about the company in question, Peter is still in great shape in this trade. The deep in-the-money strike sold ($55.00) generated an 11.9% downside protection of the time value component of the original option sale (4.2%). This means that Peter was guaranteed a 4.2% one-month return as long as share value did not decline below $55.00. Even if the $2.00 drop in share value does occur, there is still another $3.06 in downside protection protecting that profit. At this point, the trade is still a classic "take no action" situation again as long as there was no unusual news reported by the company.

When do we start losing money?

Well we always have our exit strategy arsenal in place to avoid or mitigate losses but our *breakeven* is always share price – total option premium. In this case:

$62.46 – $9.75 = $52.71

With the stock currently trading at $60.06, even a share drop of $2.00 will leave us a galaxy away from the breakeven. Sometimes the best action to take is no action at all.

Calculating Protective Puts: The Collar Strategy

Covered call writing exit strategies play a major role in mitigating losses in our BCI methodology. In most cases, we can keep losses to a minimum, turn losses into gains and enhance profits as well. Some covered call writers want the security of protecting against a catastrophic gap-down which can occur rarely. This can be accomplished by purchasing a *protective put* in what is known as the *collar strategy*. Here's how it works:

The collar strategy

- Buy a stock
- Sell an out-of-the-money call option (strike higher than current market value)
- Buy an out-of-the-money put option (strike lower than current market value)

Goals of this strategy

- Generate cash flow
- Protect against catastrophic price decline in the underlying security (an advantage)

Disadvantages

- Lower returns than traditional covered call writing due to the cost of the put option
- Managing three positions instead of two (stock, call option and put option)

Real-life example

In this article we will calculate the hypothetical returns using no puts in one case and evaluating three different strike prices for implementing the collar strategy with protective puts. I am using Facebook, Inc. (FB) in this example as it has been appearing in our Premium Watch List for several months, has decent returns and several choices of strike prices. Here are the stats at the time I am writing this article:

Facebook Stats on 3/11/2014

- Current price is $71.98
- Call strike selected is $72.50
- Put strikes to evaluate are $70.00, $68.00 and $66.00

FB options chain (Figure 43)

FB: $71.98

CALLS

PUTS

10.80	10.48	10.55	11.05	[illegible]	[illegible]	[illegible]	[illegible]	0.00	0.29	0.35	0	29
10.35	9.97	10.10	10.60	[illegible]	[illegible]	[illegible]	[illegible]	0.00	0.35	0.39	0	6
9.85	9.47	9.65	10.05	[illegible]	[illegible]	[illegible]	[illegible]	0.00	0.3[illegible]	[illegible]	[illegible]	206
9.50	8.97	9.30	9.70	[illegible]	[illegible]	[illegible]	[illegible]	0.00	0.4[illegible]	[illegible]	[illegible]	0
9.05	8.47	8.85	9.25	[illegible]	[illegible]	[illegible]	[illegible]	0.00	0.5[illegible]	[illegible]	[illegible]	42
8.60	7.97	8.40	8.80	0	33	64.00	0.59	0.00	0.5[illegible]	[illegible]	[illegible]	24
8.18	7.47	8.00	8.35	0	34	64.50	0.66	0.00	0.64	0.68	0	0
7.75	6.97	7.55	7.95	5	135	65.00	0.74	0.00	0.72	0.76	173	296
7.35	6.47	[illegible]	[illegible]	0	22	65.50	0.82	0.00	0.80	0.85	3	2
6.95	5.97	[illegible]	[illegible]	[illegible]	13	66.00	0.93	0.00	0.91	0.94	60	650
6.58	5.47	[illegible]	[illegible]	[illegible]	25	66.50	1.04	0.00	1.01	1.06	11	82
6.15	4.97	6.00	6.30	0	47	67.00	1.16	0.00	1.14	1.18	67	399
5.78	4.47	5.70	5.85	0	192	67.50	1.29	0.00	1.27	1.31	1	99
5.45	3.97	5.35	5.55	0	69	68.00	1.44	0.00	1.41	1.46	0	1,037
5.12	3.47	5.05	5.20	0	144	68.50	1.59	0.00	1.57	1.61	17	397
4.75	2.97	4.70	4.80	1	59	69.00	1.76	0.00	1.74	1.78	0	683
4.45	2.47	4.40	4.50	4	87	69.50	1.94	0.00	1.92	1.96	7	32
4.15	1.97	4.10	4.20	25	447	70.00	2.13	0.00	2.11	2.16	5	199
3.85	1.47	3.80	3.90	0	372	70.50	2.34	0.00	2.32	2.37	5	84
3.60	0.97	3.55	3.65	0	1,058	71.00	2.57	0.00	2.55	2.59	10	162
3.30	0.47	3.25	3.35	0	254	71.50	2.80	0.00	2.77	2.83	0	115
3.05	0.00	3.00	3.10	145	595	72.00	3.05	0.03	3.00	3.10	0	45
2.82	0.00	2.80	2.84	0	508	72.50	3.33	0.53	3.30	3.35	0	82
2.60	0.00	2.58	2.62	0	517	73.00	3.60	1.03	3.55	3.65	10	40
2.40	0.00	2.37	2.42	4	189	73.50	3.90	1.53	3.85	3.95	0	6
2.20	0.00	2.18	2.22	10	254	74.00	4.20	2.03	4.15	4.25	15	18
2.02	0.00	2.00	2.05	10	55	74.50	4.50	2.53	4.45	4.55	0	27
1.85	0.00	1.83	1.87	24	1,752	75.00	4.85	3.03	4.80	4.90	19	235

Figure 43- Facebook Options Chain as of 3/11/2014

We glean the following stats from this options chain

- Short call ($72.50) generates $2.80
- $70.00 put costs $2.16
- $68.00 put costs $1.46
- $66.00 put costs $0.94

The protective put gives us the right to sell at the strike price so *the higher the strike, the greater the protection and the more expensive is the put*. To determine our initial profit (ROO), we subtract the cost of the put from the cash generated from the sale of the call option ($2.80) and divide by our cost basis of $7198.00 per contract. From there, we can calculate returns if the share price moves above the call strike or moves below the put strikes. We will make the assumption that if no put is purchased, BCI members will employ our arsenal of exit strategies to manage our positions to maximum profits or minimum losses. Such strategies, if needed, all start with buying back the option and frequently using our 20%/10% guidelines as detailed in my books and DVDs. Next the calculations in Figure 44:

Spreadsheet using protective puts versus exit strategy management only

FB PRICE	Buy Put?	Call Strike	Call $	Put Strike	Put $	Net $	ROO	> Call Strike	< Put Strike
71.98	N	72.5	2.8	NA	NA	2.8	3.90%	4.60%	USE EXIT STRATEGIES
71.98	Y	72.5	2.8	70	2.16	0.64	0.90%	1.60%	(-)1.9%
71.98	Y	72.5	2.8	68	1.46	1.34	1.86%	2.60%	(-)3.7%
71.98	Y	72.5	2.8	66	0.94	1.86	2.60%	3.60%	(-)5.7%

Mathematics of protective puts

Figure 44- Calculations with and without Protective Puts

It is impossible to make specific final determinations using the information provided in this hypothetical because so much depends on the skill of the investor in terms of using position management when indicated as well as the amount of price decline if the put is needed. However, certain generalizations of interest can be made:

Determinations

- The initial return not using protective puts is significantly higher than when using them (ROO column)
- If the share price closes above the call strike price (> call strike column), not buying a put produces the best results (4.60%)
- If the share price closes below the put strike price (< put strike column), the smallest losses occur for the higher strike put prices but all still result in losses
- Position management can also be used in the collar strategy but is more involved and may require more time because the investor is in three, rather than two positions

Commentary

Using protective puts or the collar strategy for covered call writing is a viable and sensible approach to this strategy. However, it does have its advantages and disadvantages. *The main advantage is that the call writer is protected against catastrophic share depreciation below the put strike. The main disadvantage is that the profits generated from the sale of the call option will be substantially lower due to the debit resulting from the purchase of the put.* The main reason for a stock price gap-down is a disappointing earnings report and we always avoid those situations in our BCI methodology. However, unexpected bad news can come out at any time. Although that scenario is rare, some investors may prefer the protection afforded by protective puts. There is no right or wrong here. Each investor must make his (her) own decisions. I personally do not buy puts but have absolutely no problem with members who do.

Calculating Two-Month Returns when Rolling Out and Up

Options calculations will give us an accurate assessment of our covered call writing profits. It's more meaningful to use percentages rather than dollar amounts when executing these calculations. For example, a $1000.00 profit on a $10,000.00 investment (10%) is much more impressive than a $1000.00 return on a $100,000.00 investment (1%). That's why percentages form the foundation for both versions of the Ellman Calculators (Basic and Elite) as well as the BCI Put Calculators.

A few months ago, one of our members, Jonathan, shared me with one of his successful covered call writing trades and inquired about percentage returns month-to-month. In this article, I will breakdown that trade and use the Ellman Calculator to demonstrate the second leg of the trade where Jon rolled out and up:

The trade in a one hundred-share format

- 2/10/2014: Buy 100 x AGN at $120.36
- 2/10/2014: Sell 1 x February $120.00 call at $2.52
- 2/21/2014: Share value is $125.59
- 2/21/2014: Buy back February $120.00 call at $6.20
- 2/21/2014: Roll out and up to the March $125.00 call at $4.10

- 3/21/2014: Option expires in-the-money and shares are sold for $125.00

The calculations

You will note that the trade was established midway through the February contract. Here are the final returns from the first twelve days of the trade as shown in the "multiple tab" of the Ellman Calculator in Figure 45:

RETURN ON OPTION (ROO) CALCULATOR - MULTIPLE STOCKS

Stock Name or Symbol	Stock $/sh	Option $/sh	Strike $	Expires	Intrinsic	Upside	Breakeven	ROO	Up Potential	Down Protect
BC…				06/20/14	$ 7.46	$ -	$ 52.71	4.2%	0.0%	11.9%
AGN	$ 120.36	$ 2.52	$ 120.00	02/21/14	$ 0.36	$ -	$ 117.84	1.8%	0.0%	0.3%

12-day return in month #1

Figure 45- AGN Returns: First Twelve Days

Jon achieved a very nice short-term return (1.8% in twelve days) and then decided to roll out (next month) and up (higher strike price). For this computation (Figure 46) we use the "what now tab" of the Ellman Calculator and first fill in the blue cells on the left:

	A	B	C	D	E	F
	OKAY, YOU BOUGHT YOUR STOCK LAST MONTH AND SOLD AN OPTION AGAINST IT. TOMORROW IS EXPIRATION FRIDAY. WHAT DO YOU DO NOW? BELOW YOU WILL FIND SOME CHOICES FOR VARIOUS SITUATIONS.					
	1) IS THIS COMPANY REPORTING EARNINGS NEXT MONTH? (Y or N)				N	
	2) ENTER THE STOCK NAME, SYMBOL AND PRICES PER SHARE OF YOUR STOCK.					
	Stock name >>	AGN				
	Stock symbol >>	AGN		Stock share price you paid >>	$	120.36
	Number of shares you bought >>	100		Stock share price today >>	$	125.59
	3) ENTER THE INFORMATION BELOW FOR THE OPTION YOU SOLD.					
		Symbol	# Contracts	Strike Price	Exp Date	Price / share
	Option you sold >>	$120	1	120.00	02/21/14	2.52
	Today's option price is >>					6.20
	4) ENTER THE INFORMATION FOR THE NEW OPTION CHOICES YOU MAY SELL.					
		Symbol	# Contracts	Strike Price	Exp Date	Price / share
	Roll out >>					
	Roll out and up >>	125	1	125.00	03/21/14	4.10
	Roll out and down >>	See note on printed results page.				
	5) PRESS THE PRINTER ICON OR CLICK ON THE "FILE" MENU, SELECT "PRINT" AND CLICK "OK"					

Figure 46- Calculating Rolling Out and Up Returns: Entering the Stats

The option was bought back at $6.20 and the next month's higher strike was sold for $4.10. Note that although Jon rolled out-and-up, he did so to an in-the-money strike which was lower than the current market value of AGN. The key point here is that our cost basis is now $120, not $120.36 or $125.59. The reason is that since we are deciding whether to roll the option or allow assignment we must compare "apples-to-apples" If we permit assignment we will receive $120.00 per share due to our initial option obligation. If we roll the option, our cost basis must be the same so we can decide which approach is in our financial best interest. Once the blue cells on the left side of this tab our filled in as shown in Figure 46, the white cells on the right side become populated with results as shown in Figure 47:

WHAT IF I ROLL OUT AND UP?	w/upside pot.		w/o upside pot.	
The proceeds for 1 AGN MAR 125.00 is:	$	410.00	$	410.00
The cost to buy back 1 AGN FEB 120.00 is:	$	(620.00)	$	(620.00)
Your net loss on this option position is:	$	(210.00)	$	(210.00)
The "bought up" value in the closing option is:	$	500.00	$	500.00
Your upside potential return is:	$	-		
Your net return will be:	$	290.00	$	290.00
Your comparative basis in the stock is:	$	12,000.00	$	12,000.00
Your comparative returns are:		2.42%		2.42%
You downside protection is:		0.50%		$59.00

CODE D1 | CODE D2 | CODE D3 | CODE D4 | CODE D5 ...

Figure 47- AGN: Final Rolling Calculations

Once the shares were sold at $125.00 as a result of option exercise on 3/21/2014, a 2.42%, one-month return was realized and Jon had $12,500.00 per contract in cash to use the following week for the April contracts.

Two-month final returns

In reality this is a six-week return because the trade was initiated mid-contract in February:

1.8% + 2.42% = 4.22% = 36% annualized

Summary

Although calculations can be challenging for many of us, using percentages and the Ellman Calculators will make our covered call writing decisions more meaningful and help elevate our returns to the highest possible levels. For a detailed discussion of covered call writing calculations see pages 99 – 152 in Volume I of the *Complete Encyclopedia for Covered Call Writing*.

Covered Call Writing with a Twist: Selling Two Calls per One Hundred Shares

Covered call writing is a strategy that can be applied in several different manners. I have written about generating monthly cash flow, the main reason we use this great strategy. But it also can be used to augment long-term buy-and-hold portfolios, enhance dividend distributions by decreasing our cost basis and protect us in bear market environments with some downside protection. The common thread is the goal of more cash in our pockets in all these scenarios.

Recently, one of our members, Rick from upstate NY, wrote me suggesting a twist to our covered call writing strategy where both in-the-money and out-of-the-money options are sold after buying one hundred shares of stock. My reaction was probably the same as yours…we are now "covered" in only half of our short positions. So my initial concerns are:

- We are undertaking added risk
- Will our brokerage approve us for naked call options trading (selling call options without owning the stock first)?
- Is this an appropriate strategy for the level of risk tolerance we are willing to undertake?

For most of us it is not an appropriate strategy nor will our brokerage likely approve us for this level of trading. More sophisticated traders with substantial cash balances will get the broker approval for these riskier strategies.

Despite this, I do feel that it would be a valuable exercise to set up hypothetical trades that will give us some ideas as to the risks and benefits of such a combination strategy.

The stock I selected from our Premium Watch List is SWKS (Skyworks Solutions, Inc.). Have a look at the beautiful price chart in Figure 48 as of the penning of this article:

Figure 48- Price Chart for SWKS: 3/13/2014

Here are the hypothetical parameters I'll use in this article (initial stats taken from the options chain for SWKS on March 13, 2014 and a five-week return):

Initial stats

- Buy 100 x SWKS at $37.00
- Sell $35.00 call at $2.65 (1.9% return; 5.4% downside protection of the profit)
- Sell $38.00 call at $1.00 (2.7% return; 2.7% upside potential)

Hypothetical closing prices to be evaluated

- $30.00
- $36.50
- $44.00

We will evaluate the returns if share price rises or falls by $7.00 and closes between the two strikes.

If stock price drops to $30.00 by expiration

- Neither option is exercised
- Unrealized share loss = $7.00
- Total premiums collected total $3.65
- Net unrealized loss calculates to (-) $3.35 = (-) 9.1%
- **The risk and unrealized loss are magnified as share price declines below $30.00, if no exit strategies are instituted**

If stock price rises to $44.00

- Both options will be exercised
- We will need to buy 100 shares at $44.00 to cover the naked option
- Average cost per share calculates to $40.50: [($44.00 + $37.00)/2]
- Average sale price is $36.50: [($38.00 + $35)/2]
- Share loss is $4.00
- Total premiums collected total $3.65
- Net loss is $0.35 = 0.9% ($0.35/$40.50)
- **The risk and loss are magnified if share price moves above $44.00 and no exit strategies are initiated**

If stock price closes at $36.50

- The $35.00 call will be exercised and generate $35.00 per share
- The $38.00 call will not be exercised
- Share loss is $2.00 per share (buy at $37.00 and sell at $35.00)
- Total premiums collected = $3.65
- Net profit = $1.65 = 4.5% ($1.65/$37.00)

Takeaways from these hypothetical trades

- A closing price between the two strikes will result in a handsome return
- Extreme share acceleration or depreciation will result in a loss, perhaps a catastrophic loss because half our position was uncovered initially

Conclusion

Adding an uncovered or naked component to covered call writing changes everything. We are incurring more risk for a strategy that is geared to conservative investors with capital preservation as a key requirement. There are many ways to make money in the stock and options markets and each investor must evaluate his (her) own risk tolerance level before deciding which of those strategies are appropriate for the family portfolio.

Ellman Calculator: Enhancements made in the 2014 Version

Options calculations are an integral part of our BCI methodology both in guiding us in making the best investment decisions and also in determining our trading success. To assist in achieving these goals I developed the *Ellman Calculato*r in 2008 and with the benefit of your suggestions, my team and I have been enhancing the tools and information this spreadsheet provides. In this article, I will describe the enhancements we are proud to announce for the 2014 versions of both the Basic and Elite versions of the Ellman Calculators.

Enhancements made to both versions (Basic and Elite)

Multiple tab

We have added a breakeven column, based on the feedback from many of our members. This is quite different from the *downside protection* column which applies only to in-the-money strikes where the intrinsic value of the premium protects the time value of the premium. In Figure 49, I have highlighted the breakeven column which is calculated as the price paid for the shares or current market value minus the entire option premium:

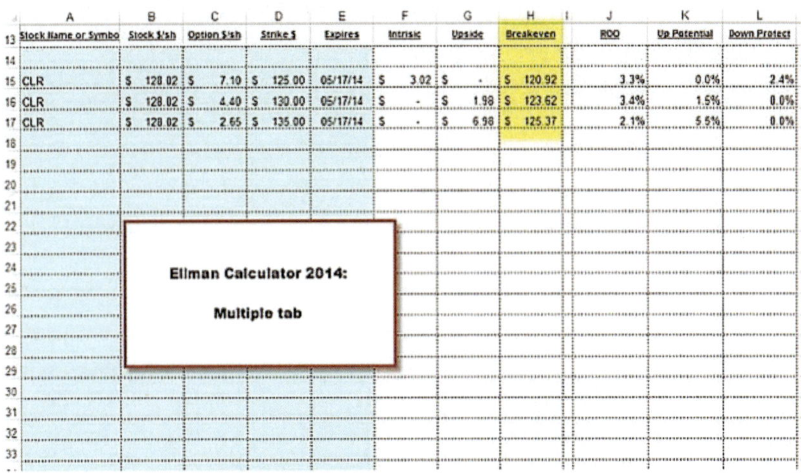

Stock Name or Symbo	Stock $/sh	Option $/sh	Strike $	Expires	Intrisic	Upside	Breakeven	ROO	Up Potential	Down Protect
CLR	$ 128.02	$ 7.10	$ 125.00	05/17/14	$ 3.02	$ -	$ 120.92	3.3%	0.0%	2.4%
CLR	$ 128.02	$ 4.40	$ 130.00	05/17/14	$ -	$ 1.98	$ 123.62	3.4%	1.5%	0.0%
CLR	$ 128.02	$ 2.65	$ 135.00	05/17/14	$ -	$ 6.98	$ 125.37	2.1%	5.5%	0.0%

Figure 49- Ellman Calculator: Multiple Tab Showing the Breakeven Column

In the top row, we paid $128.02 for the stock and sold the $125.00 call for $7.10 resulting in a breakeven of $120.92. Once the share price drops below $120 92 we can suffer an unrealized loss.

What now tab for rolling options

This tab is used for calculating our returns when rolling options on or near expiration Friday. We have added a statistic for the percentage of downside protection we generate when rolling out or rolling out and up to an in-the-money strike as shown in the screenshot below:

WHAT IF I ROLL OUT?		w/o upside pot.
The proceeds for UTHR JAN 0.00 is:		$ -
The cost to buy back 1 UTHR MAR 150.00 is:		$ (1,550.00)
Your net return will be:		No Entry
Your comparative basis in the stock is:		$ 15,000.00
Your comparative returns are:		#VALUE!
You downside protection is:	8.10%	$1,322.00
WHAT IF I ROLL OUT AND UP?	**w/upside pot.**	**w/o upside pot.**
The proceeds for 1 UTHR APR 160.00 is:	$ 950.00	$ 950.00
The cost to buy back 1 UTHR MAR 150.00 is:	$ (1,550.00)	$ (1,550.00)
Your net loss on this option position is:	$ (600.00)	$ (600.00)
The "bought up" value in the closing option is:	$ 1,000.00	$ 1,000.00
Your upside potential return is:	$ -	
Your net return will be:	$ 400.00	$ 400.00
Your comparative basis in the stock is:	$ 15,000.00	$ 15,000.00
Your comparative returns are:	2.67%	2.67%
You downside protection is:	2.00%	$322.00

Figure 50- What Now Tab Showing Percentage of Downside Protection

The past versions of the Ellman Calculators showed only a dollar amount per contract of downside protection. For example, if a stock was trading at $32.00 and we rolled out to the $30.00 call, our downside protection was displayed as $200.00. With this enhancement, it will also be shown as 6.25% ($2.00/$32.00), similar to the downside protection column used in the multiple tab. In the above screenshot, the downside protection for rolling out (next month's same strike) came to 8.10% and rolling out and up to the next month's higher in-the-money strike came to 2.00%, both circled in the screenshot). This is the percentage amount the intrinsic value of the premium protects the time value of the premium.

Enhancements only to the Elite version of the Ellman Calculator

Unwind now tab (adjacent to the what now tab)

This tab is used to determine if the *mid-contract unwind exit strategy* (see pages 264 – 271 of the *Complete Encyclopedia Covered Call Writing* Volume I) makes financial sense. This is when the stock price rises well above the original strike sold and the time value of the option approaches zero. The goal is to close the entire position at little or no cost and to then use the cash to generate a second income stream in the same month with the same cash. The enhancement we created is the time value cost to close and the percentage of the cost basis we are paying to close this position. We can then determine if the cash freed up by closing can generate a significantly higher return than the cost to close. Figure 51 is a screenshot of this enhanced tab in action:

RETURN IF I UNWIND THE POSITION TODAY			
Cost of shares			$ 7,979.00
Option premium received			$ 153.00
Option close-out			
Cost to buy back the option			$ 575.00
Premium received on sale			$ 153.00
Gain (loss) on close-out			**$ (422.00)**
Stock close-out			
Proceeds from sale of stock			$ 8,531.00
Cost of shares			$ 7,979.00
Gain (loss) on close-out			**$ 552.00**
Net Gain (Loss) to UNWIND			**$ 130.00**
NET RETURN ON POSITION			
Net gain (loss) to unwind position today	$ 130.00	=	**1.60%**
Net cash to open position	$ 7,979.00		
Number of days position was open			4
Annualized return			**130.00%**
Time Value Lost To Close			
Time value of option remaining ($)			$ (44.00)
Percentage lost to time value			-0.55%

Figure 51- Unwind Now Tab of the Ellman Calculator 2014

In this case, the cost to close is $44.00 or a fraction of 1% (0.55%). If the cash generated from the sale of the stock can produce more than 0.55% in a new covered call trade, then it makes sense to unleash the mid-contract unwind exit strategy.

Schedule D entry codes

Previous versions of the Elite Calculator displayed dollar amounts of capital gains (losses). We have now added two columns on the right side of the page (gray field) that will calculate percentage gain (loss) and annualized percentage gain (loss) as demonstrated in Figure 52:

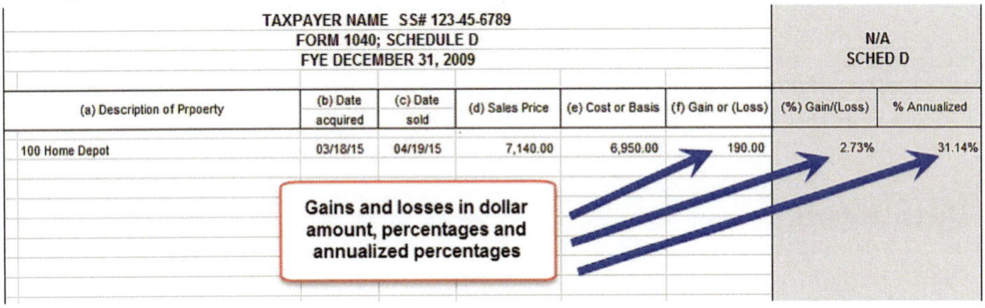
TAXPAYER NAME SS# 123-45-6789
FORM 1040; SCHEDULE D
FYE DECEMBER 31, 2009

N/A
SCHED D

(a) Description of Prpoerty	(b) Date acquired	(c) Date sold	(d) Sales Price	(e) Cost or Basis	(f) Gain or (Loss)	(%) Gain/(Loss)	% Annualized
100 Home Depot	03/18/15	04/19/15	7,140.00	6,950.00	190.00	2.73%	31.14%

Figure 52- The Elite Calculator- Schedule D Enhancements

In the original versions, the calculator showed only a gain of $190.00 per contract. Now we can visualize this return as a 2.73% return which annualizes to 31.14% based on the number of days the trade was active.

Where can I get these calculators?

The Basic Ellman Calculator is free to all and can be downloaded to your computer directly from the "free resources" link located on the top black bar of our web pages. A free BCI Put Calculator is also available. Just enter your email address and you're in. The Elite version of the Ellman Calculator is available for purchase in the Blue Collar store or free to premium members in the "resources/ downloads" section of the premium site. Just scroll down to "Elite Calculator"

Exit Strategy Calculations versus Final Calculations

Mastering options calculations is an essential skill needed to attain the very highest covered call writing returns. Although the *Ellman Calculators* will do most of the heavy lifting for us, understanding the reasons behind these calculations and when and how to apply them, will make us all more skilled investors.

Recently a BCI member sent me a hypothetical trade that involved two of our exit strategy choices: *rolling down* and the *mid-contract unwind exit strategy*.

Definitions

Rolling down: Closing out an option position at one strike and simultaneously opening another at a lower strike price.

Mid-contract unwind exit strategy (MCU): Closing an entire covered call position mid-contract when the time value of the premium approaches zero and using the cash (generated from the stock sale) to establish a second income stream in the same month with a new position.

The hypothetical trade

- Buy shares at $74.00
- Sell-to-open $74.00 calls (at-the-money) at $2.50
- Buyback $74.00 calls at $0.50
- Roll down to $70.00 strike at $2.00
- Price rockets up to $78.00
- Buyback $70.00 calls at $8.20
- Sell the shares at $78.00

The questions from our BCI member

- Now what I want to know is that if I am correct here in knowing that the intrinsic value of the last option ($70.00) is $8.00, and the time value is at $0.20 (from the $8.20 premium for the $70.00 strike), then am I to also take the MCU share gain as $8.00 (from $70.00 to $78.00)?

- It can't surely be from $75.00 up to $78.00 (can it?) as time value would be too large?
- Is my calculation correct for a (-) $4.20 total options loss, and + $8.00 for price gain to net to a $3.80 profit?

The mathematics of the trade

Based on this example, I see the confusion commonly experienced by covered call writers. There are two sets of calculations that should be viewed individually but frequently are combined and that will cloud the situation. The first calculation relates to whether to pull the trigger on the MCU strategy or not. The second is the overall profit (loss) results.

Let's address the MCU first

We base our decision whether to completely close our short option and long stock positions based on the current market value of our shares which was rolled down to $70.00 (our current option obligation). We do not base it on some value from the past ($74.00). The time value component to accomplish this is $0.20 because the shares can be sold for $78.00 and therefore we stand to gain $8.00 in share value at this point in time (based on our option obligation to sell at $70.00). If we can generate more than $20.00/$7000.00 or .28% (a fraction of 1%) by re-investing that newly-acquired cash, we should pull the trigger on the MCU strategy.

Final results

We don't know yet because the cash generated from instituting the MCU strategy hasn't been re-invested so the final chapter hasn't been written. However, to date we have an options debit of:

[$2.50 + ($2.00 – $0.50) – $8.20] = (-) $4.20 (sum of all options credits and debits)

We have a share credit of $78.00 – $74.00 = + $4.00 (bought at $74.00 and sold at $78.00)

Total loss to date = (-) $0.20

This tabulates to a fraction of 1% as shown in Figure 53:

RETURN IF I UNWIND THE POSITION TODAY					
Cost of shares				$	7,400.00
Option premium received				$	400.00
Option close-out					
Cost to buy back the option				$	820.00
Premium received on sale				$	400.00
Gain (loss) on close-out				$	(420.00)
Stock close-out					
Proceeds from sale of stock				$	7,800.00
Cost of shares				$	7,400.00
Gain (loss) on close-out				$	400.00
Net Gain (Loss) to UNWIND				$	(20.00)
NET RETURN ON POSITION					
Net gain (loss) to unwind position today	$	(20.00)	=		-0.30%
Net cash to open position	$	7,400.00			
Number of days position was open					7
Annualized return					-16.00%
Time Value Lost To Close					
Time value of option remaining ($)				$	(20.00)
Percentage lost to time value					-0.29%

Cost to close is a fraction of 1%

Figure 53- Mid-Contract Unwind Exit Strategy

Now, it's up to us to write the final chapter that month and re-invest the $7800.00 per contract to turn that small loss into a gain. We turn to our watch list of eligible stocks, find an appropriate price per share and check options chains. The information is fed into the *Ellman Calculator* as we make our final decisions.

This is a great example of how being active with position management opportunities can, in many cases, allow us to manage our positions to mitigate losses, turn losses into gains and enhance gains.

Generating Profit when Share Price Declines 10% in Two Months

Can we use covered call writing and selling cash-secured puts to generate profits when share price declines by 10% in two months during a bear or volatile market environment? I am writing this article on January 5th, 2015, the worst day the market has experienced in over three months. This hypothetical trade represents an unscientific study based on a real-life options chain and many of the BCI guidelines and rules. Here are the assumptions for this two-month trade:

- We are in a bear or volatile market environment that will last for at least two months
- Share price will decline 10% in two months, we'll assume 5% per month
- Market concern dictates the use of out-of-the-money puts (strike price below stock price) and in-the-money calls (call price below stock price)
- We will estimate monthly returns for the calls and puts by using a six-week options chain and converting to monthly percentages

- We will assume no exit strategies will be required
- The stock selected is KORS as of January 5, 2015

With the price of KORS at \$73.11 near market close on January 5, 2015 this is the real-life options chain for the six-week February expiration:

CALLS							PUTS					
33.10	33.07	32.30	33.90	0	1	40.00	0.05	0.00	0.05	0.05	0	7
28.05	28.07	[illegible]	[illegible]	0	4	45.00	0.05	0.00	[illegible]	[illegible]	0	63
23.10	23.07	[illegible]	[illegible]	8	21	50.00	0.08	0.00	[illegible]	[illegible]	0	614
18.15	18.07	[illegible]	[illegible]	0	76	55.00	0.15	0.00	[illegible]	[illegible]	0	118
13.40	13.07	13.00	13.80	0	83	60.00	0.45	0.00	0.40	0.50	0	1,818
11.05	10.57	10.60	11.50	4	36	62.50	0.70	0.00	0.65	0.75	21	534
9.15	8.07	8.90	9.40	4	160	65.00	1.07	0.00	1.00	1.15	23	6,684
7.20	5.57	7.00	7.40	0	16	67.50	1.62	0.00	1.55	1.70	170	2,975
5.55	3.07	5.40	5.70	21	1,492	70.00	2.45	0.00	2.40	2.50	570	7,172
4.10	0.57	[illegible]	4.20	61	769	72.50	3.50	0.00	3.40	3.60	23	585
2.90	0.00	2.80	3.00	61	1,503	75.00	4.80	1.93	4.70	4.90	83	4,811
2.00	0.00	1.90	2.10	13	595	77.50	6.35	4.43	6.20	6.50	5	827
1.32	0.00	1.25	1.40	411	5,224	80.00	8.20	6.93	8.10	8.30	51	1,512
0.53	0.00	0.45	0.60	1,468	4,002	85.00	12.00	11.93	10.90	13.10	0	1,072
0.23	0.00	0.20	0.25	0	1,712	90.00	16.75	16.93	15.60	17.90	0	212
0.10	0.00	0.05	0.15	25	3,041	95.00	21.60	21.93	20.50	22.70	0	99
[illegible]	[illegible]	[illegible]	[illegible]	0	985	100.00	26.55	26.93	25.40	27.70	0	33
[illegible]	[illegible]	[illegible]	[illegible]	10	511	105.00	31.60	31.93	30.30	32.90	0	0
[illegible]	[illegible]	[illegible]	[illegible]	0	258	110.00	36.70	36.93	35.30	38.10	0	0
[illegible]	[illegible]	[illegible]	[illegible]	0	292	115.00	41.55	41.93	40.30	42.80	0	0
[illegible]	[illegible]	[illegible]	[illegible]	0	118	120.00	46.70	46.93	45.30	48.10	0	0
0.05	0.00	0.05	0.05	0	56	125.00	51.95	51.93	50.10	53.80	0	0
0.05	0.00	0.05	0.05	0	4	130.00	56.65	56.93	55.10	58.20	0	0
0.05	0.00	0.05	0.05	0	0	135.00	61.95	61.93	60.10	63.80	0	0

1-5-15

KORS: \$73.11

Spreads for Fri Feb 20 00:00:00 PST 2015 Options: Bull Call Spreads | Bull Put Spreads | Bear Call Spreads | Bear Put Spreads

Figure 54- KORS Options Chain on 1/5/2015

Initial trade

Since we are concerned about current market conditions, we will start by selling an out-of-the-money cash-secured put and converting the six-week return into a one-month return. With KORS trading at \$73.11, the \$70.00 out-of-the-money put generates \$2.40. Let's calculate:

[\$2.40/ (\$70.00 – \$2.40)] = 3.55%, six-week return = 2.6%, one-month return. Note that our breakeven is \$70.00 – \$2.40 = \$67.60. If share price declines by 5% to \$69.45, we are still in a profitable situation.

Status at first month expiration

Let's assume share price drops by 5% and the shares are put to us at $70.00. Since we are still concerned about the overall market environment, we will write an in-the-money covered call. Using the same formula as we did for the put calculations, we see a six-week return for an in-the-money call of $5.40. Since the current call ($70.00) is more than $3 in-the-money, we will assume the call strike for the second month to be $66.00 (we are projecting the value of the $66.00 call based on current market data of the $70.00 call). The six-week return for the front-month $70.00 in-the-money call is [($5.40 – $3.11)/ ($73.11 – $3.11)] = 3.27% which converts to a one-month return of 2.36%. Note that our new breakeven in the second month is between $64.00 and $65.00 dollars with current share value at $69.45 (using $5.40 as a projected premium for the next month $66.00 strike price). Once again, we will assume another 5% decline in share value from $69.45 to $65.97, near the $66 in-the-money call strike and well above breakeven.

What is our cost basis?

Let's calculate without using time value profit to reduce our cost basis (don't do this for tax purposes!). Shares were put to us at $70.00 and the intrinsic value of the call premium "bought down" our cost basis to about $66.00. This is very close to the current projected price of $65.97. Our two-month profit is 2.6% + 2.36% = 4.96% which annualizes to 30%. Now, even if the numbers fall less favorably for us, we still have plenty of room for a palatable outcome in a bear market environment.

Summary

Option selling can result in monthly profits even in bear and volatile market conditions. This article, although unscientific in nature, represents some general points to support this conclusion.

How much did that Stock Cost Us? / How much did we Receive when we Sold it? / When Options are Exercised

Covered call writing and put-selling generate monthly cash flow because we are selling option contracts and getting paid for undertaking the contract obligations. When a contract is exercised, we then enter another phase where we either buy or sell shares. The purpose of this article is to review and (hopefully) simplify the mathematics of exercise in four scenarios:

- Buying call options
- Selling call options
- Buying put options
- Selling put options

Buying call options

In this scenario, we are paying for the right to buy a stock at the strike price by the expiration date. Since we are paying for this right, we must add the cost of the option to the strike price to determine the actual cost basis of this purchase should we decide to exercise. Let's set up a hypothetical example:

- Buy 1 x BCI call $40.00 strike at $1.00
- If exercised, we pay $40.00 + $1.00 = $41.00 (our cost basis)

Selling call options (covered call writing when buying the underlying shares first)

Here we are selling the right to the option buyer to buy our shares at the strike price by the expiration date. If the option holder chooses to exercise (not our decision), we sell at the strike plus factor in the option premium received. For example:

- Sell 1 x BCI call $40.00 strike at $1.00
- If exercised, we receive $40.00 + $1.00 = $41.00 (our sale price)

For call options, we add in the premium to determine our purchase or sale price.

Buying put options

In this situation, we are purchasing the right to sell our shares at the strike price by the expiration date. If we decide to exercise, we sell at the strike minus the cost to buy that option. Here's an example:

- Buy 1 x BCI put $50.00 for $1.50
- If exercised, we sell for $50.00 less the cost of the option: $50.00 – $1.50 = $48.50 (our sale price)

Selling put options (as when we sell cash-secured puts)

This trade allows the option buyer (not us) the right to sell her shares to us at the strike by the expiration date. For example:

- Sell 1 x BCI put $50.00 for $1.50
- If exercised, we buy the shares for $50.00 less the premium of $1.50: $50.00 – $1.50 = $48.50
- In my put book, *Selling Cash-Secured Puts*, I allude to this as "buying at a discount"

For put options, we subtract the premium to determine our purchase or sale price.

Summary

As option sellers we are generating monthly cash flow. When selling call options that are then exercised, our sale price will include both the strike price plus the option premium. When selling cash-secured puts which are subsequently exercised, our purchase price is the strike price less the premium received from the put sale.

Option Premiums: How Intrinsic Value Protects Time Value

Meaningful option calculations are essential in determining if the premiums meet our goals. To this end, we must understand the mathematics of these calculations to become elite covered call writers. Now don't worry…we don't have to become Albert Einstein to be successful. But we do have to have a general understanding of the components of the option premium and how they influence our investment decisions.

Let's start with the basic equation that many of you have seen in my books and DVDs:

Option premium = intrinsic value + time value

Intrinsic value for calls applies only to *in-the-money strikes* and is the amount the strike price is below the current market value. As an example, if we bought Company BCI for $32.00 and sold the $30.00 call for $3.00, of that $3.00, $2.00 is intrinsic value (NOT profit) and $1.00 is time value (our true initial profit). Now, at-the-money and out-of-the-money strikes have premiums associated with them that are all time value since the strike price is not in-the-money. Examples:

- At-the-money: Buy BCI for $30.00 and sell the $30.00 call

- Out-of-the-money: Buy BCI for \$28.00 and sell the \$30.00 call

In this article, I will discuss and show hypothetical and real life examples of how intrinsic value protects time value when selling in-the-money strikes.

Hypothetical example

- Buy BCI at \$32.00
- Sell \$30.00 call for \$3.00
- Intrinsic value = \$2.00
- Time value = \$1.00
- Initial profit = \$1.00/(\$32.00 – \$2.00) = 3.3%

Since we only count \$1.00 of the \$3.00 premium as initial profit and we did, in fact, receive a total of \$3.00, what happened to the other \$2.00? We use it to "buy down" our cost basis from \$32.00 to \$30.00. This means we are guaranteed our 3.3%, one-month return as long as share depreciation does not drop from \$32.00 to below \$30.00. I call this *downside protection* which is quite different from *breakeven*. It is protection of the initial profit and is calculated as follows:

Downside protection = \$2.00/\$32.00 = 6.3%

I view the downside protection as an insurance policy which is paid for by the option buyer. When evaluating this trade, the calculations tell us the following:

We are guaranteed a 3.3%, one-month return as long as share value does not decline by more than 6.3% by expiration. If that trade meets our goals then it's time to make some money.

As an aside, to calculate *breakeven* we deduct the entire option premium from the initial cost:

$32.00 – $3.00 = $29.00

Real-life example: MYGN

At the time I am writing this article, Myriad Genetics (MYGN) is a stock on our *Premium Watch List* and the options chain shows the following stats with three weeks remaining until expiration:

- Price = $36.21
- $35.00 call strike = $2.30
- Therefore, time value = $1.09 and intrinsic value = $1.21

Let's allow the "multiple tab" of the Ellman Calculator in Figure 55 to do the work for us:

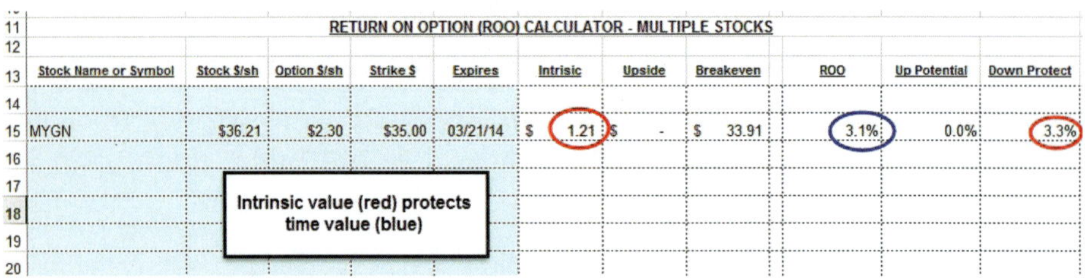

RETURN ON OPTION (ROO) CALCULATOR - MULTIPLE STOCKS

Stock Name or Symbol	Stock $/sh	Option $/sh	Strike $	Expires	Intrisic	Upside	Breakeven	ROO	Up Potential	Down Protect
MYGN	$36.21	$2.30	$35.00	03/21/14	$ 1.21	$ -	$ 33.91	3.1%	0.0%	3.3%

Figure 55- Calculating In-The-Money Strikes

The calculator shows that we are guaranteed a 3.1%, three-week return as long as share value does not decline by more than 3.3% by expiration. One of the many perks of being a covered call writer is that this "insurance policy" is paid for by the option buyer, not by us.

Summary

When using in-the-money strikes, the intrinsic value protects the time value or our initial profit. These strikes are most appropriate in bearish or volatile markets, when chart technicals are mixed and when the investor's risk-tolerance is extremely conservative. The disadvantage of in-the-money strikes is that the option seller will not benefit if stock price accelerates prior to expiration.

Selecting a Specific Strike Price for our Covered Call Positions

We must master strike price selection to maximize our covered call writing returns. In our BCI methodology, strike price selection is ultimately determined as a result of our careful stock screening analysis and overall market assessment. By developing a watch list of eligible candidates with elite fundamentals and strong price chart technicals along with passing our common sense screens (like minimum trading volume) we are off to a great start in constructing our monthly covered call writing portfolios. Next we make our overall market assessment (bullish vs. bearish) and that will dictate the percentage of in-the-money (conservative) and out-of-the-money (bullish) strikes we will select.

Whether we are favoring in-the-money or out-of-the-money strikes we may have several choices to choose from. So the question now becomes *which specific strike price should we select?* At this point the calculations become a key factor. The first consideration is to decide what our initial one-month goals are for our positions (mine are 2-4%). From there, we look at the amount of upside potential if bullish or the amount of downside protection of the option profit if bearish or have a low-risk tolerance. Let's make some generalizations:

- The more bullish we are, the further out-of-the-money we will go after meeting our initial goals

- The more bearish we are, the further in-the-money we will go after meeting our initial goals

Let's look at a real life example, using EDU, a stock on our Premium Watch List at the time I wrote this article. Figure 56 shows a one-month options chain:

EDU- 1-month options chain
Price: $33.68

Calls						Feb 14
Last	Intrinsic Value	Bid	Ask	Vol	Open Interest	Strike
13.00	12.68	12.40	13.60	0	0	21.00
[illegible]	[illegible]	[illegible]	12.60	0	0	22.00
[illegible]	[illegible]	[illegible]	11.60	0	0	23.00
[illegible]	[illegible]	[illegible]	10.60	0	0	24.00
[illegible]	[illegible]	[illegible]	9.60	0	2	25.00
[illegible]	[illegible]	[illegible]	8.70	0	0	26.00
6.90	6.68	6.10	7.70	0	0	27.00
6.20	5.68	5.70	6.70	2	8	28.00
5.25	4.68	4.80	5.70	1	11	29.00
4.45	3.68	4.00	4.90	2	34	30.00
3.50	2.68	3.20	3.80	10	35	31.00
2.67	1.68	2.55	2.80	15	97	32.00
2.08	0.68	2.00	2.15	47	237	33.00
1.55	0.00	1.45	1.65	24	75	34.00
1.15	0.00	1.05	1.25	71	309	35.00
0.80	0.00	0.75	0.85	38	8	36.00
0.57	0.00	0.50	0.65	34	13	37.00
0.38	0.00	0.30	0.45	0	15	38.00
0.25	0.00	0.20	0.30	5	1	39.00
0.17	0.00	0.10	0.25	0	0	40.00
0.25	0.00	N/A	0.25	0	0	41.00

Figure 56- EDU One-Month Options Chain

Note the following:

- EDU is trading at $33.68
- We will evaluate in-the-money strikes of $32.00 and $33.00 (yellow fields)
- We will evaluate out-of-the-money strikes of $34.00 and $35.00 (pink fields)
- We will use the published "bid" prices with the understanding that we can frequently negotiate better sale prices (pages 223 – 227 in Volume I of the *Complete Encyclopedia...*)

Next, let's take these stats and enter them into the Ellman Calculator (Figure 57):

Stock Name or Symbol	Stock $/sh	Option $/sh	Strike $	Expires	Intrisic	Upside	Breakeven	ROO	Up Potential	Down Protect
EDU	$33.68	$2.55	$ 32.00	02/21/14	$ 1.68	$ -	$ 31.13	2.7%	0.0%	5.0%
EDU	$33.68	$2.00	$33.00	02/21/14	$ 0.68	$ -	$ 31.68	4.0%	0.0%	2.0%
EDU	$33.68	$1.45	$34.00	02/21/14	$ -	$ 0.32	$ 32.23	4.3%	1.0%	0.0%
EDU	$33.68	$1.05	$35.00	02/21/14	$ -	$ 1.32	$ 32.63	3.1%	3.9%	0.0%

Figure 57- EDU Calculations with the Ellman Calculator

Note the following:

- All initial returns meet the goal of 2-4% (ROO column)
- The more bearish or conservative an investor is, the more likely he (she) is to select the $32.00 strike and sacrifice some initial return for more protection
- The more bullish an investor is, the more likely he (she) is to select the $35.00 strike to create an opportunity for greater upside and a potential 7%, one-month return (3.1% + 3.9%).

Summary:

The key takeaway here is that there is no one strike price that is best suited for every investor in all situations. The factors that need to be considered are:

- Chart technicals
- Overall market assessment
- Personal risk tolerance
- Individual monthly goals

By factoring in these considerations we will be able to make an appropriate decision for ourselves based on sound fundamental, technical and common sense principles.

Show or Fill Rule/ How to Negotiate Better Option Prices

Covered call writers generate cash flow by selling call options associated with a stock or exchange-traded fund. Our goals are to generate the highest possible returns with low-risk trades that also meet our requirement for capital preservation. The three required skills for achieving these goals are stock (or ETF) selection, option selection and position management (exit strategies). In this article, I will discuss a fourth, less apparent skill, negotiating a better price with the market-maker.

Market-makers generate profits from the bid-ask spreads… the greater the spread the more money they make. From their perspective, they want to buy as low as possible and sell as high as possible. To protect retail investors from large spreads, the SEC has established the *Show or Fill Rule* also known as the *Limit Order Display Rule* or technically the *Exchange Act Rule 11 Ac1-4*. This regulation requires market-makers to show or publish any order that improves the current *"bid"* or *"ask"* prices unless it is filled. Any order between the *bid* and the *ask* will improve the market.

When the spread is small, say \$2.50 – \$2.60, we don't have that much to work with. But what if the spread was \$2.50 – \$3.00? If we placed a market order, we would most likely get filled at the bid price of \$2.50 and there may have been an opportunity lost. Instead, let's leverage the *Show or Fill Rule*: Find the *mark* or mid-point of the bid-ask spread and drop down slightly in favor of the market-maker and place a limit order at that price. In this case, the mark is \$2.75. I would place a limit order to sell the call option at \$2.70, not \$2.50. Now the market-maker is faced with a dilemma...execute our trade for \$2.70 or publish the new spread at \$2.50 – \$2.70. The \$0.50 spread now becomes a \$0.20 spread. It is now in the hands of the market-maker. In many cases, we will get executed at \$2.70 and the published spread will remain at \$0.50 as we pocket an additional \$20.00 per contract. Covered call writers are in the business of selling options. These \$20.00 "bonuses" will add up over an investment lifetime.

Figure 58 shows a real-life example for AKRX (Akorn Inc.) as of market close 4/17/2015

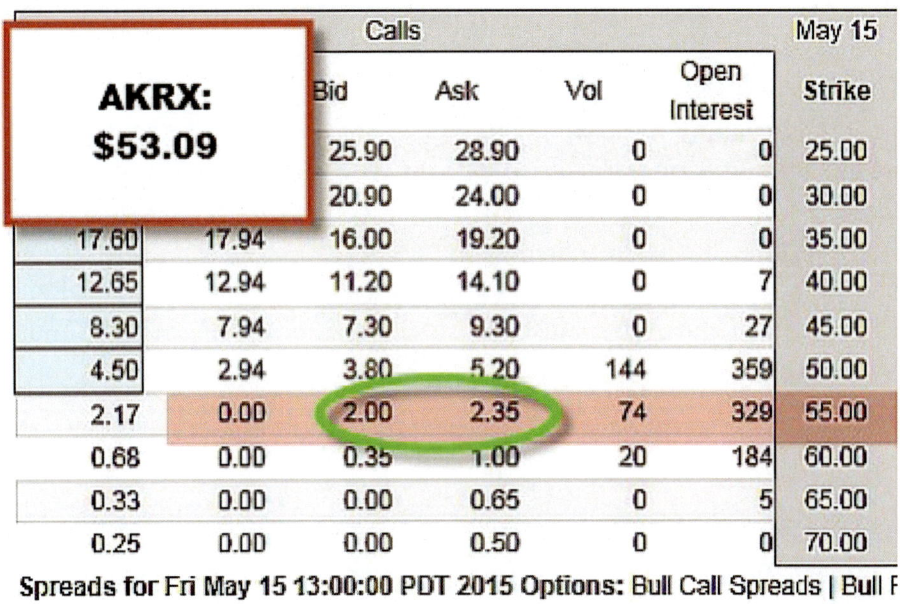

AKRX:
$53.09

		Calls				May 15
		Bid	Ask	Vol	Open Interest	Strike
		25.90	28.90	0	0	25.00
		20.90	24.00	0	0	30.00
17.60	17.94	16.00	19.20	0	0	35.00
12.65	12.94	11.20	14.10	0	7	40.00
8.30	7.94	7.30	9.30	0	27	45.00
4.50	2.94	3.80	5.20	144	359	50.00
2.17	0.00	2.00	2.35	74	329	55.00
0.68	0.00	0.35	1.00	20	184	60.00
0.33	0.00	0.00	0.65	0	5	65.00
0.25	0.00	0.00	0.50	0	0	70.00

Spreads for Fri May 15 13:00:00 PDT 2015 Options: Bull Call Spreads | Bull F

Figure 58- Bid-ask spread for AKRX

- Spread: $2.00 – $2.35
- Mark: $2.17.50
- Place limit order to sell covered call at $2.15

One more thing: Our trade execution forms have an *All or None (AON) box*. Do not check this box. If we do, the market-maker is no longer obligated by terms of the Show or Fill Rule.

Enjoy the extra cash!

Stock Exchanges: The New Way to Calculate Trading Volume

In the BCI methodology for covered call writing, we require a minimum average daily trading volume for the underlying security of 250,000 shares. This is important because it increases the likelihood of favorable trade execution pricing and decreases the chances of price manipulation characteristic of highly illiquid stocks. For our premium members, the BCI team screens all securities for trading volume and for those of you who do your own screening there are many free sites where that information can be accessed. For example, from the http://finance.yahoo.com/ site, Figure 59 shows a screenshot showing the average daily trading volume (3-month average) for PRXL, a stock frequently on our Premium Watch List:

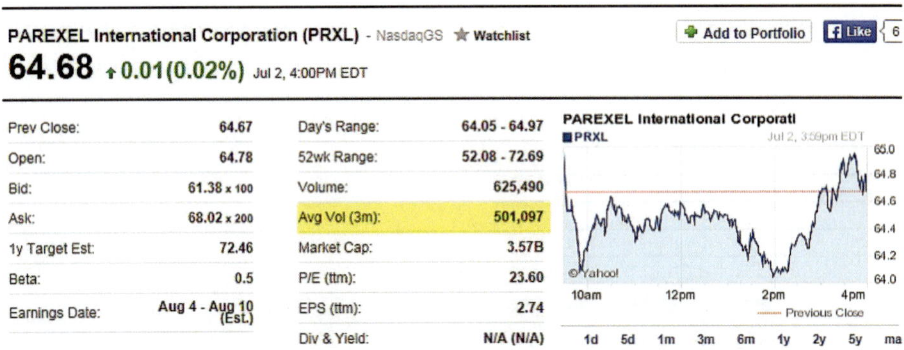

Figure 59- Average Daily Trading Volume for PRXL

In this case, the average daily trading volume is 501,097, double our 250,000 requirement.

How is trading volume currently calculated?

Currently trading volume is calculated based on 100-share blocks of trades, ignoring odd lots (anything less than 100 shares).

What is wrong with this current method?

Due to rising share prices and the popularity of computer strategies, the size of current stock trades has been reduced. Another factor is the reduction in stock splits. A company like Apple Computer used to split as the price of the stock rose but hadn't done so in many years until June 2014 when it split seven-for-one. As a result, the average cost per share for an S&P 500 company now stands at $65.00, almost double what it was a decade ago. Ten years ago, the average trade for an S&P 500 company was eight hundred shares. Today it is less than two hundred shares. High-priced stocks like *Google* now have more than 50% of their trades under one hundred shares accounting for 23% of its trading volume. Nearly 40% of Apple's trades are also under one hundred shares. According to a paper published by Maureen O'Hara, a finance professor at Cornell University, on average, 24% of stock trades fall under one hundred shares. It is estimated that by adding odd lots the published volume on US exchanges can increase up to an additional 5% and give a more focused vision of what is taking place in our markets.

What's being done to correct this issue?

The New York Stock Exchange, the Nasdaq Stock Market and FINRA (Financial Industry Regulatory Authority, Inc.) have agreed to add odd lots to the official records of daily trading volume for individual stocks and the overall market.

Will this bring trading volume back to the levels of 2008?

NO. According to *Bloomberg*, the average daily trading volume in the second half of 2008 was ten billion shares. The average in 2013 was 6.4 billion shares.

Conclusion

Adding odd lots to the stock and market trading volume will provide a much more accurate picture of market and equity activity. It may add a few more eligible candidates for our covered call writing portfolios as well. The need for this change has been a combination of a rising market, the decline of stock splits and the popularity of computer trading.

Chapter 7

Factors that Impact the Value of Our Option Premiums

Chapter outline

1. Buy a Stock and Wait Before Selling the Option: Is this a Good Strategy?
2. Deep In-The-Money Strikes: A Can't Lose Strategy?
3. Earnings Reports and Covered Call Writing in our BCI Methodology
4. Expanded Weekly Options: When should we Enter a Trade?
5. How to Use Implied Volatility in our Covered Call Writing Decisions
6. Implied Volatility and our Premium Exchange-Traded Funds (ETF) Report
7. Implied Volatility: General Market Conditions that Make Option Values Move Up or Down
8. Implied Volatility: More Important than Historical Volatility to Covered Call Writers and Put-Sellers
9. Mini Options- A New Product for Retail Investors
10. Mini Options: The Impact of Commissions and Liquidity on Final Returns
11. Option Prices: The Role of Interest Rates and Dividends

12. Put-Call Parity: Understanding Option Pricing
13. RHO: Why Interest Rates Effect our Option Premiums
14. Role of VIX and Market Volatility in our Covered Call Writing Decisions
15. Special One- Time Cash Dividends and Our Covered Call Positions
16. Unusual Options Activity: Speculation or Cheating?
17. Using Beta to Capture Higher Premium Returns
18. Vega: An Option Greek and How it Impacts our Option Premiums
19. Volatility Skew- Understanding Option Premiums over Different Time Frames and Strikes
20. What is Slippage and How Does it Impact our Trading Success?

Buy a Stock and Wait Before Selling the Option: Is this a Good Strategy?

The goals of covered call writing include generating monthly cash flow and preserving capital. We use specific fundamental, technical and common sense principles available to maximize our profits and protect our cash. Paul A. recently sent me an excellent question that motivated this article:

"…if the market has a down day and drags down the price of the stocks I am interested in, is it reasonable to buy the stocks and wait a few days in hopes the market will tick back up and allow me to generate higher option returns"

You can tell from the inquiry that Paul is a seasoned investor. Frequently, the overall market direction will cause a price decline in outstanding performing stocks and should the market recover, these elite stocks should come back with a vengeance. Let's evaluate the proposed strategy in three distinct circumstances:

The three things that can happen to the share price after the long stock position is entered

- Price goes up
- Price goes down
- Price stays the same

The price goes up

Paul's strategy works like a charm. The price increase leads to an increase in option premium (for a specific strike price) and the trade turns out more profitable than had the option been sold when the shares were purchased.

The price goes down

This time the strategy does not have a happy ending. The option premium generated will be less and in some cases we may have to write for a lower strike price in order to generate the returns required by our initial goals (2% - 4% per month in my case). In addition to that, we have capital depletion due to a lower share value. Exit strategy execution should help mitigate losses.

The price stays the same

On the surface it may appear that in this situation there is no harm but that's not the case. Despite the fact that the price remains the same, the option value will decline (assuming implied volatility remains the same). This is because of *theta* or time value erosion of the option premium. Every calendar day that passes will result in time decay of the option premium and that decay will accelerate as we move later into the contract. Theta is not linear for near-the-money strikes, it is logarithmic as time value erosion starts off slowly and then eventually "falls off a cliff". Figure 60 is a graph showing theta's impact on the time value of an option premium:

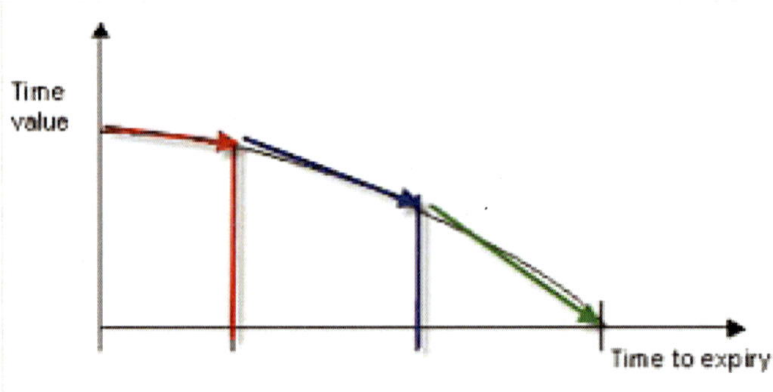

Figure 60- Theta and Covered Call Writing Premiums

In two of the three scenarios, we lose. These are odds I try to avoid. By selling the option at the time we purchased the security, we will generate the returns that meet our goals or we would not have selected that underlying. That being said, there are tactics we can employ to take advantage of this situation without incurring the risk suggested. We do survey the overall market and, if bullish, we can favor out-of-the-money strikes. What this accomplishes for us is that we generate the initial profit that meets our goal and then have the opportunity for an additional income stream from share appreciation up to the strike price. For example, if a stock price had dropped from $30.00 to $28.00 and we purchased it at that lower price, we can immediately sell the $30.00 out-of-the-money call. Let's assume we generate $0.90 per share or $90.00 per contract for an initial one-month return of 3.2%. Not bad so far. Now, since we are bullish on price movement (inherent in Paul's question) we anticipate a price increase. If the price does move up to the $30.00 strike, we generate an additional $2.00 per share or $200.00 per contract. In this scenario our total one-month profit is $290.00 on a cost basis of $2800.00 or a 10.4% one-month return.

Conclusion

After a market decline and shares are purchased at a lower price, it is to our advantage to immediately sell the option to generate our target goal. If we are bullish on the overall market's anticipated movement, we can take advantage of that situation by favoring out-of-the-money strikes. This way we are guaranteed our initial target returns and have an opportunity to take advantage of a market recovery. Of course, we are always prepared with our exit strategies if any trade turns against us or turns out much better than anticipated.

Deep In-The-Money Strikes: A Can't Lose Strategy?

Covered call writing is a strategy we use to generate consistent monthly cash flow, to re-invest profits and ultimately to become financially independent. We strive to beat the market by using sound fundamental, technical and common sense principles. But why are we getting paid more than treasuries, CDs or money market accounts? The answer is that we are generating these higher returns for undertaking risk. The whole basis of the BCI methodology is to undertake modest risk and mitigate that risk through a series of guidelines and principles set forth in our books and DVD Programs. Wouldn't it be great if we were to receive these higher returns and not be subject to any risk? That was a rhetorical question…deep down inside we all know that there is no legal way of accomplishing that goal. But it's always fun trying to find that ultimate strategy that even the most sophisticated of computers has yet to uncover.

Recently, I responded to a comment made by Tony and felt it was worthy of a journal article because of the impressive thinking that went behind the inquiry as well as the lessons learned. The question presented: *Is the following strategy, a "can't-lose" approach to covered call writing?*

Proposed strategy

- Sell a deep in-the-money strike with a 2% time value premium and downside protection of that profit
- If share price drops less than the downside protection (intrinsic value of the premium), take no action
- If share price drops below the strike mid-contract, close the entire position and generate the 2% profit or a little less if the position is closed below the strike

Principles used to develop this strategy

Tony used his knowledge of the advantages presented to us of using in-the-money strikes. We can generate a time value component of the option premium which represents our initial profit and also have an insurance policy to protect that profit in the form of the intrinsic value component of the premium…*intrinsic value protects the time value*. It appears on the surface that if the shares depreciate and the positions are closed as the strike price is approached that we are fully protected and cannot lose (do you sense a "but" coming?).

The reality of options and why there is no free lunch

- A stock price can gap-down and even if we wanted to sell at the strike, there is no guarantee that we will get our price
- To generate a time value component of 2%, the strike can certainly be in-the-money but not <u>deep</u> in the money unless the stock has huge implied volatility which we

generally try to avoid. This means that the strike selected will be below market value but not out-of-sight

- ***As the price of the stock approaches the strike originally sold that strike which was initially in-the-money is now ***at-the-money***. Since the time value component of premiums is greatest for at-the-money strikes, the cost to close will most likely result in an options debit despite the impact of theta (time value erosion) mid-contract
- There will also be a small debit from the bid-ask spread, less of a factor than the option time value debit

Time value components for different strikes for Facebook (FB)

The chart in Figure 61 shows the option premiums for in-the-money and near-the-money strikes for FB:

Calls — May 14

FB: $62.72

Last	Intrinsic Value	Bid				Strike
17.88	17.72	17.60				45.00
13.28	12.72	13.00				50.00
11.18	10.22	11.00				52.50
9.15	7.72	9.05	9.25	0	71	55.00
7.35	5.22	7.25	7.45	0	134	57.50
5.83	2.72	5.75	5.90	0	2,361	60.00
5.55	2.22	5.45	5.65	0	446	60.50
5.30	1.72	5.25	5.35	0	365	61.00
4.97	1.22	4.85	5.10	0	144	61.50
4.75	0.72	4.65	4.85	0	533	62.00
4.45	0.22	4.35	4.55	0	264	62.50
4.22	0.00	4.15	[illegible]	0	800	63.00
4.00	0.00	3.95	4.05	0	637	63.50
3.78	0.00	3.70	3.85	0	624	64.00
3.58	0.00	3.50	3.65	0	496	64.50
3.33	0.00	3.25	3.40	0	5,079	65.00
3.12	0.00	3.05	3.20	0	318	65.50
2.91	0.00	2.85	2.97	0	835	66.00
2.73	0.00	2.69	2.78	0	343	66.50
2.56	0.00	2.51	2.61	0	340	67.00
2.39	0.00	2.34	2.44	0	604	67.50
2.23	0.00	2.18	2.28	0	959	68.00
2.08	0.00	2.04	2.13	0	154	68.50
1.94	0.00	1.90	1.99	0	838	69.00
1.81	0.00	1.77	1.85	0	166	69.50
1.69	0.00	1.65	1.72	0	2,901	70.00
1.55	0.00	1.49	1.61	0	107	70.50
1.46	0.00	1.42	1.49	0	483	71.00
1.34	0.00	1.31	1.38	0	25	71.50

Figure 61- Option Premiums of Different Strike Prices for FB

- The time value of the near-the-money strike $62.50 is $4.55 – $0.22 = $4.33 (cost to close or buy-to-close). This demonstrates the increased time value for near-the-money or at-the-money strikes
- The time value of the in-the-money strike $60.00 is $5.75 – $2.72 = $3.03 (original premium generated or sell-to-open)
- The option debit to close in this case would be $1.30 or $130.00 per contract, about a 2% loss. It will actually be slightly less due to the impact of theta or time value erosion but there will be a loss. I created this chart to demonstrate the ***higher cost to buy back an at-the-money strike compared to the cash generated from selling an in-the-money strike and why there is no free lunch***

If we thought about it and there was, in fact, a "can't lose" strategy, who would be the folks taking the other side of our trades? They can't win if we can't lose! Eventually, they would wise up and such trades would no longer exist. We trade in markets, hopefully we all trade in fair market conditions. Our edge ("the BCI edge") over everyone else is the due-diligence we execute regarding the major three aspects of covered call writing:

- stock selection
- option selection
- position management

This is what gives us our edge in this low-risk, but not no-risk, strategy.

With thanks to Tony.

Earnings Reports and Covered Call Writing in our BCI Methodology

In the BCI methodology, our covered call writing strategy has several guidelines and one rule. The rule is to **never sell a covered call option when there is an upcoming earnings report prior to expiration**. Some may ask why not? With the added volatility, aren't our options going to generate additional premium and if the report disappoints will not the premium help mitigate losses? True and true but the rule stands.

BCI history

When I started teaching myself this strategy in the early 1990s I would find that periodically one stock's price decline would wipe out my entire month's option profits. I would always research the cause of a loss and more often than not it was a disappointing earnings report. I, like you, don't like to lose money so ultimately I created the rule to avoid earnings reports and the number of catastrophic gap downs decreased dramatically (they will, however, still pop up from time to time usually due to unexpected negative corporate or global news).

What can cause an earnings report gap down?

So what is it about these reports that can create a gap-down? Why is it that a company can have a stellar report and still decline in price? Market reaction, to a great extent, is based on analyst expectations or *consensus*. If a company's earnings and revenues rose by 20% year-to-year but the market was anticipating a 25% increase, look out below. Then there's the *whisper number*. This is the unofficial, unpublished earnings forecasts that circulate among professionals on Wall Street. This number may be different from consensus and can impact market interpretation of a report. There is also corporate *guidance* where a company forecasts future earnings and revenues. This too can be a source of market disappointment. The point here is that so much can go wrong and we are generally conservative investors, using low-risk strategies with capital preservation a critical goal. Why take the chance?

Evaluating earnings reports from a mathematics perspective

The implied volatility of an option reflects the market anticipation of price movement in the future. It is greater when earnings are due to be reported prior to expiration. Let's say in a non-earnings report contract month a stock traditionally trades in a $4.00 price range. So a stock trading at $38.00 may trade between $36.00 and $40.00. Writing a $40.00 call for $1.60 on an uptrending stock with strong fundamentals is a low-risk and sound investment. Now let's say earnings is approaching and the market is anticipating a drop as low as $30.00 or a move up as high as $46.00, a $16.00 range. Admittedly, I am using an extreme example, but I feel that it is important to make this point as graphically as possible. Selling that same $40.00 strike will limit the upside to $2.00 but protect the downside by only the premium generated. We are susceptible to greater losses despite the fact that we had knowledge of the date that enhanced our risk liability.

What if the report does not disappoint and I still like the stock?

Time to get on board. You now have two months to use this great-performer after the volatility of the report reaction passes. Never look back and say what could have been. But rather congratulate yourself for circumventing a potential disaster. The cash you would have spent on this stock didn't go to waste. You used it to invest with another financial soldier…a safer one.

What if I think the report will be a positive one?

Okay so now we're getting away from covered call writing but

I must admit that from time to time I will own a stock through an earnings report. Years ago I did this frequently with CSCO and AAPL with huge success. Although it is not part of our BCI methodology when a stock is owned through a report, we take full advantage of the positive surprise (the last few years there have been more positive than negative surprises) and then write the call after the report passes and get the best of both worlds. However, be prepared that you could be wrong and get spanked with this approach if the report disappoints. Whether we should own a stock through an earnings report (and then write the call after that report passes) depends on our personal risk-tolerance and the confidence we have in a positive surprise.

Sample chart

Figure 62 shows a chart of YNDX, a stock frequently found on our Premium Watch List showing both a gap up (pink field) and a gap down (yellow field) resulting from earnings reports:

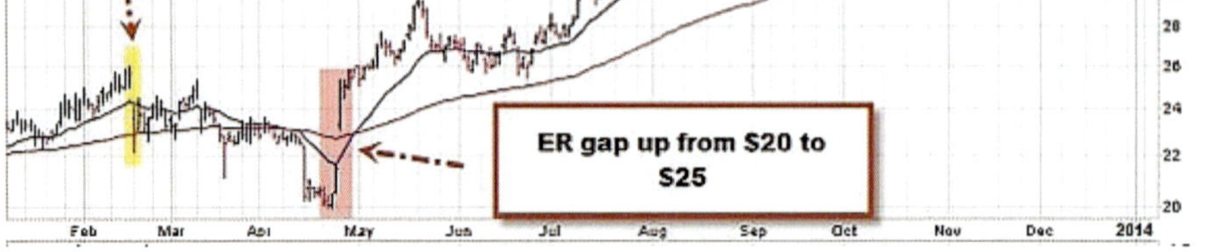

Figure 62- YNDX and Earnings Reports

Premium Report earnings dates

Premium Member Stock Reports highlight earnings dates for the current contract month in gold rows (red arrow) with the projected dates for all eligible stocks in the column highlighted by the blue arrow as seen in Figure 63:

Week 1 06/26/15	Week 2 07/03/15	Week 3 07/10/15	Expiry ▼ Week 4 07/17/15	Week 5 07/24/15	Running List	Price	Wks On Run List	Next ER Date	Industry Segment	Segment Rank	Risk / Reward	Beta	% Div. Yield	Wkly Avail	NTM OI >100 Cntr.	Comments (The last or next Ex-Div date is shown)
0 & OTHER - PASSED CURRENT WEEK					PASSED PREVIOUS WEEKS & PASSED CURRENT WEEK											
AAN	AAN				UNH	121.81	7	**07/16/15**	Medical	A/A	8	1.17	1.60	Y	Y	06/11/15
ABG	**ACHC**				EBAY	61.85	1	**07/16/15**	Retail	A	7	0.92		Y	Y	
ACHC	**ADVS**				ABG	91.06	4	07/21/15	Retail	C/C	5	1.30			Y	
ADVS	**AFSI**				MANH	59.84	30	07/21/15	Software	A/A	9	1.35			Y	
AFSI	AGN				SBNY	147.74	4	07/21/15	Banks	B/B	10	1.06			N	
AGN	AOS				ILMN	220.07	9	07/22/15	Medical	A/A	6	1.30		Y	Y	
AHS	ATHM				LAD	113.71	17	07/22/15	Retail	C/C	7	1.52	0.70		Y	05/13/15
AMBA	**AYI**				TCBI	62.34	3	07/22/15	Banks	A/A	10	1.08			Y	
AMSG	**BIIB**				ROL	27.11	1	07/22/15	Busn Svcs	A	9	0.61	1.20		N	05/06/15
BIIB	**CELG**				UCBI	20.99	1	**07/22/15**	Banks	B	7	1.04	1.00		N	06/11/15
CELG	CRI				AOS	72.76	11	**07/23/15**	Building	B/B	8	0.93	1.00		Y	04/28/15

Figure 63- Premium Stock Reports and Earnings

Conclusion

Never write a covered call on a stock with an upcoming earnings report. If you feel strongly about owning the stock through the report or own it in a long-term buy and hold portfolio, write the call after the report passes. Some stocks have Weekly options which will allow you to write calls up to the week of the earnings report.

Expanded Weekly Options: When should we Enter a Trade?

With the rising popularity of stock option strategies and covered call writing in particular, we have seen the creation of more option products like Weekly stock options. *Weeklys* expire each Friday of the month whereas the more traditional *Monthlys* generally expire only on the third Friday of each month. Weeklys fall into one of two categories: *standard Weeklys* or *expanded Weeklys*. In the last quarter of 2012, the options exchanges received regulatory approval for extended Weekly expirations. The options exchanges can now list up to five consecutive Weekly expirations for selected securities. Although any product with Weekly expirations can be part of the extended Weekly program, the exchanges will typically select the most actively traded options.

If the regular monthly expiration is three weeks away, then investors would most likely see Weekly, Weekly, Monthly, Weekly and Weekly expirations listed over a five-week period. There are no new Weeklys added that would expire during the expiration week for traditional Monthlys, which is typically the third Friday of each month, nor are they listed if they would expire on the same date as a Quarterly option on the same underlying security. *Quarterlys* are options that expire at the ends of quarters.

With so many more choices than we previously had available, I thought it would be interesting to evaluate the returns for one, two, three and four-week options on the same underlying securities and then annualize those returns to give us a sense as to which time frame may be in our best interest. Although this is far from a long-term scientific study, I did find the results interesting as a preliminary view into the world of Weekly stock options. Here's how I set things up:

Weekly evaluation setup

- I selected two stocks from our Premium Watch List dated 7/18/2014
- These stocks had to have expanded Weeklys associated with them
- Neither stock could have an upcoming earnings report prior to expiration
- Data was taken immediately after expiration of the July contracts
- One, two, three and four-week options were calculated
- The two stocks selected were SWKS and TTM

Calculating results

Figure 64 shows the results in the "multiple tab" of the Ellman Calculator:

RETURN ON OPTION (ROO) CALCULATOR - MULTIPLE STOCKS

Stock Name or Symbol	Stock $/sh	Option $/sh	Strike $	Expires	Intrisic	Upside	Breakeven	ROO	Up Potential	Down Protect	Annualized returns
SWKS	$54.33	$0.35	$ 55.00	07/25/14	$ -	$ 0.67	$ 53.98	0.6%	1.2%	0.0%	33%
SWKS	$54.33	$0.75	$55.00	08/01/14	$ -	$ 0.67	$ 53.58	1.4%	1.2%	0.0%	36%
SWKS	$54.33	$ 1.00	$55.00	08/08/14	$ -	$ 0.67	$ 53.33	1.8%	1.2%	0.0%	32%
SWKS	$54.33	$1.30	$55.00	08/15/14	$ -	$ 0.67	$ 53.03	2.4%	1.2%	0.0%	31%
TTM	$ 42.65	$ 0.30	$ 43.00	07/25/14	$ -	$ 0.35	$ 42.35	0.7%	0.8%	0.0%	37%
TTM	$ 42.65	$ 0.60	$ 43.00	08/01/14	$ -	$ 0.35	$ 42.05	1.4%	0.8%	0.0%	37%
TTM	$ 42.65	$ 0.85	$ 43.00	08/08/14	$ -	$ 0.35	$ 41.80	2.0%	0.8%	0.0%	35%
TTM	$ 42.65	$ 1.15	$ 43.00	08/15/14	$ -	$ 0.35	$ 41.50	2.7%	0.8%	0.0%	35%

Figure 64- Calculating Weekly Options with the Ellman Calculator

Summary of results

- The options in weeks one and two showed slightly higher annualized returns than those in weeks three and four for both stocks
- Is this small difference enough for us to favor Weeklys over the more traditional Monthlys?

In my humble opinion

From this initial, admittedly cursory view of weekly calculations there appears to be no clear reason for favoring Weeklys or Monthlys based on annualized returns although the Weeklys in weeks one and two did slightly outperform. This may be motivation enough for some. Therefore, I would make a decision based on an overview of the pros and cons of Weeklys as compared to traditional Monthlys.

Pros and cons of Weeklys as I see them

Positives:

- Annualized returns can be higher as shown in Figure 64

- Can avoid exposure over weekends
- Can generate greater premium as earnings report dates are approached and trade up to the week before earnings

Negatives:

- The pool of stocks with Weeklys is much smaller than those with Monthlys
- Position management is much more time-consuming as "rolling" possibilities come up every week
- Less time for exit strategy execution
- Quadruple the number and amount of trading commissions
- Lower option liquidity
- Wider bid-ask spreads

Conclusion

There are many ways to make money in the stock market and using Weeklys is certainly one of them. There is no one strategy appropriate for every single investor so when deciding between Weeklys and Monthlys we must make sure we understand all the nuances (pros and cons) associated with each choice in order to come to the conclusion that is in our personal best interest.

How to Use Implied Volatility in our Covered Call Writing Decisions

Understanding the Greeks, or factors that impact the value of our covered call premiums, is essential to mastering options trading basics and becoming an elite covered call writer. One of the Greeks (although not truly a Greek letter) is *Vega*, the amount an option price will change for every 1% change in volatility of the underlying security. As the anticipated or implied (implied by the option premiums) volatility of the underlying security moves higher, so does the value of the option premium if all other factors remain the same. This *implied volatility* is different from the *historical or statistical volatility* which is based on actual price fluctuation over a specific time frame.

This understanding of the impact that volatility has on our option profits has led some investors to look for divergences between historical and implied volatility, specifically when implied is well above its historical statistics. The theory here is that the greater the divergence, the greater the opportunity to generate higher returns. Here is an example of such a trade made a few months ago by one of our members:

The company is Alcobra (ADHD), a pharmaceutical company known for dealing with attention deficit medical conditions.

- Buy ADHD at $20.92
- Sell October 17, 2014 $20.00 call at $7.20

Let's feed this information into the "multiple tab" of the Ellman Calculator (Figure 65):

RETURN ON OPTION (ROO) CALCULATOR - MULTIPLE STOCKS

Stock Name or Symbol	Stock $/sh	Option $/sh	Strike $	Expires	Intrisic	Upside	Breakeven	ROO	Up Potential	Down Protect
ASHR	$54.72	$5.80	$ 50.00	07/17/15	$ 4.72	$ -	$ 48.92	2.2%	0.0%	8.6%
ASHR	$54.72	$2.95	$55.00	07/17/15	$ -	$ 0.28	$ 51.77	5.4%	0.5%	0.0%
ASHR	$54.72	$ 1.40	60	07/17/15	$ -	$ 5.28	$ 53.32	2.6%	9.6%	0.0%
ADHD	$20.92	$7.20	$20.00	10/17/14	$ 0.92	$ -	$ 13.72	31.4%	0.0%	4.4%
CRUS	$ 36.84	$ 2.00	$ 35.50	06/19/15	$ 1.34	$ -	$ 34.84	1.9%	0.0%	3.6%
UTHR	$ 184.14	$ 7.60	$ 180.00	06/19/15	$ 4.14	$ -	$ 176.54	1.9%	0.0%	2.2%
NXPI	$ 103.15	$ 5.20	$ 100.00	06/19/15	$ 3.15	$ -	$ 97.95	2.0%	0.0%	3.1%

Figure 65- Initial Returns for ADHD (yellow-highlighted row)

The results show a HUGE return of 31.4% in less than two months and also downside protection *of that profit* of 4.4%. In other words, share value can drop by no more than 4.4% by expiration and we still would have generated a two-month return of 31.4%. Equally as impressive is the trade breakeven point of $13.72. Can this be the free lunch we all have been searching for?

So why are option buyers willing to pay us such a generous premium? It is so important to understand the other side of a trade in addition to looking at it from our perspective. The answer goes back to implied volatility or the market's anticipation of future price movement of the underlying security. The option buyers are expecting substantial price movement of this security by expiration and we are being paid for undertaking the associated risk. To determine the implied volatility of this specific option, I turned to the options calculator (Figure 66) found at www.cboe.com:

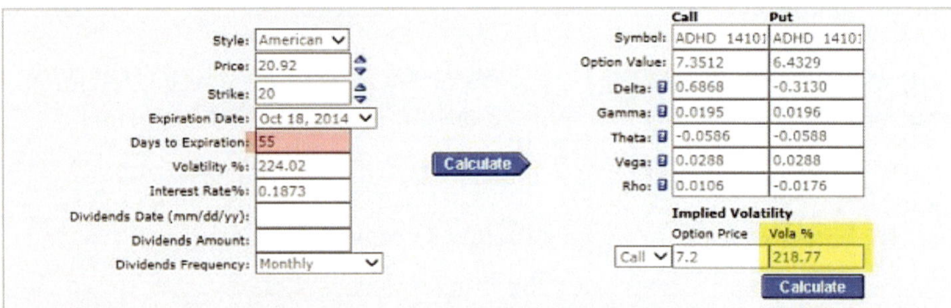

Figure 66- Implied Volatility of ADHD

On the lower right side of this screenshot (highlighted in yellow) we see the implied volatility of the October $20.00 call is a whopping 218.77%. Now, I have this thing for math so please bear with me…there is a formula that we can use to determine the market's anticipated price movement based on this implied volatility and it is based on one standard deviation which just means that it will be accurate 68% of the time…hang in there:

One Standard Deviation = stock price x implied volatility x [the square root of the number of days in the trade/365]

1 SD = \$20.92 x 2.18 x .39 = plus or minus \$17.78

Let's bring this down to human talk: Based on this implied volatility of 218%, the market is anticipating a price range for this stock as low as \$3.14 and as high as \$38.70 by expiration (in fifty-five days), 68% of the time. This is why the premium is so generous but do we want to hang our hats on such a security? Covered call writing is a conservative strategy for investors with low-risk-tolerance who stress capital preservation.

I wonder how many of you are wondering why the market is anticipating such a monumental price change over the next fifty-five days. Me too. Like many pharmaceuticals, the company is involved in a drug trial with the FDA and initial results were due out in the fourth quarter, 2014. A positive report and the share price can go to the moon; a negative report and...well you get the idea.

So what happened?

Figure 67- ADHD after Negative News

The market expectation was correct on the negative side as share price dropped from over $20.00 per share to under $6.00 per share. Remember how safe that breakeven at $13.72 felt? Once again, no free lunch.

Conclusion

Understanding how the Greeks (and implied volatility in particular) impact our covered call writing decisions is critical to becoming an elite options trader. Screening for stocks that show a large divergence between implied and historical volatility may be a way to *eliminate* (as opposed to locate) covered call writing candidates and should only be embraced by those with a high risk-tolerance.

Implied Volatility and our Premium Exchange-Traded Funds (ETF) Report

Our study of option trading basics and stock option strategies includes an analysis of implied volatility. This is the market's forecast of the underlying security's volatility as implied by the option's price in the market place. Frequently, the mid-point of the bid-ask spread, called the *mark*, is used to calculate implied volatility. In this article, I am highlighting a feature we have added to our Premium ETF (exchange-traded funds) Reports involving implied volatility statistics.

Reason for adding this additional information

Based on member feedback, which is so important to us, it has come to our attention that some members have made the assumption that the exchange-traded funds in our reports are all low-risk securities with low implied volatility (IV). This conclusion was based on the fact that BCI is a low-risk approach to covered call writing and investing in general, and by using ETFs our investment approach is even more conservative in nature. A point well-taken. Our ETF screening process involves selecting securities that are out-performing the S&P 500 over the past three months, have a relative strength rating (price performance compared to overall market) above 60, have adequate trading volume and option liquidity in the form of open interest (OI) of more than one hundred contracts for near-the-money strikes. Although most of the ETFs presented in our reports have associated low implied volatility, some do not. As we have done throughout the years, when we can enhance the products we provide to our members we take action.

Information provided on pages seven and eight of the report

Our BCI team will be sharing the current implied volatility of the S&P 500 (SPX) and that of the eligible ETF candidates. This will allow our members to compare the expected movement of a particular security to that of the overall market. We are using the average IV for the call and put options for that underlying security. Let's have a look at a past page seven of our Premium ETF Report in Figure 68:

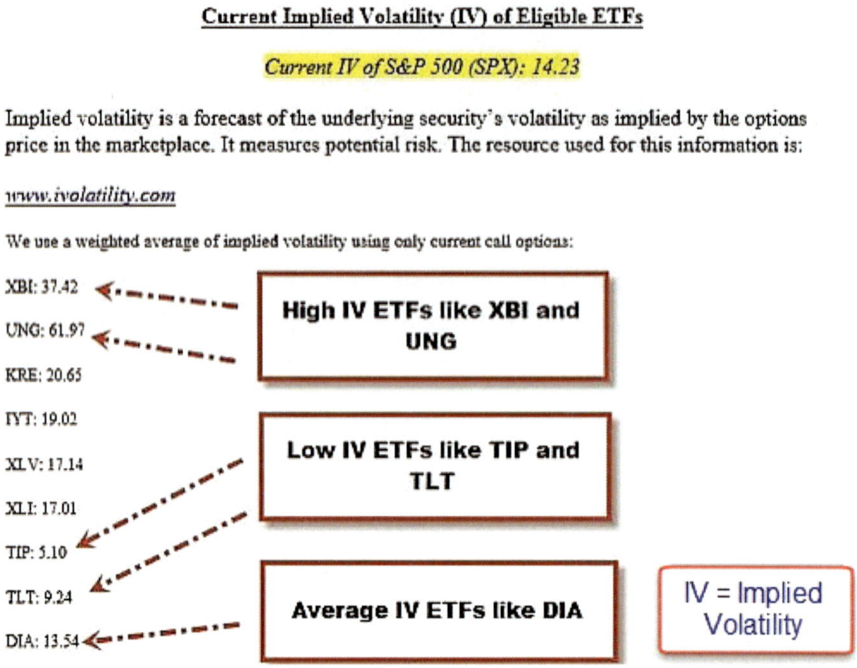

Figure 68- Exchange-Traded Funds and Implied Volatility

Features of the report

- The current implied volatility of SPX (S&P 500) is 14.23 (highlighted in yellow)
- ETFs like XBI and UNG have implied volatilities triple and quadruple that of SPX
- ETFs like TIP and TLT had implied volatilities one half to one third that of SPX
- ETFs like DIA have similar implied volatilities to that of SPX
- The resource we use is: www.iVolatility.com
- High implied volatility ETFs are expected to be riskier securities with higher call premiums

- Low implied volatility ETFs are expected to be safer securities with lower call premiums
- Selections can be made based on personal risk-tolerance and overall market assessment

Summary

Based on member feedback, the BCI team has added another feature to our premium ETF Report. Pages seven and eight of the reports will now show the current implied volatility based on the average of call and put options for all eligible ETFs and a comparison stat with that of the S&P 500 (SPX). This will allow our members to select the appropriate securities for their personal risk tolerance and overall market assessment.

Implied Volatility: General Market Conditions that make Option Values Move Up or Down

Option trading basics teaches us that selling call and put options is actually selling time value. Time value consists mainly of time to expiration stats and the implied volatility (IV) of the underlying security. Since most of us are selling monthly options, the main distinguishing factor in our option prices is the implied volatility… therefore, *we are selling volatility*.

In this article we will take a look at how implied volatility is impacted by individual stock events and then we will take a broader look as to how implied volatility is influenced by supply and demand for options based on market perception.

Individual stocks events

There are certain events that can cause the market to anticipate a significant price change in our stocks and exchange-traded funds (ETFs) and therefore elevate the implied volatility of the associated options. The most common of these circumstances is earnings reports, a topic I will never stop discussing because I consider it so important to our ultimate success. Other events, like impending FDA announcements of drug approvals and Federal Reserve announcements (among others) will also elevate implied volatility and therefore our option prices. However, higher implied volatility also means greater risk as share value can decline significantly thereby resulting in substantial losses. This is why a BCI golden rule is to never sell a covered call or put option when there is an upcoming earnings report prior to expiration Friday. Although implied volatility is influenced by a myriad of factors, earnings reports are one of the most common and important as shown in the chart below (Figure 69) highlighting the volatility spikes (as shown by the CBOE Volatility Index or VIX) in each of the last four earnings quarters:

Figure 69- Implied Volatility and Earnings Seasons

General market perception

Options are used for three major reasons:

- Generating cash flow (that's us!)
- Speculation (betting a stock price will move up or down)
- As a risk management tool (hedging)

Speculation

There is a greater demand for call options as implied volatility increases because shares of stock can be controlled at a much lower cost and if the trade turns against the investor, there is less capital risk than if the shares had been purchased. In addition to this, during times of low volatility, speculators will turn to selling options (just like us) to elevate the returns they are not receiving due to the low-implied volatility environment.

Hedging

Institutional investors (mutual funds, hedge funds, banks and insurance companies) use options to protect their multi-million dollar portfolios. When there is an impression that risk is increasing, there is a greater demand for option hedging (buying puts for example) and as a result, prices of these securities will rise. On the other end of the spectrum, when the market is presuming a period of lower volatility the demand for option protection is lessened and therefore options are sold and prices decline.

Summary

Long option positions are supported by high volatility conditions while short option positions benefit from low volatility situations. Buying and selling options is equivalent to buying and selling volatility.

Implied Volatility: More Important than Historical Volatility to Covered Call Writers and Put-Sellers

Understanding the concept of implied volatility is essential for successful covered call writing and put-selling. First, implied volatility gives us a window into the market's perception of future price movement. It will also allow us to calculate probability of a stock price reaching a certain level. Like all other parameters, implied volatility, although quite important and useful, does have its limitations. Let's first compare the two major types of volatility:

Historical vs. implied volatility

Historical volatility is the actual price fluctuation as observed over a specific time frame. More specifically, it is the annualized standard deviation (discussed below) of past stock price movements.

Implied volatility is a forecast or market opinion of the underlying security's volatility as implied by the option's prices in the current market.

For short-term option sellers like us, current information is much more important than historical data which may be more significant to longer-term investors.

Implied volatility and our option premiums

We know that the time value component of our option premiums is impacted by time to expiration and the implied volatility of the underlying security. Since most of us sell one-month or one-week options, time to expiration will remain constant when comparing premiums. That leaves the implied volatility as the main factor influencing premium (remember we are talking time value, not intrinsic value). The good news is that the greater the implied volatility, the more premium our option sales will generate. The bad news is that the greater the volatility, the more risk to the downside we are susceptible to as calculated by using the implied volatility stat. *Understanding implied volatility will allow us to make informed decisions as we compare premium to implied risk.*

How is implied volatility calculated?

To calculate implied volatility, we need (or someone needs...) an option pricing model like the *Black-Scholes Option Pricing Model*. Of these six inputs below, implied volatility is the only one not directly observable in the market and therefore we need the other five inputs to calculate implied volatility:

- Call premium
- Exercise price
- Price of underlying
- Risk-free interest rate
- Time to expiration
- Implied volatility

Standard deviation and implied volatility

The implied volatility generated from an option pricing model will tell us the probability of a certain price movement <u>in either direction</u> on an annualized basis. Let's say a stock is trading at $30.00 and has an implied volatility of 20% for the at-the-money strike. This means that the share price, based on current option pricing, is expected to move up or down by $6.00 during the next year. In other words, the anticipated trading range is $24.00 to $36.00. This stat is for one standard deviation as it relates to a bell curve distribution of potential prices. Stated differently, we would expect a trading range of $24.00 to $36.00 68% of the time. Now, two standard deviations would be $12.00 in either direction or a range of $18.00 to $42.00 and is expected to stay in that range 95% of the time. Three standard deviations would represent a range of $12.00 to $48.00 and would be expected to stay in that range 99% of the time. Still with me? Figure 70 shows what that distribution curve looks like:

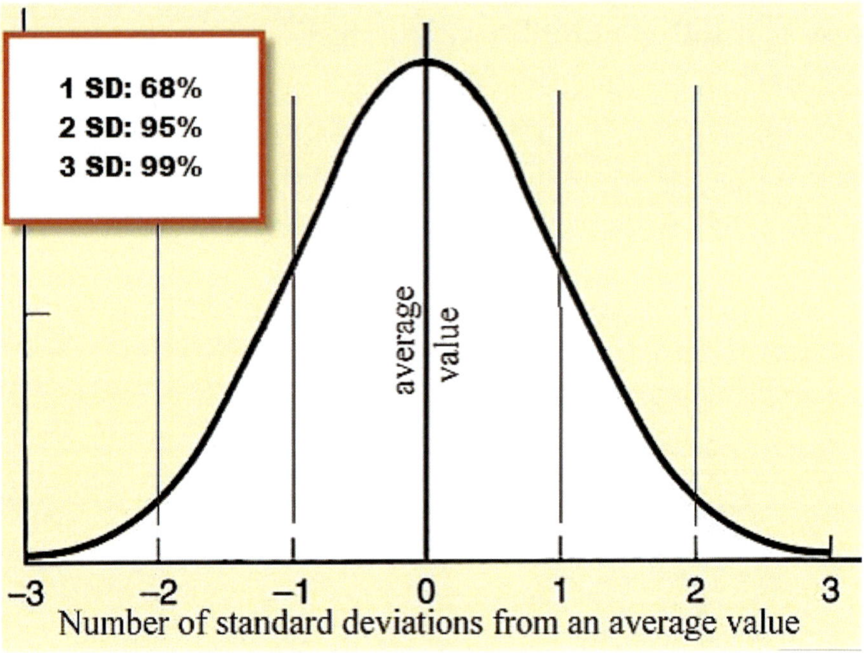

Figure 70- Standard Deviation: Normal Bell Curve

Calculations for one month and one standard deviation

Since very few of us trade one-year options, these implied volatility stats must be customized to our shorter-term periods. It's not necessary to remember this math but you're getting it anyway...

For a thirty-day option and one standard deviation for this $30.00 stock, we multiply the implied volatility stat by the square root of 30/365:

$30.00 x 20% x .286 = $1.72

This means that based on current option pricing, we would expect this stock to trade between $28.28 and $31.72 68% of the time during the next thirty days (I'm beginning to give myself a headache!).

Summary

Implied volatility is more important to short-term option sellers than is historical volatility. It demonstrates market sentiment about future price movement although it does not define direction. We can use it to determine price probability and therefore risk parameters that will allow us to decide if a trade is consistent with our personal risk-tolerance and monthly goals. A quick, user-friendly way to estimate implied volatility is to look at the returns on an option. For example, if a one-month at-the-money strike generates more than 6%, we are dealing with a high-implied volatility trade. This may be appropriate for some but not for others.

Mini Options- A New Product for Retail Investors

There is a new options product that will begin trading on March 18, 2013 which has the potential to add great flexibility to our covered call writing strategy. They are called *mini options* and I'm excited to present this information to you because the product is geared to average retail investors (aka Blue Collar Investors) like us. Like all new securities we must take our time to evaluate the efficacy of instituting them into our portfolios as we evaluate the pros and cons of implementing these new products.

What is a mini option?

These are contracts that deliver ten shares of an underlying security, whereas standard contracts deliver one hundred shares. They will have the same expiration dates and strike prices as the standard contracts. The International Securities Exchange (ISE) also expects the bid-ask spreads to be the same. We'll see about that. These new products are not superior to their standard counterparts, just smaller with reduced risk and reduced reward.

What will the commissions be?

Right now, I would frame this as a big unknown. I haven't received a firm response from the exchanges or brokerages that I have contacted. One would hope (expect) that the commissions would be 1/10th of that of the standard contract but there are no guarantees at this time.

***Note: As of 2015 trading commissions for minis are the same as standard options, a big disappointment for retail investors.

What are the available underlying securities and why were they selected?

It appears that the exchanges, initially, are requiring underlying stocks and exchange-traded funds to have a minimum price of $100.00. In addition, the exchanges surveyed various brokerages to see which tickers tended to trade in *odd lots* or fewer than one hundred shares. For example, according to TD Ameritrade, 77% of executions with AAPL occur in odd lots. Here are the five securities that will be trading mini options as of March 18, 2013:

- Apple Inc. (AAPL)
- Google Inc. (GOOG)
- Amazon.com, Inc. (AMZN)
- SPDR S&P 500 ETF Trust (SPY)
- SPDR Gold ETF (GLD)

Here are a few potential additions in the near future but NOT available initially:

- Master Card Inc. (MA)
- Visa Inc. (V)
- Priceline.com Inc. (PCLN)

- Netflix Inc. (NFLX)
- Chipotle Mexican Grill Inc. (CMG)
- Goldman Sachs Group Inc. (GS)
- iShares 20+ Year Treasury Bond Fund (TLT)

Sample portfolio with $50,000.00 cash available (Figure 71)

I created a hypothetical covered call portfolio assuming a cash balance of $50,000.00 using the BCI requirement of similar cash allocation per position and using current bid-ask spreads with three weeks remaining until expiration of the March contracts:

MINI OPTIONS/SLIGHTLY OTM STRIKES				
STOCK/ETF	**PRICE**	**# SHARES**	**COST**	**OPTION $**
GOOG	$800	10	$8,000	$112
AMZN	$263	30	$7,890	$154
AAPL	$445	20	$8,900	$216
SPY	$152	50	$7,600	$75
GLD	$155	50	$7,750	$78
			$40,140	**$635**
	3-week return = 1.6%= 27% annualized			

Figure 71- Mini Options: Sample Covered Call Portfolio

Benefit to Blue Collar Investors

Since the average portfolios of retail investors has between $10,000.00 and $50,000.00 in assets, the mini options will allow many of us to trade with high-priced underlying securities. For example, to sell a traditional covered call on AAPL, we would currently (before minis) have to purchase one hundred shares at about $500.00 per share (prior to 7-for-1 stock split) or invest $50,000.00 before we could sell the option. That one trade would create too much risk for most of us and prevent appropriate diversification. With minis, we could purchase just ten shares for $5,000.00, sell the mini call and have plenty of cash left over for additional positions.

Potential pitfalls and why we should watch and wait

As I stated at the beginning of this article, I am truly excited about these new products. However, I would not jump in right away for the following reasons:

- The commissions involved have not been published by the brokerages. My hope is that they will reflect 1/10 that of standard options but only time will tell (update... commissions were not reduced)
- Since option liquidity plays a major role in bid-ask spreads, this will be another unknown until the minis actually begin trading
- We must familiarize ourselves with the new tickers to make sure we are entering the correct tickers when executing a trade. You're probably sick of hearing me say this but paper-trading a new product first makes good sense to this investor
- We must be sure that the brokerages, market makers and market vendors are prepared for the March 18th launch. Let's allow others to be the guinea pigs and then we can jump in once the "bugs" are ironed out.

Conclusion

The new mini options appear to be a product that will benefit average retail investors. It will allow us to trade high-priced securities while still being properly diversified as well as allowing for balanced cash allocation. However, it is prudent to wait a bit for the launch of these new products and then re-evaluate their value to us a few months down the road.

Mini Options: The Impact of Commissions and Liquidity on Final Returns

Our stock options strategies have a new product to consider: mini options. These options have a deliverable ten shares of underlying security instead of the traditional one hundred shares. *The options symbols for these minis begin with the security ticker followed by the number 7:*

- AAPL7
- AMZN7
- GOOG7
- GLD7
- SPY7

These five securities are the only ones currently available with mini options although many more will likely follow. These new products allow average retail investors to sell covered call options without having to layout huge sums of money to purchase the underlying shares of high-priced stocks. For example, to sell one traditional covered call option for Apple Computer would require us to invest over $50,000.00 to enter the long stock position. With minis that investment would be reduced to $5,000.00 (prior to the seven-for-one stock split).

My initial concern, as with the introduction of all new products, is the liquidity of trading and how that impacts the bid-ask spreads. My second, specifically with minis, is the question of commissions. Will the brokerages reduce commissions since the per-share commission percentage amount would be ten times greater if they didn't…they didn't as it turned out. In today's article I will use Apple Computer to demonstrate the impact that lower liquidity, higher bid-ask spreads and higher per-share commissions have on our annualized returns. At the time that I am writing this article AAPL was trading at $545.78 and the March, 2014 monthly contracts were five weeks away from expiration. Figure 72 shows the options chain for the traditional monthly contract with one hundred shares deliverable:

AAPL trading @ $544.78

Traditional option for $545 strike returns $14.25

84.62	84.79	83.90	85.35	6	346	460.00
					231	465.00
					541	470.00
					431	475.00
					921	480.00
					287	485.00
					600	490.00
					207	495.00
					543	500.00
					918	505.00
					159	510.00
33.95	29.79	33.70	34.20	99	1,990	515.00
30.10	24.79	29.90	30.30	835	4,643	520.00
26.43	19.79	26.25	26.60	580	2,961	525.00
22.90	14.79	22.80	23.00	482	4,117	530.00
19.82	9.79	19.70	19.95	798	4,112	535.00
16.90	4.79	16.85	16.95	1,356	7,120	540.00
14.28	0.00	14.25	14.30	725	3,526	545.00
11.93	0.00	11.85	12.00	3,649	10,366	550.00
9.88	0.00	9.80	9.95	1,498	3,423	555.00
8.07	0.00	8.00	8.15	2,201	5,586	560.00
6.60	0.00	6.55	6.65	1,181	3,802	565.00
5.35	0.00	5.30	5.40	1,007	4,252	570.00
4.28	0.00	4.20	4.35	912	5,048	575.00
3.42	0.00	3.35	3.50	865	16,263	580.00
2.76	0.00	2.73	2.79	584	2,577	585.00
2.21	0.00	2.18	2.24	1,327	10,362	590.00
1.79	0.00	1.77	1.82	542	1,359	595.00
1.46	0.00	1.44	1.48	1,880	11,097	600.00
1.21	0.00	1.18	1.23	174	1,221	605.00
1.00	0.00	0.99	1.02	81	2,245	610.00

Figure 72- AAPL Traditional Contracts

For the near-the-money $545.00 strike

- High open interest of 3,526 contracts
- Tight bid-ask spread of $0.05 ($14.25 – $14.30)
- Premium generated from sale of a covered call is $14.25 per share

The math

- ROO (return on option before commissions) = $1425.00/$54,478.00 = 2.62%, five-week return, 26.2% annualized
- ROO (after a $10.00 commission) = $1415.00/$54,478.00 = 2.60%, five-week return, 26% annualized
- Commission resulted in a five-week return reduction of 0.02%

***ROO = initial return on option or initial profit**

The options chain for the minis, also for March, 2014 expiration with ten shares deliverable (Figure 73)

74.40	74.79	72.95	75.85	0	22	470.00
69.53	69.79	68.10	70.95	0	7	475.00
64.50	64.79	63.25	65.75	4	99	480.00
					22	485.00
					40	490.00
					15	495.00
					244	500.00
					204	505.00
					192	510.00
					113	515.00
					395	520.00
					278	525.00
22.93	14.79	22.55	23.30	12	371	530.00
19.75	9.79	19.25	20.25	9	281	535.00
16.85	4.79	16.40	17.30	69	433	540.00
14.20	0.00	13.70	14.70	42	246	545.00
11.68	0.00	11.30	12.05	117	937	550.00
9.73	0.00	9.30	10.15	38	476	555.00
8.02	0.00	7.85	8.20	56	343	560.00
6.53	0.00	6.45	6.60	48	223	565.00
5.30	0.00	5.15	5.45	29	263	570.00
4.17	0.00	4.10	4.25	41	480	575.00
3.40	0.00	3.30	3.50	8	228	580.00
2.73	0.00	2.63	2.84	9	108	585.00
2.21	0.00	2.10	2.32	2	244	590.00
1.78	0.00	1.68	1.89	2	55	595.00
1.40	0.00	1.35	1.45	4	315	600.00
1.19	0.00	1.10	1.27	0	60	605.00
1.02	0.00	0.91	1.12	0	397	610.00
0.84	0.00	0.75	0.93	0	36	615.00

AAPL Minis: $13.70

Figure 73- AAPL Mini Options Chain

For the near-the-money $545.00 strike

- Significantly lower open interest of 246 contracts
- Much wider bid-ask spread of $1.00 ($13.70 – $14.70)
- Premium generated from sale of a covered call is $13.70 per share, $0.55 less than the traditional option

The math

- ROO (before commissions) = $137.00/$5447.80= 2.51%, five-week return, 25.1% annualized
- ROO (after a $10 commission) = $127.00/$5447.80 = 2.33%, five-week return, 23.3% annualized
- Commission resulted in a five-week return reduction of 0.18%

Annualized difference in returns

- Traditional: 26%
- Minis: 23.3%
- Traditionals outperform minis by 2.7%

AMZN stats

I then evaluated the same process using AMZN as the underlying when the stock was trading at $357.20 and looking at the $360.00 strike for both the traditional and mini options. The result was even more significant with the traditionals out-performing the minis by an annualized rate of 4.7%

Conclusion

Using the mini options at the current time will allow us to take positions in the five securities with a much lower cash investment. However, the returns will suffer because of the impact of commissions and wider bid-ask spreads due to lower option liquidity. I do believe that this liquidity will increase as time goes by, thereby decreasing the size of bid-ask spreads and perhaps brokerages will lower commissions for these products. In the interim, choosing other underlying securities that will generate higher returns may be the prudent approach.

Option Prices: The Role of Interest Rates and Dividends

Mastering options trading basics includes understanding the factors that impact our option premiums. The original Black Scholes pricing model was designed to evaluate *European Style options* which can only be exercised on expiration Friday, not earlier. Here is a brief summary of the factors considered in these original pricing models:

Factors for original option pricing models

- Stock price
- Option strike price
- Time to expiration
- Implied volatility

These four main factors have been detailed in my books, DVDs and many of my journal articles and videos. We must know and understand the concept of these pricing factors to become elite options traders. In today's article I will discuss two additional factors that have been added to more recent option pricing models, interest rates and dividends. These factors apply more to *American Style options*, which can be exercised at any time from option purchase to 4 PM ET on expiration Friday. The main significance interest rates and dividends have is related to the possibility of early exercise of our American Style options.

Interest rates

As interest rates rise, the difference in the cost of a share of stock versus the cost of an option becomes more significant. A trader can buy an option instead of a stock and invest the unused cash to generate income from the higher interest rate. Therefore, the call buyer is willing to pay a higher price for the call option. Rising interest rates also make it more enticing to exercise a put early and use the cash generated from the sale of the underlying securities to benefit from the higher interest rates.

Dividends

Call buyers benefit from share appreciation and put buyers benefit from share depreciation. When a dividend is distributed (or more accurately, when the *ex-dividend date* approaches) the value of the underlying security drops in value by the amount of the dividend. This makes the value of the call option lower and the value of a put option higher as dividends rise. Early exercise of call premiums is more likely when the strike is in-the-money and the time value of the option premium is less than the dividend about to be distributed. Early exercise, when it occurs, usually takes place 1-2 days prior to the ex-dividend date. Figure 74 summarizes the minor factors found in the more recent option pricing models:

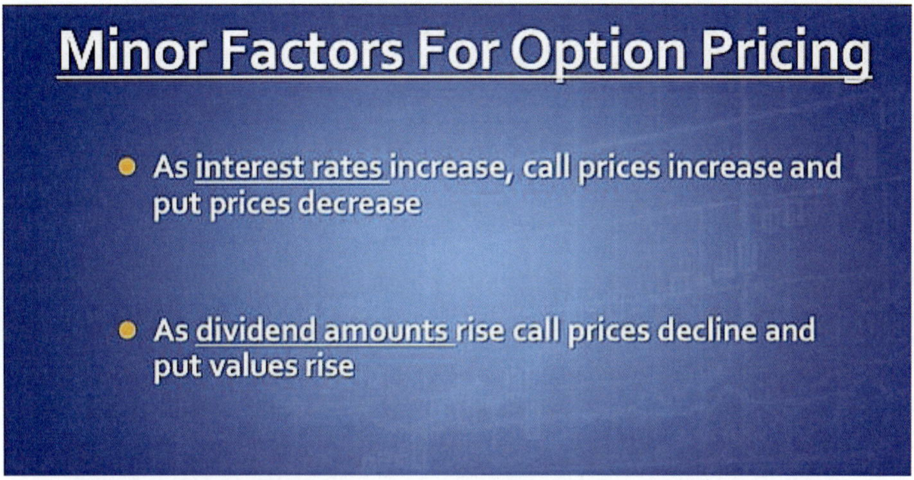

Figure 74- Factors Included in Recent Option Pricing Models

Summary

There were four major factors included in the original option pricing models which were geared to European Style options. These were the stock price, the strike price, the expected volatility of the stock and the time to expiration. Newer pricing models now also include statistics for interest rates and dividends which apply to potential early exercise of American Style options.

Put-Call Parity: Understanding Option Pricing

One of the mission statements of The Blue Collar Investor is to share information so that we can master option trading basics and become better investors. Many times I will research and write an article based on inquiries from our members and that is why I am able to continue to write weekly articles year after year. Today's topic is an interesting one that we haven't discussed in quite a while: *put-call parity*.

***This article has a few advanced concepts that I hope you find interesting but are NOT necessary to master or memorize. Some of the material may make your head spin a bit as it did mine as I was writing the article!

Definition and example

Put-Call Parity is an option pricing concept that requires the time (extrinsic) values of call and put options to be in equilibrium so as to prevent arbitrage (*Arbitrage* is the simultaneous purchase and sale of an asset in order to profit from a difference in the price). It is when the value of a call option, at one strike price, implies a certain fair value for the corresponding put, and vice versa. The argument, for this pricing relationship, relies on the arbitrage opportunity that results if there is difference between the value of calls and puts with the same strike price and expiration date. Arbitrageurs would step in to make profitable, risk-free trades until the departure from put-call parity is eliminated. This relationship is mainly for European style options, but the concept also applies to American-style options, adjusting for dividends and interest rates. *If the dividend increases, the puts expiring after the ex-dividend date will rise in value, while the calls will decrease by a similar amount. Changes in interest rates have the opposite effects. Rising interest rates increase call values and decrease put values.*

Figure 75 represents a put-call parity graph:

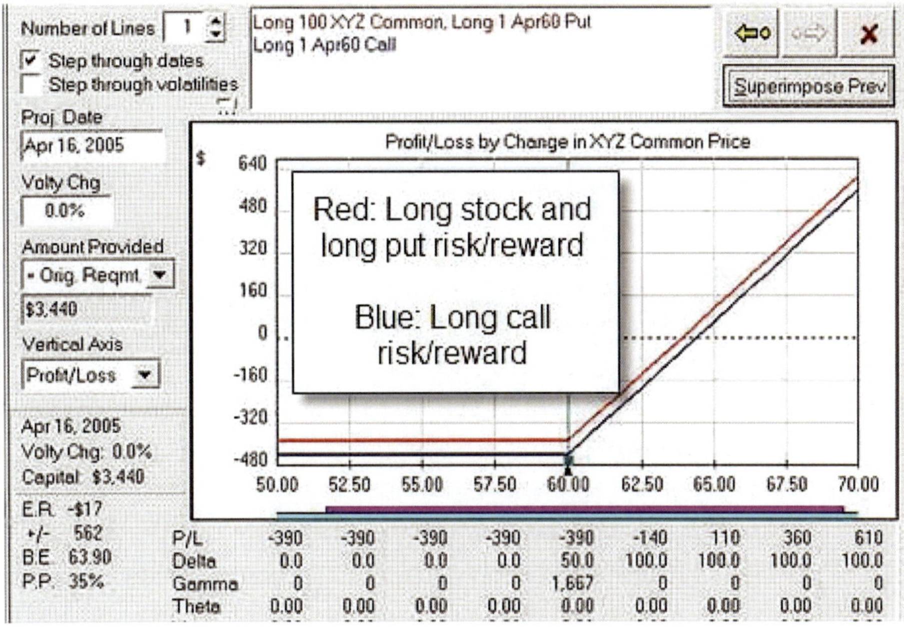

Figure 75- Put-Call Parity Graph

The above chart depicts a put-call parity relationship. We see that a long-stock/long-put position (red line) has the same risk/return profile as a long call (blue line) with the same expiration and strike price. The only difference between the two lines is the assumed dividend that is paid during the time to expiration. The owner of the stock (red line) would receive the additional amount, while the owner of the call (blue line) would not. However, if we assume no dividend would be paid to stockholders during the holding period, then both lines would overlap. From this chart one can see that if you sold a cash-secured put instead of writing a covered call, the put-call parity concept would account for that dividend difference.

When you buy a call, your loss is limited to the premium paid while the possible gain is unlimited. Now, consider the simultaneous purchase of an at-the-money long put and one hundred shares of the underlying stock. Once again, your loss is limited to the premium paid for the put, and your profit potential is unlimited if the stock price goes up.

Put Call Parity – An Example

Assumptions

- BCI trading at $50.00 per share
- $50.00 call = $2.00
- $50.00 put = $2.00
- At expiration BCI still trading at $50.00

The trades

- Buy 1 x $50.00 call for $200.00
- Buy 100 x BCI and 1 x $50.00 put for $5200.00

Results

Calls expire worthless = $200.00 loss

Puts expire worthless, no loss or gain on shares = Net $200.00 loss

Since Put Call Parity exists, the net losses on both positions are exactly the same so that there is no arbitrage opportunity to be exploited by being long one position and shorting the other simultaneously.

Why are call premiums sometimes higher than put premiums?

Look at many option prices in which the stock price is close to the strike price. You are likely to see that put premiums are lower than call premiums (a dividend distribution prior to expiration will have the opposite effect). Are puts cheaper than calls? In fact, the time premiums of puts and calls at the same strike price (and the same expiration) are theoretically the same. Why then do call premiums frequently appear to be higher?

The answer is that with the stock price equal to the strike price, the calls are considered in-the-money and the puts are considered out-of-the-money. This is because the real price of the underlying is the stock's *future delivery price*, which is determined by the stock's dividend and the current interest rate in addition to the stock price. If the interest rate is higher than the dividend rate (as it usually is) then the stock's future delivery price will be higher than its current price.

As an example, if you are a market maker and you need to buy the stock (and guarantee a price) for one-year delivery, you need to borrow the funds (at the one-year interest rate) to buy the stock. This increases your actual cost of the stock. However, you also collect the dividends (if any) on the stock. This will reduce your price. Thus, if the current stock price is $100.00, the one-year interest rate is 5% and the dividend rate is 1% annually, then the real cost of the stock for a one-year option is $104.00.

The equation therefore is:

Effective stock price = current stock price
plus Interest minus Dividend

An arbitrage opportunity: Why put and call prices are equal

If call or put time premiums get out of line with each other, option market makers can make a risk-free arbitrage profit. Here's an example:

Let's assume that the time premium of a particular put is greater than the time premium of the corresponding call (same stock, strike and expiration). Here the market maker can take advantage of the difference in the time premiums by selling the put and buying the call. What the market maker has done is to create a "synthetic" long stock position with a free credit of premium. The market maker can fully offset his risk by selling the stock. The net credit of time premium from this transaction will be his arbitrage profit.

Put/call parity rules: Synthetic trades (this is the head-spinning part!)

From the above paragraph, you get the first of the put/ call parity rules: If you buy a call and sell a put at the same strike price and expiration, you get the equivalent of a long stock position.

The six rules

- Rule 1: (+) Buy Call & (-) Write Put = (+) Buy Stock
- Rule 2: (-) Write Call & (+) Buy Put = (-) Short Stock
- Rule 3: (+) Buy Stock & (+) Buy Put = (+) Buy Call
- Rule 4: (-) Short Stock & (-) Write Put = (-) Write Call
- Rule 5: (-) Short Stock & (+) Buy Call = (+) Buy Put
- Rule 6: (+) Buy Stock & (-) Write Call = (+) Write Put = Covered Call

Notice that if you move any of these transactions to the other side of the equal sign, you change the strategy from a short to a long (or vice versa) and the "+" sign to a "-" sign (or vice versa).

Practical application of put-call parity

Since the market maker has a clear advantage in trading options, it is unlikely that the average blue collar investor will capture profit from "risk-free" arbitrage opportunities. However, these rules are helpful, because knowing them can help you determine what your strategy alternatives are. Here are two examples:

1- Let's say you see attractive covered call opportunities, where the call is in-the-money. Here you may be reluctant to establish the position for fear of having the call exercised and perhaps be susceptible to tax liability. Here you can write a cash-secured put instead of the covered call (Rule 6).

2- Let's assume you are interested in buying a particular stock, but you are concerned about the risk and may want to hedge it with a put. Knowing rule 3 tells you that buying the call will give you the same risk/reward as buying the stock and the put.

Put-Call Parity – In the real world

As you might have noticed above, put-call parity requires that the extrinsic (time) value of call and put options of the same strike price to be the same. However, in reality, the extrinsic value of put and call options are rarely in exact parity in option trading even though market makers have been charged with the responsibility of maintaining put-call parity. When the outlook of a stock is bullish, the time value of call options tend to be higher than put options due to higher implied volatility and when the outlook of a stock is bearish, the time value of put options tends to be higher than call options. When the put option is valued much higher than the call, look for a dividend distribution to be the reason why.

However, such option trading arbitrage opportunities are rare even under *put-call disparity* as the presence of bid/ask spreads and commissions tends to neutralize gains from such disparities.

Conclusion

Put-call parity is one of the foundations for option pricing, explaining why the price of one option can't move very far without the price of the corresponding options changing as well. So, if the parity is violated, an opportunity for arbitrage exists. *Arbitrage strategies are not a useful source of profits for the average retail trader.*

RHO: Why Interest Rates Effect our Option Premiums

Interest rates and the option *Greeks* play an important role in understanding option trading basics. *Rho*, not considered a major

Greek, measures the change in an option's price resulting from a one percent change in interest rates. When interest rates do change, it is normally by twenty five basis points (one quarter of one percent), not a full percentage point and that's why option prices will not be heavily impacted in the short-term by interest rates.

However, as Blue Collar Investors, we need to be educated in all aspects of our investment strategies and interest rates do play a role. Let's start with a basic premise:

When the interest rate rises by 1%, call value will increase by the amount of its rho and put value will decrease by the amount of its rho.

Figure 76 shows an example from an options calculator (www.cboe.com) showing a positive rho for calls and a negative rho for puts as interest rates increase (highlighted in the pink row):

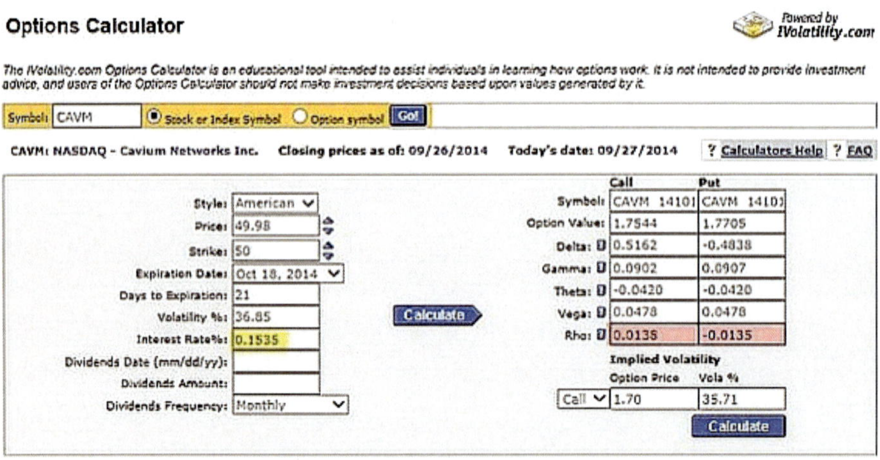

Figure 76- Rho for Calls and Puts

For the twenty one-day period until expiration, the interest rate is 0.1535 (left side, highlighted in yellow), the cost to own the shares (if the money to purchase the shares is borrowed or the interest lost, if not borrowed). Should interest rates increase by 1%, the call value will increase by 1.38 cents and the put value will decline by

1.35 cents from the current value of $1.70 (right side). Given that interest rates generally change by twenty five basis points when there is an adjustment, the practical impact on our option premiums would be one fourth these amounts. We can now understand why *rho is considered a minor Greek*.

Why rising interest rates increase call value

There is an interest advantage to buying call options. Let's assume for a moment that we are interested in a $60.00 stock and want to purchase three hundred shares. The cost before commissions is $18,000.00. Now if a $30.00 deep in-the-money call can be purchased at parity (intrinsic value only or $30.00, the amount the strike is in-the-money), the cost to control three hundred shares would be cut in half to $9,000.00. The risk is cut in half and the reward is nearly the same. Now the $9,000.00 not spent on buying the shares can be deposited into an interest-bearing account to generate income. The higher the interest rates, the more valuable call options become and so the rho impacts calls in a positive manner as interest rates rise.

Why rising interest rates decrease put value

There is an interest disadvantage to buying puts. There is a theoretical cost to buying puts, the interest cost to buy the options. *Put holders benefit when share price declines* and put value then accelerates in much the same way professional traders benefit from shorting stocks. When a stock is shorted, cash is generated into the brokerage account which will result in an interest credit (professional traders do pay a small amount of interest for borrowing shares that were shorted). The choice then becomes do these traders pay interest as puts are purchased or do they receive interest as shares are shorted? As interest rates increase, put-buying becomes less attractive and stock shorting becomes more attractive (mainly for professional traders who impact option value much more than we do).

Summary

Rho is a minor Greek, impacting option premiums as interest rates change. Call and put premiums are impacted inversely as rates rise or fall. Understanding how and why interest rates effect option premiums make us all better investors.

Role of VIX and Market Volatility in our Covered Call Writing Decisions

Options trading basics teaches us that the *VIX or CBOE Volatility Index* demonstrates the market's expectation of a future thirty-day volatility. It measures market risk and is also known as the *investor fear gauge*. With this in mind, covered call writers are faced with a dilemma. Increased market volatility will translate into higher option premiums because the time value component of the premium is directly related to this *implied* volatility. On the other hand, a high overall market volatility increases our risk as share value can plummet and erase our initial gains. So is a higher VIX a positive or a negative?

One question that is frequently posed to me is that if the VIX is low do we stop selling calls because of lower premiums? This suggests that a high VIX is a positive for covered call writers. Let's take a look at an extreme example in 2008 when the VIX went from the 20 - 30 level to the 70 - 80 level in the last four months of the year as depicted in Figure 77:

Figure 77- VIX in 2008

As a general rule, the movement of the VIX and the performance of the overall market (S&P 500) are inversely related as demonstrated in Figure 78 where the market takes a dive in the last four months of the year 2008:

Figure 78- S&P 500 in 2008

To confirm this relationship, let's look at a comparison chart of the VIX and the S&P 500 since the decline in 2008. In Figure 79 note how the VIX has been declining while the overall market has been accelerating. Whenever there was a short-term spike up in the VIX, there was a corresponding decline in the market performance:

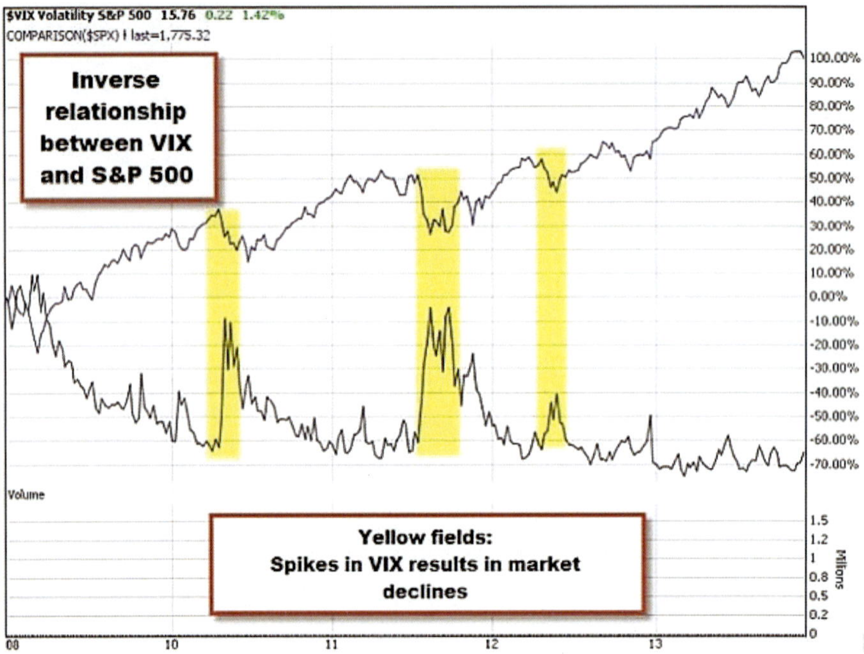

Figure 79- VIX (lower line in chart) vs. the S&P 500 from 2008 – 2013

VIX and covered call writing

Covered call writing is a conservative strategy and those who use it are generally cautious investors looking to generate cash flow with capital preservation in mind. As such, a high VIX is no friend of covered call writers although we can use our common sense principles to manage those scenarios. A low VIX is usually a positive for us because it means a more stable market and oftentimes a rising market as we have experienced since early 2009.

How to manage a high VIX

We can "stay in the game" by selling in-the-money strikes, using options with lower implied volatility (set goals at 1 - 3% instead of 2 - 4% for initial monthly returns) and use low beta stocks from our

Premium Watch List and ETF reports. We can also turn to selling out-of-the-money cash-secured puts to enter a covered call trade "at a discount" if the put is exercised.

How to manage a low VIX

This is one of the factors that will give us the confidence to take a more bullish stance and sell at-the-money and out-of-the-money strikes with higher beta stocks and higher implied volatility options. The exit strategies selected in these environments are detailed in my books and DVD Programs.

Conclusion

The VIX is a factor that should be considered in our covered call writing decisions. It should neither be feared nor embraced but rather managed using the fundamental, technical and common sense principles of the BCI methodology.

Special One- Time Cash Dividends and our Covered Call Positions

Every so often we will see a company declare a "special dividend" which is separate and apart from the typical recurring dividend cycle, if there is one. It is frequently a reflection of exceptionally strong earnings and/or a company with a large cash balance. It is a positive sign regarding the financial health of this corporation. Some of you may remember the $3.00, one-time cash dividend announced by Microsoft in 2004 to "relieve its balance sheet of a large cash balance"...such problems we should all have! When a stock generates a special cash dividend, of let's say $1.00 per share, the price of the stock is then adjusted by decreasing by that amount. Option contract strike prices are adjusted accordingly on the ex-dividend date.

Now let's bring this information into our world of covered call writing. We sell call options which implies that someone is buying them (we're the "casino" ...they're the players). Let's say we buy a stock for $69.00 and sell the $70.00 call. The holder of that call option bought the call with the strike $1.00 higher than the market value of the stock. If a $1.00 cash dividend is distributed prior to expiration causing the stock price to be adjusted down by $1.00, the option buyer's position would be dramatically compromised. To make this situation fair and the option buyer "whole" the strike price is decreased by the dividend amount or by $1.00 in this scenario. So a $70.00 call becomes a $69.00 call. All other factors being equal, the market value and strike drops an equal amount and so the strike is still $1.00 from the market value.

Where to get information on special cash dividends

www.cboe.com

www.optionsclearing.com

Real life example

On August 11, 2011, HollyFrontier announced a special, one-time cash dividend of $1.00. Figure 80 depicts what that information looked like on the second site listed above where the $66.00 hypothetical settlement price is reduced by the $1.00 dividend amount:

OCC

#29315

Back to Infomemo Search

DATE: AUGUST 9, 2011

SUBJECT: HOLLYFRONTIER CORPORATION – CASH DISTRIBUTION
FUTURE SYMBOL: HFC1C
DATE: 8/11/11

HollyFrontier Corporation (HFC) has announced a Special Cash Distribution of $1.00 per HFC Common Share. The record date is August 15, 2011; payable date is August 22, 2011. The ex-distribution date for this distribution will be August 11, 2011.

CONTRACT ADJUSTMENT

Pursuant to Article XII, Section 3 of OCC's By-laws, all HFC1C futures will be adjusted as indicated below.

EFFECTIVE DATE: August 11, 2011

SYMBOL: HFC1C remains unchanged

MULTIPLIER: 100 (e.g., 1.00 equals $100.00)

NUMBER OF CONTRACTS: Unchanged

SETTLEMENT PRICES: All previous day's settlement prices shall be reduced by $1.00

For example:

Future Symbol	Before Ex-Date	Start of Business Ex-Date
HFC1C	$66.00	$65.00

DELIVERABLE PER CONTRACT: 100 HollyFrontier Corporation (HFC) Common Shares

CUSIP: 436106108

Figure 80- HFC- Special Cash Dividend

Figure 81 shows a chart taken from the CBOE site reflecting the change in the strike prices:

EXISTING SERIES					ADJUSTED SERIES*			
HFC	50.00	2011-08-20	C/P	=>	HFC	49.00	2011-08-20	C/P
HFC	55.00	2011-08-20	C/P	=>	HFC	54.00	2011-08-20	C/P
HFC	60.00	2011-08-20	C/P	=>	HFC	59.00	2011-08-20	C/P
HFC	65.00	2011-08-20	C/P	=>	HFC	64.00	2011-08-20	C/P
HFC	70.00	2011-08-20	C/P	=>	HFC	69.00	2011-08-20	C/P
HFC	75.00	2011-08-20	C/P	=>	HFC	74.00	2011-08-20	C/P
HFC	80.00	2011-08-20	C/P	=>	HFC	79.00	2011-08-20	C/P
HFC	85.00	2011-08-20	C/P	=>	HFC	84.00	2011-08-20	C/P
HFC	90.00	2011-08-20	C/P	=>	HFC	89.00	2011-08-20	C/P

Figure 81- HFC- Change in Strike Prices

How to calculate our adjusted covered call returns

If we bought a stock for $69.00 and sold the $70.00 call for $3.00, our initial calculation would be:

ROO= $3.00/$69.00 = 4.3%

When we receive a cash dividend of $1.00, in essence our cost basis is reduced by $1.00 or $69.00 becomes $68.00:

ROO = $3.00/$68.00 = 4.4%

Our long stock position is decreased by $1.00 and that is why I don't like to calculate the extra $1.00 as additional option premium. It would skew the results and not account for the reduced share value:

$4.00/$69.00 = 5.8% (exaggerated result)

These calculations are NOT for tax purposes. They are used to assess the best covered call decisions at that specific point in time.

Strike prices if the dividend were not an even number

The OCC Security Committee evaluates each situation on a case-by-case basis but generally speaking **if a dividend is greater than 12 1/2 cents the strike price can be adjusted by the amount of the dividend.** If HFC had declared a one-time cash dividend of $1.25, the $70.00 strike would become $68.75. As new series of options are published after the contract adjustments, the standard strike prices will return.

Special dividends in the form of shares instead of cash

Once again contract adjustments are done on a case-by-case basis but generally speaking if a 5% stock dividend was declared on a $30.00 stock:

- Share value is determined by the following equation: $30.00/1.05 = $28.57
- The new strike price will be $28.57
- Each contract will now deliver 105 shares instead of the original 100

Conclusion

Special cash dividends will frequently impact our strike prices due to the decrease in share value after the ex-dividend date. Because these are handled on a case-by-case basis it is important to understand how your position has changed due to the unexpected cash or stock distribution. The websites I referenced above are great resources for locating this information as are the specialists who work at our brokerages.

Unusual Options Activity: Speculation or Cheating?

Covered call writers are average retail investors looking to generate monthly cash flow in small but consistent increments and then compounding those profits. In time, it could lead to financial independence. Other investors look to make a lot of money in a short time frame by undertaking much greater risk than we do. Still others look to cash in using illegal activities. In today's article I will ask you to draw your own conclusions.

The day is Friday July 12th and the stock is LEAP Wireless International Inc. (LEAP) which is a takeover candidate by AT&T. In the late afternoon, the share price was near $8.00 per share, the July $9.00 call option was priced at $0.10 and the August $9.00 call at $0.40. Covered call writers could generate an initial profit (ROO) of 1% and 5%, respectively. The average daily option trading volume for this company was 1320 contracts over the last three months. It appeared to be a normal trading day until the last hour of trading when option volume went through the roof. By days end, 7139 contracts were traded, all but 350 were calls as traders were taking a bullish stance on this stock. I think you know what's coming!

After market close, there was an announcement of a takeover bid by AT&T for $15.00 per share, almost doubling the value of the share price. That would move the $9.00 call strike price $6.00 in-the-money. In Figure 82, we see a chart of LEAP showing the gap up in share price on July 12th (after hours trading):

Figure 82- LEAP Share Price Gaps Up after July 12th Announcement

Figure 83 reflects the options chart for the August $9.00 call options:

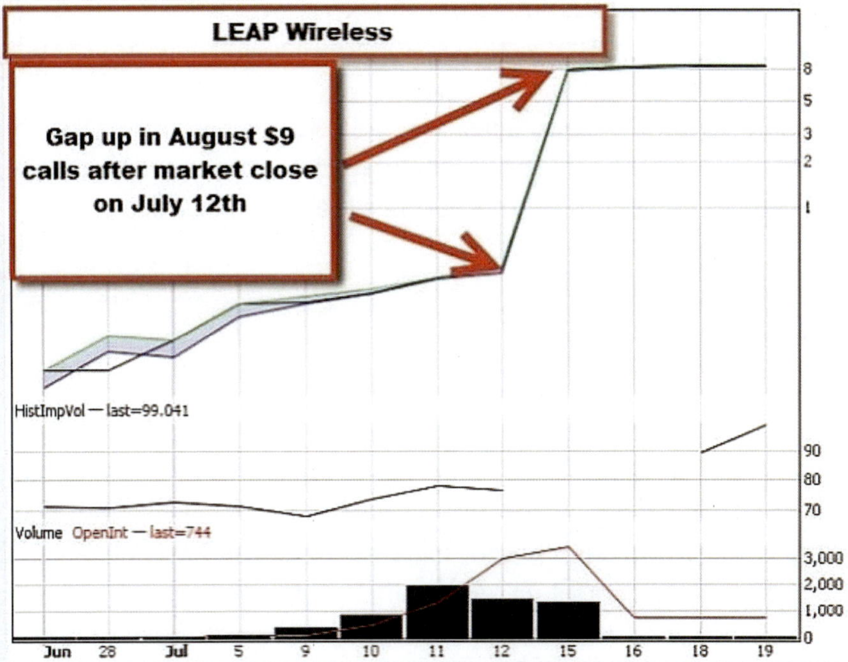

Figure 83- LEAP $9.00 Call Options Gap Up

According to *Trade Alert*, an option analytics company, there were unusual trading patterns in a three-minute window just before market close where substantial numbers of call options were purchased. I report, you decide.

Other examples

I have been hypothesizing the past few years that the playing field for average retail investors is leveling off thanks to the hard work of the SEC and FINRA. Recently, the SEC has been investigating insider trading on Onyx Pharmaceuticals Inc. Assets and accounts have also been frozen for potential illegal trading on Smithfield Foods and Heinz Co.

So what does this all mean for Blue Collar Investors in the case of LEAP share price acceleration? Well here's the good news...

nothing negative for us in this example. Had we taken a covered call position with LEAP we would have generated the call premium plus any profit up to the strike price. The time value of the $9.00 call would then approach zero and we could have closed the short call, sold the stock and used the cash to generate a second income stream or at the very least, maxed out the initial trade.

Discussion:

Whether this is an example of incredibly lucky speculation or illegal trading activity is for others to determine. I will be shocked if there is no investigation although those involved are innocent until proven guilty. As I say in my books and DVDs, we look to hit singles and doubles, not grand slam homeruns. The latter can be much too risky and could ultimately get us into trouble (wink, wink).

Using Beta to Capture Higher Premium Returns

When using covered call writing and put-selling strategies it is important to set goals for initial returns in order to select the most appropriate underlying security and option. My goal for initial returns in normal market conditions is 2% – 4% per month and a bit higher in a bull market environment. Recently, several of our members have contacted me inquiring about a way to scan eligible stocks for premiums that may meet these goals. This article will address this issue using our *Premium Watch List* although other resources may be used as well. One of the columns inherent in our member reports is titled *"beta"*. This is a measure of the volatility of a security as compared to that of the S&P 500. A stock with a beta of "1" has the same statistical or historical volatility as the S&P 500 and would be expected to perform similarly. Stocks with betas greater than 1 have higher-than-market volatility and those with betas less than 1 have lower-than-market volatility Beta is therefore based on actual historical statistics.

Implied volatility, on the other hand, is a market forecast of the underlying's volatility as implied by the current option's pricing. Implied volatility impacts option premium more directly than does beta. However, it makes sense that those securities with higher betas will generally also have higher implied volatilities, admittedly with some exceptions. With that in mind, we will set up a screen for higher option returns by screening for eligible stocks (passed our fundamental, technical and common sense screens) that have betas greater than 1.50. We also want to be sure that the stocks have no earnings reports due out before contract expiration and the associated options have adequate open interest.

Figure 84 shows a screenshot of the information gleaned from the Premium Watch List dated 2/13/2015 and from the associated option chains:

STOCK	BETA	IND	STOCK $	STRIKE	Option $
SWKS	1.78	Chips	82.17	85	1.8
QRVO	1.9	Chips	68.56	70	2.25
CAVM	1.91	Chips	64.71	65	2.75
HAR	1.91	Consumer	135.71	140	3
IDTI	1.79	Chips	20.69	21	0.85
DATA	2.05	Software	99.01	100	3.8
NXPI	1.54	Chips	83.93	85	2.6
LCI	2.06	Medical	61.13	65	1.5
SAVE	1.6	Transport	78.65	80	2.75

Beta > 1.50
No earnings due out
Adequate open interest

Figure 84- High-Beta Stocks

You will note that five of the nine candidates are in the "Chips" industry segment so we must be cautious not to over weigh our portfolio in one particular segment. If more candidates are needed, we can always drop our beta requirement a bit, perhaps to more than 1.30. Next, we will enter the options data into the multiple tab of the *Ellman Calculator* (Figure 85). For the purposes of this article, we will view out-of-the-money strikes only but this can be expanded to other strikes as well:

RETURN ON OPTION (ROO) CALCULATOR - MULTIPLE STOCKS										
Stock Name or Symbol	Stock $/sh	Option $/sh	Strike $	Expires	Intrinsic	Upside	Breakeven	ROO	Up Potential	Down Protect
SWKS	$82.17	$1.80	$85.00	03/20/15	$ -	$ 2.83	$ 80.37	2.2%	3.4%	0.0%
QRVO	$68.56	$ 2.25	$ 70.00	03/20/15	$ -	$ 1.44	$ 66.31	3.3%	2.1%	0.0%
CAVM	$64.71	$2.75	$65.00	03/20/15	$ -	$ 0.29	$ 61.96	4.2%	0.4%	0.0%
HAR	$135.71	$3.00	$140.00	03/20/15	$ -	$ 4.29	$ 132.71	2.2%	3.2%	0.0%
IDTI	$ 20.69	$ 0.85	$ 21.00	03/20/15	$ -	$ 0.31	$ 19.84	4.1%	1.5%	0.0%
DATA	$ 99.01	$ 3.80	$ 100.00	03/20/15	$ -	$ 0.99	$ 95.21	3.8%	1.0%	0.0%
NXPI	$ 83.93	$ 2.60	$ 85.00	03/20/15	$ -	$ 1.07	$ 81.33	3.1%	1.3%	0.0%
LCI	$ 61.13	$ 1.50	$ 65.00	03/20/15	$ -	$ 3.87	$ 59.63	2.5%	6.3%	0.0%
SAVE	$ 78.65	$ 2.75	$ 80.00	03/20/15	$ -	$ 1.35	$ 75.90	3.5%	1.7%	0.0%

Figure 85- Calculations for Stocks with High Betas

The column highlighted in yellow, ROO, represents the actual time value initial returns which do meet our 2% – 4%, one-month goals. The column featured in brown, upside potential, shows additional profit that may be generated if share price moves up from current market value to the strike. For example, should SWKS (top row) move up from its current price of $82.17 to the $85.00 strike, the total one-month return would be 5.6% (2.2% initial profit + 3.4% from share appreciation to the strike).

Summary

One approach to screening eligible stocks for higher option returns is to look at beta statistics. The process includes setting initial goals, establishing a minimum beta requirements, checking options chains and then running the calculations. All this should take less than twenty minutes for those with a quality watch list.

Vega: An Option Greek and how it Impacts our Option Premiums

Covered call writing generates monthly cash flow by selling short-term options. The main factor in determining the amount of this premium is the *implied volatility (IV)* of the underlying security. The impact that implied volatility has on the premium is known as *Vega*, one of the option *Greeks*.

What is Vega?

Vega is the expected change in the value of an option with a 1% change in implied volatility whether up or down. It is expressed in decimal form (.040 as an example) and represents cash amount per share. As with the other *Greeks*, it is based on all other pricing factors remaining the same. Calls and puts both have positive Vega amounts so that if implied volatility increases the option value on both will rise by the Vega amount. If implied volatility decreases the option value will fall by the Vega amount. A change in implied volatility or Vega does not require an associated change in stock price. Vega has its greatest dollar impact on at-the-money strikes and its greatest percentage impact is on out-of-the-money strikes. Also, the greater the time to expiration, the higher the Vega.

A stock's implied volatility can vary dramatically from its *historical volatility* (actual price fluctuation as observed over a period of time. Also known as *statistical volatility*). It can also change quickly and dramatically and is considered the most significant price factor in option value. In addition, *implied volatility is rarely the same through the various strike prices and expiration dates* as shown in Figure 86:

Implied Vola (%)	Call Delta	Change (%)	Call Bid/Ask Mean	Expiry	Strike
50.58%	86.82%	0.97 (35.14)	3.750	May 17, 2014	25.0
42.03%	32.83%	0.28 (84.62)	0.600	May 17, 2014	30.0
49.97%	90.87%	1.25 (25.00)	6.250	Jun 21, 2014	22.5
43.59%	80.61%	0.93 (29.60)	4.050	Jun 21, 2014	25.0
42.23%	40.60%	0.40 (47.06)	1.250	Jun 21, 2014	30.0
57.52%	20.98%	0.32 (0.00)	0.325	Jun 21, 2014	35.0

Figure 86- Implied Volatility and Vega for Covered Call Writing

The red line separates strikes prices for GLOG, a stock from our Premium Watch List, for both May and June expirations. Note how the implied volatility differs from strike to strike and between expiration dates as well.

Using Vega when selling covered calls

We know that Vega is mainly impacted by implied volatility and the higher the Vega, the higher option premium, all other pricing factors remaining constant. We also know that the greater the implied volatility, the higher the risk. We can use this knowledge to tailor our trading decisions to our personal risk tolerance and overall market assessment. My goal for initial, one-month returns is 2%-4% per month. More aggressive investors will set higher goals and vice-versa. Another factor to consider is that implied volatility rises prior to news announcements and therefore will enhance our risk exposure. That is why we *avoid selling covered calls prior to earnings announcements*.

When to consider options with high Vegas

- Higher personal risk tolerance
- Bullish market outlook
- Strong and confirming chart technicals

When to favor options with low Vegas

- Low personal risk tolerance
- Bearish or volatile market outlook
- Chart technicals mixed

This assessment and determination can be accomplished without looking up the Vega stats for every option on every stock although many brokerages provide options chains that incorporate much of this information. I make my investment decisions based on a quick and user-friendly observation. I set a goal based on initial option premium return (time value only). My goal as stated above is 2%-4% per month for these initial option returns. I have found over the years that adhering closely to this parameter will allow me to generate favorable monthly returns and minimize the risk of higher-Vega options. In strong bull markets I may get a bit more aggressive and set higher monthly goals and in strong bear markets I may set lower monthly goals.

Call Vega example

- BCI call option has a value of $4.00 and a Vega of 0.06
- Current contract value = $400.00
- Implied volatility increases by 1%
- New contract value would be $406.00, a gain of $6.00
- If implied volatility decreases by 2%, the contract value would decline to $388.00 ($400.00 – $12.00) assuming all other pricing factors remain the same

Summary

Our option premium amounts are impacted mostly by the implied volatility of the underlying security. The impact that implied volatility has on the option value is measured by the *Greek* known as Vega. We can tailor our covered call writing plan to meet our personal risk tolerance needs and overall market assessment by factoring in Vega as a key determining factor.

Volatility Skew- Understanding Option Premiums over Different Time Frames and Strikes

For covered call writing, our option premiums are influenced by the volatility of the underlying security. Using the Black Scholes option pricing model, we can calculate the volatility of the underlying by entering the market prices for the options. Common sense would seem to dictate that for options with the same expiration date, we would anticipate the implied volatility (IV) to be the same regardless of which strike price we use. However, in reality, the implied volatility we see is different across the various strikes. This disparity is known as the *volatility skew*.

Definitions reviewed

Implied Volatility- This is a forecast of the underlying stock's volatility as implied by the option's price in the marketplace. This differs from historical volatility:

Historical volatility- This *is* the actual price fluctuation as observed over a period of time.

Calculating implied volatility

As discussed in my books and DVDs, an options pricing model such as the *Black-Scholes* model uses six inputs to determine the theoretical price of an American Style option:

- asset value (stock or ETF)
- time left until expiration
- strike price
- risk-free interest rate (treasuries for example)
- dividends (if applicable)
- *asset volatility

To determine the implied volatility of an American Style option the model uses these inputs:

- asset value (stock or ETF)
- time left until expiration
- strike price
- risk-free interest rate (treasuries for example)
- dividends (if applicable)
- Option price

Option premiums will rise and fall with volatility. These pricing models make the incorrect assumption that volatility is constant throughout each respective strike price and regardless of duration. Supply and demand will never allow these conditions to exist. It is, however, possible to calculate implied volatility for different strike prices and over different time frames by using the current options price as a given, using the other five inputs listed above and then solving for that specific implied volatility. The difference in implied volatility levels for options with the same underlying security is known as ***volatility skew***. Stated differently, it is the difference in implied volatility between out-of-the-money, at-the-money and in-the-money options and also between different expiration periods.

Types of Volatility Skews

Vertical skews (different strike prices):

The two types of vertical skews are *forward* and *reverse*. The reverse skew which is common to the equity market is where the lower option strikes have higher implied volatilities and the higher strikes have lower implied volatilities. The downside options are being priced more aggressively to put more premium on fast downward moves, which intuitively makes sense. If we plotted the implied volatilities over the various strike prices, Figure 87 shows what a typical skew chart would look like:

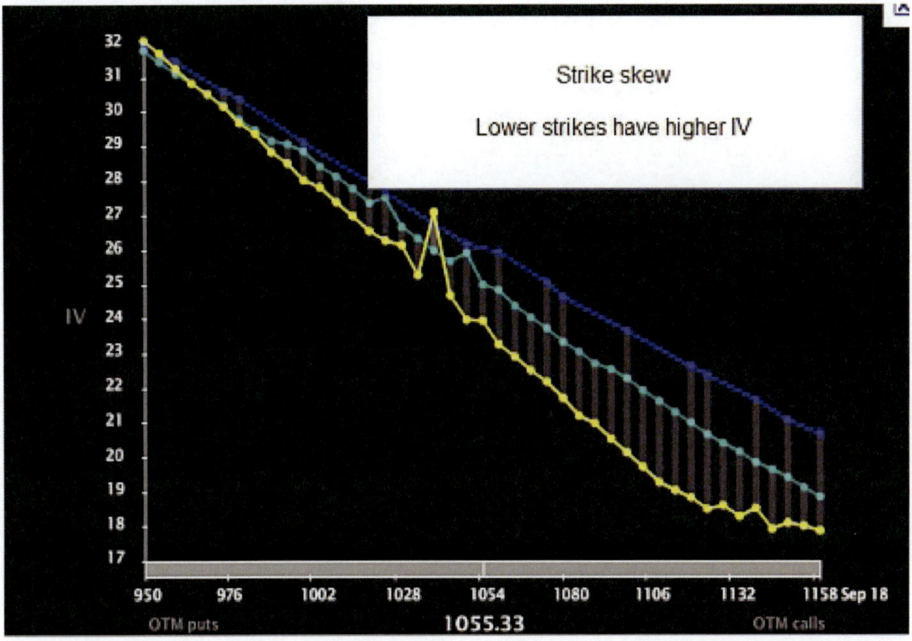

Figure 87- Skew Chart for Strike Prices and Implied Volatility

Horizontal skews (same strike, different expirations):

Horizontal skew refers to the situation where at a given strike price, implied volatility will either increase or decrease as the expiration month moves forward into the future. A forward horizontal skew occurs when volatilities increase from near to far months. This is typical of the equity market. A reverse horizontal skew occurs when volatilities decrease from near to far months. Figure 88 is a chart showing a forward horizontal skew for the S&P 500:

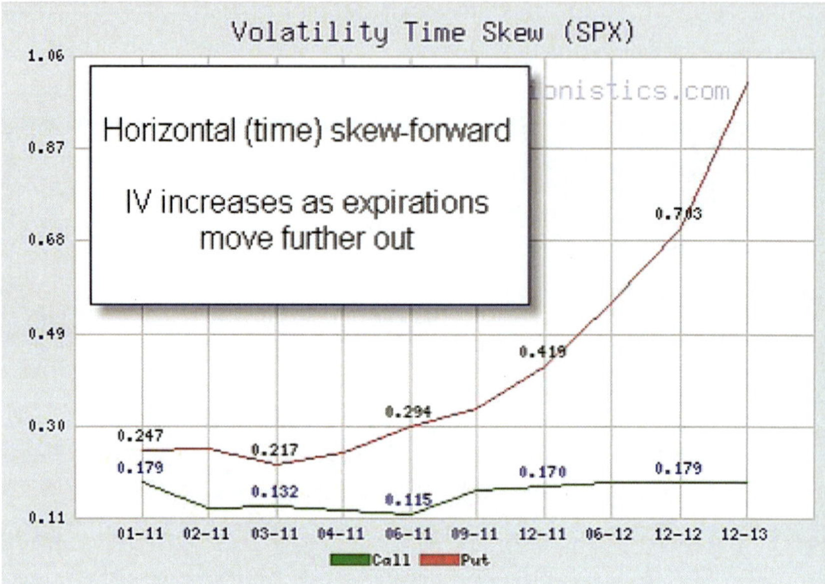

Figure 88- Forward Horizontal Skew

Skew smirks and smiles

Although volatility skew is most typical for an equity strike price, we occasionally see a *volatility smile or smirk*. This could occur when there is anticipation of extreme market or stock price movement like an earnings report or other corporate news. This can result in speculators buying the out-of-the-money options to take advantage of the potential price movement. As a result the implied volatility of the higher strikes will rise thereby changing the skew to a smile or smirk pattern as shown in Figures 89 and 90:

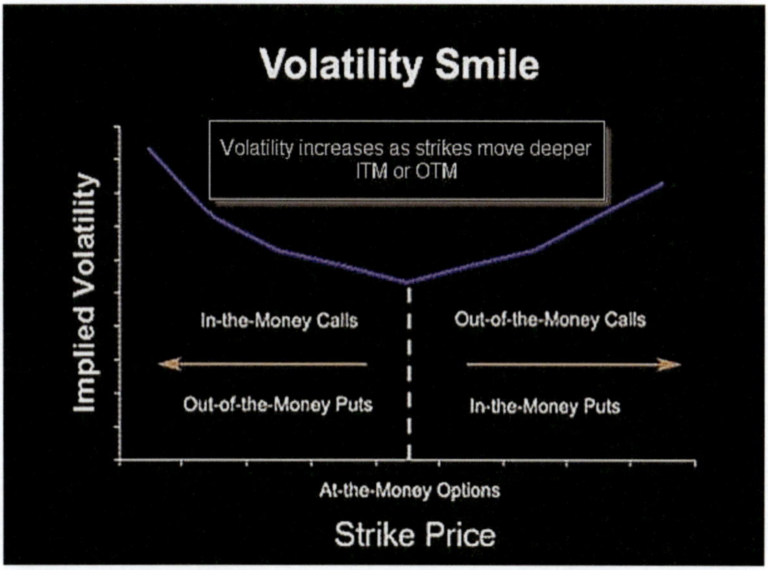

Figure 89- Classic Volatility Smile Pattern

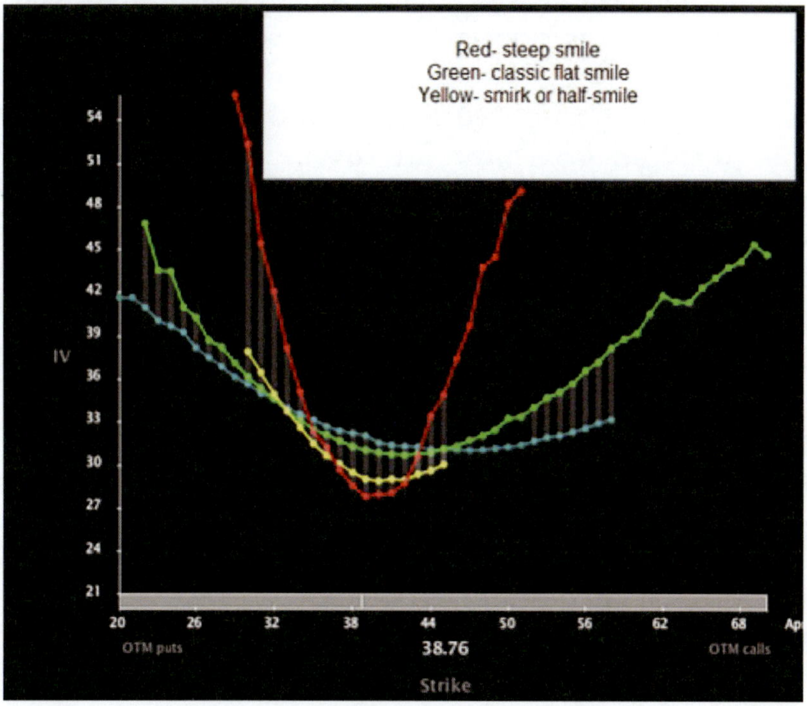

Figure 90- Volatility Smiles and Smirks

In these instances the in-the-money and out-of-the-money strikes have higher implied volatilities (more expensive) than the at-the-money strikes.

Sites to build skew charts

Free:

http://www.optionistics.com/f/volatility_skew

Not free but sophisticated:

www.livevol.com

Conclusions

By studying implied volatility chart patterns we know that the volatility assumptions made by option pricing models rarely exist in the real world. Implied volatilities ARE different across different strikes and time frames. **Generally the market assigns a higher implied volatility for lower strikes and higher implied volatilities for longer durations for the same strikes**. These typical stock implied volatility patterns result in skew patterns. When a skew develops into a smile there is an expectation of greater price movement in the future causing the chart pattern to turn up into a smirk or a smile. Some sophisticated options traders will trade with or against the skew. That discussion is beyond the scope of this book. For our community of Blue Collar Investors we use our knowledge of skew and smile patterns to better understand the relationship between implied volatility and our option premiums and to red flag potential risk in the future.

What Is Slippage and how does it Impact our Trading Success?

When studying investment basics, the term *slippage* has two applications. In general, it means having a trade executed at a price less favorable to the trader. Let's look at the two areas where we may see this term used:

An order is executed at a worse-than-expected price

Stock and options

Slippage occurs when there is an unexpected change in the bid-ask spread. If we place a market order to buy a stock at the "ask" it may get executed at a higher price. This is usually the result of a period of higher volatility, low trading liquidity or unexpected bad news. Let's say the bid-ask spread for Company BCI was $31.00 – $31.25. If we placed a market order to buy one hundred shares we would expect to pay $3125.00 plus commissions. However, in a highly volatile market environment or if some unexpected news is reported about the company the spread may change against us and we may pay $3200.00 plus commissions or more as an example. On the other side of the spread, if we placed a market order to sell one hundred shares of BCI for $31.00 (the "bid") we may end up generating $30.50 minus commissions or less.

Stop loss order

Let's say we purchased BCI for $32.00 and placed a stop loss order at 10% or $28.80. This means that if the price reaches the stop price, the order will become a market order and sold at the best price of $28.80 or less. What if unexpected news came out regarding a disappointing earnings report and the share price gapped down to $26.00? The stop order is now a market order (unless otherwise specified) and our shares are sold for $2.80 less than we anticipated.

An order is executed at the published bid-ask spread

The difference between the bid and ask prices (the "spread") is a normal aspect of trading. If the spread is $30.00-$30.50, the moment we buy the shares for $30.50 we can only sell for $30.00. That $0.50 difference is also called *slippage* as you are immediately at a 1.6% deficit. This is true of both stocks and options.

How to minimize the impact of slippage in our accounts

1. Favor stocks that have a significant average daily trading volume. In my covered call writing accounts, **my guideline is to require a minimum average daily trading volume of 250,000 shares per day or more**. In my longer term accounts, I favor equities with a minimum average daily trading volume of 500,000 shares per day or more (I have addressed a long-term trading strategy for high school and college students as well as all those not near retirement in my fourth book, *Stock Investing for Students*).
2. **Favor options that have an "open interest" of 100 contracts or more and/or a bid-ask spread of $0.30 or less for near-the-money strikes**. In Figure 91, we see that the January $50.00 calls for EBAY do meet our system requirement with 145 contracts of open interest and a bid-ask spread of $0.03:

		Calls				Jan 13
Last	Intrinsic Value	Bid	Ask	Vol	Open Interest	Strike
12.53	12.31	10.80	14.25	0	0	37.50
9.32	9.81	8.30	10.35	0	0	40.00
9.18	8.81	8.60	9.75	0	0	41.00
8.18	7.81	7.70	8.65	0	0	42.00
7.65	7.31	7.20	8.10	0	0	42.50
7.18	6.81	6.70	7.65	0	0	43.00
6.17	5.81	5.75	6.60	0	0	44.00
5.07	4.81	4.80	5.35	0	0	45.00
4.40	3.81	3.75	5.05	0	0	46.00
3.13	2.81	2.91	3.35	0	0	47.00
2.69	2.31	2.47	2.91	0	0	47.50
2.18	1.81	2.05	2.31	0	0	48.00
1.32	0.81	1.29	1.35	0	0	49.00
0.72	0.00	0.71	0.74	272	145	50.00
0.08	0.00	0.07	0.09	130	30	52.50
0.05	0.00	N/A	0.05	0	0	55.00
0.01	0.00	0.01	0.02	13	0	57.50
0.02	0.00	N/A	0.02	0	0	60.00

Figure 91- Open Interest and Bid-Ask Spreads for EBAY

3. Avoid trading during volatile market hours. I avoid early morning and late afternoon trading to circumvent volatile computerized institutional trading. My favorite trading hours are between 11 AM ET and 3 PM ET.

4. Negotiate your trade order price. I call it 'playing the bid-ask spread" Place the limit order slightly below or above the midpoint of the spread (depending on if you are buying or selling), favoring the market maker. You'll be amazed at how many orders will get filled at the better price. For tight bid-ask spreads ($0.10 or less) there is no room for negotiation. See pages 225 – 227 of Volume I of the *Complete Encyclopedia for Covered Call Writing*.

Conclusion

Slippage is a normal part of trading stocks and options. To maximize our returns we must execute all measures that will minimize the impact slippage has on our trading success.

Chapter 8

Common Sense Factors

Chapter Outline

1. Airline Stocks now "Banned" from Covered Call Writing and Put-Selling Strategies
2. Economic Reports and our Covered Call Writing Decisions
3. Managing Covered Call Trades while Working a Full-Time Job

Airline Stocks now "Banned" from Covered Call Writing and Put-Selling Strategies

Stocks eligible for our covered call writing and put-selling portfolios are screened using a three-pronged approach: fundamental analysis, technical analysis and *common sense principles* like avoiding earnings reports. One of the categories under the common sense umbrella is *banned stocks* which are excluded due to monthly same store retail sales reports. This list, once eighty-long, is now down to eight companies as the others opted out of reporting on a monthly basis and reverted to quarterly reporting. Monthly reports like these create the same type of risk as do earnings reports. If they disappoint, share value can take a major hit and wipe out our profits for the month.

Recently, one of our members, Ryszard from Tempe, Arizona, was kind enough to share with me that airlines have analogous monthly reports that can create a high level of risk. These reports are known as *capacity reports* and are published in the first or second week of every month depending on the airline. Airlines report *ASM* or *available seat miles* as their maximum capacity and then these monthly capacity reports reflect the actual percentage of ASM used. Like earnings and revenues, analysts make predictions regarding the statistics of these reports and if they disappoint, the shares can decline significantly. I back-checked and found that disappointing capacity reports occur frequently enough where I felt the protection of banning these stocks was justified. Figure 92 is a screenshot of the updated list of *banned stocks*.

"Banned Stocks"

Stocks that Report Same Store Monthly Retail Sales

Definition:

Monthly sales volumes from individual department, chain, discount, and apparel stores are usually reported on the first Thursday of each month. Most companies have opted out of reporting monthly and the number of such corporations has gone from over 80 to under 10. Here is our latest list of "banned stocks"

- **BKE**
- **CATO**
- **COST**
- **GPS**
- **LB**
- **SMRT**
- **WAG**
- **ZUMZ**

Stocks that Report Monthly Capacity Airline Statistics

Definition:

Available seat miles (ASM) refers to how many seat miles are actually available for purchase on an airline. Capacity stats are published monthly in the 1st or 2nd week of the calendar month depending on the airline. Here are the "banned" airline stocks:

- **ALK**
- **ALGT**
- **AAL**
- **CPA**
- **DAL**
- **HA**
- **JBLU**
- **RJET**
- **SKYW**
- **LUV**
- **SAVE**
- **UAL**
- **VA**

Figure 92- Banned Stocks- 2015

For our premium members, these stocks are automatically screened out and will never appear in our Premium Watch List. To those of you screening the stocks yourself, print out the list and keep it by your computer for reference. We will continue to update all our members should we locate additional securities that may not fit our risk profiles.

Economic Reports and our Covered Call Writing Decisions

Covered call writing and put-selling results are enhanced by selecting the best underlying securities and most appropriate options. Stock selection involves screening via fundamental and technical analysis as well as common sense screens (like proper diversification). Option selection is based on several factors including chart analysis, overall market assessment and personal risk tolerance. In this article, we will focus in on overall market assessment using the myriad of weekly economic reports available to us. It is not necessary to memorize this information as it is presented as reference material to enhance our educational arsenal.

These reports can be categorized into four major groups:

- Labor market conditions
- Consumer health
- Business health
- General economic indicators

Here is a summary of several of the most critical reports:

Labor Market Conditions

Employment Situation

A monthly report of the number of persons on nonfarm payrolls, the rate of unemployment, and workers' average hourly earnings. It is considered a very timely and accurate reflection of labor market conditions. The unemployment rate is a key business cycle indicator.

Initial Jobless Claims

A weekly report of the number of individuals who filed for unemployment insurance for the first time the prior week.

Consumer Health

Consumer Confidence

A monthly gauge of consumers' attitudes about the present economic situation as well as their expectations regarding future conditions. Consumer confidence tends to have a strong correlation with consumer spending patterns.

Personal Income; Personal Spending

A monthly report of the income that households receive from all sources. Since income is the major determinant of spending, the report is an indicator of future consumer spending patterns.

Retail Sales

A monthly report of the dollar value of sales of a broad range of goods. Retail sales are a major indicator of consumer spending trends.

Durable-Goods Orders

A monthly measure of the number of orders for a broad range of products with an expected life of at least three years. Durable-goods orders are a leading indicator of industrial production and capital spending.

New Residential Construction

A monthly report on the construction of single-family homes and apartment buildings. When new residential construction is robust, purchases of household furnishings and appliances tend to quickly follow.

Existing-Home Sales

A monthly report of the number of previously constructed homes with a closed sale during the month. Existing-home sales make up a larger share of the market than new-home sales and indicate housing market trends.

New-Home Sales

A monthly report of the number of newly constructed homes with a committed sale during the month. The level of new-home sales is an indicator of housing market trends.

Construction Spending

A monthly measure of the dollar value of new construction activity. Construction projects contribute significantly to gross domestic product.

Business Health

Business Inventories

A monthly report of the dollar value of product inventories held by manufacturers, wholesalers, and retailers. Included in the report is the number of months it would take to deplete existing inventories at the current rate of sales, which is an important indicator of the near-term direction of production activity.

Industrial Production

A monthly measure of the changes in quantity of physical materials and items produced in the manufacturing, mining, and utilities industries. Industrial production is a significant indicator of trends in the industrial sector.

ISM Manufacturing Index

A monthly indicator of overall factory-sector trends, based on a survey of purchasing managers at several hundred manufacturing firms in a variety of industries. An index reading above 50 indicates that the manufacturing economy is generally expanding; below 50, that it is generally declining.

ISM Non-Manufacturing Index

A monthly indicator of overall service-sector trends, based on a survey of several hundred purchasing and supply executives in a variety of nonmanufacturing industries. A reading above 50 indicates that the nonmanufacturing economy is generally expanding; below 50, that it is generally declining.

General Economic Indicators

Leading Economic Indicators

A monthly composite index of ten economic indicators that typically lead overall economic activity. The index includes indicators such as housing permits, new orders for consumer goods, consumer expectations, and performance of the S&P 500 Index.

Consumer Price Index (CPI)

A widely followed indicator of inflation. The CPI is a monthly measure of the average change over time in the prices paid by urban consumers for a fixed market basket of consumer goods and services. The "core" CPI excludes food and energy prices, which account for roughly one-quarter of the broad CPI and tend to fluctuate widely, providing a truer reflection of inflationary trends.

Producer Price Index (PPI)

A monthly measure of the average change over time in the selling prices of a fixed basket of goods by stage of production, industry, and commodity. It is considered a leading indicator for consumer inflation. The "core" PPI excludes food and energy prices—which account for roughly one-quarter of the broad PPI and tend to fluctuate widely—providing a truer reflection of inflationary trends.

Gross Domestic Product (GDP)

A quarterly record of the country's economic health. GDP represents the total value of the country's production and consists of purchases of domestically produced goods and services by individuals, businesses, foreigners, and the government.

The role of these reports

A generalization can be gleaned from these reports evaluating them as favorable, mixed or unfavorable. Assuming favorable chart technicals and an average risk-tolerance, a favorable overall market assessment would lead us to select out-of-the money call options or put options that are closer to at-the-money than out-of-the money strikes. Both represent more aggressive option-selling positions. If our overall market evaluation was less favorable, we may opt for in-the-money call options and deeper out-of-the-money put options, both more conservative approaches to option-selling.

Accessing the information

Each week I summarize the weekly economic reports at the end of my blog articles and on page 1 of our Premium Stock Reports. We also publish the overall market assessment of *Investor's Business*

Daily and that of Dr. Eric Wish, a Professor at The University of Maryland who teaches an honors finance course. His *GMI indicator* is a fabulous resource for overall market evaluation. This, of course, is in addition to the market appraisal of BCI as shown in the screenshot below:

WEEKLY SUMMARY:
For the week: The S&P 500 Index fell by 0.40% for a year-to-date return of 2.07%.

IBD: Uptrend Under Pressure

GMI: 5/6- Buy signal since market close of May 11, 2015
The GMI is an independent index developed by Dr. Eric Wish, Professor at the Univ. of MD. The GMI uses 6 specific market measurements to determine the direction of the market. (http://wishingwealthblog.com/)

BCI: Cautiously bullish but still concerned over situation with Greece and how the markets respond. Until this is resolved, I am selling an equal number of in-the-money and out-of-the-money strikes but expect to get more aggressive once this matter is settled.

Figure 93- Summary of Overall Market

Managing Covered Call Trades while Working a Full-Time Job

Covered call writing is a popular and potentially highly rewarding strategy geared to retail investors. But most blue collar investors work nine-to-five jobs and managing investment positions can be challenging if no common sense plan is in place. The purpose of this article is to discuss ways that we can keep track of our positions and generate cash flow from passive income (investments) while still generating active income (going to work). Let's first breakdown the four stages of covered call writing:

- Stock selection
- Option selection
- Trade execution
- Position management

Stock selection

This aspect of our strategy can be accomplished in the evenings or on weekends. For those of you who are or will become premium members, the BCI team will do the screening for you and save you a significant amount of time by providing you with our Premium Watch Lists. Figure 94 shows a view of the top portion of our *running list* which is the watch list we provide to our members as located in the mid-portion of our stock reports:

Running List	Next ER Date	Industry Segment	Segment Rank	Beta	% Div. Yield	Wkly Avail	NTM OI >100 Cntr.	Comments (The last or next Ex-Div date is shown)
PASSED PREVIOUS WEEKS & PASSED CURRENT WEEK								
THRM (13)	03/05/14	Auto	B/B	1.41			Y	
WX (2)	03/05/14	Medical	A/A	1.20			Y	
AYI (6)	04/02/14	Building	A/A	1.30	0.40		Y	01/16/14
GIII (1)	04/02/14	Apparel	B	1.18			N	
AMTD (1)	04/15/14	Finance	B	1.36	1.40		Y	02/03/14
GOOG (14)	04/17/14	Internet	A/A	1.00		Y	Y	
SWKS (5)	04/17/14	Chips	B/B	1.18			Y	
HXL (1)	04/21/14	Aerospace	A	1.33			Y	
MANH (2)	04/22/14	Software	A/A	0.85			Y	
FFIV (4)	04/23/14	Internet	A/A	1.25			N	
URI (10)	04/23/14	Finance	A/A	2.00			Y	
NTCT (3)	04/24/14	Software	A/A	1.13			Y	
SYNA (9)	04/24/14	Computer	A/A	1.28			Y	
ALK (1)	04/24/14	Transport	A	1.58	1.20		Y	02/21/14
EFII (5)	04/29/14	Computer	A/A	1.20			Y	
IACI (2)	04/29/14	Internet	A/A	1.08	1.20		Y	02/12/14
JLL (4)	04/29/14	Real Estate	A/A	1.14	0.40		Y	11/13/13

Figure 94- Premium Watch List or "Running List"

All stocks located in the "white cells" are eligible candidates for consideration. Our typical running list has between forty to sixty eligible stocks for covered call writing in addition to our twenty to twenty five exchange-traded funds candidates which we provide to our members in a separate report.

Option selection

Once our watch list has been established, we can check the calculations by accessing the options chains and using the multiple tab of the Ellman Calculator. Ninety percent of this work can also be accomplished in evenings and weekends but will need to be re-checked prior to trade execution during hours when US markets are open (9:30 AM ET to 4:00 PM ET, Monday through Friday).

Trade execution

Here is where we need to find a small time slot mid-day once or twice a month. Most of our trading will take place just prior to expiration of our contracts (the third Friday of the month) or the beginning of the following week. All the preparation can be done in advance but market pricing changes so all orders need to be re-checked prior to execution. As you master the strategy this will not take a lot of our time. I like to *enter my covered call trades between 11AM ET and 3PM ET* when the market volatility is at a minimum. How about during a lunch hour? Again, it's only once or twice a month as you set the tables in the evenings or on weekends.

Position management

For this aspect of the strategy we must become creative. In my books and DVDs, I detail the 20%/10% guidelines which dictate when and if to buy back an option if share price declines. Once our trades are entered, we can immediately enter *limit orders* (at a specified price or better) to buy back the options at 20% in the first half of the contract and at 10% during the second half. In essence, we are instructing our broker to close our short options positions if the price of the option we originally sold declines to 20% or 10% of its original value or less depending on the week of the current contract. If the price does not reach that level, the trade is never executed. However, if it does, the option will automatically be bought back and an email sent to us notifying us of the trade.

We can then make a decision that night or over the weekend what path to follow now that our option obligation no longer exists. Once again, position management techniques are highlighted with examples in my books and DVDs. Follow-up exit strategy trades may require a small number of lunchtime sessions of five to ten minutes. It will be time well spent. The chart in Figure 95 shows what a trade execution form may look like after entering a covered call position and setting up a limit order to buy back that option (buy-to-close). In this hypothetical, we buy EDU at $28.00 and sell the $30.00 call for $1.00 (sell-to-open). We then set a limit order (that amount or cheaper) at 20% or $0.20 to buy back the short call:

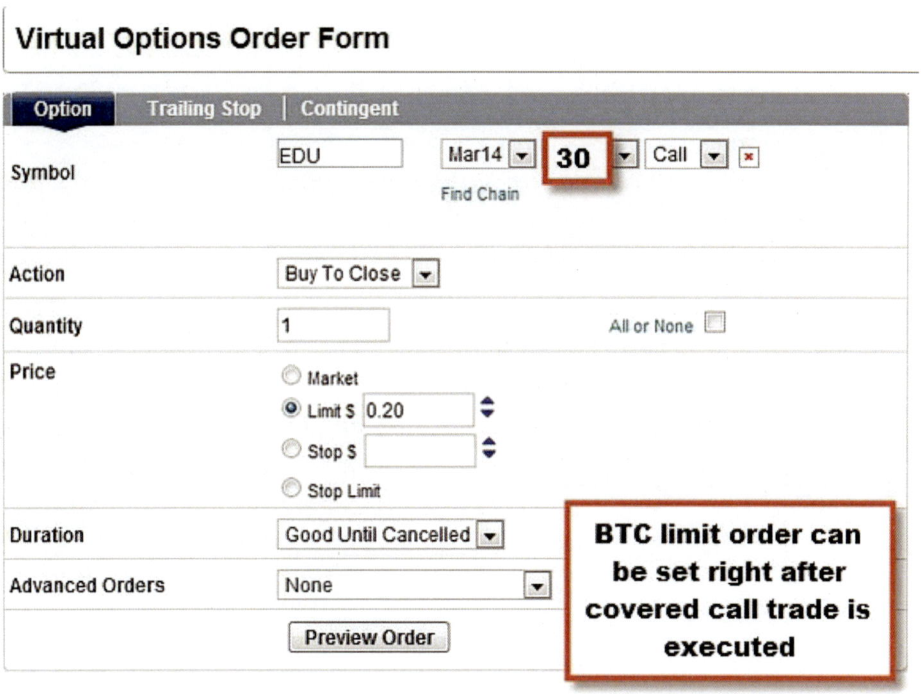

Figure 95- Limit Order-Options Trade Execution Form

Using this technique means we don't have to constantly watch our positions and by placing "good until cancelled" orders, they remain in effect until executed or until we change them (also accomplished after hours). Now, mid-way through the contract we change the

20% limit order to 10% (evenings or weekends), in this case the limit order will be at $0.10 and also "good until cancelled"

Summary

Covered call writing does require us to be available during market hours for an hour or two a month. By educating ourselves and mapping out a non-emotional common sense plan based on sound fundamental, technical and common sense principles, the time required during these hours can be minimized and made manageable while still working a full-time blue collar job.

THE BLUE COLLAR INVESTOR

Chapter 9

Executing Covered Call Trades

Chapter outline

1. Covered Call Writing, Leveraged ETFs, Weekly Options and Protective Puts
2. Covered Call Writing: Setting Up a Stop Loss Order
3. Covered Call Writing when there is Overall Market Concern
4. Evaluating Brokerages and Comparing their Commissions
5. Executing a Covered Call Trade: A Step By Step Look at our Broker Statement
6. Option Approval Levels for our Brokerage Accounts
7. Options Clearing Corporation: Guaranteeing our Options Trades
8. Should I Enter my Trades on Expiration Friday or the Following Monday?

Covered Call Writing, Leveraged ETFs, Weekly Options and Protective Puts

Traditional covered call writing consists of buying a stock or exchange-traded fund (ETF) and selling a call option to generate cash flow. Frequently, BCI members will think outside the box and add additional strategies and products to create a covered call writing-like strategy. The goal in these cases is not to complicate a relatively straightforward strategy but rather to generate even higher returns. Here is a strategy recently proposed to me by a BCI member that I thought you would find interesting. The strategy involves the use of covered call writing, leveraged ETFs, Weekly options and protective puts. Let's first define the latter three terms.

Definitions

Leveraged ETFs: Exchange-traded funds that use financial derivatives (like options) and debt to magnify the returns of an underlying index.

Protective puts: A put option purchased for a stock already owned by the put buyer. It protects against a decrease in share price below the put strike price and ensures a minimum sale price of the stock.

Weekly options: Options which exist for eight days. They are introduced each Thursday and expire eight days later on Friday. *Expanded Weekly options* are also available up to five weeks in advance of expiration and have expiration dates in between the third Fridays of the months.

Leveraged ETF Example TNA (Drexion Small Cap Bull 3x Shares):

This leveraged ETF seeks a return that is 300% the return of its benchmark index (small cap bull fund) ***for a single day***. **The fund should not be expected to provide three times the return of the benchmark's cumulative return for periods greater than a day.** By nature, these securities are highly volatile and therefore generate higher option premiums.

The prosed trade

- Buy 300 x TNA at $54.70
- Buy the six-month $77.50 put option for $27.51 (three contracts)
- Total position cost (stock price plus put price) = $82.21 x 300 = $24,663.00
- Guaranteed sales price because of put option is $77.50 per share, leaving a debit before covered call writing of $4.71 per share

Theory behind the trade

- Sell weekly, slightly out-of-the-money call options on TNA making sure to generate at least $1.00 per share premium
- Continue selling these options weekly for twenty six weeks generating $7800.00 ($300.00 x 26)
- By put expiration the shares are sold for $77.50 or $23,250.00
- Total returns = $7800.00 + $23,250.00 = $31,050.00
- Less cost basis of $24,663.00 = $6387.00 which represents a 25.9%, six-month return

Selecting the short calls

Figure 96 depicts a recent options chain for TNA which shows which strike we would have to sell to generate a weekly return of $1.00 per share:

Calls						Sep 13
Last	Intrinsic Value	Bid	Ask	Vol	Open Interest	Strike
10.75	10.70	9.25	12.25	0	0	44.00
9.70	9.70	9.50	9.90	0	0	45.00
8.70	8.70	8.45	8.95	0	0	46.00
7.78	7.70	7.55	8.00	0	0	47.00
6.92	6.70	6.80	7.05	0	0	48.00
6.05	5.70	5.95	6.15	0	0	49.00
5.47				0	0	49.50
5.15				0	0	50.00
4.62				0	0	50.50
4.28				0	0	51.00
3.95				0	0	51.50
3.58				0	0	52.00
3.12				0	0	52.50
2.85	1.70	2.79	2.91	0	0	53.00
2.51	1.20	2.46	2.57	0	0	53.50
2.21	0.70	2.15	2.26	0	0	54.00
1.92	0.20	1.89	1.96	0	0	54.50
1.63	0.00	1.59	1.67	19	0	55.00
1.40	0.00	1.35	1.45	2	0	55.50
1.16	0.00	1.11	1.21	24	0	56.00
0.97	0.00	0.91	1.02	1	0	56.50
0.78	0.00	0.73	0.84	26	0	57.00
0.64	0.00	0.61	0.66	7	0	57.50
0.52	0.00	0.48	0.55	149	0	58.00
0.40	0.00	0.37	0.42	54	0	58.50
0.31	0.00	0.27	0.34	6	0	59.00
0.21	0.00	0.18	0.25	0	0	59.50
0.18	0.00	0.17	0.20	11	0	60.00

TNA weekly options chain with stock price @ $54.70

Figure 96- TNA: Recent Options Chain

The $56.50 strike generates $0.91 close to our $1.00 target. To avoid assignment the stock cannot go higher than $56.50.

Security volatility

Next let's view a recent one-month chart of this security (Figure 97) to see how realistic avoiding assignment for twenty six consecutive weeks is:

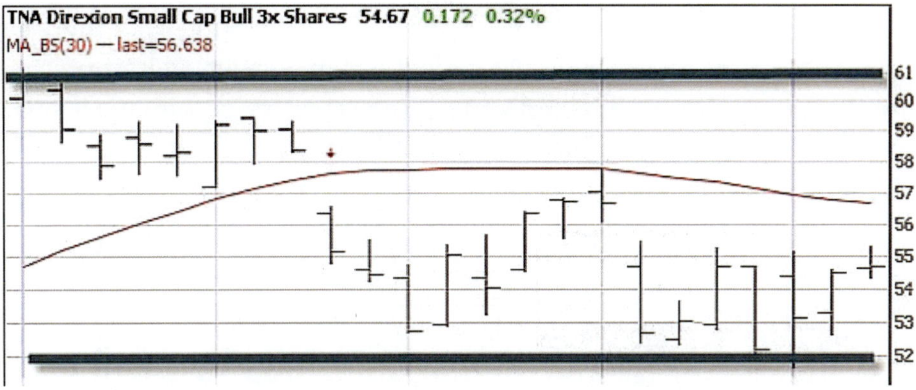

Figure 97- TNA: One-Month Chart

Practical application

TNA has traded in a $9.00 price range ($52.00 to $61.00) in the past month and so the expectation of assignment during that twenty six-week time frame is highly probable. To avoid assignment we can buy back the option but that is an option debit not accounted for in the original trade proposal. If we allow assignment we would have to repurchase the security at a higher price also incurring an additional, unaccounted for debit.

Assumptions made and related concerns

For twenty six consecutive weeks you will never be assigned on the short call. Herein lies the weakness of the strategy. We are dealing with a highly volatile, leveraged security which will generate high option returns but also put us at *assignment risk*. We are protected to the downside because of the put purchase but vulnerable to the upside.

Conclusion

Traditional covered call writing can be altered through the use of additional strategies like put buying and other option products like Weekly options and leveraged ETFs. These strategies will have their advantages and disadvantages which must be fully understood before implementing them into our portfolios and risking our family's hard-earned money. Once all aspects of the multi-level strategy are understood, only the individual investor can determine if the strategy is appropriate. The one rule of thumb you can always take to the bank is that there is no free lunch.

Covered Call Writing: Setting up a Stop Loss Order

Successful covered call writing requires the appropriate use of exit strategies to mitigate losses and enhance gains. In this article, we will focus on actions that can be taken when a stock price declines and capital preservation becomes a concern. Once we enter our covered call position we are in two distinct trades. We are long the stock (purchased the stock) and short the option (sold the option). Without the stock, we would be in a *naked options position* and susceptible to extreme capital risk. As a matter of fact, most brokerages will not allow retail investors naked options trading privileges for our own protection and for their own preservation as well (we do live in a litigious society). This means that we must close our short options position first before selling the stock or close both simultaneously. The latter is now possible with the new advanced trading platforms offered by many online discount brokerages. In this article we will discuss two ways to manage our covered call trades with a declining underlying security.

Simultaneous closing of long and short positions: One Triggers Other Order (OTO) (Figures 98 and 99)

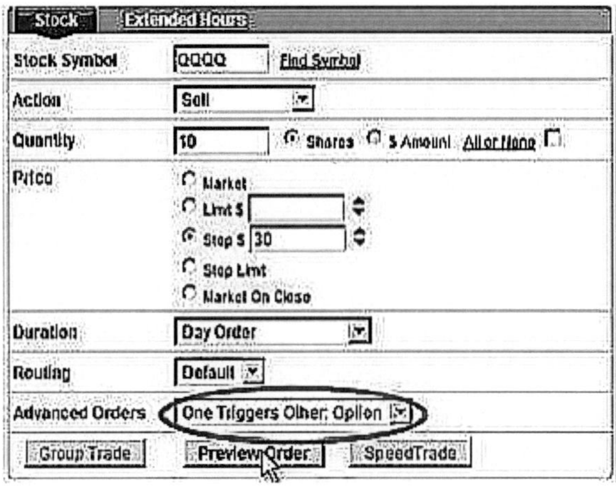

Figure 98- Stop orders on Covered Calls

After navigating to the stock order form, we enter a sell stop order at a specific price and then select *one triggers other* from the advanced orders drop down box. Then click *preview* (highlighted by arrow) to enter the options order entry screen:

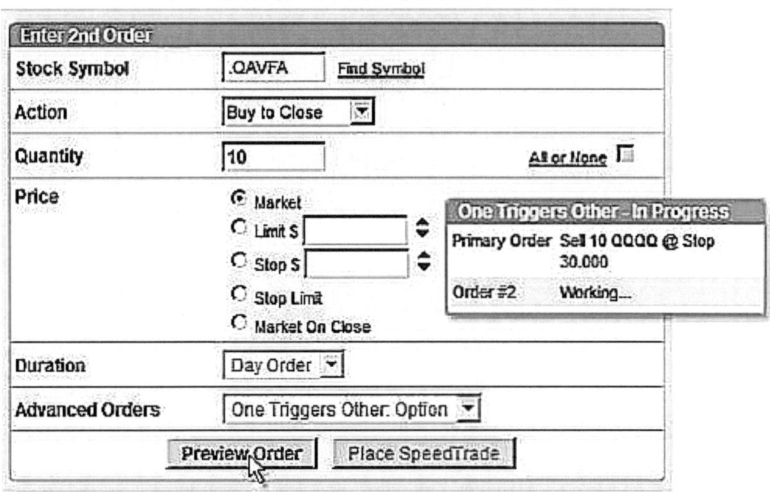

Figure 99- Closing Short Options Position

Trade logistics of the OTO order

Here are the logistics as to how this trade executes successfully:

- The sell stop of the long stock position is executed first
- Since most of us are not approved for naked options trading, we must enter a market order (best published price) for the closing of the short options position
- The options order is immediately sent to the trading floor once the long position is closed

Advantages

- Orders can be entered without having to be in front of our computers monitoring positions
- Affords protection against catastrophic losses in most cases

Disadvantages

- Market orders limit our ability to negotiate more favorable option prices when closing the short options position
- Closing our entire covered call trade may not be the best exit strategy to execute
- Closing the short options position first will give us the greatest amount of position management flexibility

Using the 20%/10% guideline

In my books and DVDs I discuss a guideline concept that I have developed over the years called the 20%/10% guideline. I call it a guideline for a reason. You can veer from the exact percentiles a slight amount and still be a successful covered call trader. For example, in bear or volatile market conditions I may spend a little more than 20% or 10% to buy back my options. Here are the steps if the original option sale was for $3.00:

- Place a limit order to buy back (buy-to-close) the option for $0.60 or less in the first half of the contract and for $0.30 or less in the latter part of the contract
- Request that your brokerage company send you an email notification if the short position is closed
- Once the short position has been closed we now own our shares without any obligation
- We now have the ability to roll down, take no action and look to "hit a double" (re-sell the same option), or close the entire position

Advantages

- We can negotiate a better options price leveraging the Show or Fill Rule
- We have much more flexibility as to the type of exit strategy opportunities we can take advantage of
- Excellent protection against catastrophic loss in most cases (barring a gap down in price on unexpected bad news…remember no earnings reports!)

Disadvantage

- More time required for proper management

Conclusion

Placing stop loss orders on our covered call writing positions can be accomplished using the *OTO* or *one triggers other order* or by closing the short options position first and then taking the best appropriate action. The latter will afford more opportunities to raise our profit level if time permits.

Covered Call Writing when there is Overall Market Concern

Covered call writing is a stock option strategy with primary goals of income generation and capital preservation. Most of us are conservative investors who use the power of education to master an investment strategy better than most everyone else using the same strategy. That is what the Blue Collar Investors are all about.

In the past few weeks, I have heard from many of our members (international members as well) who are concerned about a possible severe market correction and want to be prepared in case a significant downturn does take place. Although I do not personally share this degree of concern, I do feel that a review of some of the management techniques we can implement in the event that the market corrects to a significant extent will be useful:

Sell in-the-money strikes

Using in-the-money strikes is our most commonly used approach to protecting ourselves against share depreciation. We are generating downside protection of the time value of the premium, a perk paid for by the option buyer, not by us. If we sold a $30.00 call on a stock currently trading at $32.00 for $3.00, our initial profit is 3.3% ($1.00/$30.00) and that profit is protected by the intrinsic value ($2.00/$32.00) = 6.25%. In other words, our share price can drop by 6.25% and we would still generate a 3.3%, one-month return.

Use low-beta stocks

Our premium watch list gives beta stats and historically low-beta stocks tend to outperform in bear market situations.

Lower monthly goals using options with less implied volatility

As an example, lower your monthly goals for initial returns from 2-4% to 1-3%. This means that the implied volatility of the underlying securities is less and therefore carries lower risk.

Use exchange-traded funds (ETFs) instead of stocks

ETFs or exchange-traded funds are baskets of stocks with some going up and some going down in value. As a whole, and generally speaking, these securities have less implied volatility (IV) than individual stocks. In our weekly ETF Reports for premium members we also give implied volatility stats for the eligible ETFs allowing our members to tailor their portfolios to personal risk tolerance levels and overall market assessment. Here, too, I would establish my goal to perhaps 1%-2%.

Buy protective puts

A put will give us the right, but not the obligation, to sell our shares at a certain price. When used in conjunction with covered call writing, the strategy is called the *collar strategy*. It usually is set up by selling an out-of-the-money call and buying an out-of-the-money put. Here's an example:

- Buy BCI at $48.00
- Sell the $50.00 out-of-the-money call for $2.00
- Buy the $45.00 out-of-the-money put for $1.00

Our initial options credit is cut in half in this hypothetical example but we are protected against a catastrophic price decline below $45.00.

Sell cash-secured puts

We can enter our covered call positions "at a discount" when we are bearish on the overall market. Here's an example:

Using Cash-secured puts to enter covered call positions

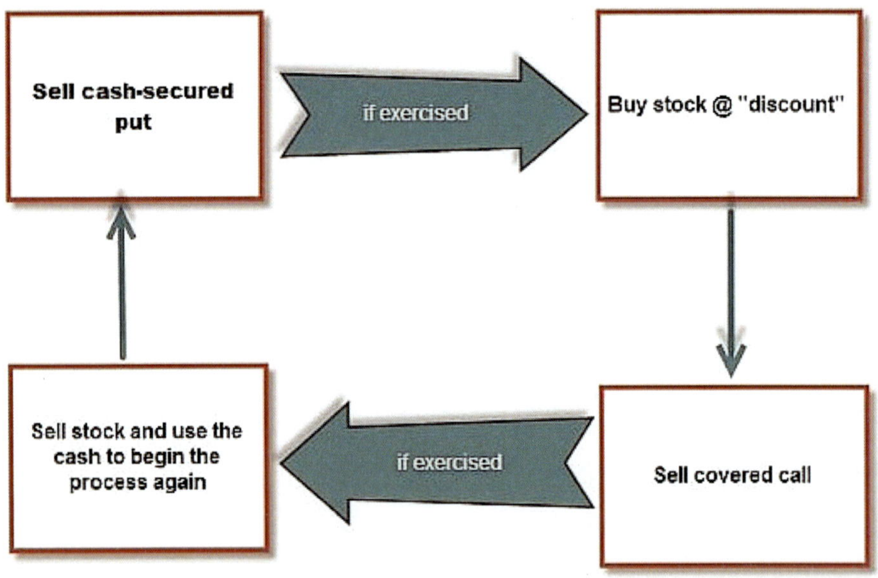

Figure 100- Cash-Secured Puts and Covered Call Writing: The PCP Strategy

This strategy is detailed in my fifth book, *Selling Cash-Secured Puts*.

Summary

One of the advantages of covered call writing is that it can be molded and modified to meet the challenges of current market conditions. An elite and educated covered call writer, which is where I want all of you to be, will change the strategy approach based on overall market assessment, chart technicals and personal risk tolerance. One size does not fit all.

Evaluating Brokerages and Comparing Their Commissions

Option trade executions include a discussion of the levels of trading approval needed to use various options strategies. You will recall that these defined levels will vary slightly from one brokerage to another. Figure 101 shows one example of these trading levels:

Option Approval Levels

OPTION LEVELS	STRATEGIES
Level 1	Covered Call, Long Protective Puts
Level 2	Long call/put
Level 3	Spreads
Level 4	Uncovered or Naked

Figure 101- Levels of Options Trading Approval

In this article, I will review the commission structure of some (but not all) of the more prominent brokerages that offer options trading platforms and services.

Covered call writing as well as put-selling are short-term strategies that require frequent trading. This is the antithesis of a buy-and-hold strategy. Therefore, commission costs will play a significant role in our annualized returns much like expense ratios can substantially impact the returns we realize from mutual funds. For this reason, we cannot consider using full-service brokers to execute the sales of our covered calls or cash-secured puts. They simply charge too much. So we turn to *online discount brokers* who allow us to execute our trades online at reduced commissions, absent the investment advice and other perks full-service brokers offer.

Most of the major brokerages are reliable, ethical and efficient as it relates to the execution of our trades. They also offer phone support if we experience any problems with the trading platform. They just won't offer advice unless we are willing to pay for it. Don't pay for it. You don't need it. Education is power and will lead to the confidence we need in order to trade like an expert.

When doing our due-diligence as to which online discount broker to select we should factor in an evaluation of the quality of the research platforms, minimum cash deposits, and interest earned on deposited cash. But most importantly we should look at the commissions, the fees we pay to have our broker execute our trades. This is especially important to us due to the number of trades option sellers execute.

The major distinguishing factor between discount brokerages is the cost, or commission, charged to execute trades. As the competition has heated up over the years between these firms, commission rates have fallen precipitously, with some predicting commissions to eventually approach zero! Today (mid-2015) the rates are low, but not quite zero. The chart below (Figure 102) lists eleven of the top brokerages and the commissions charged by each to enter an options position and for assignment (our shares being sold or shares being "put" to us). Web links for each of these firms have also been provided so that you can conduct further research to find the brokerage firm that best meets your needs:

BROKERAGE OPTION COMMISSIONS

Brokerage	URL	Commission to enter	Commission if exercised
Options House	www.optionshouse.com	$5 up to 5 contracts $8.50 + .15/contract if >5	$5
Trade King	www.tradeking.com	$4.95 + .65/contract	$9.95
TD Ameritrade	www.tdameritrade.com	$9.99 + .75/contract	$19.99
OptionsXpress	www.optionsxpress.com	$14.95 up to 10 contracts $1.50/contract if > 10	$9.95
E-Trade	www.us.etrade.com	$9.99 + .75/contract	$7.99
Trade Monster	www.trademonster.com	$12.50 min. or .50/contract	$7.50
Fidelity	www.fidelity.com	$7.95 + .75/contract	$7.95
Scottratde	www.scottrade.com	$7 + 1.25/contract	$17.00
ING Direct	www.sharebuilder.com	$6.95 + .75/contract	$20.00
USAA	www.usaa.com	$5.95 + .75/contract	$5.95
Interactive Brokers	www.interactivebrokers.com	$0.70/contract Min. $1	$0.005/share $1 min.

Figure 102- A Comparison of Brokerage Commissions

A few pennies or a couple of dollars may not seem like a big issue for a single trade but multiply those stats by the number of trades executed in a month, a year and an investment lifetime and all of a sudden we have a significant cash amount that is better off in our pockets than those of the brokers. The world of online discount brokers is highly competitive and they are all vying for our business so it behooves us to do our due-diligence and keep as much of our hard-earned money as possible. *Many times, making a phone call to your broker requesting lower commission rates will result in a successful negotiation.*

Executing a Covered Call Trade: A Step By Step Look at our Broker Statement

Executing a covered call trade and understanding the accounting procedures of our online discount broker statements can be confusing to the new option trader. I have recently received a few emails regarding this topic so I thought it would be useful to show an actual trade I made using Michael Kors Limited (KORS), a stock on our Premium Watch List at the time this article was written. The four steps we will review are:

- Purchase four hundred shares of KORS
- Confirm purchase
- Sell four September call contracts
- Confirm sale

Entering a covered call trade in this manner is known as *legging-in*. For information on using a *buy-write combination form* see pages 219 – 223 of my *Complete Encyclopedia for Covered Call Writing Volume I*.

Steps 1 and 2

Since the bid-ask spread is tight (small difference between the *"bid"* and the *"ask"*), I placed a market order to purchase four hundred shares and got executed at $72.36 as seen at the top of Figure 103:

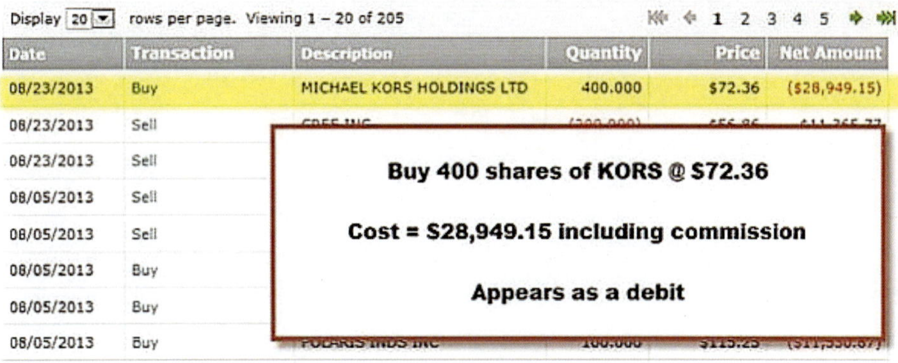

Figure 103- Confirmed Purchase of Four Hundred Shares of KORS at $72.36

Note that the total cost, including commissions is $28,949.15 and appears as a debit (red parenthesis on top right). This information appears in the "Activities" section of the brokerage statement.

Step 3

Now that I own the shares and I'm in a "covered" or protected position, I am free to sell the call option. I decided to sell the near-the-money $72.50 September call option with slightly less than one month to contract expiration. Figure 104 shows the trade execution form:

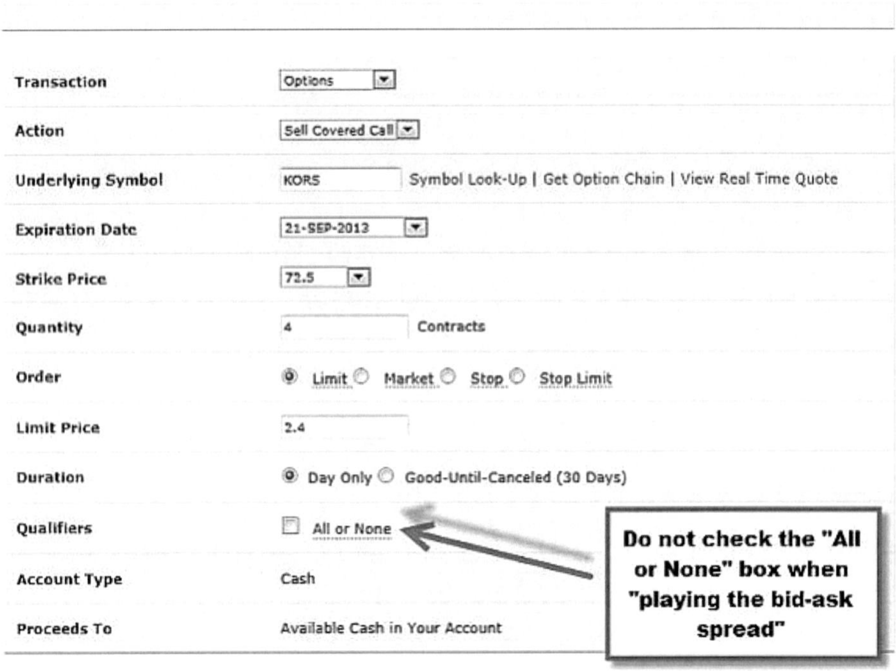

Figure 104- Selling a Covered Call Option for KORS

Please note the following:

- The first 6 lines are self-explanatory
- We enter a limit order, not a market order
- We enter a limit price based on the bid-ask spread shown in an options chain
- The order is day only
- ***DO NOT CHECK THE ALL OR NONE BOX when playing the bid-ask spread (pages 224 – 228 of Volume I)

Step4

Next I checked the activity section of the broker statement (order status can also be checked) to see if the option sale was executed (see Figure 105):

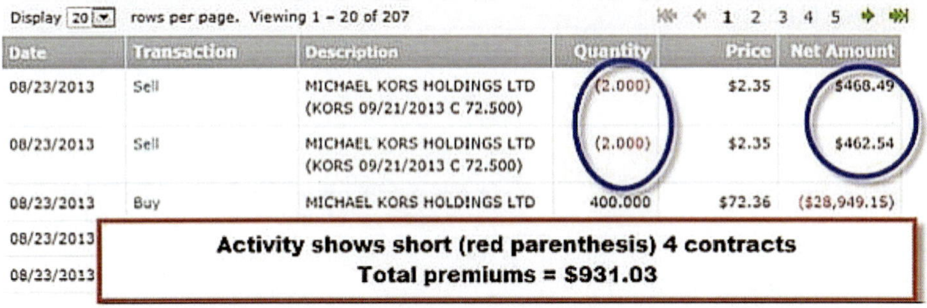

Figure 105- Four September $72.50 Calls Sold for KORS

Please note:

- Four contracts (two plus two) were confirmed sold for a total of $931.03, including commissions
- My initial one-month return is $931.03/$28,949.15 = 3.2%, after commissions
- Notice the option price dropped from $2.40 to $2.35 while I was creating these slides so I had to adjust the limit order down (took one for the team!)
- The contracts appear in red parenthesis (middle of chart) because I am short these contracts (I sold them and have an obligation to sell my shares and may have to buy back the options)
- Since I am long the 400 shares, they appear in black and NOT in parenthesis

Positions section of brokerage statement

This is the section that can get quite confusing. Although I generated $931.00 in cash from the sale of the four contracts, the option value will appear as a debit in this portion of the statement because the position is still open and may have to be bought back. Let's have a look a couple of minutes after the trade was executed as shown in Figure 106:

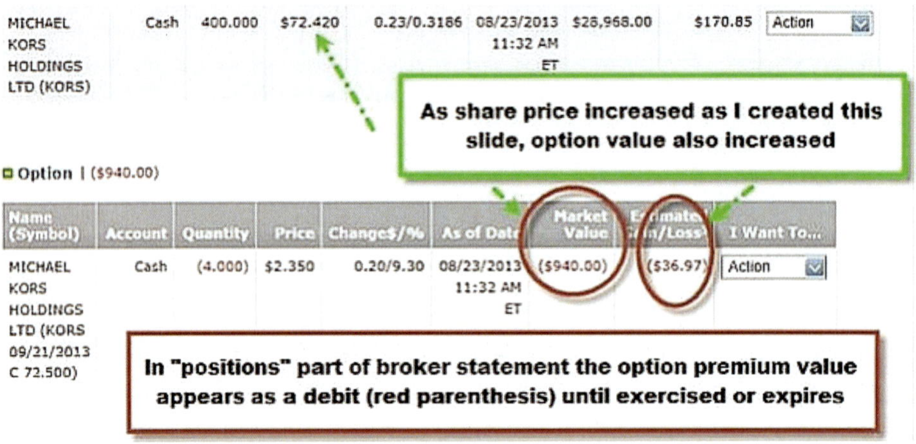

Figure 106- KORS: Stock and Options Positions

Please note:

- As share value started to rise after the trade was executed so did the value of the option premium
- Option value appears as a debit (red) because the cost to buy back is greater than the premium received.
- This is deceiving because an increase in share value is a positive for us. This is simply an accounting technique used by brokerages which we must understand
- The four contracts also appear in red because I am short these contracts and still hold an option obligation
- The cash generated from the sale of the options IS in the cash portion of my account and available to trade with
- Once the options expire, are bought back or are exercised the apparent debits and short positions are deleted from

the positions section of the broker statement. The cash, of course, is ours to keep.

Conclusion

Brokerage statements will not all appear precisely the same but will be similar in many respects. When executing our covered call trades it is important to be aware of the accounting methods used by our respective brokers to avoid confusion. Be sure to fully understand your brokers platform before entering your first covered call trade.

Option Approval Levels for our Brokerage Accounts

Covered call writing along with all other stock and option strategies require us to open a brokerage account. This process will take more than a simple phone call. All brokerages will require us to fill out an options approval form as designed by its compliance department. Based on the information gleaned from this form, the brokerage will decide which level of trading approval the investor is sanctioned for. So how do we get the necessary experience without first getting approval to trade? This is a dilemma that is easy to overcome by starting out with simpler and less risky strategies like covered call writing (I may be biased but as you will soon see, the brokerages agree with me). So *before you locate and fund a* brokerage account, *make a phone call to find out the policy regarding options trading approval*. For those looking for a place to start searching for a broker, see the "free resources" link on the top black bar of the Blue Collar web site. One of the files is a list of several online discount brokers with the associated contact information.

Options Approval Form

The reason brokerages require us to fill out this form is because of FINRA rule 2090 called the *Know Your Customer Rule* or *KYC Rule*. Brokerages are required to undertake reasonable diligence when opening accounts to assist in avoiding inappropriate risks on the part of retail investors. They also have their own interests in mind so as to avoid regulatory and legal issues. The form will ask about our trading experience and knowledge as well as our financial resources.

Levels of trading approval

There are no official standards and levels may vary from broker to broker but in all cases the higher levels incorporate the lower level approvals. Figure 107 is a graphic of a typical brokerage format for trading levels (similar concept to the one shown in Figure 101):

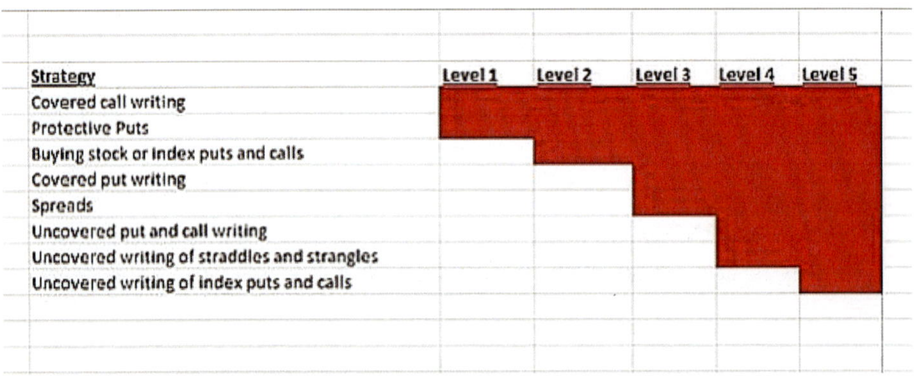

Figure 107- Levels of Option Trading Approval

Level 1:

- Covered call writing (writing as you know means selling)
- Protective puts
- Approved for self-directed IRA accounts

Level 2: Level 1 +

- Call and put buying

Level 3: Levels 1 and 2 +

- Covered put writing (bearish strategy where a put is sold and the stock is shorted)
- Spreads (simultaneous purchase and sale of options on the same stock and class)

Level 4: Levels 1, 2 and 3 +

- Uncovered call and put writing
- Uncovered writing of straddles (both call and put positions with same strike and expiration)
- Uncovered writing of strangles (both call and put positions with different strikes but same expiration)

Level 5: Levels 1,2,3,4 +

- Uncovered writing of index puts and calls

Which level should I apply for?

Sophisticated options traders know the level appropriate for their needs. For Blue Collar Investors, Level 1 is the place to be in most (but not all) instances, at least initially. It will allow us to write covered calls and use protective puts if that is part of our strategy. It will also allow us to incorporate our trading into our self-directed IRA accounts. It may also keep us out of trouble! We will be less inclined to try riskier strategies while we are developing our trading skills. We can always move up to higher levels as our skills are enhanced.

Quick story

A few years ago, a wealthy group of investors flew me out to the west coast to do a private seminar. One investor immediately (way too soon) started trading hundreds of thousands of dollars in covered calls. His brokerage gave him a high level of trading approval because the account was funded with millions of dollars. One day he inadvertently sold the underlying (thousands of shares) and was left in a risky naked (uncovered) options position. It cost him about $150,000.00 …not so bad for him but a killer for most of us! (He still needed a box of Kleenex). Had he not had a high level of trading approval, selling the long stock position would not have been permitted and there would not have been the significant loss.

Conclusion

Find the appropriate level of trading approval and avoid unnecessary risks. For most of us that's level 1 at least to start.

Options Clearing Corporation: Guaranteeing our Options Trades

Covered call writing and selling cash-secured puts involve investing our hard-earned money. Did you ever wonder who guarantees these trades? It's not our broker or even our broker's clearing firm. It's the *Options Clearing Corporation* or the OCC.

This is an organization that acts as both the issuer and guarantor of options and futures contracts. The Options Clearing Corporation operates under the jurisdiction of the U.S. Securities and Exchange Commission (SEC) and the Commodities Futures Trading Commission (CFTC). Under its SEC jurisdiction, the OCC clears transactions for put and call options, stock indexes, foreign currencies, interest rate composites and single-stock futures. It is the ultimate resource in buy/sell option transactions as well as the exercise and the subsequent assignment. In effect, the OCC guarantees every trade.

Let's say that John buys option A through broker B. Broker B then submits the trade to its clearing firm C which then sends the trade information to the OCC.

Meanwhile, Ann, an option seller (possibly a market-maker) submits her trade to clearing firm D which also sends the trade information to the OCC. The OCC then matches up the two trades. Now what if John, the option buyer, wants to exercise the option and own the underlying shares while Ann, the option seller, wants to buy back the option to close her position? Both trades then go from broker to clearing firm and to the OCC. The OCC will then locate the appropriate customer who was short the option to then deliver the shares to John's clearing firm and then to John as well as a different appropriate customer to take the other side of Ann's trade. The process of exercise and assignment is done either randomly or *first in, first out (FIFO)* where the oldest inventory is sold to the most recent buyer. Figure 108 is a flow chart showing how these trades are executed:

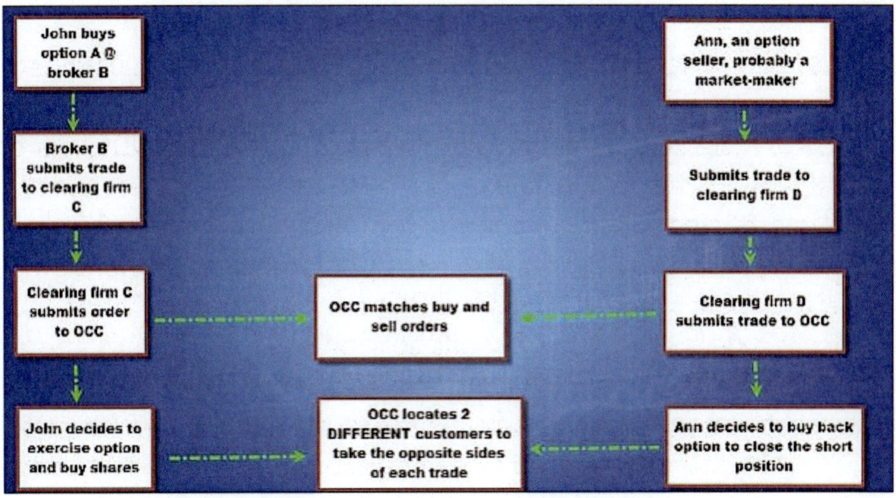

Figure 108- Options Clearing Corporation Flow Chart

Many retail investors frequently wonder what happens to the option buyer who bought the contracts we sold and then bought back. The purpose of this article is to demonstrate how the system works to accommodate both buyers and sellers and therefore guarantees all trades executed.

Should I Enter my Trades on Expiration Friday or the Following Monday?

The timing of our option trade executions will impact the success of our covered call writing returns. The BCI methodology prides itself on having rules and guidelines for buying back options, re-selling options and selling long stock positions. One question that many of us have inquired about is when to enter our one-month trades. My books and DVDs have guidelines for this as well:

- For a four-week contract (eight of these per year), we enter the trade within the first few days of the contract
- For a five-week contract (four of these per year), we enter the trade within the first seven trading days of the contract

The reason we don't want to wait longer than these time frames is due to the impact of *theta* or time value erosion. Theta is an estimate of how much the theoretical value of an option declines when there is a passage of one calendar (not trading) day while there is no change in stock price or volatility. For near-the-money strikes, theta is logarithmic in nature (not linear) and causes time value erosion to start off slowly and then impact our premiums to a greater extent as expiration approaches as shown in Figure 109:

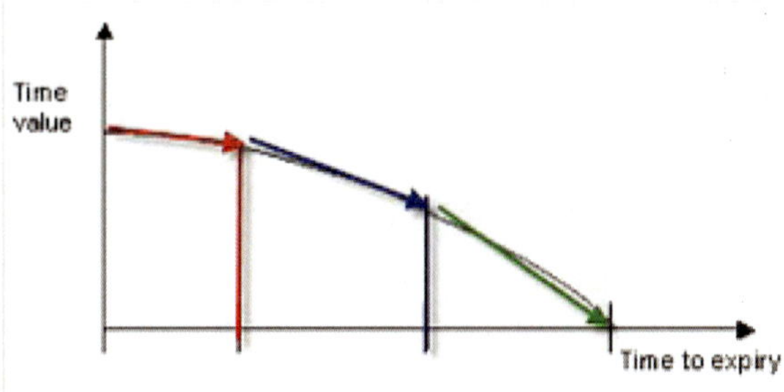

Figure 109- Theta: Time Value Erosion of our Option Premiums

With this in mind, many covered call writers intuitively feel that they should establish new positions on expiration Friday rather than the following Monday to capture some extra time value and negate the impact that theta will have over the weekend. To see if this approach will benefit us in most cases we must further investigate how traders value the options when using option pricing models. For every calendar day that passes, the option value will decline by the amount of the theta. To really dissect this in a blue collar manner we must ask ourselves when the calendar day is deducted from the pricing model…Friday…Saturday…Sunday…once each day?

It is fair to say that many traders assume the day is deducted and option premium value is decreased at the end of each calendar day and base their trades on that assumption. However, that frequently is not the case as traders anticipate the price decline and calculate option value prior to the end of a trading day or prior to the weekend. We may notice option values declining on the Thursday before expiration Friday and more so mid-day on expiration Friday as options are now being priced at Monday's theta value. In other words, the weekend days are already deducted and so *there may be no added value of entering trades on expiration Friday compared to the following Monday. In addition to this, we are now exposed to weekend risk for very little reward, if any at all.*

Of course, there are many other factors that impact option value (the Greeks) so we can't make a blanket statement that we are always better off waiting until Monday. However, we can say that based on the manner in which theta is factored into option value, *waiting until the beginning of the week after expiration is generally a better way to enter new covered call trades.*

Chapter 10

Exit Strategies

Chapter outline

1. Closing a Covered Call Writing Position Mid-Contract: A Real Life Example: Example 1
2. Closing our Entire Covered Call Position when Share Price Rises: The Mid-Contract Unwind Exit Strategy: Example 2
3. Emergency Management Report: Dealing with Volatile and Bearish Markets
4. Evaluating Returns when Rolling Out and Up
5. How to Avoid Early Exercise when Dividends are About to be Distributed
6. Rolling Out and Up to Capture Share Appreciation: A Good Idea?
7. When do we Sell our Covered Call Writing Stocks?

Closing a Covered Call Writing Position Mid-Contract: A Real Life Example: Example 1

The use of exit strategies will elevate our profits to the highest possible levels. Mastering the skill of position management is one of the main reasons why Blue Collar Investors outperform other covered call writers. A favorite exit strategy of mine is the *mid-contract unwind exit strategy* used in the first half of an options contract when share price has risen well above the strike price sold. In this article I will show a real-life example of a trade I made last year using TAN (Guggenheim Solar ETF), an exchange-traded fund that was a top-performer on our Premium Member ETF Report at the time.

The trade

- 8/19/2013: Buy 500 x TAN at $25.83
- 8/19/2013: Sell 5 x September $26.00 calls at $0.90
- 9/6/2013: Share price rises to $29.66, leaving the $26.00 call deep in-the-money

Accessing the options chain

Since there were still two full weeks remaining in the contract, I investigated the options chain to see how much time value was associated with the $26.00 call option and whether it paid to unwind. Here's the option chain on 9/6/2013 (Figure 110):

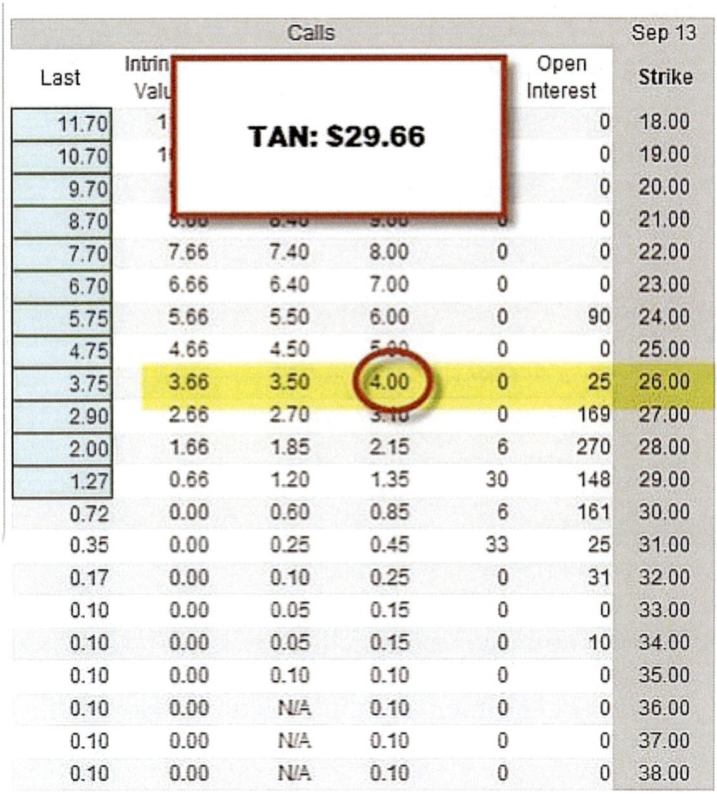

Calls						Sep 13
Last	Intrin Valu				Open Interest	Strike
11.70	1				0	18.00
10.70	1				0	19.00
9.70					0	20.00
8.70	[illegible]	[illegible]	[illegible]	[illegible]	0	21.00
7.70	7.66	7.40	8.00	0	0	22.00
6.70	6.66	6.40	7.00	0	0	23.00
5.75	5.66	5.50	6.00	0	90	24.00
4.75	4.66	4.50	[illegible]	0	0	25.00
3.75	3.66	3.50	4.00	0	25	26.00
2.90	2.66	2.70	[illegible]	0	169	27.00
2.00	1.66	1.85	2.15	6	270	28.00
1.27	0.66	1.20	1.35	30	148	29.00
0.72	0.00	0.60	0.85	6	161	30.00
0.35	0.00	0.25	0.45	33	25	31.00
0.17	0.00	0.10	0.25	0	31	32.00
0.10	0.00	0.05	0.15	0	0	33.00
0.10	0.00	0.05	0.15	0	10	34.00
0.10	0.00	0.10	0.10	0	0	35.00
0.10	0.00	N/A	0.10	0	0	36.00
0.10	0.00	N/A	0.10	0	0	37.00
0.10	0.00	N/A	0.10	0	0	38.00

Figure 110- TAN: Options Chain on 9/6/2013

The bid-ask spread was \$3.50 – \$4.00. I leveraged the *Show or Fill Rule* to negotiate the cost to buy-to-close down to \$3.80 of which \$3.66 was intrinsic value (\$29.66 – \$26.00). This left \$0.14 of time value, the actual cost to close (plus small trading commissions) or about one half of 1% (\$0.14/\$26.00). This means that if we can generate significantly more than 0.54% with the cash freed up by closing our entire position (\$2600.00 x 5 =\$13,000.00), it makes sense to move forward with this exit strategy. With two weeks remaining until expiration, this goal should be easily achievable.

The Ellman Calculator

That said, let's use the "Unwind Now" tab of the Elite version of the Ellman Calculator to calculate our results prior to generating our second income stream:

Entering the stats (Figure 111)

1) ENTER THE ORIGINAL TRADE INFORMATION BELOW			
Stock name >>	TAN		
Stock symbol >>	TAN		
Date of transaction >>	08/19/13	Today's date >>	09/06/13
Stock purchase price >>	$ 25.83		
Option STRIKE price >>	$ 26.00		
Option sale price/share >>	$ 0.90		
2) ENTER TODAY'S INFORMATION			
Current stock price >>	$ 29.66		
Current option price/share >>	$ 3.80		
3) PRESS THE PRINTER ICON OR CLICK ON THE "FILE" MENU, SELECT "PRINT" AND CLICK "OK"			

Figure 111- Ellman Calculator- Unwind Now Tab

Calculation results (Figure 112)

Once the information is entered into the blue cells, the white cells on the right side of the spreadsheet automatically become populated:

RETURN IF I UNWIND THE POSITION TODAY				
Cost of shares				$ 2,583.00
Option premium received				$ 90.00
Option close-out				
Cost to buy back the option				$ 380.00
Premium received on sale				$ 90.00
Gain (loss) on close-out				$ (290.00)
Stock close-out				
Proceeds from sale of stock				$ 2,966.00
Cost of shares				$ 2,583.00
Gain (loss) on close-out				$ 383.00
Net Gain (Loss) to UNWIND				$ 93.00
NET RETURN ON POSITION				
Net gain (loss) to unwind position today		$ 93.00	=	3.60%
Net cash to open position		$ 2,583.00		
Number of days position was open				19
Annualized return				70.00%

Figure 112- Calculations if Position is Closed Mid-Contract

We see that we have generated a 19-day return of 3.60% which annualizes to 70%. Next we take the approximately $13,000.00 cash from the sale of TAN and use it in a new covered call position to generate a second income stream. In stage two of this exit strategy, our goal (in this case) is to glean a significantly higher return than .54%. All this is thought out in advance of closing the position. If for any reason, we couldn't generate a return that meets our goal for this second position, using this exit strategy would not make sense. In that unlikely event, we would leave the original position as is and re-evaluate as contract expiration approaches.

Summary

The use of the mid-contract unwind exit strategy is most appropriate in the first half of the options contract when the time value of the premium approaches zero and the ability to generate a second income stream greater than the cost to close the first one is apparent. Using the "unwind now" tab of the Elite version of the Ellman Calculator will make the process much easier.

Closing our Entire Covered Call Position when Share Price Rises: The Mid-Contract Unwind Exit Strategy: Example 2

Exit strategies or position management is one of the three major skills we must master to become elite covered call writers. The other two are stock (or ETF) and option selection. In my books and DVDs I mostly focus on scenarios that can result in losses and how to mitigate those losses or turn them into gains. However, there are times we need to take action when the trade turns out to be much better than we anticipated…a short-term acceleration in price. I refer to this strategy as the *mid-contract unwind exit strategy*. With the market rebounding significantly recently, opportunities have been created. Several of our members (we have a very smart group I'm proud to say) have recognized these favorable circumstances and inquired as to the best time to close a position when share price rises substantially in a short time frame. These inquiries motivated this article.

If we purchased a stock at $48.00 and sold the $50.00 call for $1.50, we generated a 3.1% initial option return. If share price moves up to $60.00 in the first half of the contract, we have another $2.00 in share profit ($48.00 to the $50.00 strike price). That is a 7.3%, one-month return which appears to be maxed out because there is no benefit to us if share price rises higher due to our option obligation to sell at $50.00. The only way we would not achieve maximum return on this trade is if share price drops more than $10.00 to under $50.00. The BCI guideline as it relates to the mid-contract unwind exit strategy is to **always close the entire covered call position (short option and long stock) when the time value component of the option premium approaches zero in the first half of a contract**. When an option is trading at intrinsic value only it is said to be trading at *parity*.

Let's look at a real-life example taken from the Premium Watch List dated 10/24/2014. The stock is JAZZ Pharmaceuticals (JAZZ). Here's the trade:

- 10/20/2014: Buy JAZZ at $152.26
- 10/20/2014: Sell $155.00 out-of-the-money call at $3.35 for a 2.2%, initial one-month return (maximum share profit = $2.74 per share or an additional 1.8%)
- 10/20/2014: Max profit possible = 4% (option profit + share appreciation)
- 10/30/2014: JAZZ is trading at $168.36
- 10/30/2014: $155.00 call's last trade was $13.35 with intrinsic value of $13.43

Figure 113 depicts a linear price chart of the $155.00 call option showing initial and subsequent values:

Figure 113- JAZZ: $155 Call Option Price Chart

Next, we will review the options chain for JAZZ on 10/30/2014 (Figure 114):

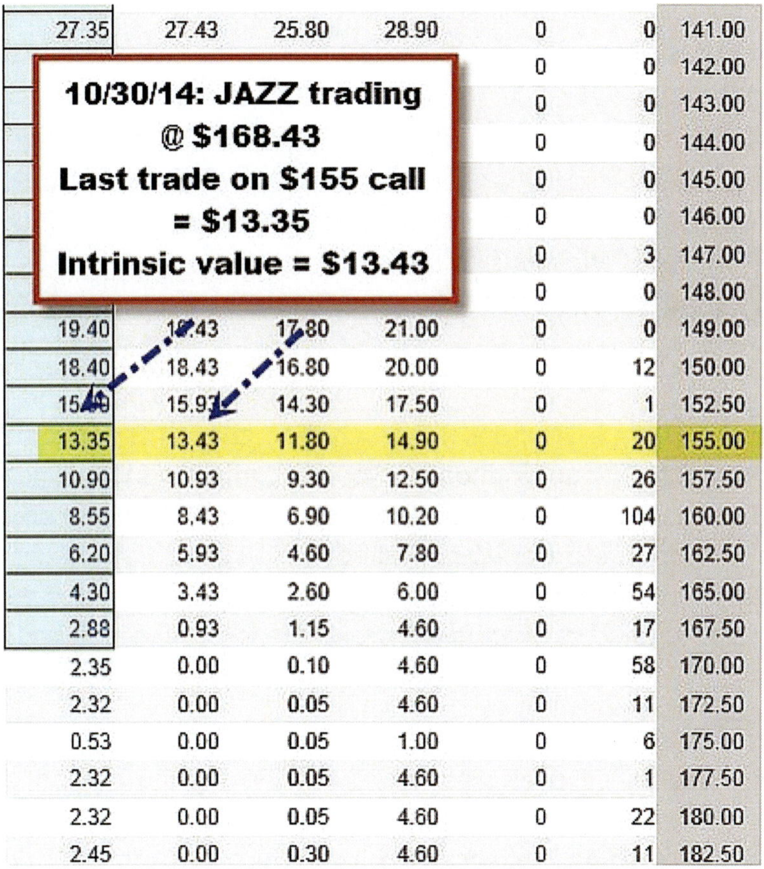

27.35	27.43	25.80	28.90	0	0	141.00
				0	0	142.00
				0	0	143.00
				0	0	144.00
				0	0	145.00
				0	0	146.00
				0	3	147.00
				0	0	148.00
19.40	[illegible]	17.80	21.00	0	0	149.00
18.40	18.43	16.80	20.00	0	12	150.00
[illegible]	[illegible]	14.30	17.50	0	1	152.50
13.35	13.43	11.80	14.90	0	20	155.00
10.90	10.93	9.30	12.50	0	26	157.50
8.55	8.43	6.90	10.20	0	104	160.00
6.20	5.93	4.60	7.80	0	27	162.50
4.30	3.43	2.60	6.00	0	54	165.00
2.88	0.93	1.15	4.60	0	17	167.50
2.35	0.00	0.10	4.60	0	58	170.00
2.32	0.00	0.05	4.60	0	11	172.50
0.53	0.00	0.05	1.00	0	6	175.00
2.32	0.00	0.05	4.60	0	1	177.50
2.32	0.00	0.05	4.60	0	22	180.00
2.45	0.00	0.30	4.60	0	11	182.50

Figure 114- JAZZ Options Chain on 10/30/2014

If we can execute the trade to close our short position at or near a cost of $13.43, it will meet our requirement to close when time value approaches zero. Let's assume we can close for $13.50, an amount above the last trade. Of that $13.50, $13.43 is intrinsic value, the amount the $155.00 strike is in-the-money. In this case we have an option debit of $13.50 to close the short call but a stock price credit of $13.43 because we are no longer obligated to sell at $155.00. Our net cost to close (excluding commissions) is $0.07 or $7.00 per contract. When the shares are sold, we have maxed our initial trade in the month (November contract in this case), less $7.00, and have now freed up all the cash from the stock sale to initiate another covered call trade in the same month with the same cash. We have created two incomes streams from this same cash amount. To make this a successful exit strategy, all we need to do is generate an amount greater than $7.00 per contract.

Good lesson for option liquidity

We made the assumption that we could negotiate a buy-to-close at $13.50, above the mid-point of this extremely wide spread. Low option liquidity will result in wider bid-ask spreads and make favorable trade executions more challenging. This demonstrates why we prefer to use options with open interest of one hundred contracts or more and/or bid-ask spreads of $0.30 or less. Of course, when the trade was initiated the $155.00 strike did meet our system criteria.

Summary

When share value rises significantly in the first half of an option contract after entering a covered call trade, buy back the option when its time value component approaches zero and the amount that can be generated in a subsequent trade in the same contract month exceeds the debit incurred in closing the initial position.

Emergency Management Report: Dealing with Volatile and Bearish Markets

With the stock market declining over 5% in the past month as a result of geo-political and global economic concerns exacerbated by the fears of an Ebola epidemic we find ourselves in a position that may lead to "panic" in our investment decisions. The stock market seemed to stabilize a bit on Friday but we are not out of the woods yet based on just that one day. Whether you are an experienced investor who has "been there, done that" or a newbie who is experiencing this discomfort for the first time, patience and non-emotional responses are the most prudent. In this article I will highlight strategies to manage existing positions in these extreme circumstances and strategies to initiate new positions for those who want to "stay in the game". Much of the information has been taken from my books and DVD Programs as well as articles I have published in the past.

Managing existing positions

1. We always buy back the option when it approaches our *20%/10% guidelines* (declines in value to or below 20% or 10% of initial sale value depending on when in the contract cycle that decline takes place). This eliminates our option obligation and allows us to sell another option or to close our long stock position. Limit orders can be set up to close our short option positions to make this automatic.

2. When market tone is negative (which it currently is) and equity technicals are also negative, we *sell the stock*. Many investors will also use a percentage price decline to dictate when to sell a stock. This percentage will usually range from between 8% to 10% of the initial stock purchase price or a percentage from its highest subsequent price. Once sold, a personal decision needs to be made as to whether you want to "stay in the game" and enter a new position. See below for some strategies to consider. Many investors are more comfortable staying in cash until a firm bottom is identified.

3. *Rolling Down*:

   Rolling down occurs when we buy back a previously sold option (buy-to-close our short position) and simultaneously sell another option at a lower strike price in the same contract month (open a new short position).

We lean towards implementing a rolling down strategy when the market tone and technicals are mixed to negative. I would also be more inclined to use this strategy later, rather than earlier, in the contract period (late in week two and week three, rather than in week one of a one-month contract).

Entering new positions- staying in the game

For those who have a higher risk tolerance and want to remain in the market, it is prudent to implement strategies that are appropriate for bearish or volatile market conditions, especially extreme ones like we are experiencing now. Selling out-of-the-money strikes may work out but it makes little sense to take an aggressive stance until the market tone improves and stabilizes. Here are a few strategies that will allow us to generate an initial profit and provide us with some protection of that profit:

1. *Sell only in-the-money strikes*:

   If we buy 100 shares of XYZ for $32.00 and sell a $30.00 call for $3.50, we have sold an in-the-money call option because the strike price of the call option ($30.00) is lower than current price of XYZ ($32.00). The sale of this call option obligates us to sell 100 shares of XYZ for $30.00 per share (or $3,000.00 per contract) if the option is exercised. Should XYZ increase in price from $32 to $40, we make no additional income due to our obligation to sell our shares at $30.00. The option premium we receive from the sale of this option has $2.00 of intrinsic value ($32.00 – $30.00). The remainder of the option premium is solely time value, which represents our true initial profit (ROO). Thus, if we received $3.50 in *total* option premium from the sale of the $30.00 call option, the $3.50 premium we receive consists of $2.00 of intrinsic value and $1.50 ($3.50-$2.00) of time value. Because our true profit is represented by time value only, in this example we generated an option profit of $1.50 per share or $150.00 per contract, which represents a

5% ROO (the $2.00 intrinsic value "buys down" our cost basis to $30.00 per share). The protection of that 5% initial profit is the intrinsic value divided by the current market value of the stock or $2.00/$32.00 = 6.25%

2. *Buy protective puts- the collar strategy:*

   As safe a strategy as covered call writing is there is some risk; the risk is in purchasing the stock, not in selling the option. For this reason, some investors who sell covered calls also buy *protective puts* to alleviate some of the risk. A protective put is a put option that is purchased for an underlying stock that is already owned by the put buyer. It defends against a catastrophic decrease in the share price of the underlying security. When a protective put is used in conjunction with covered call writing, the strategy is referred to as a *collar strategy*. A *collar* is the simultaneous purchase of a protective put option and the sale of a covered call option. In a true collar strategy, the puts and calls are both out-of-the-money and have the same expiration dates and an equal number of contracts. Thus, we sell an out-of-the-money call and add additional downside protection for the underlying equity by purchasing a protective put option. This strategy protects against disastrous share devaluation but also decreases our initial option profits.

3. *Sell out-of-the money cash-secured puts*:

   With this strategy we are selling the right, but not the obligation, for the buyer of the put to sell a stock to us at a specified price, by a specified date. In return for undertaking this obligation, we also receive a premium. For example, a stock is trading at $32.00 per share and we sell a $30.00 out-of-the-money put for $1.50, receiving a return of $150.00 per contract. The returns in these scenarios are generally similar to the returns generated from selling covered calls, and if the put is exercised, we are required to buy the stock for $30.00 per share, meaning we purchase the shares at a cost basis of $28.50 ($30.00 less the $1.50 premium). Some investors consider this "buying at a discount" from the original $32.00 share price. We can then write a covered call on the newly-acquired shares. For most brokerages, we will need a higher level of trading approval for selling cash-secured puts even though the risk-reward profiles for both strategies are the same.

4. *Use inverse ETFs:*

   Inverse ETFs use derivatives to bet against the direction of financial markets. These are known as *short* or *bear ETFs* and will make money if markets decline in value. **They will lose money, however, if markets move against the bet**. Covered call writers who have a bearish market outlook may find these funds useful.

   Many sophisticated covered call writers can benefit from the use of inverse ETFs *in the short run when the market is bearish*.

   Inverse ETFs with options to consider:

   - PSQ: short QQQ
   - DOG: short Dow 30
   - SH: short S&P 500
   - RWM: short Russell 2000

Summary:

What is transpiring now is an aberration. Market forces are being torn between both positive local economic news and negative geo-political and global economic influences. This will pass because it always does. The greatest error we can make is to act emotionally without employing the critical investment parameters that will make us all succeed in the long run...fundamental, technical and common sense principles. In challenging times there may not be great choices to make but there will ALWAYS be the best choices to make under the circumstances. Finding these and implementing the most sensible strategies are some of the prime mission statements of Blue Collar Investors all over the world. The purpose of this article was to summarize and highlight these doctrines.

Evaluating Returns when Rolling Out and Up

Covered call writing and put-selling calculations must be accurate and preferably understood by option-sellers. I created the Ellman Calculators to facilitate the practical computations we depend on. In this article, I will review a successful trade executed by one of our members, David L, who used United Therapeutics Corp. (UTHR) from our Premium Watch List as the underlying security.

Initial trade for the March contract

- Buy UTHR at $155.90
- Sell March $150.00 in-the-money call for $9.25
- Intrinsic value = $5.90 (amount the strike price is in-the-money)
- Time value (Dave's initial profit) = $3.35 per share
- ROO = $3.35/$150.00 = 2.2%
- Downside protection (different from breakeven) of ROO = 3.8%

Figure 115 shows these calculations from the multiple tab of the Ellman Calculator:

RETURN ON OPTION (ROO) CALCULATOR - MULTIPLE STOCKS										
Stock Name or Symbol	Stock $/sh	Option $/sh	Strike $	Expires	Intrisic	Upside	Breakeven	ROO	Up Potential	Down Protect
UTHR	$155.90	$9.25	$ 150.00	03/20/15	$ 5.90	$ -	$ 146.65	2.2%	0.0%	3.8%

Figure 115- Initial Returns for UTHR

This represented an excellent conservative position to take on one of our outstanding performers.

Trade status one week prior to expiration

- Share price = $163.22
- Cost to close = $15.50
- Considering rolling out and up
- April $160.00 call generates $9.50

Rolling Out and Up

Using the "What Now" tab of the Ellman Calculator to calculate rolling out and up one week prior to expiration (Figure 116):

WHAT IF I ROLL OUT AND UP?	w/upside pot.	w/o upside pot.
The proceeds for 1 UTHR APR 160.00 is:	$ 950.00	$ 950.00
The cost to buy back 1 UTHR MAR 150.00 is:	$ (1,550.00)	$ (1,550.00)
Your net loss on this option position is:	$ (600.00)	$ (600.00)
The "bought up" value in the closing option is:	$ 1,000.00	$ 1,000.00
Your upside potential return is:	$ -	
Your net return will be:	$ 400.00	$ 400.00
Your comparative basis in the stock is:	$ 15,000.00	$ 15,000.00
Your comparative returns are:	2.67%	2.67%
You downside protection is:	2.00%	$322.00

Figure 116- Rolling Out and Up with UTHR

The computations show a five-week return of 2.67% with 2% downside protection of that profit (not breakeven).

Return if we opened the position today for the April contract

David astutely pointed out that if the position were entered one-week prior to expiration that the initial return would be 3.9% with 2.0% downside protection of that initial profit as shown in the screenshot in Figure 117:

RETURN ON OPTION (ROO) CALCULATOR - MULTIPLE STOCKS

Stock Name or Symbol	Stock $/sh	Option $/sh	Strike $	Expires	Intrisic	Upside	Breakeven	ROO	Up Potential	Down Protect
UTHR	$155.90	$9.25	$ 150.00	03/20/15	$ 5.90	$ -	$ 146.65	2.2%	0.0%	3.8%
UTHR	$163.22	$ 9.50	$160.00	04/17/15	$ 3.22	$ -	$ 153.72	3.9%	0.0%	2.0%

Figure 117- UTHR Calculations One-Week Prior to Expiration

What is our real return, 2.67% or 3.9%?

It's 2.67%. To own the shares at $163.22 (current market value) we would have to buy back the option at $15.50. That would raise the real-life value of the shares from $150.00 (the option obligation) to $163.22 or + $13.22, leaving a net debit of $2.28 or 1.5%. This must be factored into our real-life returns. Rolling the option will also result in one less trading commission than closing the entire original position and re-opening at $163.22.

When should the option be rolled?

Next week. Dave had huge downside protection of his initial option profit and was fairly safe to max the returns from his original trade. Time value erosion of the option premium is logarithmic in nature, not linear, so the near term option time value will deteriorate faster than the next month option. It will be advantageous to us to wait closer to expiration to begin the rolling process.

Congratulations to David on an outstanding trade.

How to Avoid Early Exercise when Dividends are about to be Distributed

Covered call writing is a low-risk strategy that allows us to generate monthly cash flow by selling stock options. Since we are obligated to sell our shares to the option buyer (holder), one of the understood possibilities is that we will "lose" our shares, at the *strike price* or the price we have agreed to sell our shares for, mid-contract. For most of us, this is not a disadvantage but rather a positive because, if it occurs, we will have maxed our initial trade results and now have the cash from the sale of the stock to re-invest mid-contract.

The chance of *"early assignment"* (option exercised and shares sold prior to expiration Friday) is extremely rare. When it does occur it is usually related to a dividend distribution. The general rule is that *if the ex-dividend date (date we must own the shares to be eligible to earn the dividend) is prior to the expiration date of the option and the time value of the premium is less than the dividend about to be distributed, the chance of early exercise is much greater but not guaranteed.*

This article is geared to members of our BCI family who use covered call writing in their *buy and hold portfolios* to generate higher annualized returns but do not want their shares sold. Usually, these portfolios are held in non-sheltered accounts with securities that have a low cost basis and there may be tax issue concerns if shares are sold. For some of our members, these shares have been generating monthly dividends that they would like to continue.

Let me premise my remarks by saying that we can never guarantee that our shares will not be sold early because retail investors make mistakes. So even if early exercise makes no financial sense, some may opt to exercise anyway, and those exercise notices may randomly end up in our accounts. Likely? No. Possible? Yes.

Assumptions

- Ex-dividend date is prior to expiration Friday
- Time value component of the option premium is less than the dividend about to be distributed
- We don't want our shares sold

Method to dramatically reduce the likelihood of early exercise

The first step is to locate ex-dividend date data for the security as shown in Figure 118 for *American Express*:

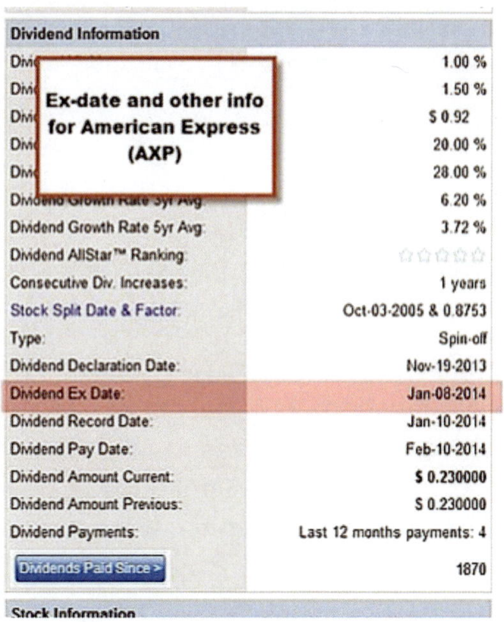

Figure 118- Ex-Dividend Date Stats for American Express

The site I used to access this information:

www.dividendinvestor.com

How to benefit from this information

1- If the ex-date is in the first week of a contract, sell the option the day after the ex-date (and still capture 3 weeks of time value).

2- If the ex-date is later in the contract, sell a two-month option after expiration of the previous contract. *When the ex-date is not close to the expiration of the contract, an option holder will rarely exercise early*.

Conclusion

There are methods we can employ to dramatically decrease any chance of early exercise due to dividend distribution but we can never be one hundred percent certain of avoiding such events because of potential errors made by retail investors (may "spend a dollar to make fifty cents").

Rolling Out and Up to Capture Share Appreciation: A Good Idea?

Covered call writing has some drawbacks as do all investment strategies. Profit limitation by the strike price is one such disadvantage. How do we manage a situation where the price of the stock moves well above the strike sold? Some covered call writers will roll out and up (to a higher strike price at a later date) in an effort to *capture the share appreciation previously limited by the original option sold*. This is very different from rolling out and up to continue to capture option profit perhaps in addition to some share appreciation. In this article, I will use Facebook (FB), a stock recently on our Premium Watch List to evaluate if this is a good idea. *Keep in mind that I am alluding to a strategy where the goal is to capture share appreciation when a stock price moves well above the original strike sold, not option profit*. This can be appropriately named "sellers remorse".

In early December, 2013, FB moved above its 20-day exponential moving average (red arrow in Figure 119) and seemed like a great candidate for covered call writing. Let's look at Figure 119, a chart depicting when this bullish event took place:

Figure 119- Facebook Price Moves Above the Short-Term Moving Average

At the time, a near-the-money strike (December contract) could have been sold for a 4%, one-month return. The price of the stock continued to increase and near expiration FB was trading at $54.69, leaving the $50.00 call $4.69 in-the-money. In an effort to capture the $4.69, some investors looked to roll out and up to a strike above $54.69. Let's have a look at an options chain (Figure 120) showing the cost to close our short $50.00 strike position:

11.12	11.20	10.95	11.30	0	0	43.50
10.73	10.70	10.65	10.80	8	10,370	44.00
10.12	10.20	9.95	10.30	0	10	44.50
			9.80	71	12,074	45.00
			9.30	0	437	45.50
			8.80	35	15,269	46.00
			8.30	0	483	46.50
			7.80	166	9,160	47.00
7.20	7.20	7.10	7.30	35	123	47.50
6.67	6.70	6.60	6.75	343	11,616	48.00
6.20	6.20	6.10	6.30	0	374	48.50
5.72	5.70	5.65	5.80	156	12,080	49.00
5.20	5.20	5.10	5.30	0	644	49.50
4.75	4.70	4.70	4.80	816	28,203	50.00
4.28	4.20	4.25	4.30	17	870	50.50
3.77	3.70	3.75	3.80	162	3,744	51.00
3.30	3.20	3.25	3.35	86	3,348	51.50
2.85	2.70	2.84	2.87	719	13,225	52.00
			2.42	1,061	22,363	52.50
			2.03	3,540	6,653	53.00
			1.64	2,771	3,737	53.50
			1.31	3,941	9,947	54.00
			1.02	4,587	6,471	54.50
0.77	0.00	0.76	0.77	9,251	46,653	55.00
0.58	0.00	0.58	0.59	3,135	5,078	55.50
0.44	0.00	0.43	0.45	5,912	10,378	56.00
0.33	0.00	0.32	0.33	1,276	3,280	56.50
0.24	0.00	0.24	0.25	2,431	10,859	57.00

FB Trading @ $54.69 near expiration

Cost to close short options position is $4.80

Figure 120- Facebook Options Chain near Expiration

The cost to close is $4.80 and that will allow our shares to now be worth current market value since there is no longer an options obligation. Next, as the proposed strategy goes, we must sell another option to negate the $4.80 cost-to-close. Let's check the January options chain for the $55.00 call for FB (Figure 121):

Rolling out and up to the January $55 generates $2.41

15.65	15.69	15.50	15.80	0	5,361	39.00
14.62	14.69	14.45	14.80	109	29,667	40.00
13.68	13.69	13.50	13.85	20	10,684	41.00
12.70	[illegible]	[illegible]	[illegible]	64	26,598	42.00
11.70	[illegible]	[illegible]	[illegible]	16	6,367	43.00
10.78	[illegible]	[illegible]	[illegible]	0	13,483	44.00
9.85	[illegible]	[illegible]	[illegible]	819	38,381	45.00
8.95	[illegible]	[illegible]	[illegible]	166	18,086	46.00
8.05	[illegible]	[illegible]	[illegible]	020	23,889	47.00
7.18	6.69	7.15	7.20	1,268	12,787	48.00
6.32	5.69	6.30	6.35	230	10,186	49.00
5.53	4.69	5.50	5.55	2,370	87,574	50.00
3.77	2.19	3.75	3.80	4,349	34,548	52.50
2.42	0.00	2.41	2.43	6,929	53,132	55.00
1.46	0.00	1.46	1.47	6,072	26,124	57.50
0.87	0.00	0.86	0.88	4,846	86,877	60.00
0.49	0.00	0.49	0.50	263	5,411	62.50
0.29	0.00	0.28	0.30	4,039	56,736	65.00
0.11	0.00	0.11	0.12	325	46,677	70.00
0.07	0.00	0.06	0.07	108	10,760	75.00
0.04	0.00	0.04	0.05	85	12,292	80.00
0.03	0.00	0.02	0.04	25	3,785	85.00

Figure 121- Facebook: January Options Chain

Rolling out and up to the January $55.00 call will result in an options debit of $2.39 ($4.80 – $2.41). Investors may then attempt to roll further out so that the time value will compensate them for the cost to close the original option. Here are the stats for other later date expiration $55.00 calls:

- February: $4.40
- March: $5.00
- June: $6.90

To get fully compensated for the cost to close we would have to roll out and up to the March $55.00 call and there the option credit would be minimal, almost a wash. It will also limit our upside over the next three months to $0.31 ($54.69 to $55.00).

If we rolled out and up to the $60 call to give additional opportunity for more share appreciation, here are the stats:

- January: $0.86
- February: $2.60
- March: $3.15
- June: $5.00

In this scenario, we would have to commit to June to make up for the cost-to-close and, like the March $55.00 call, it would almost be a wash.

Why this is not a good idea

I don't like this idea because we are changing our goals. Originally, we wanted to generate monthly cash flow by selling stock options. Our training has taught us that one of the risks with this strategy is profit limitation by the strike price. This is the obligation we undertook when we sold the option and the reason the option holder paid us all that cash. In this scenario, we were successful in maximizing our one-month option goal and we must accept (although we can still manage this position) the limitations of the strategy. By rolling out farther and farther from the current month we are obligated to hold the stock through earnings reports, a gigantic drawback. In addition, we are undertaking a longer-term obligation when we may not want to own the underlying security in the future.

What then can we do?

We are in the driver's seat, having maxed our one-month position:

1. Wait for expiration Friday to see if a rolling strategy makes sense from an option perspective. It could mean rolling out or

rolling out and up but not to capture share appreciation only. In this scenario, we are paying less time value to close our short position than had we closed it earlier in the contract.

2. If the strike is deep-in-the-money mid-contract, look to close the entire position if the time value approaches zero and use the cash from the stock sale to start a new covered call position with a different underlying security and a second income stream. This is the *mid-contract unwind exit strategy* detailed in my books and DVD Programs (see pages 264 – 271 of the original *Complete Encyclopedia for Covered Call Writing*).
3. Take no action and allow assignment where our shares are sold at the strike price. Perhaps the calculations from an options perspective do not meet our goals or maybe there is an earnings report due out the next month.
4. Set up two separate accounts. One for covered call writing and one for stock buying and selling only. This will allow us to make the best decisions for each strategy and not have different goals cloud our investment decisions.

Conclusion

Covered call writing is a strategy that generates monthly cash flow by selling stock options. The main drawback is that share appreciation is limited by the strike price. We cannot eliminate this disadvantage, just manage it. It is critical to avoid poor investment decisions by using one strategy with a defined goal and trying to also gain the benefit of another strategy with different goals. *Don't get greedy!*

When do we Sell our Covered Call Writing Stocks?

Covered call writers know how important exit strategies are to our ultimate success. Position management skills must be initiated when share price rises or falls dramatically, when dividends become an issue or when a strike is in-the-money as expiration of the contract nears. Using our 20%/10% guidelines assists us in defining when to close our short positions (options) as stock price falls but then what?

When our short options positions (called short because we sold the option without owning it first) are closed and we no longer have an option obligation, the next step is determined by factors detailed in my books and DVDs such as time to expiration, overall market assessment, chart technicals and personal risk tolerance. In this article we will focus in on a situation that challenges so many covered call writers: when do we sell our stock after closing the options positions due to a price decline? The task of making this decision is quite imposing for most retail investors for two reasons:

1. These stocks that have "let us down" were, in fact, great-performers recently. They're bound to recover…right? Absolutely, just like Bear Stearns, Enron, Tyco and WorldCom (he said sarcastically). Cynicism aside, it's understandable why so many of us hold out hope for such a security that has performed so well prior to the current contract month.

2. I respectfully submit that there is also a psychological component in play here as well. Nobody likes to take a loss and it's not a "realized" loss until we sell the shares. So we tell ourselves that price recovery is right around the corner (did I mention Bear Stearns…). We've all experienced these feelings, especially me (years ago). We must train ourselves to react in a non-emotional manner.

Stock price is declining and we close our short options position…now what?

We must check for news updates related to the company. A reliable FREE site for accessing stock news is:
www.finviz.com

If the news is egregious like corporate fraud or the loss of key contracts, we must close our long stock position and use the cash to enter a new covered call trade. Yes, realize the loss and move on.

Now for the key aspect of this article

When there is no news available to explain the decline, I compare the price action of the security in question to that of the S&P 500. If the stock is significantly under-performing the overall market, realize the loss and exit the trade. If not, rolling the option down or waiting to "hit a double" are two strategies still in play.

Real life examples

Four of the stocks on our Premium Watch List dated 12/19/2014 were:

- AMBA
- AVGO
- AMGN
- BIDU

All four experienced price declines during the January contracts and began dropping off our weekly 'running list" Figure 122 is a one-month price chart of these four securities and that of the S&P 500:

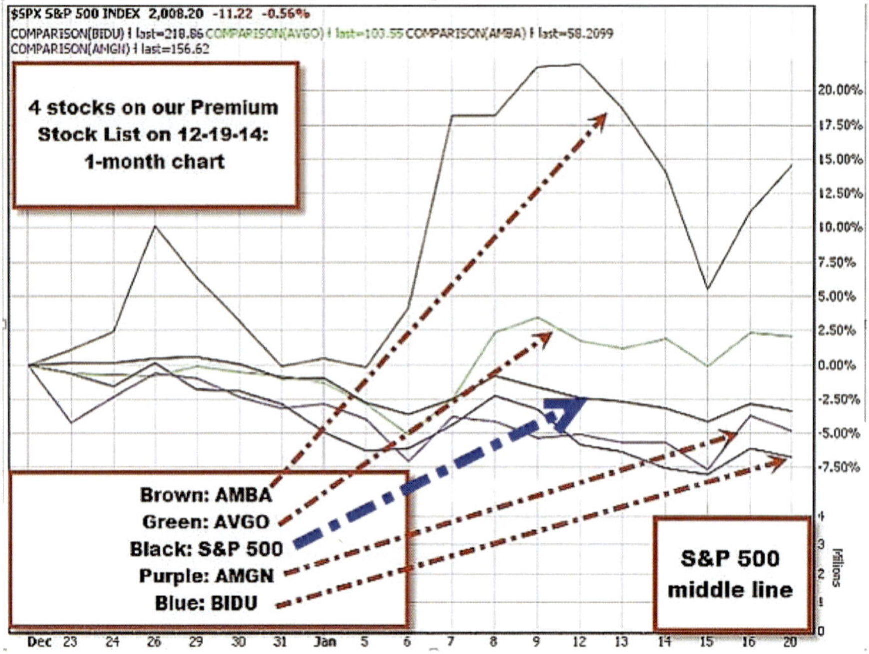

Figure 122- Comparing Declining Stocks to the S&P 500

Please note:

- The S&P 500 is the black line, third from bottom (blue arrow)
- AMBA: Brown line (top of chart) never broke below the S&P 500 so I'm more likely to stay with this stock
- AVGO: Green line mirrored the S&P 500 (very slight dips below) and then moved above it in early January. Here, I'm also more likely to keep this security
- AMGN and BIDU (purple and blue lines): Both securities under-performed the overall market for the entire contract month. If we reached the 20%/10% threshold, I am more likely to realize those losses (sell the shares) and use the cash generated from the sale of the stocks to move into new covered call trades.

Summary

We are most likely to close our long stock positions when the 20%/10% thresholds are approached and either there is negative news reported that makes this a dangerous position to stay in or the security is under-performing the overall market. No one approach will generate positive results one hundred percent of the time but we, as Blue Collar Investors, constantly strive to follow rules and guidelines that will dramatically throw the odds in our favor as we weed out the *Enrons* of the world.

Chapter 11

Dollar Cost Averaging and Exchange-Traded Funds

Chapter outline

1. Exchange-Traded Fund (ETF) Option Trading vs. Index Option Trading
2. Exchange-Traded Funds: Funding Option-Selling Portfolios with ETFs
3. Implied Volatility of ETFs and our Covered Call Writing and Put-Selling Decisions
4. Index Options and Exchange-Traded Funds Options: A Comparison
5. The Mechanics of Leveraged Exchange-Traded Funds: Appropriate for Covered Call Writers?
6. Why Covered Call ETFs Under-Perform
7. Writing Covered Calls on Broad Market Exchange-Traded Funds

Exchange-Traded Fund (ETF) Option Trading vs. Index Option Trading

Most options traders including covered call writers are familiar with exchange-traded funds (ETFs) and many trade options on these securities. Some have also heard of, but are not as familiar with, index options. The purpose of this article is to detail the differences between ETF option trading and index option trading.

Definitions

Exchange-traded fund (ETF):

This is a security that tracks an index, a commodity or a basket of assets but trades like a stock on an exchange. It can be bought and sold throughout the trading day and has price fluctuations as do individual stocks. One major advantage is that these securities provide diversification. Many ETFs have options associated with them and the BCI team provides a weekly ETF Report for our Premium Members showing twenty to twenty-five eligible ETFs for covered call writing or put-selling. Figure 123 represents one of the eight pages found in each report:

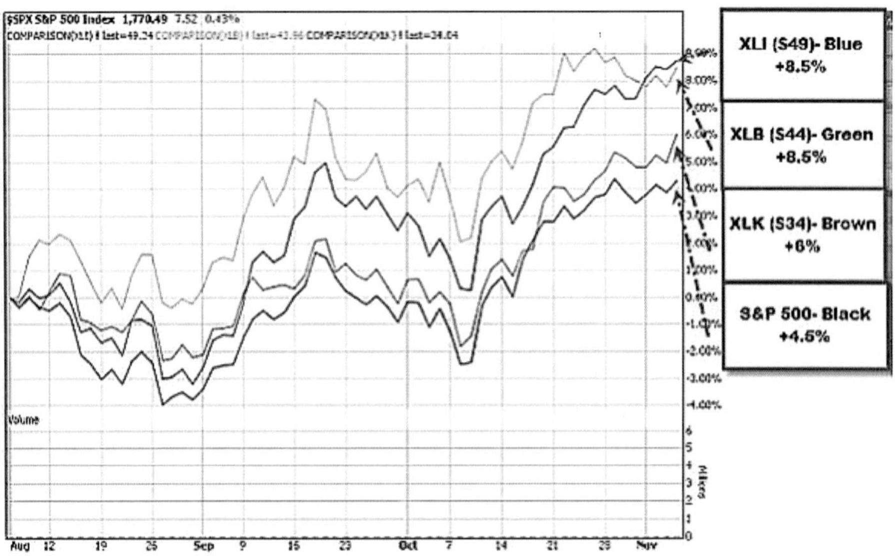

Figure 123- Blue Collar Investor ETF Report

Index:

This is an imaginary portfolio of securities representing a particular market or segment of a market. The S&P 500 is an example of a commonly used index. Another example is the Russell 2000 Index which tracks two thousand small-cap stocks. Here are a few such indexes that have actively traded options:

- DJX- Dow Jones Index Options
- NDX- Nasdaq 100 Index Options
- SPX- S&P 500 Index Options

Note that there is no trading taking place in the underlying index but rather has a calculated value that exists on paper only. Options allow the trader to speculate on price direction.

Mutual funds:

These are professionally managed, diversified portfolios that do not trade like stocks and do not have options associated with them. I include this in the definitions section so that there is clarity regarding the fact that ETFs and Indexes are very different from the much more well-known mutual funds.

Differences between ETF and Index Options

Rights conferred

The holder of an ETF call option (that we sold) has the right but not the obligation to purchase our ETF shares whereas the holder of an index option does not. Instead, the holder of an index option has the right to demand the equivalent cash value from the option seller (that's us) upon exercise of the option. *All index options are cash-settled*. Here is the formula:

Settlement amount = (Difference between index value and the strike price) x $100.00

Style of options traded

When we sell options on stocks or ETFs, we are selling *American Style* options. This means that they are settled in shares of the underlying security and can be exercised at any time up to expiration (usually 4 PM ET on the third Friday of the month). Early exercise of American Style options is rare but possible.

When options on indexes are sold, *European Style Options* are generally used (OEX- S&P 100 Index Options are an exception). These are cash-settled, can be bought and sold prior to expiration but can only be exercised on the expiration date. There are no concerns of early exercise with index options.

Settlement styles

ETF options are settled based on the closing price as of 4 PM ET on expiration Friday (or the Thursday before if Friday is an exchange-recognized holiday). Index options can have an *AM Settlement* (based on opening prices of the day of exercise) or *PM Settlement* (based on closing prices on the day of exercise). For European-style index option contracts, the last trading day will be the business day (generally a Thursday) preceding the day on which the exercise settlement value is calculated (generally the third Friday of the month unless that day is a holiday).

One more factor to consider

Trading volume can be light on many ETFs and therefore should be evaluated before entering a covered call position. The BCI guidelines are that we look for an *open interest of 100 contracts or more and/or a bid-ask spread of $0.30 or less*.

Conclusion

Most Blue Collar Investors trade American Style Options on stocks and ETFs. Understanding the difference between American and

European Style Options as well as between ETFs and Index Options will only make us better investors as we fulfill one of our mission statements...*Education is Power*.

(More on index options in an article later in this chapter).

Exchange-Traded Funds: Funding Option-Selling Portfolios with ETFs

For the strategies of covered call writing and selling cash-secured puts, we are selling the right, but not the obligation, to buy or sell one hundred shares of the underlying security. That security can be a stock or an exchange-traded fund (ETF). In this article, I will highlight ETFs and demonstrate a few approaches to funding our option-selling portfolios with these securities.

Pros and cons of ETFs

Pros

ETFs consist of a basket of stocks and, as a result, are instantly diversified to some extent. Therefore, to achieve appropriate portfolio diversification, we would require less cash to purchase the underlying securities. For individual stocks, the BCI guideline is that *no one stock or industry should represent more than 20% of our total portfolios*. Furthermore, ETFs require less management because we are not concerned about earnings reports, so we can actually stay with an ETF indefinitely if it remains a top-performer.

Cons

Since ETFs are baskets of stocks (in most cases), some are going up in value, some down, so as an aggregate the implied volatility (IV) of the security is lower than that of a typical stock. Lower implied volatility means lower option premiums so when using ETFs we should set lower goals for our initial returns. I use 2% – 4% per month in my portfolios with individual stocks and 1% – 2% in my mother's portfolio with ETFs. There are some ETFs with high implied volatility (IV) and that is why we provide IV stats in our premium member ETF Reports each week.

Considerations when selecting ETFs for option-selling

In the BCI methodology, we favor one-month options (some BCI members use Weeklys and others longer-term options but most use Monthlys as I do...all can work). Market segments fall in and out of favor with institutional investors so we want to utilize those currently in favor. As with stocks, we insist on minimum average trading volume of 250,000 shares per day and adequate open interest for the associated options. To assess if an ETF is currently in favor, we compare the three-month price performance of that security to that of the S&P 500 and require that the ETF is an out-performer with a relative price strength (RS) rating greater than 60. The chart below (Figure 124) is an example of ETF out-performers taken from our *Premium Member ETF Report* (produced weekly for our members):

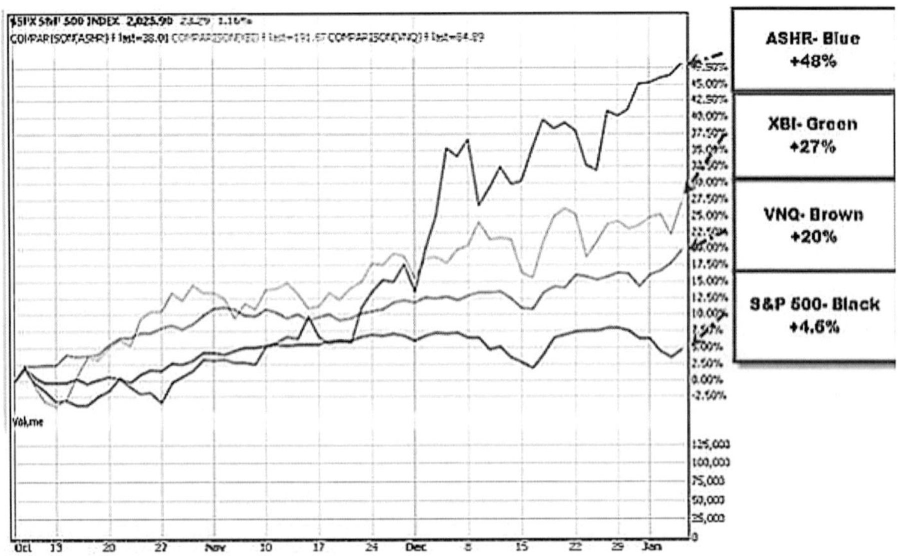

Figure 124- ETF Outperformers

The Select Sector SPDRs are unique ETFs that divide the S&P 500 into nine sector index funds. Many of our members use the current top three of these sectors to fund their option-selling portfolios as shown in the screenshot below in Figure 125 taken from a Premium ETF Report:

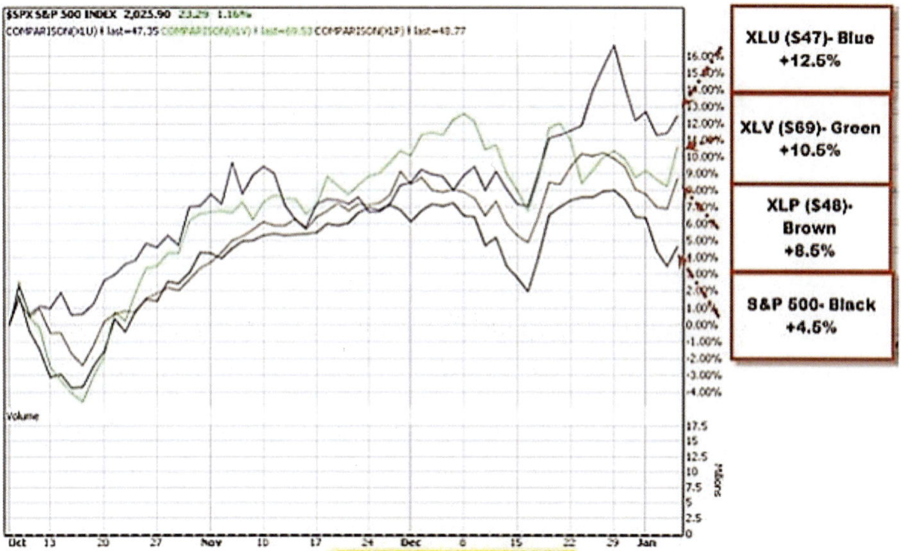

Top 3 Select Sector SPDRs

Figure 125

Extreme bear market considerations- Inverse ETFs

Although it is rare that we would resort to these securities (2008 was an exception), *Inverse ETFs* use derivatives to bet against the direction of the financial markets. These are also known as *bear or short ETFs*. Many have options associated with them as well as adequate open interest for the near-the-money option strikes. Since the market historically goes up in value in the long run, these securities historically go down in value but may have some value in unusual circumstances. Figure 126 is a screenshot taken from a *Premium ETF Report* showing the inverse ETFs under-performing the S&P 500:

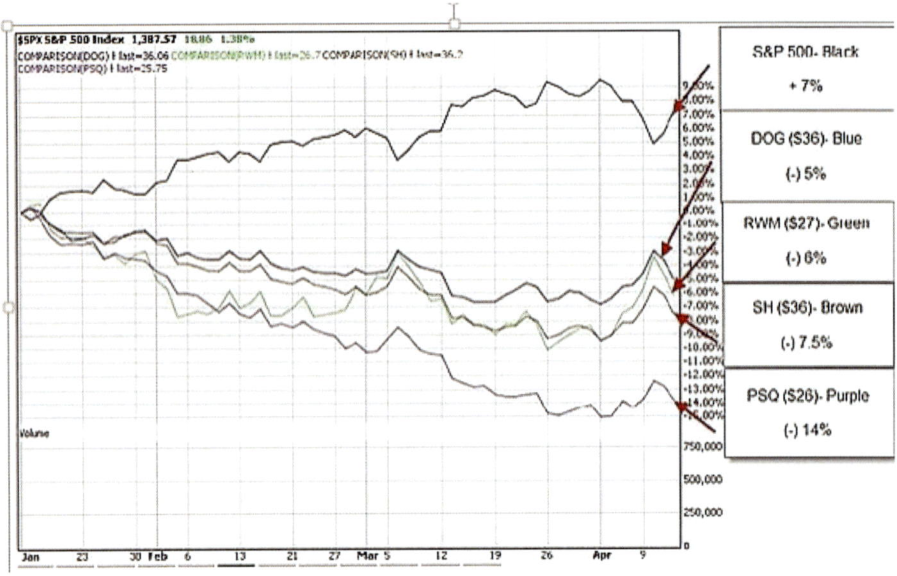

Figure 126- Inverse ETFs

Measuring ETF risk

Although most ETFs have less volatility than individual stocks as stated earlier in this article, there is still a significant range in implied volatility from one ETF to another. By looking at the implied volatility of an ETF and comparing it to the implied volatility of the overall market (S&P 500), we can make an informed decision as to the risk involved when using a specific security and whether it meets our personal initial goals and risk-tolerance profiles. Figure 127 shows a screenshot of part of the implied volatility section of our *Premium ETF Reports* (this information can be obtained for free at www.ivolatility.com):

Current IV of S&P 500 (SPX): 16.55

Implied volatility is a forecast of the underlying security's volatility as implied by the options price in the marketplace. It measures potential risk. Generally, the higher the IV, the greater the risk and the higher the premiums. We also show the current IV of the S&P 500 as a means of comparison.

We use a weighted average of implied volatility using put and call options. This ETF Report as well as our premium Stock Reports can be used for both covered call writing and selling cash-secured puts.

ASHR: 42.08

XBI: 37.78

VNQ: 13.89

XHB: 20.63

IYR: 12.92

ITB: 23.23

TUR: 25.19

Figure 127- Implied Volatility Stats Compared to the S&P 500

Summary

ETFs can represent valuable securities to incorporate into our covered call writing or put-selling portfolios. There are advantages and disadvantages as with every approach but the selection process is equally as important as when using individual stocks. Initial return goals, time for management and personal risk-tolerance play vital roles in deciding between stocks and ETFs.

Implied Volatility of ETFs and our Covered Call Writing and Put-Selling Decisions

Covered call writers and cash-secured put sellers who use ETFs (as opposed to individual stocks) tend to be novice option-sellers, more conservative investors, or have limited funds or time. If you fall into any of these categories, knowing your risk level is critical to your investment decisions and specifically, to which underlying securities you select. One way to evaluate this risk level is to view the current *implied volatility (IV)* of the associated options. IV is the forecast of the underlying security's volatility as implied by the option's price. The implied volatility is calculated by taking the market price of the option, entering it into an option-pricing model and back solving for the value of the volatility. The higher the implied volatility, the greater the option premium but also the more risk incurred regarding potential downward movement of share price. Figure 128 is an example of the implied volatility stats we provide to our members in our Premium ETF Reports (which can also be gleaned for free online as well at www.ivolatility.com) and their comparison to the overall market (S&P 500):

Current Implied Volatility (IV) of Eligible ETFs

Current IV of S&P 500 (SPX): 13.31

Implied volatility is a forecast of the underlying security's volatility as implied by the options price in the marketplace. It measures potential risk. Generally, the higher the IV, the greater the risk and the higher the premiums. We also show the current IV of the S&P 500 as a means of comparison.

We use a weighted average of implied volatility using only current call options:

JO: 54.90

UNG: 28.25

DBA: 17.10

XOP: 23.86

XLU: 14.29

CORN: 23.82

TUR: 29.43

OIL: 19.25

USO: 17.18

EPI: 33.11

EWA: 18.89

EWZ: 28.97

Figure 128- Implied Volatility Stats from a BCI Premium ETF Report

Another way to view implied volatility is as the anticipated market view of the percentage change in the price of the security on an annualized basis in either direction. In Figure 128, we see that EPI (highlighted in yellow) has an IV of 33.11 or about 33%. If the price of EPI was $21.00, then the market is anticipating a price range of $14.00 to $28.00 over the next one year ($7.00 in either direction or 33% of $21.00). The higher the IV, the more risk we are incurring for a potential price decline. As a comparison, at the top of the chart, we see the IV of the overall market (S&P 500) at the time was 13.31.

Summary

ETFs and stocks can be used as the underlying securities for covered call writers and cash-secured put sellers. The major drawback to selling options backed by ETFs is that the return or premium generated from the sale of ETF-backed options tend to be lower than the returns produced from the sale of stock-based call or put options (given that ETFs typically have lower implied volatility than individual stocks). In the context of writing options, ETFs tend to be more appropriate for the conservative investor, the investor with limited time or capital, or the novice investor. Personally, I prefer to write options that are associated with stock in my portfolio, however ETF-backed options are the preference when I invest for my mother's (more conservative) portfolio. It is up to you, the reader, to determine which is best for your portfolio based on finances and risk tolerance.

Index Options and Exchange-Traded Funds Options: A Comparison

Writers of covered calls and cash-secured puts use stocks or exchange-traded funds as the underlying securities. It is the price changes of these securities that give value to our option premiums. For example, we will buy back a call option when share price moves down causing the corresponding option to decline in value as well. We may also buy back an option when share price rises exponentially causing the strike sold to move deeper in-the-money and the time value component of that option now approaching zero. The relationship between share value and option premium is critical to our covered call writing and put-selling results. In this article, I will discuss another underlying security, the *stock index* and the options associated with them, *index options,* and I will compare them to options associated with similar exchange-traded funds or ETFs.

Definitions

Stock Index

A stock index is a statistic that reflects the composite value of a basket of stocks. Stocks listed within an index bear similar characteristics such as trading in the same stock exchange, belonging in the same industry or having comparable market capitalizations.

Exchange-Trade-Fund (ETF)

An ETF is an investment fund traded on stock exchanges, much like stocks. An ETF holds assets such as stocks, commodities, or bonds, and trades close to its net asset value (per-share dollar amount of the fund is calculated by dividing the total value of all the securities in its portfolio, less any liabilities, by the number of fund shares outstanding) over the course of the trading day. Most ETFs track an index, such as a stock index or bond index.

Charting SPY (ETF) and $SPX (Index Fund)

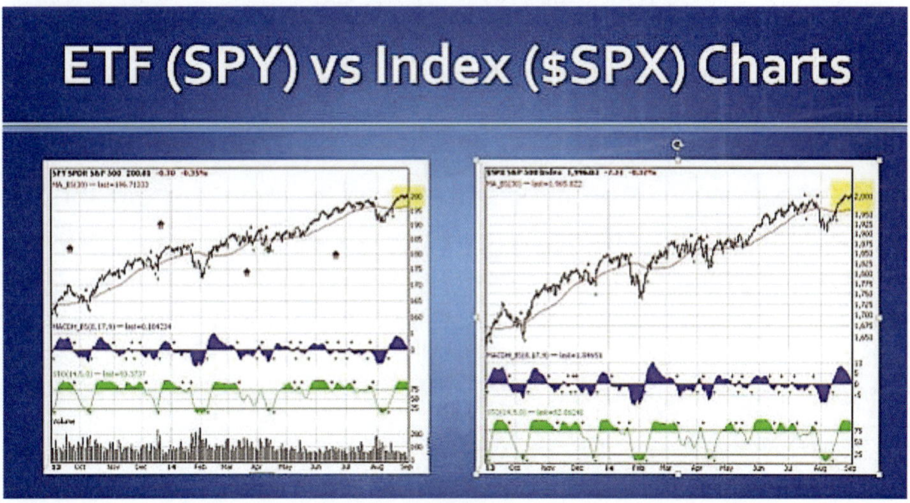

Figure 129- SPY and $SPX Charts of the S&P 500

The two charts look exactly the same with the ETF price trading at $200.00 and the Index fund price trading at $2000.00. To get a better understanding of the differences between an ETF option and an index option, I created this comparison chart in Figure 130:

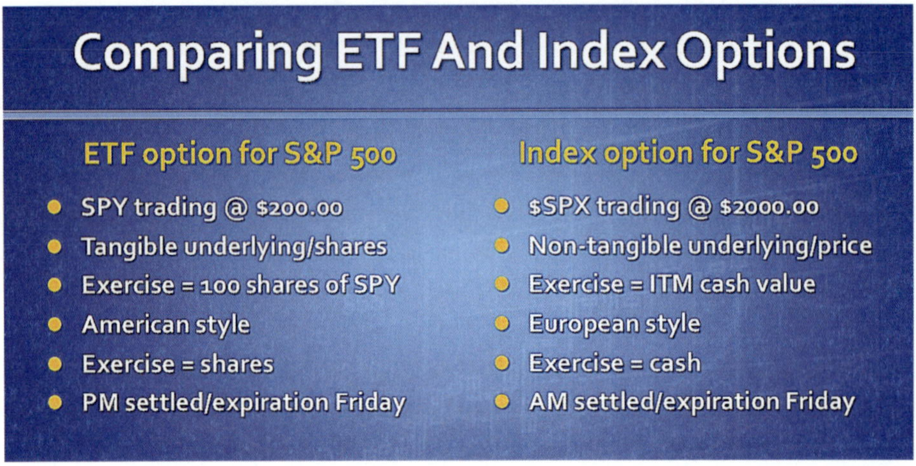

Figure 130- Comparing ETF and Index Options

Exercise of index options from the perspective of call option holders

If $SPX was priced at $2000.00 and the $2000.00 call was priced at $10.00, the breakeven would be $2010.00 and any price above $2010.00 would result in an account credit and any price below $2010.00 would cause an account debit. This is known as *cash-settlement*. The maximum loss is the amount paid for the call option. The maximum gain is theoretically unlimited. European style index options can only be exercised on the day of expiration while ETF American style options can be exercised at any time from the purchase or sale of the option through 4 PM ET on expiration Friday.

Summary

The main differences between equity (ETF) and index options occur primarily in the underlying instrument and the method of settlement. Many of our members have been using ETF options as a core income-generator in our covered call writing and put-selling portfolios. Index options can be used by buying and selling calls and puts depending on market outlook.

The Mechanics of Leveraged Exchange-Traded Funds: Appropriate for Covered Call Writers?

Our premium members receive a weekly report of exchange-traded funds (ETFs) appropriate for covered call writing and put-selling. These lists will never include a *leveraged ETF* because we feel that these securities are too risky and suitable only for sophisticated investors with high risk-tolerance. In this article, I will break down the mechanics of how leveraged ETFs work and demonstrate why they are not suitable for many retail investors. Only you can decide if they are appropriate for you.

Leveraged ETFs use a series of investment strategies such as *short-selling* (selling a security which has been borrowed from the broker), purchasing put options and using futures contracts to magnify the performance of the index that the ETF is tracking. They are constructed to return two times or three times that of the underlying index value. As an example, if an index is up 1% in a day, that leveraged ETF would be expected to rise by 2% or 3% that day. Many use the term *Ultra* in their names.

Daily re-balancing and long-term results

Fund managers are driven to trade derivative securities such that at the end of a trading day the fund meets its advertised performance. Because of this daily re-balancing of the funds, the long-term results may not be the same as its advertised objectives. As long as the index increases in value the stated leverage will be met or better. However, if the index drops in value, the leveraged ETF will be worse off than the expected value based on its stated objective. Let's set up an example to explain these concepts:

- Ultra BCI is a leveraged ETF with the objective of generating two times the returns of index XYZ
- Share value = $20.00
- Index value = $1000.00
- On day one the index rises 10% to $1100.00
- Ultra BCI rises 20% to $24.00
- On day two the index drops back to $1000.00, a decline of 9.09% ($100.00/$1100.00)
- Ultra BCI drops by 18.18% ($4.36) to $19.64
- While there was no change in the index after two days, there was a 1.8% decline in share value

QLD: A leveraged ETF looking to return 2x that of QQQ (Nasdaq 100)

To further demonstrate how the fund's leveraged objective does not usually hold true long-term, let's view a five-year comparison chart of QQQ (black line) versus its leveraged partner QLD (2x- blue line) in Figure 131:

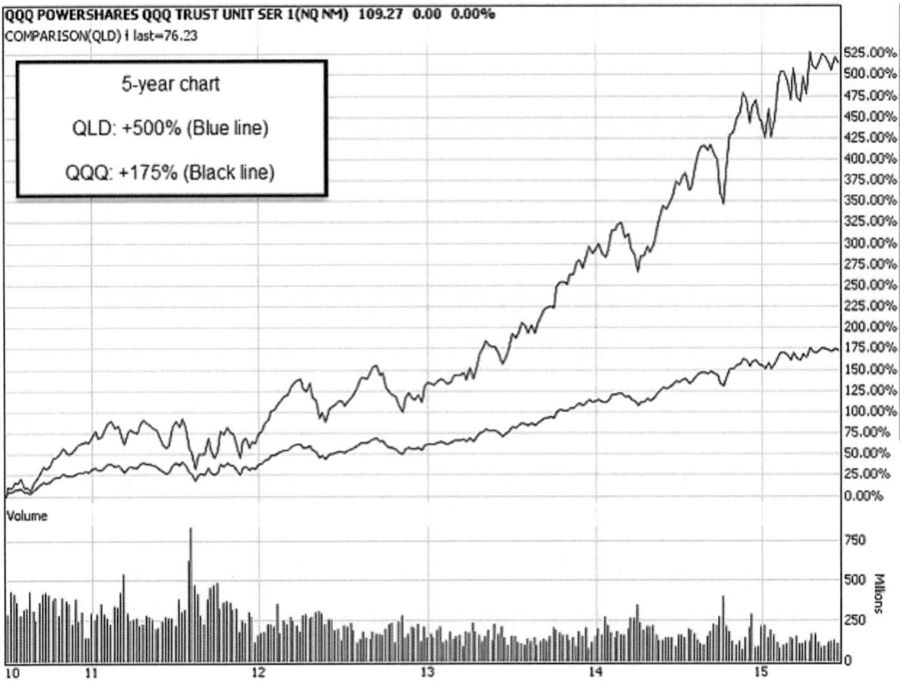

Figure 131- QLD vs. QQQ

Note how QLD performed much better than its stated two-to-one objective long-term as QQQ rose precipitously over the past five years (+500% compared to +175% for QQQ).

Tax implications

Because of the nature of the derivatives employed to reach the funds daily stated objectives, investors are subject to a complicated set of tax rules and therefore *leveraged funds are not as tax efficient as standard ETFs in non-sheltered accounts*.

Conclusion

Leveraged ETFs are not appropriate for most retail investors because of the risk and high volatility. It is particularly inappropriate (in the eyes of this investor) for conservative investors utilizing a conservative strategy like covered call writing. For sophisticated investors with high risk tolerance this may be a useful security to incorporate into their investment portfolios.

Why Covered Call ETFs Under-Perform

With the interest in covered call writing and selling cash-secured puts growing in popularity, we have witnessed the creation of new exchange-traded funds based on these strategies. **Over the last few years I have not been a proponent of these securities mainly because they under-perform the overall market and motivated retail investors can do so much better on their own.** In this article I will examine two of the newer covered call and put-selling ETFs, QYLD and HVPW. First, some explanations of the ETFs to be evaluated and the benchmarks we will use for comparison:

Benchmarks:

1. The CBOE S&P 500 BuyWrite Index (BXM^{SM})

   The CBOE S&P 500 BuyWrite Index (BXM) is a benchmark index designed to track the performance of a hypothetical buy-write strategy on the S&P 500 Index. The BXM is a passive total return index based on:

   - Buying an S&P 500 stock index portfolio, and
   - Writing (or selling) the near-term S&P 500 (SPX^{SM}) "covered" call options, generally on the third Friday of each month. The SPX calls written will have about one month remaining to expiration, with an exercise price just above the prevailing

index level (i.e., slightly out-of-the-money). The SPX call is held until expiration and cash settled, at which time a new one-month, slightly out-of-the-money call is written.

2. *S&P 500*

   An index of five hundred stocks chosen for market size, liquidity and industry grouping, among other factors. The S&P 500 is designed to be a leading indicator of U.S. equities and is meant to reflect the risk/return characteristics of the large cap universe. It is generally considered a reliable reflection of the overall stock market or its benchmark.

Option-selling ETFs

1- The Recon Capital NASDAQ 100 Covered Call ETF (QYLD)

QYLD is the only ETF that utilizes a buy-write strategy based on the NASDAQ 100. It seeks to provide investment results that will closely correspond, before fees and expenses, to the price and yield performance of the CBOE NASDAQ-100® BuyWrite Index (BXN). It is a passive total return index based on:

- Buying a NASDAQ-100 stock index portfolio, and
- Writing (or selling) the near-term NASDAQ-100 Index (NDX) "covered" call options, generally on the third Friday of each month. The NDX call written will have about one month remaining to expiration, with an exercise price just above the prevailing index level (i.e., slightly out-of-the-money). The NDX call is held until expiration and cash settled, at which time a new one-month, slightly out-of-the-money call is written.

2- ALPS U.S. Equity High Volatility Put Write Fund (HVPW)

HVPW is an income-generating fund that creates income by

selling two-month, 15% out-of-the-money puts (lower than current market value) on twenty diversified stocks with high implied volatility. The fund is fully collateralized by short-term 3-month T-bills.

Next let's set up a chart (Figure 132) showing the returns of the two benchmarks and the two ETFs over a six-month time frame in 2014:

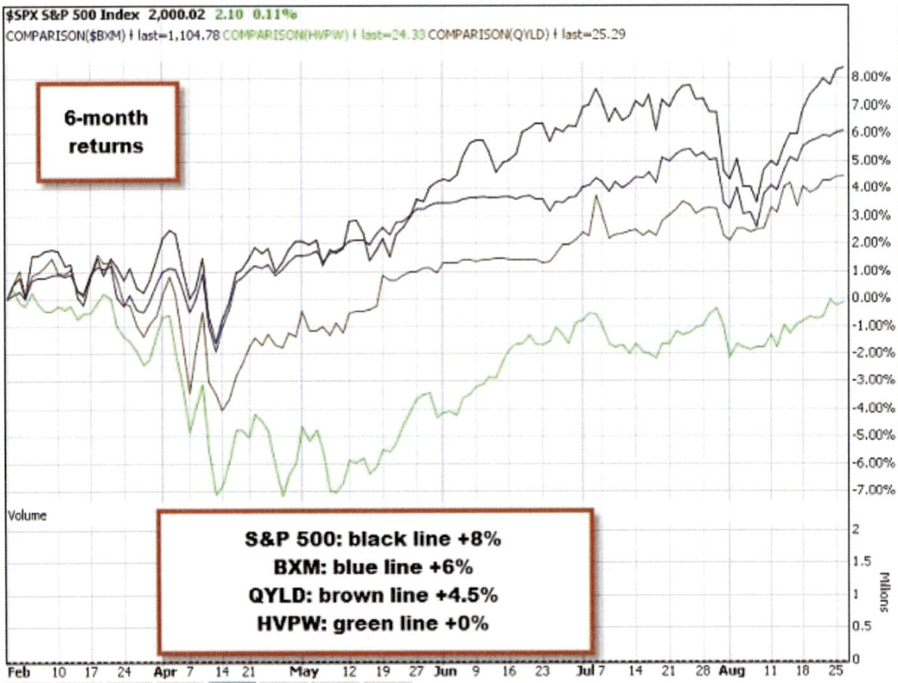

Figure 132- Covered Call Writing and Put-Selling ETFs vs Market Benchmarks

Why these ETFs underperform and retail investors can achieve higher returns

During this time frame, both ETFs under-performed both benchmarks significantly. Let's examine some of the reasons for these lower returns:

1- *Fees and expenses*

We would expect the costs required to participate in the ETFs to result in a return of least 1% lower than the benchmarks.

2- *Selection of the underlying securities*

In the case of QYLD, all 100 stocks from the Nasdaq 100 are included in the portfolio. If we were to develop our own portfolio, we could select only the best-performers from this group and the ones that generated the returns that met our goals rather than accepting all securities simply because they were members of this index. For HVPW, high-volatility stocks are stressed which may or may not be appropriate to maximize strategy results as an additional layer of risk is introduced.

3- *Only out-of-the-money strikes utilized*

Slightly out-of-the-money strikes are great because they allow us to generate two incomes streams in the same month with the same stock and cash: one from option profit and the other from share appreciation up to the out-of-the-money strike price. However, there are times when in-the-money call strikes are more appropriate or deeper out-of-the-money puts may be a better choice. I am referring to bear or volatile market conditions which may dictate a more conservative approach to covered call writing or put-selling to afford us more downside protection. Similarly, in a raging bull market, we may want to utilize deeper out-of-the-money call options or in-the-money put options to generate even higher returns. The main point here is that having more strategy flexibility will allow retail investors to generate much higher returns than a rigidly-structured ETF.

4- *No position management strategies*

Eliminating the use of exit strategy opportunities and position management techniques is a major flaw with these ETFs when comparing the strategies to how we, as retail investors, can manage them. We can take action to enhance profits to even higher levels when share price increases and also take action to mitigate losses when share price declines.

Summary

Covered call writing and put-selling ETFs allow us to participate in low-risk option strategies without having to take the time and effort to learn and manage the strategies ourselves. However, because of fees, expenses, lack of strategy flexibility and no position management components, the results will far under-perform both the market benchmarks and the even higher returns that can be achieved by elite covered call and put-writers.

Writing Covered Calls on Broad Market Exchange-Traded Funds

The initial main step for covered call writers is to select the best underlying security. This choice will vary from investor to investor based on goals and risk tolerance. Some of our members prefer exchange-traded funds (ETFs), a strategy I use in my mother's portfolio. ETFs offer the advantages of instant diversification, less volatility (in most cases) and less management time required. The main disadvantage is the lower returns generated by these securities because of the lower implied volatility and therefore smaller time value components of the option premiums.

To keep the process even simpler, some covered call writers will write calls against a broad market index ETF like SPY (S&P 500) as the underlying. This will give the writer exposure to the entire S&P 500 which historically appreciates 7-10% per year. As an example, I created a screenshot of the options chain for SPY (Figure 133) with about three and one half weeks remaining in the July, 2014 contracts:

SPY: $195.88

16.98	16.88	16.86	17.09	0	34	179.00
15.98	15.88	15.87	16.10	0	245	180.00
14.99	14.88	14.92	15.06	0	0	181.00
[illegible]	[illegible]	[illegible]	[illegible]	0	151	182.00
[illegible]	[illegible]	[illegible]	[illegible]	0	37	183.00
[illegible]	[illegible]	[illegible]	[illegible]	0	471	184.00
[illegible]	[illegible]	[illegible]	[illegible]	0	2,761	185.00
[illegible]	[illegible]	[illegible]	[illegible]	0	832	186.00
9.13	8.88	9.08	9.19	0	953	187.00
8.23	7.88	8.14	8.32	0	1,511	188.00
7.29	6.88	7.21	7.38	0	2,782	189.00
6.38	5.88	6.29	6.46	0	5,037	190.00
5.48	4.88	5.40	5.56	0	4,842	191.00
4.60	3.88	4.53	4.67	0	26,430	192.00
3.75	2.88	3.69	3.81	0	28,166	193.00
2.96	1.88	2.92	3.00	0	48,406	194.00
2.24	0.88	[illegible]	2.25	0	81,354	195.00
1.60	0.00	1.59	1.62	0	128,099	196.00
1.08	0.00	1.06	1.10	0	96,566	197.00
0.67	0.00	0.66	0.68	0	65,304	198.00
0.39	0.00	0.38	0.40	0	79,600	199.00
0.21	0.00	0.21	0.22	0	114,323	200.00
0.12	0.00	0.10	0.13	0	2,510	201.00
0.07	0.00	0.05	0.08	0	593	202.00
0.04	0.00	0.03	0.05	0	516	203.00
0.03	0.00	0.02	0.04	0	151	204.00
0.03	0.00	0.02	0.03	0	34,579	205.00
0.02	0.00	0.01	0.03	0	0	206.00
0.01	0.00	0.01	0.02	0	14,848	210.00
0.01	0.00	0.01	0.01	0	1,011	215.00
0.01	0.00	0.02	0.01	0	135	220.00

Figure 133- SPY Options Chain for July, 2014

With SPY trading at $195.88, we will view the out–of-the-money $196.00, $197.00, $198.00 and $199.00 strikes.

We feed this information into the "multiple" tab of the Ellman Calculator to see if the results meet our goals as demonstrated in Figure 134:

RETURN ON OPTION (ROO) CALCULATOR - MULTIPLE STOCKS										
Stock Name or Symbol	Stock $/sh	Option $/sh	Strike $	Expires	Intrisic	Upside	Breakeven	ROO	Up Potential	Down Protect
SPY	$195.88	$1.59	$ 196.00	07/18/14	$ -	$ 0.12	$ 194.29	0.8%	0.1%	0.0%
SPY	$195.88	$1.06	$197.00	07/18/14	$ -	$ 1.12	$ 194.82	0.5%	0.6%	0.0%
SPY	$195.88	$ 0.66	$198.00	07/18/14	$ -	$ 2.12	$ 195.22	0.3%	1.1%	0.0%
SPY	$195.88	$0.38	$199.00	07/18/14	$ -	$ 3.12	$ 195.50	0.2%	1.6%	0.0%

Figure 134- SPY Options- Calculating Covered Call Returns

With upside potential (share price moves up to strike price by expiration) the three and one half week returns range from 0.9% ($196.00 strike) to 1.8% ($199.00 strike). The more bullish we are on the overall market, the more we should favor the deeper out-of-the-money strikes.

Now another, and perhaps even better, approach to this type of investing is to use the best-performing Select Sector SPDRs. These securities are unique ETFs that divide the S&P 500 into nine sector index funds. They have the diversity of a mutual fund, the focus of a sector fund, and the tradability of a stock. Together, the nine Select Sector SPDRs represent the S&P 500 as a whole. However, each Select Sector SPDR can also be bought individually, providing us with exposure to a particular sector or industry group.

These securities all have options and can be used with our covered call strategy. Each week the BCI Team will do a three-month technical analysis of the linear price chart of each sector and compare it to the performance of the S&P 500 itself. The top three funds outperforming the market benchmark will be listed and considered to be among the best candidates for covered call writing in the near-term. We will also show a chart of all sector components. Figure 135 is a screenshot showing the three best-performing Select Sector SPDRs as of 6/18/2014:

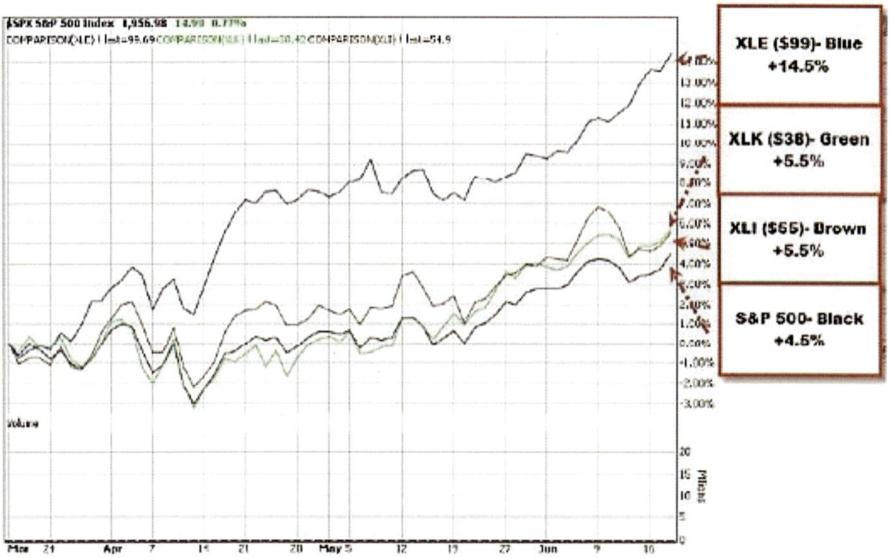

Figure 135- Select Sector SPDRs- Top Performers

Summary:

In the cases of both SPY and the Select Sector SPDRs, we have the advantages of exchange-traded funds as long as we are targeting the lower (but still significant) returns they generate compared to individual stocks. By using the SPDRs, we are limiting our exposure to the best-performers at any given point in time and can rotate in and out of them much like institutional traders do.

Chapter 12

Stock Splits

Chapter outline

1. Covered Call Writing and Contract Adjustments
2. Rolling Down and Stock Splits: A Real Life Example

Covered Call Writing and Contract Adjustments

Options trading basics include the fact that one options contract incorporates one hundred shares of the underlying security. The right or the obligation (depending on if we are looking at it from the perspective of the buyer or the seller of the option) is for the purchase or sale of one hundred shares of stock shares or exchange-traded fund shares. This is the rule but there are exceptions to this rule. From time to time a certain event will take place that will alter the terms of an equity options contract, changing the original standardized terms such as the number of deliverable shares.

Events that lead to contract adjustments

Let's first list some of the most common events that lead to contract adjustments:

- Stock splits
- Mergers

- Acquisitions
- Take-overs
- Spin-offs
- Special one-time dividends

In this article, I will highlight an example of a stock split and of a spin-off.

Stock split example

- Buy one hundred shares of BCI at $205.00
- Sell one call contract at the $210.00 strike for $530.00 ($5.30 per share)
- Initial one- month return on option = 2.6% (31% annualized)
- Upside potential (to the $210.00 strike) = 2.4%
- Total possible one-month return = 5%
- Stock splits three-for-one prior to expiration

Next let's view a pre- and post-split comparison of this trade in Figure 136:

Figure 136- Stock Splits and Contract Adjustments

In this situation, the number of shares owned and contracts sold tripled as the strike price and cost basis are cut in third. The terms of the original contract have changed but both buyers and sellers are "made whole" with these adjustments.

Spin-off example

- Buy one hundred shares of Ingersoll-Rand Plc (Ireland) (NYSE: IR) at $72.00
- Sell a one-month $72.50 call
- A part of the company called Allegion (ALLE) is spun off
- The price of IR drops from $72.00 to $55.00
- For each share of IR owned, one third share of ALLE is distributed plus cash (.3333 x price of ALLE)
- The original contracts of underlying IR are now recognized as having the underlying IR1 where:
- IR = IR1 = Current value of 100 x IR price + value of 33 shares of ALLE + .3333 x current value of ALLE
- 100 shares of IR1 are deliverable but you need a calculator to figure out if the contracts will be exercised

Figure 137 is a screenshot showing the explanation of the adjustment:

Ex-Distribution Date: December 2, 2013

Ingersoll-Rand plc ("IR") has announced a distribution of ordinary shares of Allegion Public Limited Company ("ALLE"). The distribution ratio will be one (1) ordinary share of Allegion Public Limited Company ("ALLE") for each three (3) ordinary shares of IR held of record November 22, 2013. The mail date for the distribution will be December 1, 2013.

On Monday, November 18, 2013, Allegion Public Limited Company began trading on the New York Stock Exchange on a "when issued" basis under the symbol "ALLE WI". Ingersoll-Rand plc is currently trading on the New York Stock Exchange on a "regular way" basis under the symbol IR, and on Monday November 18, 2013, began trading on an "ex-distribution"-"when issued" basis under the symbol IR WI. Allegion Public Limited Company "when issued" trading and Ingersoll-Rand plc "ex-distribution"-"when issued" trading will be suspended as of the opening on December 2, 2013. **The ex-date for the distribution will be Monday, December 2, 2013.**

THE FOREGOING IS AN UNOFFICIAL SUMMARY OF THE TERMS OF THE DISTRIBUTION, PREPARED BY CBOE FOR THE CONVENIENCE OF ITS PERMIT HOLDERS. CBOE ACCEPTS NO RESPONSIBILITY FOR THE ACCURACY OR COMPLETENESS OF THE SUMMARY. PERMIT HOLDERS SHOULD REFER TO THE NYSE INFONOTICE DATED NOVEMBER 18, 2013, FOR THE AUTHORITATIVE DESCRIPTION OF THE DISTRIBUTION AND ALL OF ITS TERMS AND CONDITIONS.

Contract Adjustments

Pursuant to Article VI, Section 11 and 11A, of OCC's By-Laws, all outstanding IR options shall be adjusted as follows. **On Monday, December 2, 2013, each adjusted Ingersoll-Rand plc contract will require the receipt or delivery of: (A) 100 ordinary shares of Ingersoll-Rand plc ("IR"), plus (B) 33 ordinary shares of Allegion Public Limited Company ("ALLE"); plus (C) cash in lieu of 0.3333 fractional ordinary share of ALLE.** Premiums for the adjusted Ingersoll-Rand plc options will continue to be calculated on the basis of a multiplier of 100, i.e., for premium and strike-price extensions, 1.00 will equal $100. The Ingersoll-Rand plc option symbol will change to **IR1.** [Any FLEX series that may exist will be adjusted in a similar manner to the standardized option.]

Figure 137- Spin-offs and Option Contract Adjustments for Ingersoll-Rand

Next, Figure 138 is a screen shot showing the contract adjustments with the strikes staying the same but a new underlying called IR1:

	EXISTING SERIES					ADJUSTED SERIES*		
IR	45.00	2013-12-21	C/P	=>	IR1	45.00	2013-12-21	C/P
IR	50.00	2013-12-21	C/P	=>	IR1	50.00	2013-12-21	C/P
IR	52.50	2013-12-21	C/P	=>	IR1	52.50	2013-12-21	C/P
IR	55.00	2013-12-21	C/P	=>	IR1	55.00	2013-12-21	C/P
IR	57.50	2013-12-21	C/P	=>	IR1	57.50	2013-12-21	C/P
IR	60.00	2013-12-21	C/P	=>	IR1	60.00	2013-12-21	C/P
IR	62.50	2013-12-21	C/P	=>	IR1	62.50	2013-12-21	C/P
IR	65.00	2013-12-21	C/P	=>	IR1	65.00	2013-12-21	C/P
IR	67.50	2013-12-21	C/P	=>	IR1	67.50	2013-12-21	C/P
IR	70.00	2013-12-21	C/P	=>	IR1	70.00	2013-12-21	C/P
IR	72.50	2013-12-21	C/P	=>	IR1	72.50	2013-12-21	C/P
IR	75.00	2013-12-21	C/P	=>	IR1	75.00	2013-12-21	C/P
IR	77.50	2013-12-21	C/P	=>	IR1	77.50	2013-12-21	C/P
IR	80.00	2013-12-21	C/P	=>	IR1	80.00	2013-12-21	C/P
IR	15.00	2014-01-18	C/P	=>	IR1	15.00	2014-01-18	C/P
IR	20.00	2014-01-18	C/P	=>	IR1	20.00	2014-01-18	C/P
IR	23.00	2014-01-18	C/P	=>	IR1	23.00	2014-01-18	C/P
IR	25.00	2014-01-18	C/P	=>	IR1	25.00	2014-01-18	C/P
IR	28.00	2014-01-18	C/P	=>	IR1	28.00	2014-01-18	C/P
IR	30.00	2014-01-18	C/P	=>	IR1	30.00	2014-01-18	C/P
IR	32.00	2014-01-18	C/P	=>	IR1	32.00	2014-01-18	C/P

Figure 138- IR- Contract Adjusted Series

To determine the likelihood of exercise the holder needs to add the value of the newly priced IR shares plus one third the value of ALLE plus .3333 x the cash value of ALLE. If that total exceeds the strike of $72.50, exercise will occur. Okay, time to summarize because my head is spinning from all of this:

Summary

Rarely, an event, like a stock split or spin-off, will take place that will necessitate the need for an option contract adjustment so that buyers and sellers are "made whole" Each situation is different so that we cannot put all changes into one specific formula. When this occurs, the best track to take is to call your broker and ask for a detailed explanation. Your broker will probably not know this information initially but will have the resources to get it for you. If we know of such an event in advance (except for a split), it is generally best, not to write calls on these stocks until the event has passed and options are again standardized...it will avoid the aggravation I alluded to before.

Rolling Down and Stock Splits: A Real Life Example

Covered call writing positions can be altered by exit strategies or contract adjustments. Contract adjustments are alterations that are typically made to option contracts when the underlying stock undergoes a stock split, pays a special cash and/or stock dividend or distribution, or is involved in a merger, acquisition or corporate reorganization. Sometimes they are impacted by both exit strategies and contract adjustments as we take full advantage of every possible opportunity to enhance our returns. In this article, I will highlight a real-life trade executed by one of our members, Mike, a few months back. In this series of covered call trades, Mike astutely used the rolling down exit strategy mid-contract and then took advantage of a stock split to continue generating income. The stock Mike used as the underlying security was Trinity Industries Inc. (TRN), a stellar-performer on our Premium Watch List and also located in the *IBD 50* at that time.

The series of trades

- 5/30/2014: Buy 100 x TRN at $87.43
- 5/30/2014: Sell 1 x $90.00 call at $1.20
- 6/6/2014: Share price declines dropping the option value to $0.20
- 6/6/2014: BTC (buy-to-close) the $90.00 call at $0.20
- 6/9/2014: STO (sell-to-open) the $85.00 call at $1.00 (This known as rolling down)

- 6/20/2014: Stock splits two-for-one doubling the number of shares owned by Mike to two hundred and cutting the strike price in half to $42.50
- 6/20/2014: Cost basis per share is cut in half to $43.72
- 6/20/2014: Option expires worthless as TRN closes at $42.23
- 6/23/2014: STO (sell-to-open) 2 x July $45.00 calls at $0.55
- 7/11/2014: Captures $20.00 cash dividend for the two contracts
- 7/14/2014: At the time I am writing this article, TRN is trading at $44.95, well above Mike's cost basis of $43.72 (one half of $87.43)

Initial calculations

- Initial return = $120.00/$8743.00 = 1.4%
- Initial upside potential = $257.00/$8743.00 = 2.9%
- Possible one-month return at the time the trade was set up = 4.3%

Two-month calculations as of 7/14/14

- Option credits: $120.00 + $100.00 + $110.00 = $330.00
- Option debit = $20.00
- Dividend credit = $20.00
- Share appreciation: $44.95 – $43.72 = $123.00 per contract = $246.00 (for two contracts)

- Two-month profit as of 7/14/2014 = $330.00 + $246.00 + $20.00 – $20.00 = $576.00
- Two-month % return = $576.00/$8743.00 = 6.6% = 39.5% annualized

Descriptive chart showing these trades (Figure 139)

Figure 139- TRN: Rolling Down with a Stock Split

1. Stock purchased at $87.43 and $90.00 call sold
2. $90.00 call bought back
3. $85.00 call sold (rolled down)
4. Stock splits two-for-one and option expires worthless… shares kept
5. Sell two contracts of the August $45.00 calls
6. Dividend distributed
7. Stock trading near $44.95

Summary

To achieve the highest possible level of covered call writing returns we must take advantage of every opportunity that arises during the course of the contract cycle. In this article, I highlighted the execution of the rolling down exit strategy and leveraging contract adjustments to maximize our returns. This demonstrates how we can benefit from stock splits on uptrending securities which are bullish events that will frequently lead us to favoring out-of-the-money strikes.

THE BLUE COLLAR INVESTOR

Chapter 13

Tax Treatment of Covered Call Writing

Chapter outline

1. Capital Gains (Losses) for Selling Cash-Secured Puts in Non-Sheltered Accounts
2. Capital Gains (Losses) for Covered Call Writing in Non-Sheltered Accounts
3. Tax Implications
4. What are Wash Sales and Wash Trading? Are they the Same Type of Transaction?

Capital Gains (Losses) for Selling Cash-Secured Puts in Non-Sheltered Accounts

In this publication I will highlight the tax ramifications as they apply to selling put options. It is imperative to check with your tax advisor before making final investment decisions as they relate to tax issues.

What is a capital gain?

A capital gain is an increase in the value of as capital asset, such as a stock or an option that gives it a higher worth than the purchase price. Capital gains must be claimed on income taxes in non-sheltered accounts.

Rules for cash-secured put writers

Premiums received for writing a put are not included as income at the time of receipt, but are held in suspense until the writer's obligation to purchase the underlying stock expires, until the put is exercised and the writer purchases the stock, or by closing the option position (buy-to-close). With that in mind, here are three possible scenarios that may occur after the sale of the option:

1. An expired option (we sold the put, we didn't close the position by buying back the option, and the holder did not exercise the option) results in a short-term capital gain. For example, we sell a BCI April $90.00 put for $4.50 in March. The proceeds are $450.00 (per contract, less commissions). Since the cost is $0.00, the short-term capital gain is $450.00. The acquisition date will be LATER than the sales date and the word "Expired" should be written in column e, the cost basis column of Form 8949.

2. If we buy back the same option in the above example to close the position (usually to initiate an exit strategy), the difference between the sale profit and the buyback cost will represent a capital gain or a capital loss. As in example 1, the acquisition date will be LATER than the sales date.

   Capital gain example: We close our position by buying back the option for $250.00. The capital gain is $200.00 ($450.00 – $250.00).

   Capital loss example: We close our position by buying back the option for $550.00. The capital loss is $100.00 ($550.00 – $450.00).

3. If the option is exercised, the option transaction becomes part of the stock transaction. The option premium is subtracted from the price we paid for the stock, reducing our basis. Example: You sold the BCI April $90.00 put for $4.50. The put is exercised and you pay $90.00 per share for the stock. Normally, your cost basis would be $90.00. However, you received $4.50 per share for the put premium. This reduces your cost basis in the acquired shares to $85.50 ($90.00-$4.50). There is no gain or loss to report on the option trade. When you sell the BCI shares you will simply enter $85.50 in the cost basis column. The holding period of the shares from the exercise date until the sale date will determine if the transaction is long or short term. The holding period of the option is ignored.

*****The Schedule D of the Elite Calculator is designed to assist your tax advisor with these long and short-term capital gains (losses) issues.**

The specific information referenced above can be found in IRS Publication 550 entitled Investment Income and Expenses, pages 59 – 61.

Personally, I choose to avoid these tax issues by trading options predominantly in tax-sheltered accounts whenever possible.

Capital Gains (Losses) for Covered Call Writing in Non-Sheltered Accounts

Whether we sell covered calls or cash-secured puts strong consideration should be given to trading in sheltered accounts whenever possible. Most, if not all, of our trades will be short-term in nature (less than one year) and therefore will be taxed at the ordinary income tax rate (up to 35%) which is much higher than the long-term capital gains tax rate (15%) if we trade in non-sheltered accounts.

What is a Capital Gain?

This is an increase in the value of as capital asset, such as a stock or an option, which gives it a higher worth than the purchase price. It must be claimed for income taxes in non-sheltered accounts.

Rules for Covered Call Writers

Premiums received for writing a covered call are not included as income at the time of receipt, but are held in suspense until the writer's obligation to deliver the underlying stock expires or until the writer either sells the stock as a result of the call assignment or by closing the option position (buy-to-close). With that in mind, here are three possible scenarios that may occur after the sale of the option:

1. An expired option (we sold the call, we didn't close the position by buying back the option and the holder did not exercise the option) results in a short-term capital gain. For example, we sell a BCI April 90.00 call for $4.50 in March. The proceeds are $450.00 (less trading commissions). Since the cost is $0.00, the short-term capital gain is $450.00. The acquisition date will be LATER than the sales date and the word "Expired" should be written in column e, the cost basis column of Form 8949.

2. If we buy back the same option in the above example to close the position (usually to execute an exit strategy), the difference between the sale profit and the buyback cost will represent a capital gain or a capital loss. As in example 1, the acquisition date will be LATER than the sales date.

3. If the option is exercised, the option transaction becomes

part of the stock transaction. The option premium is added to the strike price received, less commissions. If the stock has been held for less than one year, the entire transaction will be treated as short-term. If the stock had been held for *one year or more*, the entire transaction will be treated as long-term as the *option holding period is ignored*.

Capital gain example

We close our position by buying back the option for $250.00. The capital gain is $200.00 ($450.00 – $250.00).

Capital loss example

We close our position by buying back the option for $550.00. The capital loss is $100.00 ($550.00 – $450.00).

*****The Schedule D of the Elite Calculator is designed to assist your tax advisor with these long and short-term capital gains (losses) issues as displayed in Figures 140 and 141:**

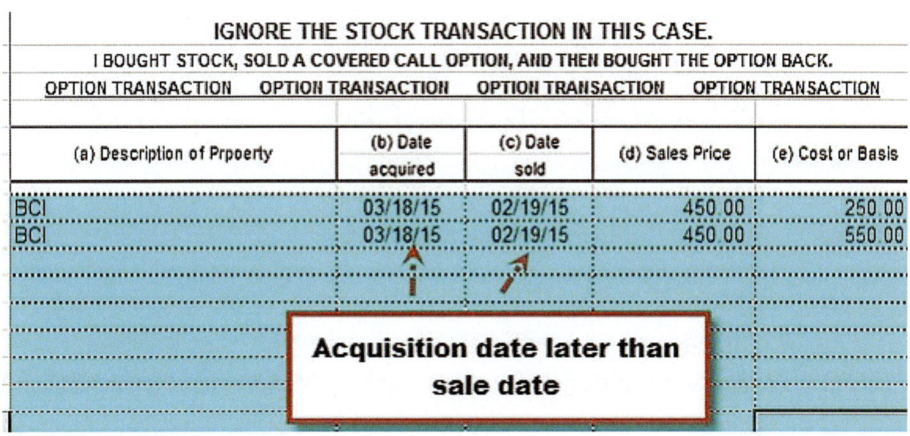
IGNORE THE STOCK TRANSACTION IN THIS CASE.
I BOUGHT STOCK, SOLD A COVERED CALL OPTION, AND THEN BOUGHT THE OPTION BACK.
OPTION TRANSACTION OPTION TRANSACTION OPTION TRANSACTION OPTION TRANSACTION

(a) Description of Prpoerty	(b) Date acquired	(c) Date sold	(d) Sales Price	(e) Cost or Basis
BCI	03/18/15	02/19/15	450.00	250.00
BCI	03/18/15	02/19/15	450.00	550.00

Figure 140- Acquisition Date Later than Sale Date

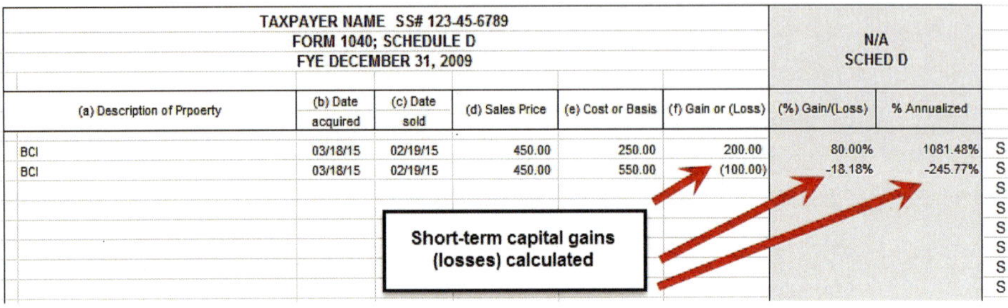

TAXPAYER NAME SS# 123-45-6789 FORM 1040; SCHEDULE D FYE DECEMBER 31, 2009						N/A SCHED D		
(a) Description of Prpoerty	(b) Date acquired	(c) Date sold	(d) Sales Price	(e) Cost or Basis	(f) Gain or (Loss)	(%) Gain/(Loss)	% Annualized	
BCI	03/18/15	02/19/15	450.00	250.00	200.00	80.00%	1081.48%	S
BCI	03/18/15	02/19/15	450.00	550.00	(100.00)	-18.18%	-245.77%	S
								S
								S
								S
								S
								S
								S

Figure 141- Capital Gain (Loss) Calculations

Notice that capital gains and losses are calculated in dollar amount, percentile and annualized percentile computations (three red arrows in Figure 141).

The specific information referenced above can be found in <u>IRS Publication 550 entitled Investment Income and Expenses, pages 57 – 58.</u>

I avoid these tax issues by trading covered call stock options predominantly in tax-sheltered accounts.

*****Contact your tax advisor before making any investment tax-related investment decision**s

Tax Implications

Let me premise my remarks by stating the obvious…I am <u>not</u> a tax expert. Nor do I play one on TV. However, I was quite fortunate to have Owen Sargent, an outstanding CPA and seasoned stock investor, agree to write this section for us.

Thus far we have discussed how to make money investing with stocks and stock options. In this section we will address how to keep those profits. If you are investing in sheltered accounts, this information does not apply. If you are investing in non-sheltered accounts, it is important to have a basic knowledge as to how you will be taxed in your investment accounts.

You will learn in this chapter that profits from stock investments can be taxed as ordinary income or long-term capital gains. When taxed as ordinary income the tax bracket is the same as the one for your wages. It includes dividends distributed by the stock plus any short-term capital gains profit (profit from a stock or option sold that was held for less than one year).

Long term capital gains usually have a much lower tax consequence and applies to a profit from a stock or option sold that was held for at least one year and one day. Losses from stock or option investments can be used to offset gains and a general rule of thumb is to keep losses to a short-term status and gains to a long-term basis. For option-selling, though, our positions are predominantly short-term.

Use the information as a reference guide. It is not necessary to become a tax expert but to have a general knowledge of tax-related issues can only make us all better investors.

Three important takeaways from this chapter are:

- Stocks and options should be bought and sold based on the principles discussed in previous chapters and tax consequences should be secondary factors
- Maintain accurate records
- Consult with your tax advisor in these matters

I now turn over the tax chapter to Owen Sargent…

This chapter is NOT just about taxes. My name is Owen Sargent. I am a New York Certified Public Accountant with twenty-nine years of accounting and tax experience. I am also a New York attorney. Hopefully, my professional experiences can benefit you, and help make you the CFO of your own, and your family's, finances. You have already taken a good step in that direction when you bought this book. You also took another good step by reading this far.

This book is designed to help you be less reliant on others for investment advice. That said, there is not a single CEO in the business world who does not rely on other professionals with expertise and advice that can help them do their jobs better. It is important that you learn when you need good professional advice. I have dealt with too many clients who tried to save money by using a friend's advice, internet advice, or bad professional advice. It often winds up being much more expensive to "fix" what has already been done, if it can be fixed, than it is to pay for good professional advice in the first place. I tell my clients there is no such thing as a stupid question. Not asking the question can be very expensive. In the paragraphs that follow I hope to answer some of your unasked questions, give you some good places to do some of your own research, and to help you formulate questions for your professional advisors that are more to the point. There are two major functions of this book. The first is to help you make some money. The second is to help you keep it.

I have laid out this chapter in four parts:

- Part One: TAXES
- Part Two: YOUNG PEOPLE (I mean you, if you are between 14 and 29)
- Part Three: NOT-SO-YOUNG PEOPLE
- Part Four: RETIREES

PART ONE – TAXES

A couple of points must be made before I discuss the taxes.

First, never let the tax laws alone drive your financial planning. Tax laws are not only subject to change, they are one of the few laws that can legally be changed retroactively. The legislature cannot pass a law in August that makes something you did in the previous March illegal. They can, however, pass a tax law in August that is effective back to March, or January.

Second, refusing to make money, as a means of getting even with the government by denying them their share, is not a sound financial plan. Tax planning is important, but taxes are a societal necessity. I tell clients that my goal in life is to have a personal income tax return with a $1,000,000 income tax. That will mean that I made two, three, or even four million dollars, depending on the types of income, and the tax rates. It is much easier to win a game if you are familiar with the rules.

Third, my discussion of various taxes here applies to the United States of America federal taxes. Many of the readers of this book are not US citizens and, therefore, subject to entirely different taxing structures and rules. Many other readers are residents of states which have no state income taxes. Generally, state income taxes are based on your federal income, with some specific adjustments. You should discuss your state's tax issues with a competent tax preparer and/or attorney in your state. You do not need to be sufficiently knowledgeable to become a tax preparer, but you should know enough to know when you should seek professional advice, or when that advice is poor.

This chapter is being written at the end of 2012. Congress has failed to pass the necessary tax laws to allow the Internal Revenue Service to even design the 2012 income tax forms. I will not even try to discuss what is coming in 2013, because nobody has those prognostication skills. One of my favorite questions: If "pro" is the opposite of "con", is "progress" the opposite of "congress"?

Ok, let's get down to the serious tax discussion. There are two major taxes that most Americans must deal with, income taxes, and estate and gift taxes. Estate and gift taxes are actually a pair of evil twins which will be discussed simultaneously below. If you are internet inclined I strongly suggest you put WWW.IRS.GOV in your favorites. Please note, it is *irs.GOV*, NOT *irs.COM*. Someone has a very nice tax information website using the dot com extension. IT IS NOT THE INTERNAL REVENUE SERVICE'S WEBSITE! Each state has its own website where you may obtain state tax forms, instructions, and publications. Just be sure it is the state's official website.

I will not provide links to the IRS website because those links are subject to change from time to time. You should spend some time browsing their website, so you can find the various forms, instructions and publications discussed below.

PERSONAL INCOME TAXES

Evading taxes is illegal. Deferring taxes is desirable. Avoiding taxes is spectacular. The discussion in this section relates to activity which is not done in a retirement account. I will discuss retirement accounts later in this chapter.

Your personal income taxes are reported on **Form 1040, "U.S. individual Income Tax Return"**. Many of the numbers appearing on form 1040 come from separate schedules which must be prepared and attached to your return. Since this book is about stock and option trading you will be dealing mostly with **Schedule D, "Capital Gains and Losses"**. You will also probably need **Schedule B, "Interest and Ordinary Dividends"**, and **Schedule A, "Itemized Deductions"**. Additionally, the IRS, as of the 2011 tax year, has now made the schedule D more complicated. The transactions are no longer entered directly into schedule D. They are entered on **Form 8949, "Sales and other dispositions of Capital Assets"**. The totals appearing on forms 8949 are then transferred to schedule D. Give up yet? It gets better. You may need to prepare up to six forms 8949, depending on the nature of your transactions. Publication 17 is an excellent source of information for your personal income tax return. Another extremely important publication is 550 Investment Income and Expenses. I suggest you download these publications onto your computer (they are Adobe .pdf files) so you can print out individual pages for future reference and documentation for your income tax return.

Schedule A Itemized Deductions

Some of the items you may be able to deduct related to your investments include investment interest, such as broker margin interest (you will also need form 4952), investment expenses, such as periodic broker account fees, tax preparation fees and attorney fees. Please read the instructions for Schedule A. You should also read Publication 529 Miscellaneous Deductions.

Schedule B Interest and Ordinary Dividends

Some of the stocks, ETFs or mutual funds you own may pay you a dividend during the period you own it. This information will be reported to you on form 1099DIV. The dividend may be subject to special reduced tax rates, or it may not. Follow the instructions for schedule B and form 1040 on where to report the dividend income reported to you by the payer. **NOTE:** ***The form 1099 does not have to be the government form you see on the IRS website. If***

you own shares of stock in a dividend reinvestment plan you may get a 1099DIV directly from that corporation or its agent. If your securities are held in a brokerage account your form 1099 will be a special report in January or February. It will have some, or all, of the same lines and descriptions as the government form, but it will probably be on 8.5 x 11 paper. Be careful. Do not to throw it out. Your tax preparer will call you many bad names, perhaps in several languages.

Schedule D Capital Gains and Losses & Form 8949 Sales and Other Dispositions of Assets

Stock sales, and option sales beginning in 2013, are reported to you, and to the IRS, using form 1099B. As noted above, in the discussion of dividends, this form may be part of a special 1099 year-end report you receive from your broker. The form also may report the basis, or cost, of the security being sold. If it an option is being sold short there will be no basis information reported. If you throw this one out your tax preparer will add two zeros to his fee for preparing your returns, and still call you many bad names.

Capital gains and losses were entered directly on Schedule D in years prior to 2011. It was a simple form, at least by my standards, as a preparer. Beginning in 2011 the IRS decided to use an additional form related to the new third party information being reported to them. Form 8949 is used to list the stock, bond and option transactions individually. First, you must decide if you have a transaction where the broker has reported the cost basis of the transaction on form 1099B. Then you must decide if the transaction is short term, or long term. Hey, WAKE UP! It gets better. If you have a sale which a broker did not report you may need to prepare a form 8949 for that, too. So, conceivably, you may need SIX different forms 8949 in order to properly report your gains and losses. I am not going to get into strange transactions, such as, you sold your car for more than you paid for it (like that ever happens!), or you sold a partnership interest to another investor. If you are involved in anything like that you should be seeing a tax professional, sooner, rather than later.

Let's follow some of the transaction types you will encounter in your trading activity. Capital gains and losses result from your purchase and sale of an asset. It is important to remember, as a covered call writer (discussed in Chapter 12), that the order of the sale date and purchase date is not always the same. When you buy shares of stock you have entered into a long position. The acquisition date will be before the sale date for a long position. When you sell a covered call option, you have entered into a short position. The acquisition date will be AFTER the sale date. Do not let this confuse you when preparing the tax forms. I will restrict the discussion of short sales, and short positions, to covered call options. It is possible to sell stock short, but that is for sophisticated investors with substantial assets and substantial nerve.

The first issue is whether you have to report a transaction, or not. A short sale (selling the option when using covered call writing) is not a completed transaction which has produced a gain or a loss. You will realize a gain or a loss on the transaction only when you have "closed" the short position, by buying it back, it expires, or it is exercised. The examples below do not include any broker commissions. Be aware that all transaction costs are included in the cost basis, or subtracted from the sales proceeds, and are reported net. So, let's get on with the examples:

Buying and selling securities

Reportable transactions involve two sides, the purchase and the sale. The transaction you are probably already familiar with is "I buy 100 shares of XYZ stock. Sometime later I sell 100 shares of XYZ stock. I have a capital gain or loss, depending on the prices of each, and it is either long term, or short term, depending on how long I owned the stock. Word of advice, check the definition of "long term" from time to time. The government has changed it a few times. As of the writing of this book long term means one year, or longer. Example of reporting this gain: You bought 100 XYZ on Mar 5, 2012 for $40 per share, with a $13 broker commission. Your basis in the stock is $4,013. You sold the stock on March 1, 2013, for $50 per share, with another $13 commission. Your gross proceeds will be $4,987. This is because the proceeds are reportable net of any transaction costs on the trade. When you prepare your Schedule D you will report a short term capital gain of $1,974 ($4,987 – $4,013). It's actually pretty simple.

It gets a bit more complex when you throw in some of the special circumstances that can change your basis. You need to be aware of these so you can keep the proper records and not pay extra taxes by mistake.

Special circumstances

Example #1: Stock splits

This happens when the company decides they want to increase the shares without selling any new ones. There are a lot of reasons why they may split the stock, but they are not important to this discussion. The split may be two for one, three for one, etc. Let's take a two for one (2:1) stock split. What this means is, you bought 100 shares of ON March 5, 2012 for $40 per share, with a $13 broker commission. In October of 2012 the company split the stock 2:1. You will receive an additional 100 shares of XYZ into your account. You do not own any more of the company than you owned before. Instead of owning 100 shares out of 100 million shares you now own 200 shares out of 200 million shares. The difference is that the price will suddenly be cut in half. Before the split you owned 100 shares at say, $58 dollars per share, $5,800 worth of stock. After the split you owned 200 shares at $29 per share (still $5,800 worth of stock). Now, this is where your record keeping becomes very important! If you sell 100 shares of XYZ on March 1, 2013 your basis is NOT $4,013. It is $2,006.50. Your capital gain will be as follows: You sold 100 shares at $29. Your net proceeds will be $2,887, after $13 commission. Your basis will be $2,006.50. Your gain will be $880.50, and you will still have 100 shares with a basis of $2,006.50. If you sell the other 100 shares on April 12, 2013 for $35 per share, your proceeds will be $3,487. Your basis will be the remaining $2,006.50. Your gain will be $1,480.50, and it will be LONG term because your holding period started on March 5, 2012, NOT October 2012 when you received the additional shares.

You MUST understand this. You do NOT own 100 shares with a basis of $4,013 and 100 shares with a basis of $0! You owned 100 shares of stock in XYZ, with a basis of $4,013, bought on March 5, 2012, BEFORE the split. You owned 200 shares of stock in XYZ, bought on March 5, 2012, with a basis of $4,013 AFTER the split. The only thing that changed is the number of shares. You do NOT have a new acquisition date for the second 100 shares. Keep an eye on your brokerage report. Make sure they report it correctly. If not, call them and tell them to correct it.

Example #2: Stock dividend

This happens when the company decides to give you a dividend in shares of stock, rather than cash. First, the dividend will usually not be reportable as a dividend. Second, the math you used in the first example will get a great deal more complex. Let's say the company gives you a 5% stock dividend. Now, the 100 shares of XYZ you bought for $4,013 on March 5, 2012 has become 105 shares of XYZ you bought on March 5, 2012. If you sell 100 shares now, you will have a basis of $3,821.90 and 5 shares with a basis of $191.10. Do yourself a favor. When you sell the shares, sell the whole 105 shares. Your basis will be the original $4,013 you paid for it and you won't have a math headache later.

Example #3: Dividend reinvestment – mutual funds

This is a spectacular way of slowly building up your stock holdings. Dividend reinvestment is very common for regular mutual funds.

Most regular funds pay their dividends at the end of the year, so it is very common to get some extra shares toward the end of December. You can keep your basis on the average price method, or the specific shares method. Your broker may select a method for you. It is probably easier to use their method.

Example #4: Dividend reinvestment – common stock

Many brokers today allow you to reinvest dividends from regular stocks trades on the stock exchanges. This allows you to buy additional shares automatically, at whatever the market price is when the dividend is paid. Again, it is a great way to build up your investment portfolio. However, it creates another record keeping nightmare. You may receive 0.21345 shares for a $16 dividend on a $75 stock. If you reinvest dividends each quarter, this will happen four times each year. You will have 41 trades, each in fractions of shares, each with a $16 basis, at the end of ten years. Don't let this keep you from investing this way. It just means you need to keep proper records so you do not pay tax on the wrong capital gain when you finally sell all of the stock.

Again, you are strongly urged to double check the information being reported by your broker. The new form 1099B includes the dates of the transactions and the cost basis of the security. This information was reported to the Internal Revenue Service. If it is not correct, the first step should be to notify the broker's tax reporting department, in writing, of precisely which transactions you disagree with, and why. If the broker refuses to correct the information, you are not lost. Do the following: Report the information as the broker reported it. Then, on another line, enter transaction information which will make the totals correct. Attach a detailed schedule to your tax return explaining the adjustments. The Internal Revenue Service uses a matching program and sends out notices that they have found a difference and you are wrong. I fight these all the time. The IRS could not match a single cork to an empty wine bottle, if they were the only two objects in the room. If you can substantiate your adjustments to arrive at the correct income you will win. You may have to rub their noses in it to make them understand it, but be persistent. You are not obligated to pay an incorrect tax simply because the IRS employees don't understand what you did. **NOTE:** ***Most preparers are required to e-file income tax returns. Again, do not let one tell you that the transactions must be entered individually because they cannot attach a paper schedule to an e-filed return. It is true they cannot attach a schedule, however, the IRS has bowed to taxpayer ire at the cost of keypunching each transaction. Tell your preparer to get form 8453, which can be used to mail paper documents for an e-filed return. You can find this information in the instructions for schedule D, and the instructions for form 8453.***

Some issues to be aware of:

The "kiddie tax"

There are special rules for minor children with unearned income. If you are trading in an account for your child, the child must file her own return. If the income exceeds a certain amount, $950 for 2011, the child's tax rate will be determined based on your tax return. This is true, even if your child is now a college student. Talk to your tax preparer if this is the case. If your child has any sales of securities she must file her own return.

The "short sale"

A short sale happens when you sell before you buy. The covered call options above are a good example. You sell the option in March and buy it back in April. That is a short sale. It is unlikely that most readers of this book will be short sellers of stock, but it is possible. If you have a substantial amount of money, you can go to your broker, borrow shares of a stock and sell them short. You do this if you think the stock is going to go down. When you buy it back at a lower price, you will make a capital gain. If you buy it back at a higher price, you will incur a loss. Just keep in mind that, for income tax reporting purposes, you report the short sale on your tax return when you buy the shares back, not when you sell the borrowed shares.

The "wash sale"

This is tricky little tax issue that you need to know about. You are not allowed to take a capital loss if you bought the stock within 30 days before or after the loss sale. Example: You buy 100 shares of XYZ for $3,000.00. You sell them for $2,000.00 on December 10 for a loss of $1,000.00. In the meantime, you bought an additional 100 shares of XYZ for $2,100.00 on December 2nd. The government figures you have not really lost the $1,000.00, because you still own 100 shares of XYZ. I'm not making this up. You pay Congress to come up with this. Anyway, you have not given up the $1,000.00 loss forever. You just need to add it to your shares bought on December 2nd. You will report the $1,000.00 loss on your tax return, and then add it back. Then you will adjust the basis of the December 2nd shares from $2,100.00 to $3,100.00. What this means is that you will essentially get your "loss" on your tax return when you finally sell the December 2nd shares. Publication 550 provides a complete explanation of the tax treatment.

Deferring Income Taxes – Individual Retirement Arrangements

Most people are familiar with Individual Retirement Arrangements. Not everyone is aware you can write covered calls in an IRA account. Ask your IRA custodian. If the custodian will not allow it, consider moving the account. It is probably not available in your company retirement plan, but it will not hurt to ask.

If you do sell covered calls in your IRA you can ignore the capital gains discussion above. Generally, the income earned in your regular IRA is taxed when you take distributions from the account, presumably, after you retire. If you have deducted all of the contributions into the account in previous years, all of the distributions will be taxable income in the year you take the money out. This is the definition of "tax deferred income".

You may have made contributions to your IRA which could not be deducted, because you or your spouse participated in a retirement account at work (See box 13 on your W2), and your income exceeded certain limits. If this is the case, part of your distributions in the future will not be taxed again, but the income earned on it will be. It important you keep records of your non-deductible contributions. The IRS does not do this for you, and the IRA custodian has no way of knowing whether you deducted the contribution in any particular year. You should discuss this with your tax preparer. You should also read Publication 590 Individual Retirement Arrangements.

Avoiding Income Taxes

This one is a beauty. The ROTH Individual Retirement Account. Contributions to a Roth IRA are taxed in the year you make the contribution. The income the account earns, and the original contribution, is not taxed when you take the distributions out! (Certain rules apply. Ask your tax preparer, or check Pub 590.)

NOTE: ***Please, before you continue reading this book put it down and call your IRA custodian. Make sure that you have a properly updated beneficiary list. When you die your IRA account must be distributed, or transferred. Improper planning can result in a disaster for your family.***

If your estate is the beneficiary the entire account will be distributed as part of the process of winding up your financial affairs. A ROTH IRA will be distributed without income tax being owed, but any future benefit that could have been derived by leaving the money in it will be lost. A regular IRA will be

subject to regular income taxes on the entire distribution, and any future benefit will be lost.

If you have a beneficiary list your IRA may continue to help your beneficiaries. You may split the account among your beneficiaries as you wish. Example: You have a husband and two children. You choose to make your children the beneficiaries, at 50% each. Upon your death, the custodian will create two new inherited IRA accounts, one in each childs name. Each child must begin taking distributions each year over his or her life expectancy. The advantage is that the undistributed funds continue to earn money tax deferred. There is a special exception for your husband. He, as the beneficiary, may leave the funds in the account until he reaches 59 1/2, or he may roll the account into his own IRA that he may already have. You may read more about inherited IRAs in Publication 590.

You should update, or review the beneficiary list any time there is a change in your life. If your beneficiary list includes your ex-wife, your children and current wife will not be happy with the outcome. If you had two children when you prepared the last beneficiary list, and now you have three, your youngest child may not remember you fondly. The custodian is obligated to distribute the account according to your beneficiary list. You may not change these instructions using your will.

That pretty much covers the personal income tax subject. You need to be aware of the rules so you can better tell if your return is correctly prepared, and your preparer is not trying to make your income tax return his entire year's income.

ESTATE AND GIFT TAXES

I am not going to go into detail regarding estate taxes. If you are reading this book you are not dead, so estate taxes should not be your highest priority. Keep in mind that all of your assets, including your IRA accounts may be subject to estate taxes on Form 706. The federal estate tax begins, as of the writing of this chapter, at $5 million dollars in estate value. This means if you leave an estate worth less than $5 million on the date you die, your estate will have no tax. If you have an estate worth more than $5 million you should go see an attorney and a CPA tomorrow to do some estate tax planning. Most important: You should have a will.

Various states have estate or inheritance taxes. The difference is who the tax is levied upon, and the threshold at which the tax begins. An estate tax is levied on the estate left by the deceased individual. An inheritance tax is levied on the beneficiaries of the estate. You should have this discussion with your financial professionals sooner, rather than later.

Gift taxes are part of the estate tax scheme. The government does not want you to give your estate to your relatives before you die without getting the estate tax they will be due. A gift tax return, Form 709 is due for any year in which you give more than $13,000 (as of 2013) to any one individual, other than your spouse. Generally, there is no gift tax due, because most filers choose to use the estate exclusion ($5 million) on their gift tax returns. If you plan on giving more than $13,000 to any one individual, in one year, you should see a competent CPA before you make the gift. You should also be aware of what is specifically NOT considered a gift subject to gift tax. If you make medical payments for someone, braces, eye surgery, whatever directly to the provider of the service, the payments are not subject to gift taxes. The same rule applies for the payment of education tuition. Be careful. This does not mean you give your son a check for $25,000 to pay his tuition at Northwestern University. It means you sent the check directly to Northwestern for the tuition bill.

PART TWO: YOUNG PEOPLE

I wish I knew, when I was sixteen, what I know now. I started working as a hospital janitor, weekends and summers, during high school. It didn't pay much, and the Individual Retirement Arrangement had not yet been invented. I could easily have been retired ten years ago if I had started saving diligently way back then. Believe it, or not, if you are a young person today, you won't be for long.

I run into a number of issues with young people.

Some of you are simply ignorant when it comes to making money, saving money and investing money, but willing to learn. That's you because you are reading this book.

Some of you are simply are not interested in learning about money. That's your friend who has three different ipods, in different colors, because each one matches a different outfit. (Don't lend her any money. You won't get it back.).

Some of you have helicopter parents who do everything for you, including your income tax returns you did not know about, for that summer job you had. They give you a credit or debit card. They give you enough money so you do not need to get a job. They remove any incentive to learn to make money, save money and spend money intelligently.

Well, there is little we can do about those not interested, and those overly sheltered by their parents. But, for those of you who want to learn to be less dependent on your parents and grandparents, welcome.

<u>Suggestion #1</u>

Buy another book. I have given my nephews and my niece each a copy. It is another excellent book to consider. The title is *The Automatic Millionaire*, by David Bach. The premise is simple. Begin investing today. Invest regularly. Retire early.

Suggestion #2

Sign up for your company pension plan. Have some money invested out of each paycheck. If your employer has no pension plan, have some money deposited directly into a savings account each week. Open an IRA or Roth IRA account. Contribute each month. You may even be able to have a regular amount withdrawn from your checking account each month by the IRA custodian.

Suggestion #3

Start as early as you can. The expression "time is money" is not just some irritating phrase your boss uses to get you to hang up your cell phone and get back to work. I do not sell widgets. I am a CPA/ attorney. I sell my time. The value of my time, $100.00 per hour, $350.00 per hour, $750 per hour, depends on the experience I have and my knowledge, but it is still my time that I sell, not a tangible product. There are many tables available online, or programs, that will tell you how much you can end up with if you invest $X each week or month, at Y%, for Z years. Here is a quick comparison:

If you invest $10,000.00 each year for twenty years, at 4% per year, you will have $309,692.00 at the end of twenty years. If you do not invest any additional funds for the next twenty years, the account will grow to $678,573.00.

If you invest $10,000.00 each year for forty years, at 4% per year, you will have $988,265.00 at the end of forty years.

What does this mean? Time is money. If you start when you are twenty years old, you can wind up with $678,573.00 when you are sixty years old, with an investment of $200,000.00 ($10,000.00 x 20 years). If you start when you are forty years old, you will wind up with $309,692.00. The extra 2twenty years is worth $368,881.00. See? Time IS money! To quote Albert Einstein, "Compound interest is the eighth wonder of the world. He who understands it, earns it . . . he who doesn't . . . pays it."

Suggestion #4

Invest the savings carefully. You cannot replace retirement money. There are limits to how much you can contribute to various types of plans, but you cannot replace $4,000.00 just because you picked a lousy stock in your IRA, and it went out of business. This book is an attempt to give you some investing acumen. Not everyone is going to be comfortable selling options regularly. However, even if that describes you, you will have the knowledge that they are not for you because you learned about them first, rather than just ignoring them. Who knows, one day you may own a stock that you decide is perfect for selling a covered call to make a few extra dollars.

Just as a point of interest, a Gucci handbag is NOT an investment. Gucci stock may, or may not, be an investment, but the handbag, unless it is one of a kind, and you put in an environmentally controlled vault, is definitely not an investment. Air Jordan sneakers are not an investment. Nike stock may be. An ipod is not an investment. Apple stock may be. Do you see where I am going with this?

Suggestion #5

Don't compare your finances to someone else's. You can always find someone who is wealthier than you are. You can always find someone who is less wealthy than you are. Who cares? Your goal in life is to take care of yourself, and your loved ones. If you can also take care of some others, wonderful, but nobody is going to be more concerned with your future than you are. You can control it if you take some time to learn and some time to invest. A lottery ticket is not a retirement plan.

Suggestion #6

Learn about your tax returns. Your parents can't do it for you forever, and I do not like clients who have no idea what goes on their returns. They are the types who, two weeks after their tax returns have been filed, begin a conversation with "Oh. Is this important?" My response is generally, "No. It was important two weeks ago, but now it just means I get to charge you for amending your tax returns."

Investing is not difficult. It does not require an investment advisor. If you wear a Nylon jacket, consider investing in DuPont. If you eat Cheerios, consider investing in General Mills. If you like your Chevrolet, consider investing in General Motors. If you like your light bulbs, consider General Electric. Learn about the company and its products. Buy stock you understand. That is Warren Buffet's rule. He never bought an internet stock because he could not safely understand how they made their money. And, as we have seen, many of them didn't understand it, either. You have a serious advantage over people who are older than you are. You have more time to make up for any investing losses, and you will have losses, I promise you. You also have the time to get more money invested, and working for you, for a longer period. Start now. Retire when you are fifty. Start when you are fifty. Retire when you are ninety. It's your choice. Be your own CEO. There is no age requirement and no interview process. Hire yourself and get started.

PART THREE: NOT-SO-YOUNG PEOPLE

Time is still money. Also, equally important, "Better late than never" comes to mind. There is a reason clichés become clichés. They are often appropriate, or true.

I know. You have responsibilities. You have a house, kids, two cars, a dog. You also have a responsibility to yourself and your retirement. There is nothing wrong with being selfish. Put your needs ahead of everyone else's. Read David Bach's The Automatic Millionaire, and then see how you feel about your next latte at Starbucks. Think about that cable premium package. Do you really need to watch Korean badminton at two in the morning? There are things you can stop wasting money on and put that money to better use, like making more money. You don't have to be putting away $30,000.00 per year, but $50.00 per week is better than nothing, and $60.00 per week is better than $50.00.

Do you realize that a car with a $290.00 monthly lease will get you to the same places as a car with a $490.00 monthly lease? What would you do with that "extra" $200.00 per month? The $290.00 car is not as impressive as the car next to you on your way to work? Well, smile politely at the driver next to you, and quietly tell yourself you have $200.00 going into the bank this month that he does not. At some time in the future he will still be out here going to work, and you will be sitting in your kitchen planning your day's retirement activities.

Suggestion #1

Go sit down with a fee based financial planner. He or she may have some good suggestions that are less painful than you think. One of the things you will be required to do is to make a list of each dollar coming in and going out for a month, or two. Do that anyway. You might not even need to see a planner once you realize just how much you are spending on coffee, lunches, cable, cell phones, etc. You also need to examine the service plans you have. Get rid of the Korean badminton and knitting channels. Stop playing Words with Friends, and searching for what Kim Kardashian is doing tonight, on your cell phone.

Suggestion #2

Set an example for your children. Show them what investing can do for them if they start earlier than you did. Offer to match part of their contribution to an IRA. Talk about a return on your investment! Johnny puts $200.00 in an IRA and you match it? That's a 100% return on his investment before he has earned the first dime on the money.

Suggestion #3

Sit down with an attorney. Make sure your will, durable power of attorney and health care proxy is in order. DO NOT PUT THEM IN A SAFETY DEPOSIT BOX! If you are not able to access your box, the documents allowing someone else to do so are worthless, if they have to get into the box to get them.

Suggestion #4

Use a good tax preparer. I do not answer questions for free. However, my tax clients are able to call me and ask questions as part of my tax service to them. A client took a distribution from a retirement account simply because the company he was leaving sent him the check, in June. The following March was too late to tell him to have the funds transferred to an IRA account. He had an early distribution. It cost him taxes, penalties, and worst of all, the lost investment opportunity of those funds in a tax deferred account for the next thirty years. If you drive by my office in August you can find me here. If you drive by most H&R Block offices in August you will see a sign saying, "See you in January" and "For assistance call 1-800-TOO-LATE".

Retirement is coming, whether you are prepared for it, or not. Next time you are served that Starbucks coffee by a sixty-something year old, ask yourself, "Is she here because she WANTS to be, or because she HAS to be?" Not everyone can retire at 55 with an eight million dollar portfolio. That does not mean that it is too late for you to start saving.

PART FOUR: RETIREES

First, let's dispense with the usual "I want to leave something for my children" garbage. You left them with an existence, an education, and the best guidance you could give them. They should be out of the house now, barring some unusual situation like special needs, illness or accident. It's nice to be able to help them, and your grandchildren, but, YOU COME FIRST now.

Covered call writing is a tool for making some extra money. It is risky. It is not intended to provide you with a monthly retirement income. At this point in your life the most important thing is to not outlive your money. There are numerous devices and advices out there to help you invest your money, conserve your money, and, in some cases, relieve you of your money.

You should have a fee based financial planner, a certified public accountant and an elder care attorney. It is probably best if you get recommendations from friends. Some professionals have been known to be in cahoots with other professionals in relieving people of their money. When it comes to your money, remember Ronald Reagan's détente rule with Russia, "Trust, but verify". If you give someone the power over your money, give someone totally unrelated the ability to keep an eye the first person. Many people who wind up stealing money over long periods start out only borrowing a little. Then they can't put it back, and they need a little more. Next month they will put it back. And so on.

Annuities are useful instruments. They are essentially insurance policies. You invest a certain amount today, and the annuity company will provide you with an income stream for a fixed period of time, or until you die. There are many features, so it is wise to discuss these with your CPA. Your financial planner may be receiving a commission from the annuity, so make sure the features of the plan are what are best for you. Some are what are known as "immediate pay annuities". These begin paying you a monthly sum immediately. Others begin paying when you reach a certain age, may only pay for ten or twenty years, and may have a death benefit. Do not let the range of features keep you from considering them. They may be appropriate for your particular needs. You do not need to pick only one. You may find one immediate pay annuity, and one or two deferred annuities better fit your needs.

Social Security may be part of your retirement. Delaying collection until the latest retirement age can increase your monthly benefit. Some retirees begin collecting as early as they can, just in case they don't live long enough to collect at a later age. The monthly difference can be substantial, and it changes every year. Make sure you have someone at the local Social Security office explain it carefully to you.

Enjoy your retirement. You have earned it.

CONCLUSION

There is no magic bullet. Investing is not a Ronco rotisserie, where you set it, and forget it. You must put some time into it. You need to educate yourself on various types of investments. The rules for stocks, bonds, futures, and options are not the same. The purpose for each of them is not the same. The people who invest in them are also not the same. Your option investing should be a small part of your investment portfolio.

You will also hear people discuss things like master limited partnerships, revocable trusts, insurance trusts, mutual funds, annuities, real estate investment trusts (REITS), etc. Each of these may, or may not, be appropriate for you. As you get older you should have less invested in stocks and more liquid in savings protected by the FDIC. This is because you have less time to recover from a market downturn, and more need to use the funds you have invested for your living expenses. Learn about them. Discuss them with a trusted professional to decide what is appropriate for you. However, no matter how much you trust someone, make sure you maintain control. Investing in a publicly traded mutual fund is not giving up control. You do not have control over the investments in the fund, but you have control over owning the fund.

There is an expression regarding the television pundits you see on television, like Jim Cramer, Suze Orman, etc. They call them talking heads, because you usually only see their heads, and they often contradict each other. They may have useful information, but it may not be useful for you. You can never know too much, but you can become confused by what you know. Research your investment. Decide if it meets your investing goals. If it does, buy it. If it doesn't, don't buy it, or if you already own it, get rid of it. No stock is a lifetime hold. If it no longer meets your needs, move on. Generally big losses started out as little losses. Don't wait until you have a big loss. There is a reason why AT&T is still here, and MCI is not.

I wish you all good luck with your investing.

Owen Sargent is a CPA, an attorney and a seasoned stock investor. He helped me develop the Ellman Calculator and is a frequent contributor to the BCI blog forum. If you are in need of a tax advisor I recommend Owen without hesitation:

osargentcpa@aol.com

What are Wash Sales and Wash Trading? Are they the Same Type of Transaction?

Covered call writing and put-selling involve the buying and selling of stocks and options. When executed in non-sheltered accounts, taxable events are created. Since the BCI community is populated with savvy investors, the topic of *wash sales* has come up frequently and some have used the term *wash trading* interchangeably with wash sales. This article will discuss the differences between the two terms.

Wash Sale

A wash sale loss is not deductible. A wash sale occurs when you sell a stock for a loss and, within thirty days before or after the trade, buy back the same stock or substantially the same stock (like an option). Stocks of one company are not considered substantially identical to those of another. For example, if you sell a stock for $35.00 for a loss and then buy a $35.00 call option on the same stock, you have a wash sale and cannot deduct the loss on the stock. In essence, the tax code considers the loss transaction and the purchase of the replacement security a "wash" so there aren't any deductible tax benefits to offset capital gains. **Wash sales apply only to losses**.

Wash sales also apply to options that are substantially identical.

Wash sales are not negated if you sell a stock in one account and buy it back in another or even in the account of your spouse. A tax loss is also disallowed if the stock was sold in a sheltered account and re-purchased in a non-sheltered account and vice-versa. The IRS has all bases covered!

What happens to the loss? All is not lost

The loss gets added to the basis of the replacement security so that when you sell, that disallowed loss either reduces the gain or enhances the loss. Also, the holding period of the wash sale is added to the holding period of the replacement security which increases the chances of qualifying for more favorable long-term tax rates.

Example when there is an equal amount of shares sold and re-purchased:

- 3/1/2015: Buy 100 x BCI at $3000.00
- 7/1/2015: Sell 100 x BCI at $2000.00 for a loss of $1000.00
- 7/10/2015: Buy 100 x BCI at $2200.00

In this example, the $1000.00 loss is disallowed but added to the cost basis of the replacement shares which becomes $3200.00

($2200.00 + $1000.00). The holding period of the disallowed loss (3/2/2015 – 7/1/2015) is added to that of the replacement shares. Had the purchase of the replacement shares taken place after the 30-day period, there would be no wash sale and the tax loss would be permitted.

****Wash sales apply to all investment accounts you own including those of your spouse.*

Wash Trade

Wash trading is an illegal process of repeatedly buying shares of stock from one broker and selling similar shares through a different broker. This leaves the impression of high volume activity despite the fact that the shares remained with the same owners. The purpose of doing this is to motivate other investors to buy shares of a stock that appears to be of great interest to the market. In essence, this is a form of price manipulation that US regulators are investigating especially as it relates to high-frequency traders.

Conclusion

The terms *wash sale* and *wash trade* are similar but have completely different connotations. The former relates to tax issues which impact retail investors and the latter to illegal price manipulation. Wash trading is one of the scams that should motivate retail investors to be extremely careful when it comes to buying and selling penny stocks which historically have been more susceptible to market manipulation.

Chapter 14

Portfolio Overwriting

Chapter outline

1. Portfolio Overwriting for Buy-And-Hold Portfolios

Portfolio Overwriting for Buy-And-Hold Portfolios

Covered call writing is a conservative strategy that encompasses a great deal of application flexibility. In my first three books and DVD Programs I have discussed the use of LEAPS as a stock surrogate, protective puts, the use of cash-secured puts to enter covered call trades at a discount and *portfolio overwriting*. In this article I will review the use of covered call writing as it relates to portfolio overwriting and present a more detailed approach than I have in the past. My motivation for writing this article is based on a number of requests from our members to provide more information on this topic so thank you for the suggestions and here we go.

Definition

Portfolio overwriting is a strategy we use to enhance the returns of a buy-and-hold portfolio. We sell out-of-the-money, one-month call options targeting a specific additional annualized return. For example, if we wanted to increase our portfolio annualized returns by six percent we would write calls that generated at least one half of one percent per month. The fact that we are writing out-of-the-money calls would also allow for share appreciation. In essence, we want additional income and do not want our shares sold. For some, share retention is for psychological reasons (you've become attached to your stock...almost like a family member!) but tax consequences due to a low cost basis is the major overriding concern. Of course, if you are trading in a sheltered account, there are no tax concerns and you can be more aggressive in your approach than detailed in this article.

Early exercise

Ninety nine percent of the time, exercise of a call option (your shares are purchased as per your option obligation) will not occur until the day after expiration Friday but there are rare exceptions of early exercise which I will address. First let me enumerate the reasons *why options are rarely exercised early*:

- A call holder can keep the cash in an interest-bearing account until the last minute rather than spend the money "early" prior to expiration Friday
- Early exercise is exposing the call buyer to greater risk as the cost of the shares is much greater than the cost of the option
- The most important reason is the loss of time value of the option. By exercising an in-the-money option, the holder is capturing intrinsic value only (the difference between current market price and strike price) but leaving time value on the table. The call buyer is usually much better off selling the option and ending up with a higher return

In the cases where early exercise does not occur and the strike is in-the-money (even by $0.01) we can roll the option (buy it back and then immediately sell the next month's option) prior to 4 PM ET on expiration Friday and avoid the sale of our low-cost basis stock. The most common exception to this rule relating to early exercise occurs when there is a *dividend distribution* from the underlying security (keep in mind that not all stocks distribute dividends but many high quality equities do). In these cases, early exercise is more likely when:

- The ex-dividend date (date you must own the shares in order to collect the dividend) is close to and prior to contract expiration
- The call strike price is in-the-money (lower than current market value of the stock)
- The dividend distribution amount is greater than the remaining time value of the option

How to avoid early exercise

The easiest way to circumvent this issue is to avoid selling options the four times per year when the ex-date is approaching until the day after that date. For example, if BCI's ex-dates are January1, April 1st, July 1st and October 1st, on those months we hold off on writing calls until the second day of those four months...problem solved. Granted the returns will be a bit lower those months but early exercise will most likely be avoided. The reason I say "most likely" is because there are some less sophisticated traders who may exercise early even though it will cost them money. It's the wrong move but may have an impact on us...this is rare and unlikely but possible. Here is a free link where ex-dates can be accessed:

http://www.dividendinvestor.com/

Figure 142 is a screenshot showing the ex-date for American Express (AXP):

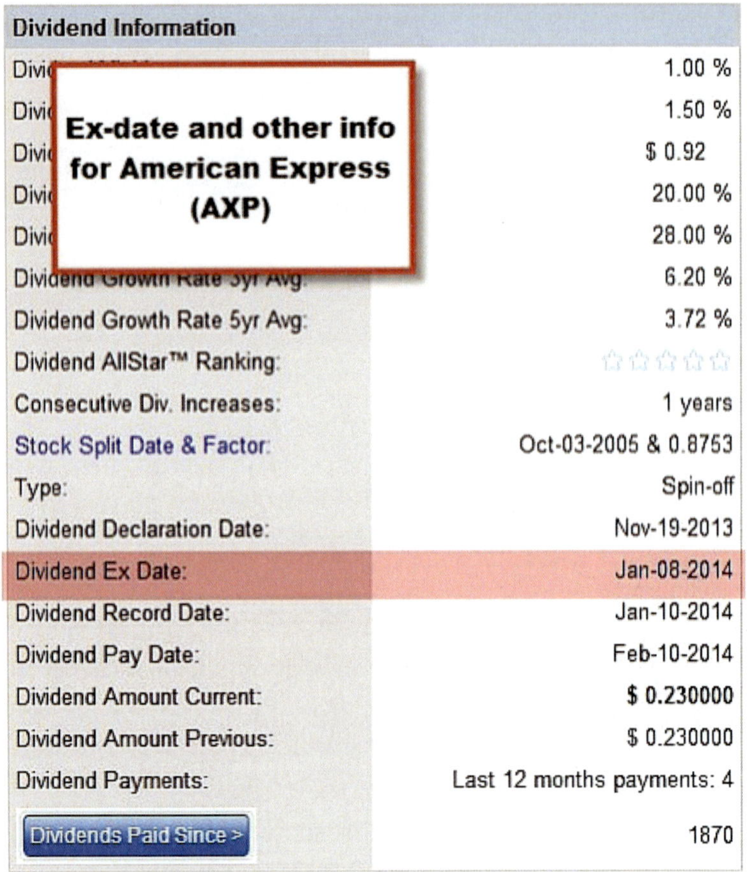

Dividend Information	
Divi	1.00 %
Divi	1.50 %
Divi	$ 0.92
Divi	20.00 %
Divi	28.00 %
Dividend Growth Rate 3yr Avg:	6.20 %
Dividend Growth Rate 5yr Avg:	3.72 %
Dividend AllStar™ Ranking:	
Consecutive Div. Increases:	1 years
Stock Split Date & Factor:	Oct-03-2005 & 0.8753
Type:	Spin-off
Dividend Declaration Date:	Nov-19-2013
Dividend Ex Date:	Jan-08-2014
Dividend Record Date:	Jan-10-2014
Dividend Pay Date:	Feb-10-2014
Dividend Amount Current:	**$ 0.230000**
Dividend Amount Previous:	$ 0.230000
Dividend Payments:	Last 12 months payments: 4
Dividends Paid Since >	1870

Figure 142- Ex-dividend Date for AXP

Another strategy that can be employed to minimize the risk of early assignment is to sell a two month option prior to the month of the ex-date. For example, after the December contracts expire and there is an ex-date on (for example) January 8th (as in Figure 142), sell the February contract rather than the January contract. This way the option holder is much less likely to consider early exercise because the time value of the option is much greater and there is a much greater exposure to share ownership because of the longer time frame. *As a guideline, if the ex-date is in the first week of a contract, sell that month's contract the day after that ex-date. If the ex-date is later in the contract, sell the next month's option (two month option) right after the previous expiration (February contract rather than the January contract in the AXP example in Figure 142).*

Summary so far:

Buy and hold portfolios, especially those with a low cost basis, can be enhanced using a conservative covered call writing strategy. It entails writing out-of-the-money calls based on our annualized goals. To avoid exercise, rolling strategies and avoidance of ex-dividend dates must be factored in. *It is also important to speak with your tax advisor should early exercise occur...it may not be a financial concern based on other investments in your portfolio.*

Step-by-step approach

Next I will walk you through the process of how this strategy can be accomplished. Keep in mind that there are many ways to approach any given strategy, this is one of them.

Assumptions

- We have a long-term buy and hold portfolio in a non-sheltered account with many securities having a low cost basis
- Our goal is for the portfolio to generate higher returns and at the same time avoid exercise and subsequent sale of the shares
- If the strike is in-the-money on or near expiration Friday we will roll the option (buy it back and sell the next month's option)
- During the four months when ex-dividend dates come up, we will hold off on selling the option until the ex-date passes or sell a two-month option
- We will set our goal to enhance our portfolio returns by six percent per year or one half of one percent per month in this example

Home Depot example

Let's have a look at Home Depot (HD) in Figure 143, a staple in many buy and hold portfolios, regarding its ex-dividend date:

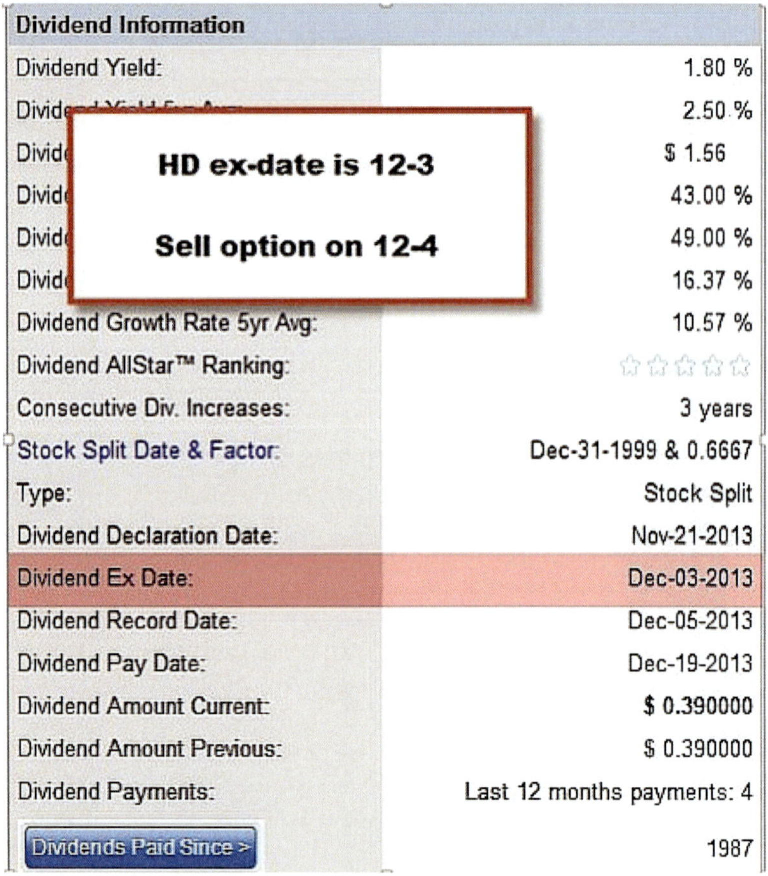

Figure 143- HD: Ex-Dividend Date

Selling a one-month option

I produced this screenshot (Figure 144) on November 29th, 2013 so I will wait through the weekend and sell the option early next week on December 4th. Our other choice would be to sell a two month option at the end of the November contracts (the Monday after the third Friday in November). Let's explore the first choice where we sold a one-month option the day after the ex-date:

Now with HD trading at $80.44 and a six percent increase in annualized returns as our goal, we will check an options chain for a one-month return of one half of one percent or about $0.40 for an out-of-the-money call option:

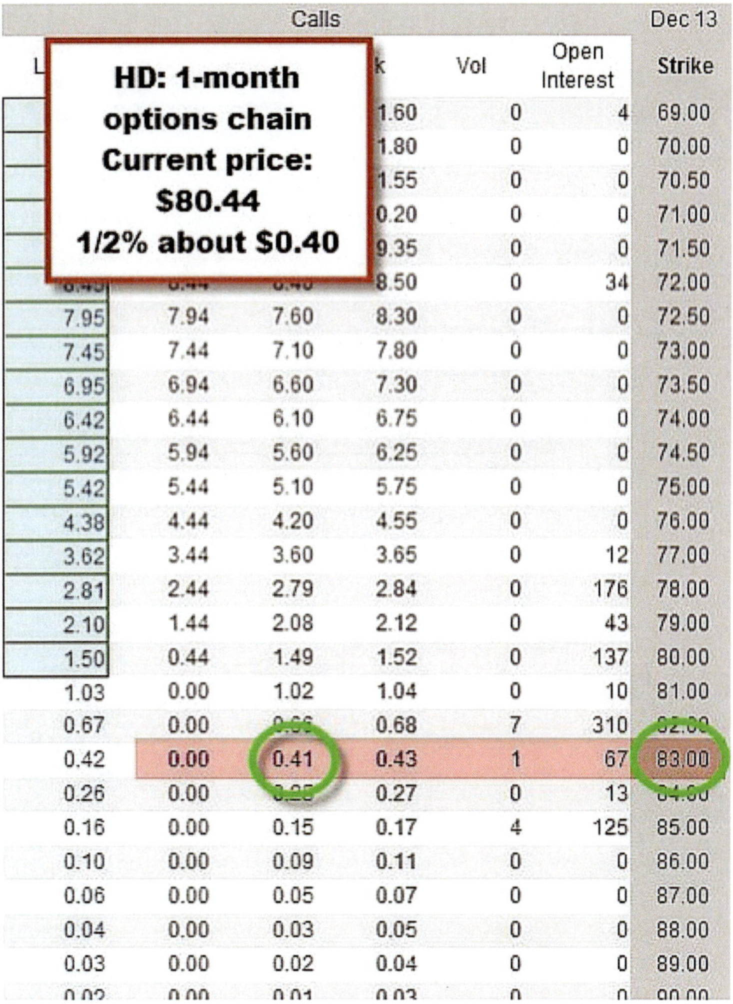

Calls						Dec 13
L[illegible]	[illegible]	[illegible]	[illegible]k	Vol	Open Interest	Strike
[illegible]	[illegible]	[illegible]	11.60	0	4	69.00
[illegible]	[illegible]	[illegible]	11.80	0	0	70.00
[illegible]	[illegible]	[illegible]	11.55	0	0	70.50
[illegible]	[illegible]	[illegible]	10.20	0	0	71.00
[illegible]	[illegible]	[illegible]	9.35	0	0	71.50
[illegible]	[illegible]	[illegible]	8.50	0	34	72.00
7.95	7.94	7.60	8.30	0	0	72.50
7.45	7.44	7.10	7.80	0	0	73.00
6.95	6.94	6.60	7.30	0	0	73.50
6.42	6.44	6.10	6.75	0	0	74.00
5.92	5.94	5.60	6.25	0	0	74.50
5.42	5.44	5.10	5.75	0	0	75.00
4.38	4.44	4.20	4.55	0	0	76.00
3.62	3.44	3.60	3.65	0	12	77.00
2.81	2.44	2.79	2.84	0	176	78.00
2.10	1.44	2.08	2.12	0	43	79.00
1.50	0.44	1.49	1.52	0	137	80.00
1.03	0.00	1.02	1.04	0	10	81.00
0.67	0.00	[illegible]	0.68	7	310	[illegible]
0.42	0.00	0.41	0.43	1	67	83.00
0.26	0.00	[illegible]	0.27	0	13	[illegible]
0.16	0.00	0.15	0.17	4	125	85.00
0.10	0.00	0.09	0.11	0	0	86.00
0.06	0.00	0.05	0.07	0	0	87.00
0.04	0.00	0.03	0.05	0	0	88.00
0.03	0.00	0.02	0.04	0	0	89.00
0.02	0.00	0.01	0.03	0	0	90.00

Figure 144- HD: One-Month Options Chain

The $83.00, out-of-the-money strike generates $0.41 or .051%, meeting our monthly goal. It also allows share appreciation up to the $83.00 strike or another 3.2% ($2.56/$80.44). If the price of the stock is above $83.00 by expiration, we can roll the option. Because we waited until December fourth to sell the option, early exercise as a result of the ex-date is highly unlikely.

Selling a two-month option

Next, let's explore our second choice where we sell a two-month option also significantly minimizing the risk of early assignment. Figure 145 is a screenshot for a two month options chain (actually seven weeks at the time I created this image) for HD:

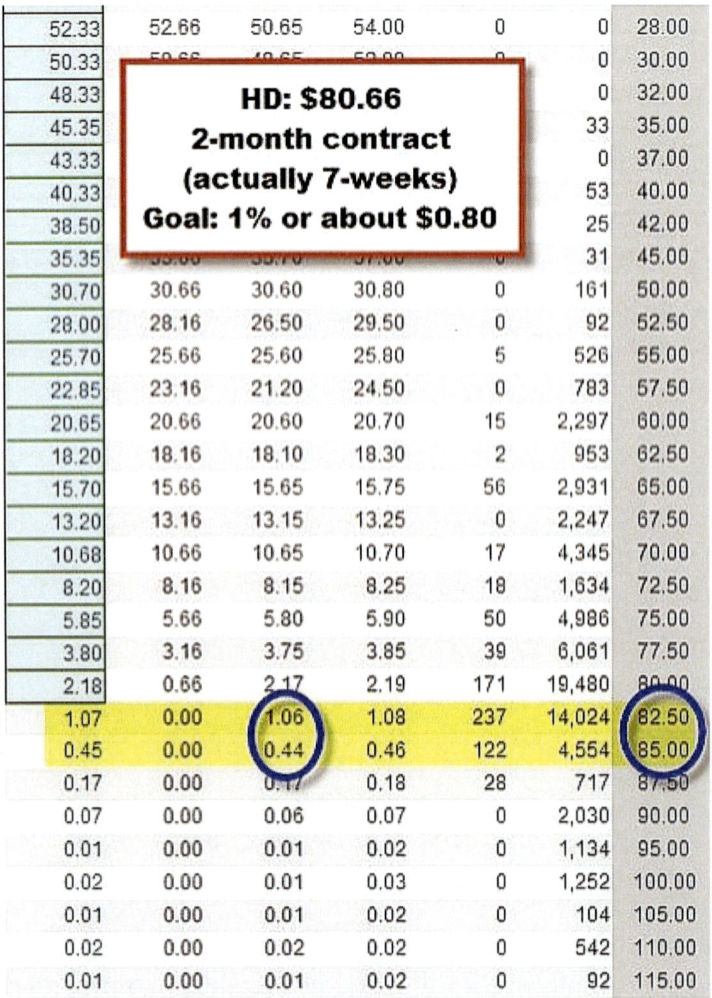

52.33	52.66	50.65	54.00	0	0	28.00
50.33	[illegible]	[illegible]	[illegible]	[illegible]	0	30.00
48.33	[illegible]	[illegible]	[illegible]	[illegible]	0	32.00
45.35	[illegible]	[illegible]	[illegible]	[illegible]	33	35.00
43.33	[illegible]	[illegible]	[illegible]	[illegible]	0	37.00
40.33	[illegible]	[illegible]	[illegible]	[illegible]	53	40.00
38.50	[illegible]	[illegible]	[illegible]	[illegible]	25	42.00
35.35	[illegible]	[illegible]	[illegible]	[illegible]	31	45.00
30.70	30.66	30.60	30.80	0	161	50.00
28.00	28.16	26.50	29.50	0	92	52.50
25.70	25.66	25.60	25.80	5	526	55.00
22.85	23.16	21.20	24.50	0	783	57.50
20.65	20.66	20.60	20.70	15	2,297	60.00
18.20	18.16	18.10	18.30	2	953	62.50
15.70	15.66	15.65	15.75	56	2,931	65.00
13.20	13.16	13.15	13.25	0	2,247	67.50
10.68	10.66	10.65	10.70	17	4,345	70.00
8.20	8.16	8.15	8.25	18	1,634	72.50
5.85	5.66	5.80	5.90	50	4,986	75.00
3.80	3.16	3.75	3.85	39	6,061	77.50
2.18	0.66	2.17	2.19	171	19,480	80.00
1.07	0.00	1.06	1.08	237	14,024	82.50
0.45	0.00	0.44	0.46	122	4,554	85.00
0.17	0.00	0.17	0.18	28	717	87.50
0.07	0.00	0.06	0.07	0	2,030	90.00
0.01	0.00	0.01	0.02	0	1,134	95.00
0.02	0.00	0.01	0.03	0	1,252	100.00
0.01	0.00	0.01	0.02	0	104	105.00
0.02	0.00	0.02	0.02	0	542	110.00
0.01	0.00	0.01	0.02	0	92	115.00

Figure 145- HD: Two-Month Options Chain

Please note the following:

- Our two-month goal is now one percent because our annualized goal is six percent
- With the shares trading at $80.66, our goal is about $0.80
- Our two closest choices are the $82.50 strike ($1.06) and the $85.00 strike ($0.44)
- If I were dealing with multiple contracts I would do half of each, averaging out to just under the one percent goal
- If I had only one contract I would favor the $85.00 strike in normal market conditions, take a lower return and allow for greater share appreciation while minimizing the chance of needing to roll the option. In a bear market environment, I would favor the $82.50 strike
- Not every month has a choice of the same strike prices... there is no $83.00 choice as there was last month

A general risk regarding covered call writing:

The strike price limits our profit potential. Most of our members reading this article already know this but I am including it in this article for those completely new to covered call writing. If a stock dramatically goes up in value, a covered call writer will not partake in any share appreciation above the strike price prior to expiration. This is the reason we are generating modest monthly returns and selling strike prices above current market value thereby having the opportunity to generate two income streams each month.

Summary

Portfolio overwriting is a low-risk (but not no-risk) way of enhancing portfolio value as long as we understand how to circumvent the issue of early exercise. Since dividend distribution is the main reason for early exercise, selling the option after the ex-date or writing a two month call option prior to the month of the ex-date will usually avoid this issue.

Chapter 15

Covered Calls and LEAPS

Chapter outline

1. LEAPS as Stock Surrogates and Covered Call Writing

LEAPS As Stock Surrogates and Covered Call Writing

LEAPS are long-term options with expirations usually greater than one year. Some investors buy LEAPS instead of stocks to then write covered calls on this leveraged type of security. This is related to, but not precisely the same, as traditional covered call writing. The best term to describe this strategy is referred to as a *calendar spread* where you simultaneously establish long and short options positions on the same underlying stock with different expiration dates.

Strategy construction

- Buy deep-in-the-money LEAPS for company BCI
- Sell near-term (I prefer one-month) options
- Construct such that, if exercised, the difference between the strikes plus the premium collected is greater than the cost of the LEAPS option
- If unassigned, continue to write short term call options

Traditional calculations for maximum returns

- Buy BCI at $35.00
- Sell the $37.50 near-term call at $1.50
- Maximum profit if BCI closes at or above $37.50 at expiration
- $150.00 (option premium per contract) plus $250.00 (stock appreciation from $35.00 to $37.50) equals $400.00, our maximum profit
- $400.00/$3500.00 equals an 11.4%, one month return

LEAPS calculations for maximum returns

- BCI is trading at $35.00
- Buy $25.00 in-the-money LEAPS for BCI at $10.00
- Sell one-month $37.50 calls at $1.50
- Maximum profit if BCI closes at or above $37.50
- $150.00 (options premium) plus $1250.00 (difference between strikes) minus $1000.00 (cost of one LEAPS contract) equals $400.00
- $400.00/$1000.00 = 40%

Traditional calculations if stock closes at $30.00

- Unrealized stock loss of $5.00 from share depreciation
- Profit of $1.50 from sale of option
- Loss of $350.00 per contract
- $350.00/$3500.00 equals a 10% loss

LEAPS calculations if stock closes at $30.00

- LEAPS value declines by $5.00 (intrinsic value)
- Option profit equals $1.50
- $350.00/$1000.00 = 35% unrealized loss (less any time value remaining on LEAPS)

Advantages of a LEAPS strategy

- Lower cost basis leads to higher return on investment (ROI)
- Pay no interest compared to leveraging via margin accounts (interest rates can also increase)
- Less likely to panic and close out a declining stock since the maximum loss is the cost of LEAPS minus option premium
- Ties up less capital
- Less downside risk

Disadvantages of a LEAPS strategy

- Deep, in-the-money LEAPS oftentimes have wide bid-ask spreads leading to unfavorable price executions
- Long-term commitment may be a negative especially if there is a high cost to close early
- If a LEAPS option is bought after a stock price decline, the cost may be high due to the inverse volatility effect (much like the VIX I have written about)
- LEAPS lose value as expiration approaches and are eventually worthless

- Generate no dividends as a LEAPS holder (but may get a cheaper price on the option buy due to this factor)
- Variability of returns: LEAPS do not behave precisely as stocks do because delta is not exactly "1" and they have a "gamma" The exact return is a range, not a precise figure

Summary

There are many ways to generate profits in the stock market and using LEAPS as stock surrogates when using a covered call writing-like strategy is one of them. This strategy is a bit more complicated than traditional covered call writing (my personal preference) and has its pros and cons. Each aspect of the strategy should be mastered before considering risking your hard-earned money employing it.

Chapter 16

Margin Accounts

Chapter outline

1. Portfolio Margining
2. Types of Brokerage Accounts

Portfolio Margining

Covered call writing and selling cash-secured puts are conservative strategies for risk-averse retail investors. This is why I feel most of us should be trading in cash accounts (no borrowing) and sheltered accounts whenever possible. For those of us who have higher risk-tolerance and are experienced investors looking for higher returns, margin accounts may be appropriate.

What is a margin account?

A *margin account* is a brokerage account where the broker lends money to the investor to purchase stocks or exchange-traded funds. The loan is secured by account stocks and cash. The investor may be required to deposit additional cash or sell some shares should the stock prices decline. By using borrowing as leverage, gains and losses are magnified. Let's have a look at margin requirements under traditional and more recent Securities and Exchange Commission's

(SEC) requirements:

Regulation T or Reg T

This is the Federal Reserve Board's regulation that governs the amount of credit a broker may extend to its clients for the purchase of stocks or exchange-traded funds. According to *Regulation T*, we may borrow up to fifty percent of the purchase price of these securities. This is known as *initial margin*. The New York and Nasdaq Stock Exchanges also require a minimum margin of $2,000.00 or the full cost of the purchase, whichever is less. A *maintenance margin* of at least twenty five percent of the total market value of the securities is required at all times, not just when purchased. Many broker-dealers require higher-than-minimum initial and maintenance margins. Figure 146 is a graphic depiction of initial margin requirements.

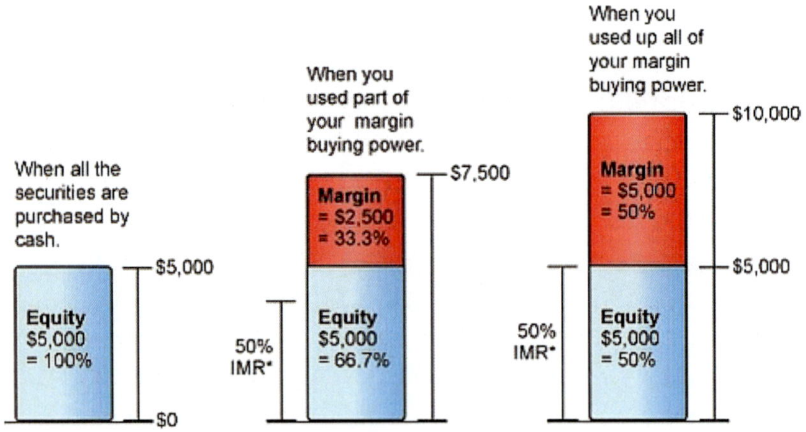

Figure 146- Initial Margin Requirements

Portfolio margining explained

Under SEC-approved Portfolio Margin rules, certain customers can increase the leverage beyond Regulation T requirements. The way it works is that highly correlated securities can be offset against each other when calculating margin requirements. For example, if a stock is purchased along with a protective put, Regulation T rules would require a deposit of fifty percent of the value of the stock plus one hundred percent of the purchase price of the put. However, when portfolio margining is used for the calculations, the decrease in overall portfolio risk would also result in a lower margin requirement.

With portfolio margining, margin requirements are accomplished utilizing a risk-based pricing model that calculates the largest possible loss for each position. This model is known as the *Theoretical Intermarket Margining System (TIMS)*. Each night, the *Options Clearing Corporation* uses this model to distribute TIMS parameter-requirements information to participating brokerage firms. The specific requirement per portfolio will reflect the actual risk of the positions in the account and may be higher or lower than the traditional Regulation T requirements.

Who is eligible for portfolio-based margining?

Not every investor is eligible for margining and requirements are broker-based usually requiring a certain minimum amount of cash in the account, a certain net worth and a minimum level of trading experience. Check with your broker for the specifics of your situation.

Goal of portfolio margining

In the end, the margin requirement will be based on the specific risk and trading strategy of our portfolios and will allow us to be margined in a way similar to professional traders. Let me re-emphasize that, in my humble opinion, **most of us should be trading in cash accounts**.

Types of Brokerage Accounts

There are three types of brokerage accounts: cash, margin and option:

- In a cash account, the client must pay in full and by the settlement date, the amount due on any transaction. All money and securities in a cash account are wholly owned by the client and entirely held in her name. This is the type of account I recommend as you initiate your investment career.
- A margin account allows the client to borrow money or securities from the broker-dealer in order to gain greater leverage on her transactions - that is, to buy as much as double what she could with a cash account. Before the account is activated, the client must sign a ***hypothecation agreement*** (applies to securities in a margin account used as collateral for money loaned from a brokerage). The broker-dealer must document that the client has been informed of all risks associated with trading on margin. A margin account must have at least $2,000.00 in invested capital; a day trader's margin account must have at least $25,000.00.
- An option account is a margin account approved by the broker-dealer for trading on the CBOE. The client will get such approval only if the broker-dealer determines that there is adequate equity in the account, that the client has adequate net worth and that the client is sophisticated enough to invest prudently in the riskier realm of options trading. A more detailed risk disclosure statement is required.

Most brokerages allow covered call writing in tax-sheltered accounts and therefore in cash accounts. Most other option strategies will require option accounts based on the level of trading approval received from the brokerage.

THE BLUE COLLAR INVESTOR

Chapter 17

Selling Naked or Cash-Secured Puts vs. Covered Call Writing

Chapter outline

1. Calculating Protective Puts: The Collar Strategy
2. Comparing Covered Call Writing and Put Selling in Bear Markets
3. Comparing Covered Call Writing and Put Selling in Bull Markets
4. Covered Call Writing with Protective Puts: A Proposed Strategy
5. Covered Combinations: Merging Covered Call Writing and Put-Selling into One Strategy
6. Covered Puts versus Covered Calls
7. Selling Cash-Secured Puts instead of Placing Limit Orders
8. Using Cash-Secured Puts to Enter a Covered Call Trade at a Discount

Calculating Protective Puts: The Collar Strategy

Covered call exit strategies play a major role in mitigating losses in our BCI methodology. In most cases, we can keep losses to a minimum, turn losses into gains and enhance profits as well. Some covered call writers want the security of protecting against a catastrophic gap-down which can occur rarely. This can be accomplished by purchasing a *protective put* in what is known as the *collar strategy*. Here's how it works:

Creating a collar

- Buy a stock
- Sell an out-of-the-money call option (strike higher than current market value)
- Buy an out-of-the-money put option (strike lower than current market value)

Goals of this strategy

- Generate cash flow
- Protect against catastrophic price decline in the underlying security (advantage)

Disadvantages

- Lower returns due to the cost of the put
- Managing three positions instead of two (call, put and stock positions)

Real-life example

In this article we will calculate the hypothetical returns using no puts in one case and evaluating three different put strike prices for implementing the collar strategy with protective puts. I am using

Facebook, Inc. (FB) in this example as it has been appearing in our Premium Watch Lists for several months, has decent returns and several choices of strike prices. Here are the stats at the time I am writing this article:

Facebook Stats on 3/11/2014

- Current price is $71.98
- Call strike selected is $72.50
- Put strikes to evaluate: $70.00, $68.00 and $66.00

FB options chain (Figure 147)

FB: $71.98

CALLS

PUTS

10.80	10.48	10.55	11.05					0.00	0.29	0.35	0	29
10.35	9.97	10.10	10.60					0.00	0.35	0.39	0	6
9.85	9.47	9.65	10.05					0.00	[illegible]			206
9.50	8.97	9.30	9.70					0.00	[illegible]			0
9.05	8.47	8.85	9.25	[illegible]	[illegible]	[illegible]	[illegible]	0.00	[illegible]			42
8.60	7.97	8.40	8.80	0	33	64.00	0.59	0.00	[illegible]	[illegible]	[illegible]	24
8.18	7.47	8.00	8.35	0	34	64.50	0.66	0.00	0.64	0.68	0	0
7.75	6.97	7.55	7.95	5	135	65.00	0.74	0.00	0.72	0.76	173	296
7.35	6.47	[illegible]	[illegible]	[illegible]	22	65.50	0.82	0.00	0.80	0.85	3	2
6.95	5.97			[illegible]	13	66.00	0.93	0.00	0.91	0.94	60	650
6.58	5.47			[illegible]	25	66.50	1.04	0.00	1.01	1.06	11	82
6.15	4.97	6.00	6.30	0	47	67.00	1.16	0.00	1.14	1.18	67	399
5.78	4.47	5.70	5.85	0	192	67.50	1.29	0.00	1.27	1.31	1	99
5.45	3.97	5.35	5.55	0	69	68.00	1.44	0.00	1.41	1.46	0	1,037
5.12	3.47	5.05	5.20	0	144	68.50	1.59	0.00	1.57	1.61	17	397
4.75	2.97	4.70	4.80	1	59	69.00	1.76	0.00	1.74	1.78	0	683
4.45	2.47	4.40	4.50	4	87	69.50	1.94	0.00	1.92	1.96	7	32
4.15	1.97	4.10	4.20	25	447	70.00	2.13	0.00	2.11	2.16	5	199
3.85	1.47	3.80	3.90	0	372	70.50	2.34	0.00	2.32	2.37	5	84
3.60	0.97	3.55	3.65	0	1,058	71.00	2.57	0.00	2.55	2.59	10	162
3.30	0.47	3.25	3.35	0	254	71.50	2.80	0.00	2.77	2.83	0	115
3.05	0.00	3.00	3.10	145	595	72.00	3.05	0.03	3.00	3.10	0	45
2.82	0.00	2.80	2.84	0	508	72.50	3.33	0.53	3.30	3.35	0	82
2.60	0.00	2.58	2.62	0	517	73.00	3.60	1.03	3.55	3.65	10	40
2.40	0.00	2.37	2.42	4	189	73.50	3.90	1.53	3.85	3.95	0	6
2.20	0.00	2.18	2.22	10	254	74.00	4.20	2.03	4.15	4.25	15	18
2.02	0.00	2.00	2.05	10	55	74.50	4.50	2.53	4.45	4.55	0	27
1.85	0.00	1.83	1.87	24	1,752	75.00	4.85	3.03	4.80	4.90	19	235

Figure 147- FB Options Chain as of 3-11-14

We glean the following stats from this options chain

- Short call generates $2.80

- $70.00 put costs $2.16
- $68.00 put costs $1.46
- $66.00 put costs $0.94

The protective put gives us the right to sell at the strike price so the higher the strike, the greater the protection and the more expensive the put. To determine our initial profit (ROO), we subtract the cost of the put from the cash generated from the sale of the call option ($2.80) and divide by our cost basis of $7198.00 per contract. The call premium must always be greater than the cost of the put so as to create an initial net credit. From there, we can calculate returns if the share price moves above the call strike or moves below the put strikes. We will make the assumption that if no put is purchased, BCI members will employ our arsenal of exit strategies to manage our positions to maximum profits or minimum losses. Such strategies start with buying back the option and frequently using our 20%/10% guidelines as detailed in my books and DVDs. Next the calculations as shown in Figure 148:

Spreadsheet using protective puts versus exit strategy management only

FB PRICE	SellPut?	Call Strike	Call $	PUT STRIKE	PUT $	NET $	ROO	> CALL STRIKE	< PUT STRIKE
71.98	N	72.5	2.8	NA	NA	2.8	3.90%	4.60%	USE EXIT STRATEGIES
71.98	Y	72.5	2.8	70	2.16	0.64	0.90%	1.60%	(-)1.9%
71.98	Y	72.5	2.8	68	1.46	1.34	1.86%	2.60%	(-)3.7%
71.98	Y	72.5	2.8	66	0.94	1.86	2.60%	3.60%	(-)5.7%

Mathematics of protective puts

Figure 148- Calculations with and without Protective Puts

It is impossible to make specific final determinations using the information provided in this hypothetical because so much depends on the skill of the investor in terms of using position management techniques when indicated as well as the amount of price decline if the put is needed. But certain generalizations of interest can be made:

Conclusions

- The initial return not using protective puts is significantly higher than when using them (ROO column)
- If the share price closes above the call strike price (> call strike column), not buying a put produces the best results (4.60%)
- If the share price closes below the put strike (< put strike column), the smallest losses occur for the higher strike put prices but all still result in losses
- Position management can also be used in the collar strategy but is more involved and may require more time because the investor is in three, rather than two positions

Comparing Covered Call Writing and Put Selling in Bear Markets

Our stock options strategies, whether writing covered calls or selling cash-secured puts require us to make an overall market assessment before entering any trades. In this article we will examine bear market environments. When selling covered calls we would favor in-the-money strikes to gain additional downside protection should share price decline. When selling cash-secured puts, we would favor selling deeper out-of-the money puts (lower than the current market value of the stock). In this article I will use the options chain for Facebook, Inc. to demonstrate the calculations for potential covered call writing and put-selling trades. Figure 149 reflects the FB options chain from May, 2014:

24.85	24.84	24.60	25.10	0	334	36.00	0.05	0.00	0.02	0.07	0	597
23.90	23.84	23.70	24.10	0	105	37.00	0.06	0.00	0.03	0.08	0	11,209
22.90	22.84	22.70	23.10	0	325	38.00	0.07	0.00	0.04	0.09	0	2,701
21.93	21.84	21.75	22.10	0	144	39.00	0.08	0.00	0.05	0.10	0	1,325
20.95	20.84	20.75	21.15	0	1,289	40.00	0.08	0.00	0.06	0.10	0	5,635
19.95	19.84	19.75	20.15	0	225	41.00	0.09	0.00	0.07	0.10	0	2,148
18.98	18.84	18.75	19.20	0	473	42.00	0.11	0.00	0.08	0.13	0	3,276
17.93	17.84	17.80	18.05	30	647	43.00	0.12	0.00	0.10	0.15	0	5,009
17.02	16.84	16.80	17.25	5	1,618	44.00	0.15	0.00	0.13	0.17	6	2,584
16.05	15.84	15.85	16.25	9	1,336	45.00	0.18	0.00	0.17	0.19	263	35,965
15.10	14.84	14.90	15.30	0	381	46.00	0.23	0.00	0.22	0.23	8	2,391
14.15	13.84	13.95	14.35	0	1,040	47.00	0.27	0.00	0.26	0.28	15	2,926
13.22	12.84	13.00	13.45	0	712	48.00	0.34	0.00	0.33	0.34	6	2,662
12.30	11.84	12.10	12.50	2	614	49.00	0.41	0.00	0.40	0.42	8	3,999
11.40	10.84	11.20	11.60	142	6,528	50.00	0.51	0.00	0.50	0.51	156	16,037
9.18	8.34	9.05	9.30	43	23,452	52.50	0.84	0.00	0.84	0.85	208	15,387
7.20	5.84	7.10	7.30	954	9,973	55.00	1.38	0.00	1.37	1.38	612	17,020
5.50	3.34	5.45	5.55	290	8,646	57.50	2.14	0.00	2.13	2.15	1,034	12,897
4.03	0.84	4.00	4.05	1,412	36,133	60.00	3.17	0.00	3.15	3.20	951	25,303
2.84	0.00	2.83	2.85	1,319	46,598	62.50	4.47	1.68	4.45	4.50	89	6,431
1.94	0.00	1.94	1.95	4,911	43,649	65.00	6.10	4.18	6.05	6.15	70	10,590
1.29	0.00	1.28	1.29	521	29,743	67.50	7.95	6.68	7.90	8.00	13	4,552
			0.85	300	38,908	70.00	10.03	9.18	9.90	10.15	0	6,645
			0.56	298	15,062	72.50	12.18	11.68	12.00	12.35	0	1,635
			0.37	63	27,454	75.00	14.50	14.18	14.30	14.70	0	1,489
			0.24	98	5,518	77.50	16.88	16.68	16.70	17.05	0	430

FB trading @ $60.84

Figure 149- Calls and Puts in Bear Market Environments: Facebook Options Chain

Bear market trade and calculations for covered call writing

We favor in-the-money strikes (ITM) which will generate time value returns that meet our goals along with downside protection of the option profit (different from breakeven). The deeper in-the-money we go, the greater our protection. With FB trading at $60.84, we will view the $57.50 in-the-money strike (highlighted in pink on the left side of the screenshot):

- Call premium = $5.45
- Intrinsic value of the premium is $3.34 (amount the $57.50 is in-the-money)

- Time value of the premium is \$2.11 (\$5.45 - \$3.34)
- Initial profit is \$211.00/\$5750.00 per contract or 3.7% (the intrinsic value "buys down" our cost basis to the strike price)
- Annualized return is 31%
- Downside protection of the 3.7% is \$3.34/\$60.84 or 5.5%
- This means that we are guaranteed a six-week return of 3.7% as long as share value does not decline by more than 5.5% by expiration Friday
- Breakeven is \$60.84 – \$5.45 = \$55.39

Bear market trade and calculations for selling cash-secured puts

We favor deeper out-of-the-money strikes which will generate more protection against share decline and less likelihood for share assignment (shares "put" or sold to us). The deeper out-of-the-money we go, the greater our protection. With FB trading at \$60.84, we will view the \$57.50 out-of-the-money strike (highlighted in pink on the right side of the screenshot). Note that we are using the same strike as shown for writing calls where the \$57.50 strike is considered in-the-money. For selling puts, that same strike is considered out-of-the-money:

- Put premium = \$2.13
- Initial profit = \$213.00/\$5537.00 per contract or 3.8% (put premium decreases our cost basis)
- Annualized return = 33%
- Downside protection of the 3.8% = \$3.34/\$60.84 = 5.5%

- This means that we are guaranteed a six-week return of 3.8% as long as share value does not decline by more than 5.5% by expiration Friday (called unexercised return)
- Breakeven is $57.50 – $2.13 or $55.37

Summary

In bear market environments we favor in-the-money call options for covered call writing and deeper out-of-the-money put options when selling cash-secured puts. The returns will be similar when utilizing a similar amount in- and out-of-the-money.

Comparing Covered Call Writing and Put-Selling in Bull Markets

Covered call writing or put-selling? In-the-money or out-of-the-money strikes? When we view an options chain there are some basic principles we must factor into our final covered call writing or put-selling decisions. First, which of these two strategies is most appropriate? Unfortunately, there is no one answer that is right for every investor. I prefer covered call writing (but use both) which is a product of the success I've enjoyed using that strategy over the past two decades. Others, favor selling cash-secured puts. When I do use put-selling, it is because I have a bearish market outlook and slightly favor put-selling in those environments. Both are great strategies that can be tailored to meet our overall market assessment and personal risk tolerances.

Once a strategy is selected, we must next choose a strike price. In both strategies, this choice is based on the following factors:

- Overall market assessment

- Chart technicals
- Personal risk tolerance

In other words, are we bullish or bearish about the market in general and the stock in particular? In the previous article I discussed a bear market scenario. In this segment I will use a bull market situation and highlight the options chain for Michael Kors Holdings Ltd (NYSE: KORS). In this example, I will show potential trade selections for both strategies. Finally, I will show the calculations for these trades which will demonstrate to us if these results meet our monthly goals. *Please note that we are showing six-week returns, so to annualize we multiply by 8.5.*

Note: Article taken from my book, *Selling Cash-Secured Puts*.

Options chain for KORS Holdings Ltd. as of May, 4, 2014- Figure 150):

Calls						Jun 14	Puts					
Last	Intrinsic Value	Bid	Ask	Vol	Open Interest	Strike	Last	Intrinsic Value	Bid	Ask	Vol	Open interest
24.00	23.90	22.70	25.30	0	5	70.00	0.20	0.00	0.15	0.25	0	238
19.25	18.90	18.00	20.50	0	1	75.00	0.42	0.00	0.35	0.50	3	248
14.90	13.90	14.00	15.80	3	12	80.00	0.88	0.00	0.80	0.95	10	1,160
12.70	11.40	12.20	13.20	0	10	82.50	1.25	0.00	1.20	1.30	21	216
10.70	8.90	10.20	11.20	0	39	85.00	1.75	0.00	1.70	1.80	12	1,022
8.80	6.40	8.60	9.00	2	65	87.50	2.38	0.00	2.3	2.45	4	197
7.10	3.90	7.00	7.20	24	220	90.00	3.20	0.00	3.10	3.30	15	89
5.60	1.40	5.50	5.70	62	313	92.50	4.20	0.00	4.10	4.30	17	69
4.35	0.00	4.20	4.50	59	141	95.00	5.40	1.10	5.30	5.50	3	35
3.30	0.00	3.20	3.40	93	75	97.50	6.85	3.60	6.7	7.00	0	32
2.40	0.00	2.30	2.50	23	746	100.00	8.50	6.10	8.40	8.60	10	89
1.23	0.00	1.15	1.30	0	299	105.00	12.35	11.10	11.90	12.80	0	0
		0	0.65	0	364	110.00	16.80	16.10	15.60	18.00	0	0
		0	0.30	0	4	115.00	21.50	21.10	20.20	22.80	0	0
		5	0.15	0	5	120.00	26.30	26.10	25.00	27.60	0	0

KORS trading @ $93.90

Figure 150- Call and Put Options Chain for KORS

In the pink-highlighted row I show strikes we may consider in bear markets. We will now focus in on the yellow -highlighted rows which are most appropriate for bull market environments.

Bull market trade and calculations for covered call writing

We favor out-of-the-money strikes which will generate time value returns that meet our goals along with upside potential from share appreciation moving from the purchase price up to the strike price. The deeper out-of-the-money we go, the greater our upside potential but the lower the initial time value profit. With KORS trading at $93.90, we will view the $97.50 out-of-the-money strike (left side of screenshot):

- Call premium is $3.20
- Upside potential from $93.90 to $97.50 is $3.60
- Time value of the premium equals $3.20 (at-the-money and out-of-the-money calls are entirely time value)
- Initial profit equals $320.00/$9390.00 per contract or 3.4%
- Annualized return equals 29%
- Upside potential is $3.60/$93.90 or 3.8%
- Maximum six-week return is 3.4% plus 3.8% equals 7.2% or 61% annualized
- Breakeven is $93.90 – $3.20 or $90.70

Bull market trade and calculations for selling cash-secured puts

We favor slightly out-of-the-money strikes as well as at-the-money and slightly in-the-money strikes which will generate higher initial returns than deeper out-of-the-money strikes. We do this to take advantage of the bull market environment to generate the highest possible returns while still having capital preservation in mind. With KORS trading at $93.90, we will view the $95.00 slightly in-the-money strike:

- Put premium is $5.30
- Initial (unexercised) profit equals [$530.00/ ($9500.00 - $530.00)] per contract or 5.9%
- Annualized return is 50.2%
- Breakeven is $95.00 – $5.30 = $89.70

Summary

By incorporating overall market assessment, chart technicals, personal risk tolerance and calculation results we can make informed, non-emotional decisions as to which strategy and strike price will be most appropriate for our portfolios.

Covered Call Writing with Protective Puts: A Proposed Strategy

When protective puts are integrated into our covered call writing strategy it is known as the *collar strategy*. The covered call aspect of the trade generates cash flow and the protective put leg serves as an insurance policy against catastrophic share depreciation. Recently, one of our members shared with me a related strategy he had heard about and I thought I'd discuss it with the BCI community. On this site we never embrace or reject a strategy approach outright but rather evaluate it from a "pros and cons" perspective and then each of us can make an informed decision as to whether it should be integrated into our portfolios based on our personal risk-tolerance. Let's break this down the Blue Collar way:

The proposed strategy

- Select a stock or exchange-traded fund (ETF) with high

implied volatility (like GILD, BIIB, IBB)

- Underlying securities should be large-cap so option open interest is high and bid-ask spreads are tight
- Associated options should have Weeklys that generate greater than one percent weekly returns
- Go one to two strikes out-of-the-money for Weeklys
- Buy protective puts six months out
- Protective puts should be fifteen to twenty percent out-of-the-money (lower than current market value)
- Cost of puts should be no more than one month of covered call profits

Theoretical returns

- One percent per week for six months equals twenty six percent
- Cost of put is 26%/6 months = 4.3% (one month of covered call profits)
- Six-month theoretical return is 21.7%
- Annualized theoretical return calculates to 43.4%

GILD example

- Real-life price is $102.22
- $85.00, six-month put is 16.8% out-of-the-money
- Cost of $85.00 put is $4.30 (less than one-month of weekly premiums as shown below)
- The $104.00 Weekly call generates $1.25 which meets the 1% system criteria

Theoretical return per contract for GILD example if share price and premiums remain constant

[(26 x $125.00) – $430.00]/$10,222.00 = 27.6% = 55.2% annualized

Advantages of this strategy if assumptions can be achieved

The advantages of this strategy are clear. A huge annualized return can be realized based on certain assumptions like share price and short call premiums remaining constant during the six month time frame. We also have protection against catastrophic share loss below the $85.00 put strike. By selecting a six-month put, the monthly cost of this protection is decreased compared to buying a put each month. In addition to this, there is opportunity to generate additional profit if share price moves up to the strike of the short call.

Potential pitfalls and possible disadvantages of this strategy

Trading commissions

One of the disadvantages of Weeklys is that we have four to five times the amount of trading commissions compared to Monthlys. Assuming a reasonable fee of $10.00 per trade, that computes to $260.00 for the six-month time frame, assuming one-contract trades. Let's add $20.00 in commissions for the purchase of the shares and the put. Therefore, over the six-month time frame, the short calls must overcome a net debit of $430.00 + $280.00 = $710.00. This represents the cost of the put plus trading commissions.

When do we breakeven?

Based on a weekly premium of $125.00, we breakeven after six weeks. Keep in mind that we paid $102.22 for the shares and we are using a security with high implied volatility as defined by the proposed strategy. If share price declines (we must be prepared for this) we start losing money and we will not break even for six weeks if share price remains constant.

What about management techniques?

For traditional covered call writing we are managing two positions: the long stocks and the short calls. In the proposed strategy, we are also managing the long put position. The investor must be capable of managing all three positions. In addition to this, if share price moves above the short call strike, we must roll the option in order to retain share ownership. This will most likely impact our $125.00/week premium goal as the time value of a short call will decline as the strike moves deeper in-the-money. Rolling out and up may actually result in a short call debit. Rolling will also result in additional trading commissions further eroding the profits from a theoretical trade.

What about earnings reports?

Two times within the six month time frame, there will be an earnings announcement. I strongly believe that a short call should not be written during those two weeks, thereby decreasing returns from the theoretical stats we archived above. The strategy, however, does require us to retain the shares through these two earnings reports and that may result in a dramatic share decline if the report (s) is disappoint(s). Now it is true that we are protected below $85.00 because of the long put but there's a lot to lose between $102.22 and $85.00.

What about dividends?

Of the three securities mentioned, IBB does distribute a quarterly dividend. Although unlikely, there is the possibility of early exercise, when expiration occurs after the ex-dividend date. Should the shares be assigned because of the ex-date, new shares would have to be purchased at the current market value and who knows how this would impact our theoretical returns. There are ways to avoid early exercise resulting from ex-dates but that would involve sophisticated management skills and would not be guaranteed.

What is the basis for selecting the underlying security?

For traditional covered call writing (according to the BCI methodology) a stock or ETF is chosen based on three factors: fundamental and technical analysis as well as common sense principles like minimum trading volume and avoiding earnings reports. In this proposed strategy, it appears that the main criteria for selection are option returns and liquidity. Quantity seems to take precedence over quality.

What about the six-month time frame?

We enter a trade today because certain system criteria are met such as those mentioned at the top of this article. By undertaking a six-month obligation, we are making the assumption that those same positive factors will be in place for half a year. We should at least be prepared that this may not come to fruition as shown in Figure 151 where the green arrows show bullish price patterns and blue arrows highlight bearish price movement:

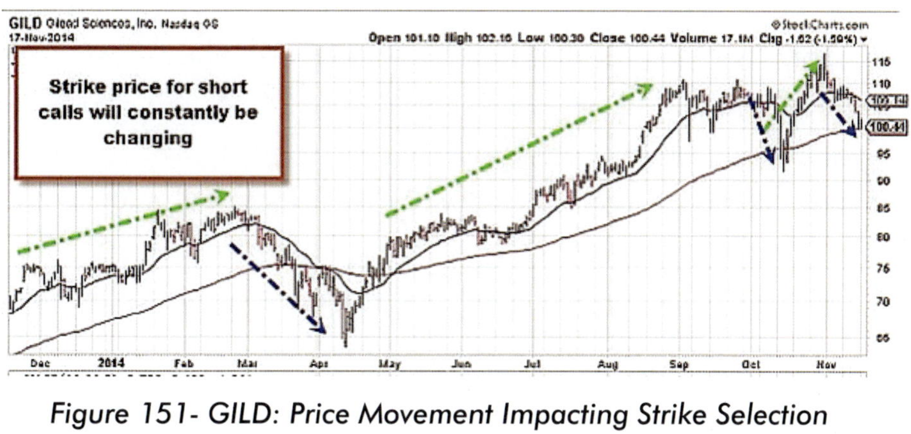

Figure 151- GILD: Price Movement Impacting Strike Selection

Discussion

There are many ways to make money in the stock and option markets. The proposed strategy may be one of those ways for certain investors. One key point is that there are no free lunches and every strategy has its advantages and disadvantages which must be evaluated before risking our hard-earned money.

Covered Combinations: Merging Covered Call Writing and Put-Selling into One Strategy

A Covered combination ("combo trade") trade is the simultaneous sale of an out-of-the-money (OTM) call and an out-of-the-money put with the same expiration date on one hundred shares of a stock or ETF (exchange-traded fund). It consists of a combination of a covered call and a short put position on a share-for-share basis. The investor generates two premiums from the sale of the call and the put, in exchange for taking on the risk of doubling his stock position should the price decline below the strike price of the put by the expiration date.

Recently, we have had several BCI members inquire about this strategy and that is the motivation for this article. This strategy is appropriate only for investors willing to hold long stock positions in two hundred share increments as this article will explain. The inspiration for using this strategy is to increase premium returns and to double a stock position half of which can be at a discount (if the put is exercised).

Hypothetical covered combination trade

- Buy one hundred shares of BCI at $52.00 per share for $5200.00
- Sell 1 x out-of-the-money $55.00 call at $1.75 (one-month expiration)
- Sell 1 x out-of-the-money $50.00 put at $1.50 (one-month expiration)
- Secure the $50.00 put sale with a deposit of $5000.00 into brokerage cash account (broker will usually allow us to deduct put premium thereby requiring a deposit of $4850.00)

Outcome if share price closes above $55.00 at expiration

This is the outcome that will maximize the returns:

- The put expires out-of-the-money and worthless
- The call is exercised and shares are sold at the $55.00 strike price
- No shares are owned after expiration
- Total option profit = $325.00 ($175.00 + $150.00)
- Stock profit = $300.00 (100 x $3.00) after buying at $52.00 and selling at $55.00
- Total profit = $625.00
- Cost basis is $5200.00 (buy 100 shares) + $4850.00 (to secure the put) = $10,050.00
- One-month percentage return = $625.00/$10,050.00 = 6.2%

Outcome if share price closes below $50.00 at expiration

This is the worst case scenario and may necessitate the implementation of exit strategy maneuvers:

- Net cost of 100 shares of BCI assigned from put = $50.00 – $3.25 (two premiums) = $46.75
- Still long 100 shares at a cost basis of $52.00
- Average cost basis of 200 shares = $49.38

Outcome if share price closes between $50.00 and $55.00 at expiration

- Both options expire out-of-the-money and worthless
- No option assignment
- Retain 100 shares originally purchased at $52.00
- Option one-month return = $325.00/$10,050.00 = 3.2%

Possible outcomes that are part of this strategy

- Obligation to sell 100 shares at $55.00
- Obligation to buy 100 shares at $50.00
- Double stock position on the downside
- Early assignment of the call is possible prior to an ex-dividend date
- Early assignment of deep in-the-money puts is possible if the time value approaches zero

Position management

BCI books, DVDs and blog articles have detailed exit strategy opportunities for both strategies and these should be utilized whenever indicated. The fact that covered combinations employ both strategies simultaneously does not eliminate the critical importance of position management to mitigate losses and enhance gains.

Discussion

I wrote this article in response to member inquiries. I am not necessarily encouraging the implementation of covered combinations but rather presenting an overview for those who are considering its use. There are many ways to make money in the stock and option markets and education is the tool that will maximize those returns.

Covered Puts versus Covered Calls

Covered call writing has been the main focus of the BCI methodology. Based on member demand and similarity of strategies we have been adding information on selling cash-secured puts, the topic of my fifth book. Recently I have received inquiries on related strategies that have led to some confusion specifically about *covered puts* so I decided to devote this article to that topic.

Defining the two strategies by formulas

Covered calls = Buy stock + sell call option = long stock + short option

Covered puts = Sell stock short (borrow shares from broker) + sell put option = short stock + short put option

Note: Selling cash-secured puts is a 3rd strategy that involves only a short put option position secured by enough cash to purchase the shares if the option is exercised.

Outlook for covered puts

A writer of covered puts has a slightly more bearish outlook than does the covered call writer as you will see as we calculate returns later in this article.

Hypothetical example of covered puts

Sell short 100 shares of BCI at $52.00 = $5200.00 cash generated into our brokerage account

Sell 1 x $50.00 out-of-the-money put for $1.50 = $150.00 cash generated into account

We now have two obligations: One is to buy the shares at $50.00 if the option holder chooses to exercise the put option and the other is to replace the one hundred borrowed shares.

Breakeven

$53.50- any move above $53.50 will result in a loss. At this price we will lose $150.00 replacing the shorted stock (sold at $52.00 and bought at $53.50) which is compensated for by the $150.00 put premium sale.

Maximum profit

$2 on the stock side ($52.00 – $50.00) for closing prices under $50.00 + **$1.50** from the put sale = **$3.50 per share** = $350.00 per contract.

No matter how low the share price moves, we purchase the shares at $50.00 due to our put obligation and this is why covered puts is a bearish strategy as we max our trade as share price declines and lose money if share price accelerates past the breakeven ($53.50 in this case).

Maximum loss

Technically, **unlimited as share price rises above $53.50, but $150.00 less than if the put was not sold and only the stock shorted**. This also assumes no position management, an unfair assumption for educated investors. Figure 152 depicts a covered put graph:

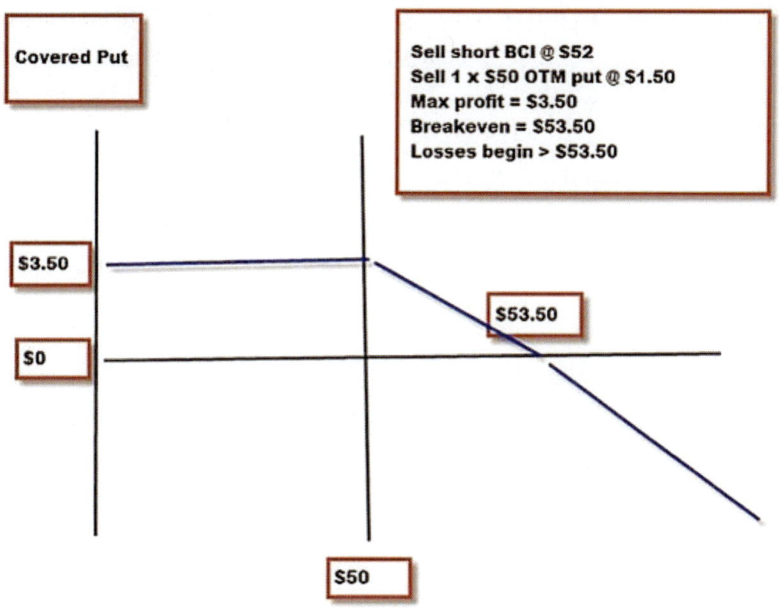

Figure 152- Covered Put Graph

Type of brokerage account required and level of trading approval needed

Since the strategy involves shorting a stock, margin accounts (not a cash account) are required with high levels of trading approval, much higher than that required for covered call writing.

Margin and interest

This will vary from broker-to-broker but a typical margin requirement of the short stock sale is 50% ($2600.00 in this case) and none on the options side. Since we are borrowing the stock from our broker, we will be required to pay interest on that loan and this should be calculated into our results.

Summary

Most strategies, if implemented and managed properly, can be profitable. For most retail investors, covered puts are not appropriate and should be considered only by experienced, sophisticated investors. **Covered puts and selling cash-secured puts are two completely different strategies**.

Selling Cash-Secured Puts Instead of Placing Limit Orders

Selling cash-secured puts is a strategy with goals of creating monthly cash flow while retaining capital preservation as a priority. However, many of our astute members are also using this strategy to purchase a stock "at a discount" instead of setting up limit order instructions to the broker. Before highlighting the strategy, let's review the key definitions.

Definitions

- Selling cash-secured puts: Giving the right, but not the obligation, to the option buyer to sell their shares to us at the strike price by the expiration date. In return for undertaking this obligation, we are paid the option premium.
- Limit order: An order instruction to our broker and placed by our brokerage to buy or sell a specified number of shares or contracts at a specific price or better. Length of time can also be indicated. In the case of buying a stock, we are agreeing to buy at the limit price or cheaper.
- Out-of-the-money put strike: The put strike, or price we agree to buy the shares for, is lower than the current market value of the underlying security

Real-life example

I am writing this article on 3/30/2015 with three weeks remaining on the April option contracts. I have selected Ambarella Inc. (NASDAQ: AMBA), a stock currently on our Premium Watch List. The price of the stock at the time was $70.35. We will make the assumption that we would like to own the stock but not at that price…$66.00 would be a great entry point in this hypothetical. A conventional approach to this scenario would be to place a limit order with our broker to buy at $66.00 or less. The advantage of this limit order is that we are controlling the price point we would enter the position. If the price point is not reached, no trade is executed and we still do not own the shares. The cash would need to be available if the trade was, in fact, executed.

Alternative approach using cash-secured puts

As an alternative to setting a limit order, we will sell a cash-secured put to accomplish the same goal but with an added perk…*we get paid if the trade is not executed*! Let's have a look at the options chain for AMBA prior to market open on 3/30/2015 (Figure 153):

67.00	1.88	0.00	1.70	2.05
67.50	2.05	0.00	1.85	2.25
68.00	2.25	0.00	2.05	2.45
68.50	2.50	0.00	2.25	2.75
69.00	2.88	0.00	2.45	3.30
69.50	3.05	0.00	2.70	3.40
70.00	3.20	0.00	2.90	3.50
70.50	3.55	0.15	3.20	3.90
71.00	3.75	0.65	3.40	4.10
71.50	4.05	1.15	3.70	4.40
72.00	4.60	1.65		
72.50	4.75	2.15		
73.00	5.05	2.65		
73.50	5.40	3.15		
74.00	5.85	3.65	5.40	6.30
74.50	6.25	4.15	5.70	6.80
75.00	6.70	4.65	6.10	7.30

AMBA: $70.35

Figure 153- AMBA Options Chain 3/30/2015

I have selected the out-of-the-money $68.00 put which generated a premium of $2.05 (perhaps higher by leveraging the Show or Fill Rule, but I will use the published bid). Let's enter this information into the BCI Put Calculator (Figure 154):

THE BCI SYSTEM PUT-SELLING CALCULATOR (ver. 1.0)

TRADE DATE (mm/dd/yyyy)		03/30/15	
STOCK SYMBOL		AMBA	
CURRENT PRICE ($)		$70.35	
EXPIRATION DATE (mm/dd/yyyy)		04/17/15	
PUT STRIKE ($)		$68.00	
PUT PREMIUM ($)		$2.05	
TOTAL PREMIUM COLLECTED PER CONTRACT ($)		$205.00	
CASH REQUIRED PER CONTRACT ($)		$6,595.00	
RETURN ON OPTION (ROO %) IF UNEXERCISED		3.11%	
STOCK COST BASIS (IF EXERCISED) / BREAK-EVEN ($)		$65.95	
PURCHASE DISCOUNT IF EXERCISED (%)		6.25%	
NUMBER OF DAYS IN THE TRADE		18	
ANNUALIZED RETURN ON OPTION (ROO %)		63.03%	

Figure 154- AMBA- Put Calculations

The following stats are gleaned from these calculations:

- The three-week unexercised return (if share price remains above $68.00) is 3.11% which annualizes to 63.03%
- The cash required to secure the put is $6595.00 per contract, similar to the cash needed to purchase 100 shares at $66.00 with a limit order
- If exercised, our cost basis is $65.95, meeting our goal to purchase at $66.00

Discussion

If a decision has been made to purchase a particular security at a specific price currently below market value, there is a distinct advantage to selling cash-secured puts over setting limit orders.

In the former, we are generating cash flow if the option is not exercised and getting paid while our cash waits to be utilized. If the limit order is not reached, we receive no cash and still do not own the desired security. Should the put option expire unexercised, the parameters of that contract can be re-set to another strike price based on current market and corporate information. A possible disadvantage to selling cash-secured puts in lieu of setting limit orders is that shares must be purchased in round lots (one hundred share increments). If an investor wants to purchase in odd lots, limit orders would be appropriate as "the only game in town".

Using Cash-Secured Puts to Enter Covered Call Positions: The PCP Strategy

Covered call writing can be used in conjunction with other strategies such as portfolio overwriting and dividend capture strategies. I have highlighted many of these covered call-related strategies in my previous books and DVDs. One of the strategies that has captured the interest of many of our members is the use of cash-secured puts. The cash-secured put involves writing (selling) a put option and simultaneously setting aside enough cash to buy the stock should the put be exercised. The strategy can be used in one of three ways:

- Generate income from premiums (you do not want exercise)
- Purchase a stock for your portfolio "at a discount" (you would like exercise at the appropriate price)
- To be used to enter a covered call position (either exercise or non-exercise will work well)

In today's article I will focus in on a strategy that incorporates both cash-secured puts and covered call writing.

Overview of the strategy

We are bearish on the overall market or have a very low risk-tolerance and do not want to pay full price for the shares before writing our call options. Selling a put option at a lower price than current market value (this is out-of-the-money for puts) gives the put buyer (holder) the right to sell us the shares at this lower strike price. The option will be exercised if the price falls below the strike. If this occurs, we can then sell a call option on this "discounted" stock.

Diagram of the strategy (Figure 155)

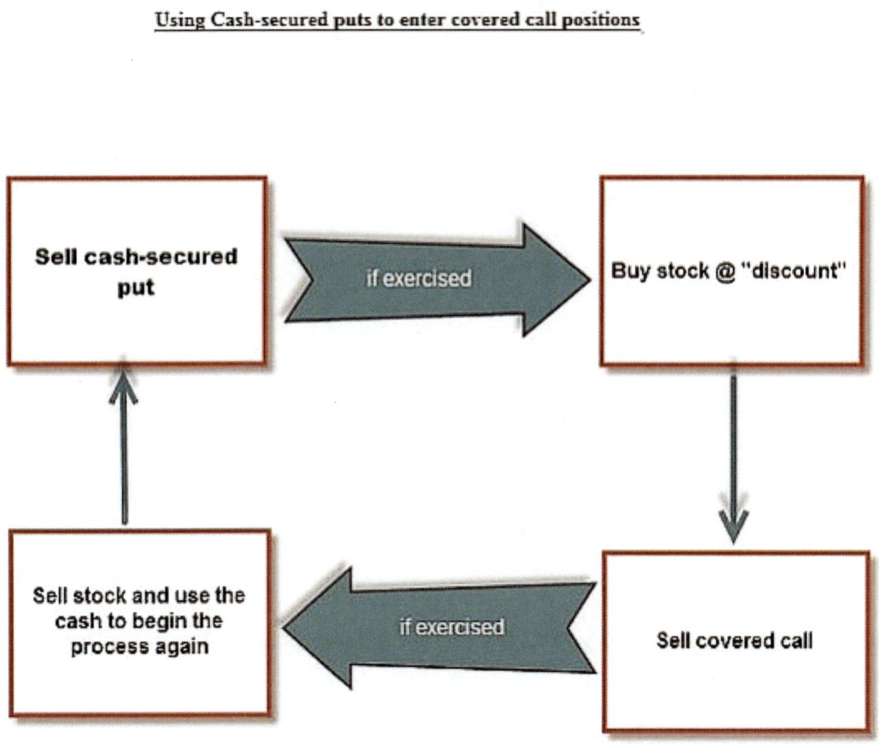

Figure 155- Cash-Secured Puts and Covered Call Writing

Real life example of entering a covered call position "at a discount"

Figure 156 shows a put options chain for EDU, a stock on our Premium Watch List as of 8/16/2013:

EDU: $22.50

Strike	Last	Intrinsic Value	Bid	Ask	Vol	Open interest
[illegible]	[illegible]	00	N/A	0.20	0	0
[illegible]	[illegible]	00	N/A	0.25	0	0
[illegible]	[illegible]	00	0.05	0.20	0	0
[illegible]	[illegible]	00	0.05	0.25	0	0
[illegible]	[illegible]	00	0.05	0.25	0	33
[illegible]	[illegible]	00	0.15	0.20	0	88
21.00	0.35	0.00	0.30	0.40	3	166
22.00	0.65	0.00	0.60	0.70	0	114
23.00	1.18	0.50	1.10	1.25	50	111
24.00	1.98	1.50	1.70	2.25	0	0
25.00	2.90	2.50	2.50	3.30	0	2
26.00	3.80	3.50	3.40	4.20	0	0
27.00	4.75	4.50	4.30	5.20	0	0
28.00	5.80	5.50	5.30	6.30	0	0
29.00	6.75	6.50	6.30	7.20	0	27
30.00	7.70	7.50	7.30	8.10	0	0
31.00	8.70	8.50	8.30	9.10	0	1

Figure 156- Put Options for EDU

The trade

- With EDU trading at$22.50 we would like to buy it at $21.50 or lower
- Sell 1 x September (one-month out) $22.00 put, giving the option holder the right to sell us the stock at $22.00
- Deposit $2200.00/contract into your brokerage account making the trade "cash-secured" or "covered"
- The broker will allow us to apply the premium against

the required cash making our cost basis $2140.00 per contract

- The initial return is $60.00/$2140.00 = 2.8%, one-month return (must be monitored if price drops dramatically)
- If stock price drops below $22.00 by expiration we will buy shares at $22.00 and a cost basis of $21.40 incorporating in the put premium
- Write covered call on newly acquired shares

Advantages

- Shares are acquired at a cost basis of $21.40 ($22.00 – $0.60), not $22.50, meeting our desired entry point
- If unexercised, we still generate a 2.8%, one-month return

Disadvantages

- Maximum profit is put premium, no share appreciation
- Monitoring is essential if share price declines dramatically (same for covered call writing)
- Must master the differences between calls and puts (in-the-money and out-of-the-money are inversely related for calls and puts)

Conclusion

Combining cash-secured puts with covered call writing is a viable strategy especially in bear market environments or if the investor has a low risk-tolerance. Before considering using this strategy an investor must master and understand the differences between call and put options. A higher level of trading approval is also required by most brokerages when selling puts in addition to covered calls. **The same stocks that are great covered call writing candidates on our Premium Watch List are also great candidates for selling cash-secured puts**.

Chapter 18

Compounding and the Time Value of Money

Chapter outline

1. Comparing Simple and Compound Interest

Comparing Simple and Compound Interest

In Volume 1 of the *Complete Encyclopedia for Covered Call Writing*, I addressed the importance of compounding profits and discussed the *Rule of 72* (the time it takes to double your money based on the annualized return on our investments). In this related article, I will highlight the difference between simple interest and compounded interest and therefore the impact re-investing our profits will have on our financial security.

When I started using covered call writing as the primary strategy in the stock portion of my portfolio, I needed the profits to support family matters like college, professional school and real estate investments. The cash generated from options sales was used to meet the needs my family had at that time. Several years later there reached a point when I no longer had those family needs and re-investing those profits took precedence. That's when I was introduced to the eighth wonder of the world...the power of compounding.

Definitions

- *Simple interest*: The interest paid on the original principle only
- *Compound interest*: Interest earned not only on the original principle, but also on all interest previously earned

Formula and example for simple interest

Interest = principle x rate of return x time

If we invested $5,000.00 at 10% per year for four years our interest would total:

$5,000.00 x 0.10 x 4 = **$2,000.00**

Four-year return = **$7,000.00**

Formula and example for compound interest

The formula is somewhat complicated and beyond the scope of this article so let's calculate the above example over the four-year time frame by compounding or re-investing our earned interest.

Year one

$5,000.00 x 0.10 = **$500.00** = $5500.00

Year two

$5500.00 x 0.10 = **$550.00** = $6050.00

Year three

$6050.00 x 0.10 = **$605.00** = $6655.00

Year four

$6655.00 x 0.10 = **$665.50** = **$7320.50**

Total interest earned via annualized compounding:

\$500.00 + \$550.00 + \$605.00 + \$665.50 = **\$2320.50**

After four years, compounding generated \$320.50 more than simple interest for the same initial investment. The results would be even more dramatic if compounding took place quarterly or monthly (as opposed to annually) and if additional funds were added to the initial investment. Needless to say, the longer the time frame the greater the impact compounding will have on our financial futures.

Compound calculators

These calculators can be found for free on the web at such sites as:

www.bankrate.com

Figure 157 shows what the above example would like when plugged into one of these tools:

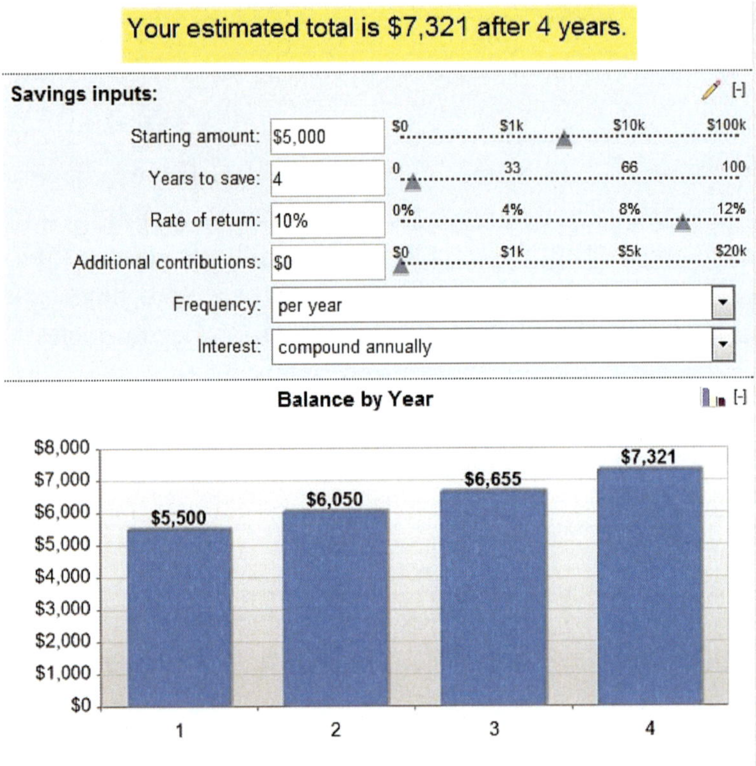

Figure 157- Compound Calculator Put to Work

Lesson-learned from the opposite perspective

Let's say we are borrowing money as opposed to generating income. Here compounding can become a nightmare and keep us in debt forever. If we borrowed $5,000.00 at 10% that would result in a yearly interest debit of $500.00. If we paid only minimum payments of let's say $100.00, the next year we would pay 10% of $5400.00 or $540.00. This why credit card companies encourage us to make only minimum payments. So which side of compounding should Blue Collar Investors reside? A rhetorical question, wouldn't you say!

Glossary

Accumulation: Buying of stock by institutional or professional investors over an extended period of time.

Acquisition: When one company purchases the majority interest in the acquired.

Actively Managed Mutual Funds: Shareholders, through a mutual fund manager, buy and sell stocks and bonds, within the fund, in an attempt to *beat the market*.

Advance-Decline Theory: Also called the *Breadth of Market Theory*, this theory states that the market direction can be determined by the number of stocks that have increased compared to those that have decreased in value. It is considered bullish if more shares are advancing than declining.

American Depository Receipt: A negotiable certificate issued by a U.S. bank representing a specified number of shares (or one share) in a foreign stock that is traded on a U.S. exchange. ADRs are denominated in U.S. dollars, with the underlying security held by a U.S. financial institution overseas. ADRs help to reduce administration and duty costs that would otherwise be levied on each transaction.

American Style Options: An option contract that may be exercised at any time between the date of purchase and the expiration date.

Arbitrage: The simultaneous purchase and sale of an asset in order to profit from a difference in the price. It is a trade that profits by exploiting price differences of identical or similar financial instruments, on different markets or in different forms.

Ask: The price a seller is willing to accept for a security. It includes both price and quantity willing to be sold.

Asset allocation: The implementation of an investment strategy that attempts to balance risk versus reward by adjusting the percentage of each asset in an investment portfolio according to the investor's risk tolerance, goals and investment time frame

Assignment: The receipt of an exercise notice by an option seller that obligates him to sell (in the case of a call) or purchase (in the case of a put) the underlying security at the specified strike price.|275

At-the-money: An option is at-the-money if the strike price of the option is equal to the market price of the underlying security.

Balance sheet: One of the major financial statements used by accountants and business owners. (The other major financial statements are the income statement, statement of cash flows, and statement of stockholders' equity) The balance sheet is also referred to as the **statement of financial position.** The balance sheet presents a company's financial position at the end of a specified date.

Banned stocks: According to the BCI methodology, this is a list of stocks that should be avoided at all times when selling short-term options because of risky monthly reports.

Bar Chart: This price chart consists of session high and lows as well as the opening and closing prices. It is also referred to as the O-H-L-C bar.

Basis: Basis is often a moving target. Generally it is what you paid for a stock or option. There are adjustments which may be necessary to report the proper capital gain. These adjustments may include special dividends, stock splits and stock dividends, and some others.

Bearish: Pessimistic investor sentiment that a particular security or market is headed downward.

Benchmark: A standard against which the performance of a security, mutual fund or investment manager can be measured. A common example is the S&P 500.

Beta: This is a measure of the volatility or *systemic risk* (market risk) of a security as compared to the market as a whole.

Bid: An offer made by an investor to buy an equity. It will include price and quantity.

BID/ASK SPREAD: The difference in price between the highest price that a buyer is willing to pay for the option and the lowest price a seller is willing to sell it.

Black-Scholes Option Pricing Model: A model used to calculate the value of an option, by factoring in stock price, strike price and expiration date, risk-free return, and the standard deviation of the stock's return.

Breakeven: The point at which gains equal losses

Brokerage statement: A broker's statement is a monthly snapshot of a brokerage account activity.

Bullish: Optimistic investor sentiment that a particular equity or market will rise.

Buy and hold portfolio: This is an investment strategy where an investor buys stocks and holds them for a long time.

Buy down price of stock: Using the intrinsic value of an in-the-money option premium to reduce the cost of the stock purchase.

Buy to close: A term used by many brokerages to represent the closing of a short position in option transactions.

Buy-write order: See net debit order

Calendar Spread: Simultaneously establishing long and short options positions on the same underlying stock with different expiration dates. For example, you buy the December, 2010 $20 call and sell the April, 2010 $20 call on the same equity.

Call: An option contract giving the owner the right (but not the obligation) to buy a specified amount of an underlying security at a specified price within a specified time.

Candlestick Chart: This chart is created by displaying the high, low, open and close for a security each day over a certain time frame.

Capacity report: A monthly report on trends in the supply of airline flights and seats.

Capital Asset: This is pretty much anything you own and use for personal, pleasure or investment purposes. The term includes such tangible assets as a boat, a coin collection, or a piece of real estate. It may also include intangible assets, such as a patent or copyright. The distinction between a capital asset and a non-capital asset is its use. Any capital asset becomes a non-capital asset if it is used in a trade or business, or is "for sale" to customers in a trade or business.

Capital Gain (Loss): A capital gain or loss is simply the difference between the proceeds of the sale and your cost basis of the asset sold. If you bought a stock for $25 and sold it for $30, you have a capital gain of $5. You can't have a capital gain or loss unless you have a sale of a capital asset. However, a sale of an asset does not necessarily mean you have a capital gain or loss. Why... because every capital gain requires two parts of the transaction, a sale AND an acquisition, or purchase.

Cash account: A regular brokerage account in which the customer is required by Regulation T to pay for securities within two days of the purchase.

Cash-secured put: When a brokerage company requires us to have the cash in our accounts to purchase the shares we are obligated to buy after selling a put option.

Cash settlement: A settlement method used in certain future and option contracts whereby, upon expiration or exercise, the seller of the financial instrument does not deliver shares but transfers the associated cash position.

CBOE S&P 500 BuyWrite Index (BXM): This is a benchmark index designed to track the performance of a hypothetical buy-write strategy on the S&P 500 Index.

CBOE Volatility Index: see VIX

Collar (strategy): A protective options strategy that is implemented after a long position in a stock has experienced substantial gains. It is created by purchasing an out of the money put option while simultaneously writing an out of the money call option.

Compound calculator: An interest calculator used to quantify the impact compound interest has on the future value of an asset.

Compound interest: Interest calculated on the initial principal and also on the accumulated interest of previous periods of a deposit or loan. Compound interest can be thought of as "interest on interest"

Compounding: The ability of an asset to generate earnings, which are then reinvested in order to generate earnings of their own.

Consolidation: *Sideways Pattern (consolidation)* - the horizontal price movement of an equity where the forces of supply and demand are equal. The stock simply cannot establish an uptrend or a downtrend.

Contract adjustment: Changes to option contract terms due to underlying corporate actions like stock splits or special cash dividends.

Contract cycle: The period of time starting with the first trading day after expiration Friday through the end of the following expiration Friday (4 PM EST unless there is an exchange recognized holiday).

Convert Dead Money to Cash Profits: An exit strategy wherein an option is bought back and the underlying equity sold. The cash is then used to buy a better performing stock which is used to sell another covered call.

Correlation: This measures the degree to which investments are related.

Cost basis: The original value of an asset. It is used to determine the capital gain, which is equal to the difference between the asset's cost basis and the current market value. Also: the amount of your original investment.

Cost to carry: When money is borrowed from our broker in a margin account, interest is charged and needs to be calculated into our results.

Covered call ETF: An exchange-traded fund that uses covered call writing as its primary income-producing vehicle.

Covered call writing: A strategy in which one sells call options while simultaneously owning the underlying security.

Covered combination: A strategy in options trading that involves selling equal number of out-of-the-money calls and puts on the same underlying security, strike price and expiration date while owning the underlying stock.

Covered put: A bearish options strategy involving the writing of put options while shorting the obligated shares of the underlying stock.

Currency carry trade: A strategy in which an investor sells a certain currency with a relatively low interest rate and uses the funds to purchase a different currency yielding a higher interest rate. A trader using this strategy attempts to capture the difference between the rates, which can often be substantial, depending on the amount of leverage the investor chooses to use.

Delta: This is the amount an option value will change for every $1 change in the price of a stock. The greater the chance of the strike ending up in-the-money, the higher the delta. Delta values for calls run from 0 to 1.

Derivative: A security whose price is dependent upon or derived from one or more underlying assets. The derivative itself is merely a contract between two or more parties. Its value is determined by fluctuations in the underlying asset. The most common underlying assets include stocks, bonds, commodities, currencies, interest rates and market indexes. Most derivatives are characterized by high leverage.

Diagonal Spread- A long and short options position with different expirations AND strikes. For example, you buy the December, 2010 $20 call and sell the April, 2010 $25 call.

Dilution: A reduction in earnings per share of common stock that occurs through the issuance of additional shares. This is avoided with stock splits by reducing the current market value of a stock by a similar ratio as was the number of shares increased.

Distribution: the selling of stock by large institutions over an extending period of time.

Diversification: A risk management technique that mixes a wide variety of investments within a portfolio. The rationale behind this technique contends that a portfolio of different kinds of investments will, on average, yield higher returns and pose a lower risk than any individual investment found within the portfolio.

Dividend: A distribution of a portion of a company's earnings to a class of its shareholders as cash payments or shares of stock.

Dollar cost averaging: The technique of buying a fixed dollar amount of a particular investment on a regular schedule, regardless of the share price. More shares are purchased when prices are low, and fewer shares are bought when prices are high.

Downside protection: The intrinsic value portion of an in-the-money call option premium divided by the original cost basis. It is the percentage of your investment that can be lost without affecting the option return on your investment. The formula is as follows:

$$\frac{\text{Intrinsic Value of option premium}}{\text{Original Cost of stock}} = \text{\% of downside protection}$$

Down trending Stock: A stock with a declining share price showing lower highs and lower lows.

The Dow Theory: This theory states that the market is in an upward trend if one of the averages (industrial or transportation) advances above a previous significant high and is accompanied by a similar advance in the other. A major trend is identified only when BOTH the Dow Industrial and Dow Transportation Averages reach a new high or a new low. Without this confirmation, the market will return to its previous trading pattern.

Early assignment: Early exercise happens when the owner of a call or put invokes his or her contractual rights before expiration. As a result, an option seller will be assigned and shares of stock will change hands.

Earnings estimate: An analyst's estimate for a company's future quarterly or annual earnings.

Earnings guidance: Information that a company provides as an indication or estimate of their future earnings.

Earnings per share: A company's profit divided by its number of common outstanding shares.

Earnings report: A quarterly filing made by public companies to report their performance. Included in these reports are items such as net income, earnings per share, earnings from continuing operations, and net sales. These reports follow the end of each quarter. Most companies file in January, April, July, and October.

Earnings surprise: When the earnings reported in a companies quarterly or annual report are above or below analysts' earnings estimates.

Efficient frontier: A line created from the risk-reward graph, comprised of optimal portfolios.

Elite Calculator: Expanded version of the basic Ellman Calculator (ESOC) which includes an *unwind tab* and a *Schedule D*.

Ellman Calculator- See ESOC.

ESOC: Ellman System Option Calculator which is an excel calculator used to compute option returns specifically for Alan Ellman's *Cashing In On Covered Calls* system.

ETFs: See exchange traded funds.

Exchange traded funds: A security that tracks an index, a commodity, or a basket of assets like an index fund, but trades like a stock on an exchange, thus experiencing price changes throughout the day as it is bought and sold. These securities provide the diversification of an index fund.

Ex-dividend date: The latest date a shareholder must own a stock to be eligible to receive an upcoming dividend distribution.

Exercise: When you exercise your stock option, you "trade in" your options for the actual stock.

Exercise notice: A broker's notification that a client wishes to exercise his or her right to buy or sell the underlying security. The exercise notice is forwarded to the option seller via the Options Clearing Corporation.

European Style Option: An option contract that can only be exercised on the expiration date.

Execution (of a trade): The completion of a buy or sell stock order.

Exit strategy: A plan in which a trader intends to get out of an investment position made in the past. It is a way of *cashing out* or *closing out a position*.

Expanded Weekly options: options that are listed to provide expiration opportunities every week. Weeklys are typically listed on Thursdays and expire on Fridays, provided that such expirations were not previously listed. Expanded Weeklys can be traded weeks in advance.

Expected Return: Possible return on a portfolio in different market conditions (bullish, bearish and neutral) weighted by the likelihood that the return will occur.

Expense ratio: A measure of what it costs an investment company to operate a mutual fund. It is determined through an annual calculation, where a fund's operating expenses are divided by the average dollar value of its managed assets Operating expenses are taken out of a fund's assets and lower the return to a fund's investors. Some funds have a marketing cost referred to as a 12b-1 fee, which would also be included in operating expenses. It is interesting that a fund's trading activity - the buying and selling of stock - is NOT included in the calculation of expense ratio.

Expiration date: The last day (in the case of an American- style) or the only day (in the case of European-style) on which an option may be exercised. For stock option, this date is the third Friday of the expiration month. If Friday is a holiday, the last trading day is the preceding Thursday.

Exponential moving average or EMA: A type of moving average that is similar to a simple moving average, except that more weight is given to the most recent data. It reacts faster to recent price changes than does a simple moving average. The 12- and 26-day EMA's are the most popular short-term averages, and they are used to create indicators like the MACD.

FIFO: See First in, first out.

Financial statement: A collection of reports about an organization's financial results, financial condition, and cash flows

First call: A company that gathers research notes and earnings estimates from brokerage analysts and forms a consensus estimate. The estimate is compared to the actual earnings reports, and then the difference between the two is the earnings surprise. The other major player in this estimate game is **Zachs.**

First in, first out: An asset-management and valuation method in which the assets produced or acquired first are then sold first.

Fundamental analysis: A method of analyzing the prospects of a security by observing the accepted accounting measures such as earnings, sales, and assets and so on.

Future delivery price: The financial value of the underlying security or commodity when a futures contract expires.

Gamma: The rate of change for delta with respect to the price of the underlying security. It is an estimate of how much the delta of an option changes when the price of the stock moves $1.

Gap: A gap is a break between prices on a chart that occurs when the price of a stock makes a sharp move up or down with no trading occurring in between.

GMI (signal): A series of six technical indicators developed by Dr. Eric Wish, a professor at The University of Maryland that generates highly accurate stock market buy and sell signals.

Globalization: The tendency of investment funds and businesses to move beyond domestic and national markets to other markets around the globe, thereby increasing the interconnectedness of different markets. It has had the effect of increasing international trade and cultural exchange.

Greeks: A mathematical means of estimating the risk of stock options. Delta measures the change in the option price due to a change in the stock price, gamma measures the change in the option delta due to a change in the stock price, theta measures the change in the option price due to time passing, Vega measures the change in the option price due to volatility changing, and rho measures the change in the option price due to a change in interest rates.

Guidance: Information that a company provides as an indication or estimate of its future earnings.

Historical volatility: This is the actual price fluctuation as observed over a period of time.

Hit a Double: An exit strategy wherein an option is bought back and then resold at a higher premium in the same contract period.

Hit a Triple: An exit strategy wherein an option is bought back and resold twice in the same contract period.

Horizontal skew: The difference in implied volatility across options with different expiration dates.

Horizontal Spread- A spread where both options have the same strike price as in the above example but different expiration dates. *The terms calendar and horizontal spreads are interchangeable*.

Hypothecation Agreement: For margin accounts, it gives the firm permission to pledge securities held on margin.

IBD 100: The Investor's Business Daily 100 is a computer-generated ranking of the leading companies trading in America. Rankings are based on a combination of each company's profit growth; IBD's Composite Rating, which includes key measures such as return on equity, sales growth and profit margins; and relative price strength in the past 12 months.

Implied Volatility- This is a forecast of the underlying stock's volatility as implied by the option's price in the marketplace.

Income statement: One of the major financial statements used by accountants and business owners. (The other major financial statements are the balance sheet, statement of cash flows, and the statement of stockholders' equity.) The income statement is also known as the profit and loss statement of operations, or statement of income.

Index fund: A type of mutual fund with a portfolio constructed to mirror, or track, the components of a market index such as the S&P 500 Index. An index mutual fund is said to provide broad market exposure, low operating expenses and low portfolio turnover. *Indexing* is a passive form of fund management that has been successful in out-performing most actively managed mutual funds.

Index option: A financial derivative that gives the holder the right, but not the obligation, to buy or sell a basket of stocks, such as the S&P 500, at an agreed-upon price and by the expiration date. An index option is similar to other options contracts, the difference being the underlying securities are indexes.

Internal rate of return: IRR is a way to analyze an investment considering the time value of money. It basically calculates the interest rate which is the equivalent of the dollar amount your investment will return.

Initial margin: The amount of a margin account as a percentage of the investment purchased on margin.

Inverse ETF: An exchange-traded fund (ETF) that is constructed by using derivatives for the purpose of benefitting from the decline in the underlying benchmark.

Inverse volatility effect: Addresses the inverse relationship between market benchmark pricing and implied volatility of the benchmark (for example, the S&P 500 and the VIX).

In-the-money: A term describing any option that has *intrinsic value*. A call option is in-the-money if the underlying security is higher than the strike price of the call.

Intrinsic value: The value of an option if it were to expire immediately with the underlying stock at its current price; the amount by which the stock is in-the-money. For call options, this is the positive difference between the stock price and the strike price.

Investor Fear Gauge: See **VIX.**

IRA: A form of an "individual retirement plan" provided by many financial institutions, that provides tax advantages for retirement savings in the United States.

Key economic indicator: Macroeconomic data that is used by investors to interpret current or future investment possibilities and judge the overall health of an economy. These are specific pieces of data released by the government and non-profit organizations. These include:

The Consumer Price Index (CPI)

Gross Domestic Product (GDP)

Unemployment statistics

The price of crude oil

Know your customer rule (KYC rule): A standard form in the investment industry that ensures investment advisors know detailed information about their clients' risk tolerance, investment knowledge and financial status.

KYC rule: See "know your customer rule"

Laddering: This is an investment technique whereby investors purchase multiple financial products with different maturity dates. I have borrowed this term and used it to describe a covered call t5echnique where different strike prices are used for the same equity.

Lagging indicator: A technical indicator that trails the price action of an underlying asset. It is used by traders to generate transaction signals or to confirm the strength of a given trend. Since these indicators lag the price of the asset, a significant move will generally occur before the indicator is able to provide a signal. It confirms long-term trends but does not predict them.

Large cap: An abbreviation for the term *large market capitalization*. Market capitalization is calculated by multiplying the number of a company's outstanding shares by its stock price per share. The expression *large cap* is used by the investment community as an indicator of a company's size. A large cap stock has a market-capitalization dollar value of over 10 billion.

LEAPS- Long-Term Equity Anticipation Securities. These are option contracts with expiration dates longer than one year. Only the more heavily traded stocks and ETFs have these types of options associated with them.

Legging in: A way of executing a covered call trade wherein we first buy the stock and, once owned, sell the corresponding call option.

Levels of trading approval: Before you can trade options, your broker will approve you for a specific *level* of options trading. Usually, brokerages have four or five levels of approval that are based on factors such as your investing objectives, investing history and your account balance.

Leveraged ETF: An exchange-traded fund (ETF) that uses financial derivatives and debt to amplify the returns of an underlying index.

Limit Order: An order placed by a brokerage to buy or sell a specified number of shares at a specific price or better. The length of time an order remains outstanding can also be specified.

Line Chart: This is a very basic chart created by connecting a series of closing prices of a particular security with a line.

Long (position): The buying of a security, such as a stock or options contract, with the expectation that the asset will rise in value.

MACD (Moving average convergence divergence): A trend-following momentum indicator that shows the relationship between two moving averages of prices. The MACD is calculated by subtracting the 26-day exponential moving average (EMA) from the 12-day EMA. A 9-day EMA of the MACD, called the *signal line,* is then plotted on top of the MACD, functioning as a trigger for buy and sell signals.

MACD Histogram: A common technical indicator that illustrates the difference between the MACD and the trigger line. This difference is then plotted on a chart in the form of a histogram to make it easy for a trader to determine a specific asset's momentum.

Maintenance Margin: The minimum amount of equity that must be maintained in a margin account.

Margin account: This is a brokerage account where the client has the ability to borrow money from the broker to purchase securities. This loan is then collateralized by the cash and securities in that specific account.

Margin call: When the value of the securities in a margin account drop to a certain level, the investor will be required to put additional cash in the account or sell certain securities.

Mark: The mid-point of a bid-ask spread.

Market capitalization: The total dollar market value of all of a company's outstanding shares. It is calculated by multiplying a company's shares outstanding by the current market price of one share. The investment community uses this figure to determine a company's size, as opposed to sales or total asset figures. Also referred to as *market cap*.

Market consensus: The average earnings estimates made by brokers and security analysts. Also known as *earnings expectations*.

Market Order: An order to buy or sell a stock at the current best available price.

Market Tone: The feeling of a market (general psychology) as demonstrated by the price activity of stocks. We use the VIX and S&P 500 chart patterns to help assess this sentiment.

Marking the close: A form of market manipulation. It is an attempt to influence the closing price of a security by executing purchase or sale orders just prior to the close of trading.

Married put: When the protective put is purchased on the same day as the stock, it is referred to as a *married put* for tax purposes.

Mergers: A general term used to refer to the consolidation of companies. It is a combination of two companies to form a new company.

Mid-contract unwind: Closing both the long and short legs of a covered call trade mid-contract after maximum profits have been achieved to then use the cash to generate a second income stream.

Mini options: These are option contracts where the underlying security is 10 shares of a stock or exchange-traded fund (ETF). This is the main difference between mini options and standard options which have 100 shares of the underlying security.

Modern portfolio theory: A portfolio optimization methodology that utilizes the mean variance of investment returns. It uses the standard deviation of all returns as a measure of risk.

Momentum indicator: Designed to track momentum in the price of a security to help identify the enthusiasm of buyers and sellers involved in the price trend development. Some indicators compare the closing price with some historical price so many periods before; others construct trend lines like the *MACD*. Others, like *Stochastics,* is a ratio using the high, low, and close values on various days.

Momentum Oscillator: A technical analysis tool that is banded between two extreme values and built with the results from a trend indicator for discovering short-term overbought or oversold conditions. As the value of the oscillator approaches the upper extreme value the asset is deemed to be overbought, and as it approaches the lower extreme it is deemed to be oversold. This oscillator is most advantageous when a stock price is in a trading range (sideways). An example is the *stochastic oscillator*

Money market securities: The securities market dealing in short-term debt and monetary instruments. These forms of debt mature in less than one year and are quite liquid. Treasury bills make up the bulk of the money market instruments. These securities are relatively risk-free.

Moneyness: Term describing the relationship between the strike price of an option and the current trading price of its underlying security. In options trading, terms such as in-the-money, out-of-the-money and at-the-money describe the moneyness of options.

Monthlys: Option contracts with monthly expiration dates, usually the third Friday of each month.

Moving average: An indicator frequently used in technical analysis showing the average value of a securities price over a set period. Moving averages are generally used to measure momentum and define areas of possible support and resistance.

Multiple Tab of the ESOC: Compare returns, upside potential, and downside protection for many stocks, all on the same page.

Nasdaq 100 index: An index composed of the 100 largest, most actively traded U.S. companies listed on the Nasdaq stock exchange. This index includes companies from a broad range of industries with the exception of those that operate in the financial industry, such as banks and investment companies.

NAV (net asset value): A mutual fund's price per share or exchange-traded fund's (ETF) per-share value. In both cases, the per-share dollar amount of the fund is calculated by dividing the total value of all the securities in its portfolio, less any liabilities, by the number of fund shares outstanding.

Near-the-money: Refers to options with strike prices which are near to the prevailing price of the underlying stock. The term is used often as a replacement for At-the-money options due to the fact that it is rare for the share price to be exactly equal to the strike price of an option.

Net debit order: This is where you buy the stock and sell the option at the exact same time, not for specific corresponding prices but for a *limit net debit*. Also called a *buy-write*.

Net effective sale price (NESP): When selling covered call options, it is the total price of the strike price plus the option premium

Non Standard Options: These are options that don't have the standard terms of an options contract, namely 100 shares as the underlying asset.

Odd Lot Theory: This theory is based on the assumption that the small investor is always wrong. Since these investors usually buy and sell in odd-lot amounts (less than 100 shares) and have low risk-tolerance (the theory continues), they tend to buy high and sell low. A bullish signal is when odd-lot sell orders increase relative to odd-lot buy orders**.**

OHLC (bar) chart: Short for *Open High, Low Close chart*. This type of chart is used to spot trends and view stock movements, particularly on a short term basis.

One triggers other: A two-stage brokerage order wherein we enter an initial order for a stock, ETF or option, and simultaneously place a second order that's contingent upon the fill of the first order. Also known as **OTO** order.

One-time special cash dividend: A non-recurring distribution of company assets, usually in the form of cash, to shareholders. A special dividend is usually larger than standard dividend distributions.

Online Discount Broker: A stockbroker who carries out buy and sell orders online, at reduced commissions, but provides no investment advice.

Open interest- The open interest of an option contract is the number of outstanding options of that type which currently have not been closed out or exercised

Option: A contract that gives the owner the right, if exercised, to buy or sell a security or basket of securities (index) at a specific price within a specific time limit. Stock option contracts are generally for the right to buy or sell 100 shares of the underlying stock.

Option account: A brokerage account where the brokerages permit the account holder to hold options.

Option chain: A way of quoting option prices through a list of all the options for a given security. For each underlying security, the option chain tells investors the various strike prices, expiration dates, and whether they are calls or puts.

Option contract: Represents 100 shares in the underlying stock. Information included consists of the underlying security, type of option (call or put), expiration month, strike price and premium.

Option premium: The price at which the contract trades. It is the price paid by the buyer to the writer, or seller, of the option. In return the writer of the call option is obligated to deliver the underlying security to an option buyer if the call is exercised or buy the underlying security if the put is exercised. The writer keeps the premium whether or not the option is exercised.

Options Clearing Corporation: An organization that acts as both the issuer and guarantor for options and futures contracts. Also known as the **OCC**.

OTO: See "**One triggers other**"

Out-of-the-money: A call option is out-of-the-money if the strike price is greater than market value of the underlying security.

Over-the-counter option (OTC): An option traded off-exchange, as opposed to a *listed* stock option. The OTC option has a direct link between buyer and seller, has no secondary market, and has no standardization of strike prices and expiration dates. This securities market is not geographically centralized like the trading floor of the NYSE. Trading takes place through a telephone and computer network.

Overbought: A technical condition that occurs when prices are considered too high and susceptible to decline. Overbought conditions can be classified by analyzing the chart pattern or with indicators such as the Stochastic Oscillator. Generally, a security is considered overbought when the Stochastic Oscillator exceeds 80. Overbought is not the same as being *bearish. It simply infers that the stock has risen too far too fast and might be due for a pullback.*

Oversold: A technical condition that occurs when prices are considered too low and ripe for a surge. Oversold conditions can be classified by analyzing the chart pattern or with indicators such as the Stochastic Oscillator. Generally, a security is considered oversold if the Stochastic Oscillator is less than 20. Oversold is not the same as being *bullish. It merely infers that the security has fallen too far too fast and may be due for a reaction rally.*

Paper trade: A hypothetical trade that does not involve any monetary transactions. It is a risk-free way to learn the ins and outs of the market.

Parity: The amount by which an option is in the money. Parity refers to the option trading in unison with the stock. This also means that parity and intrinsic value are closely related. When we say that an option is *trading at parity*, we mean that the option's premium consists of only its intrinsic value.

Passive management (of mutual funds): An investment strategy that mirrors a market index and does not attempt to beat the market.

PE Ratio: P/E Ratio or Price-Earnings Ratio is a valuation ratio that compares the price of a stock to the per share earnings.

PEG Ratio: PEG = PE Ratio/Annual EPS Growth

PEGY Ratio: = PE Ratio/ Expected Earnings Growth + Dividend Yield

Pinning the strike: This is when puts and calls are near the money on expiration Friday. There is a tendency called *pinning the strike* for the stock to move to the strike price or slightly beyond.

Portfolio management: The art and science of making decisions about investment mix and policy, matching investments to objectives, asset allocation, and balancing risk versus performance. *It requires organized lists of accurate information.*

Portfolio overwriting: This is where a call option is sold on a stock already part of an existing portfolio. That option is selected in a manner such that the option is NOT expected to be exercised as every effort is made to retain the equity.

Portfolio pumping: See "marking the close".

Portfolio rebalancing: Involves buying or selling assets in your portfolio to maintain your original desired level of asset allocation.

Premium report: The weekly stock screen and watch list published by the Blue Collar Investor Corp. This is a screen specific for candidates geared to writing one-month covered calls and selling short-term cash-secured puts.

Premium Watch List: The BCI list of screened stocks and exchange-traded funds that have passed the fundamental, technical and common sense screens and are eligible for option-selling.

Price-to-book ratio: A valuation ratio used by investors which compares a stock's per-share price to its book value (shareholders' equity). It is an indication of how much shareholders are paying for the net assets of a company.

Price-to-earnings ratio: Ratio of a company's share price to its per-share annualized earnings.

Price bar: see *OHLC*.

Profit and loss graph: Also called a *risk graph*, is a visual representation of the possible profit and loss of an option strategy at a given point in time

Protective put: A put option purchased for a stock that is already owned by the owner of the option. A *protective put* defends against a decrease in the share price of the underlying security.

Put: An option contract that gives the holder the right, but not the obligation, to sell the underlying security at a specified price for a certain fixed period of time.

Put-call disparity: Deviations from put-call parity which may be used to predict future pricing.

Put-call parity: A principle referring to the static price relationship, given a stock's price, between the prices of European put and call options of the same class (i.e. same underlying, strike price and expiration date). This relationship is shown from the fact that combinations of options can create positions the same as stock ownership.

QQQQ: This is the ticker symbol for the Nasdaq 100 Trust, which is an exchange traded fund (ETF) that trades on the Nasdaq. It offers broad exposure to the tech sector by tracking the Nasdaq 100 index, which consists of the 100 largest non-financial stocks on the Nasdaq. It is also known as the *quadruple-Qs*.

Quarterlys: Options which expire on the last trading day of each quarter to coincide with end-of-quarter accounting practices. (By comparison, traditional options generally expire on the Saturday following the third Friday of the month.).

Ratio valuation: The comparison of two more financial metrics located in a corporation's financial statements that reflect on the financial health of the company.

Regulation T: Also known as **Reg T**, governs the extension of credit by securities brokers and dealers in the United States. It's best-known function is the control of margin requirements for stocks bought on margin.

Resistance: The price level at which there is a large enough supply of a stock available to cause a halt in the upward trend and turn the trend down. Resistance levels indicate the price at which most investors feel that the prices will move lower.

Return on equity: Also called **ROE,** this is a profitability ratio that measures the ability of a firm to generate profits from its shareholders investments in the company.

Rho: Not considered a major Greek, measures the change in the option price due to a change in interest rates.

Risk-reward profile: A risk reward profile is a chart of the theoretical maximum profit or loss a particular investment can have in your portfolios.

Rolling down: Closing out options at one strike price and simultaneously opening another at a lower strike price.

Rolling out (forward): Closing out of an option contract at a near-term expiration date and opening a same strike option contract at a later date.

Rolling up: Close out options at a lower strike and open options at a higher strike.

ROI: The benefit to the investor resulting from an investment of some resource.

ROO (return on option): The percent profit realized from the sale of a covered call option based on the cost basis of the underlying stock. If an in-the-money option was sold, the intrinsic value is deducted from the option premium before calculating the return.

Rule of 72: A rule stating that in order to find the number of years required to double your money at a given interest rate; you divide the compound return into 72. The result is the approximate number of years that it will take for your investment to double.

S&P 500 (Standard and Poor's 500): An index consisting of 500 stocks chosen for market size, liquidity, and industry grouping, among other factors. It is designed to be a leading indicator of U.S. equities and is meant to reflect the risk/return characteristics of the large-cap universe.

Sarbanes-Oxley Act of 2002 (SOX): An act passed by the U.S. Congress to protect investors from the possibility of fraudulent accounting activities by corporations. It includes the establishment of a *Public Company Accounting Oversight Board* where public companies must now be registered.

Schedule D: A U.S. income tax form used by taxpayers to report their realized capital gains or losses.

Securities and Exchange Commission (SEC): A government commission, created by Congress, established to regulate the securities markets and protect investors. It also monitors the corporate takeovers in the U.S. The SEC is composed of five commissions appointed by the U.S. President and approved by the Senate. The statutes administered by the SEC are designed to promote full public disclosure and to protect the investing public against fraudulent and manipulative practices in the securities markets. Generally, most issues of securities offered in interstate commerce, through the mail or on the internet, must be registered with the SEC.

Select Sector SPDRs: Unique Exchange Traded Funds (ETFs) that divide the S&P 500 into nine index funds and managed with the objective of matching the price and yield performance of their underlying sector indexes.

Sell to open: A phrase used by many brokerages on the street to represent the opening of a short position in option transactions.

Sheltered account: A brokerage account which minimizes or decreases an investor's taxable income and, therefore, his or her tax liability.

Short (or short position): The sale (also known as *writing*) of an options contract or a stock to open a position.

Short sale: Short sale is the sale of a stock not owned by the seller. It is borrowed from the broker and eventually must be replaced. The seller anticipates a decline in equity value and realizes a profit by covering (buying back) the short sale at a lower price in the future.

Show or Fill Rule: This regulation requires the market makers to show or publish any order that improves the current bid or ask prices unless it is filled.

Short Interest Theory: This theory states that a larger short interest is the predecessor of an increase in the price of a stock.

Sideways Pattern (consolidation) – This is the horizontal price movement of an equity where the forces of supply and demand are equal. The stock simply cannot establish an uptrend or a downtrend.

Simple interest: Determined by multiplying the interest rate by the principal by the number of periods.

Simple moving average (SMA): A moving average that gives equal weight to each day's price data.

Single Tab of the ESOC: Allows you to evaluate returns from different strikes for the same stock.

Slippage: The difference between the expected price of a trade, and the price the trade actually executes at. Slippage often occurs during periods of higher volatility and when market orders are used.

Speculation: The practice of engaging in risky financial transactions in an attempt to profit from fluctuations in the market value of a stock or option.

Spin-off: Type of divestiture. Businesses wishing to streamline their operations often sell less productive or unrelated subsidiary businesses as spinoffs.

Spread: The difference between the bid and ask prices of a stock or option.

Standard Deviation: This is a statistical measurement that sheds light on historical volatility.

Standard Weekly options program: Standard Weeklys are listed on Thursdays and expire on the following Friday. They appear one week at a time.

Statement of cash flows: This is one of the main financial statements. (The other financial statements are the balance sheet, income statement, and statement of stockholders' equity). The cash flow statement reports the *cash* generated and used during the time interval specified.

Stochastic Oscillator: A momentum indicator that measures the price of a security relative to the high/low range over a set period of time. The indicator oscillates between 0 and 100. Readings below 20 are considered oversold. Readings above 80 are considered overbought.

Stock Scouter Rating: MSN Monet Central's rating of stocks from 1 to 10, with 10 being the best. It uses a system of advanced mathematics to determine a stock's expected risk and return.

Stock split: A change in the number of shares outstanding (in circulation). The number of shares is adjusted by the split ratio, e.g. 2 to 1. In this case, 1000 shares splits to 2000 shares but the opening price and current price are cut in half. The overall effect is to maintain the same cost and current value of an investment while increasing the number of shares and lowering the per share price. This makes it easier for small investors to own the stock in round lots.

Stop loss order: This is an order placed with your broker to sell a security when it reaches a certain price.

Stop Order: This is an order to buy or sell a security when its price surpasses a specific price called the *stop price*. At that point the stop order becomes a *market order*.

Stop Limit Order: This is a combination of a *stop order* and a *limit order*. Once activated, it becomes a limit order which means that it can only be executed at a specific price or better.

Street expectation: The average earnings estimates made by brokers and security analysts.

Strike price: The stated price per share for which the underlying security may be purchased (in the case of a call) or sold (in the case of a put) by the option holder upon exercise of the option contract.

Support: A price level at which there is sufficient demand for a stock to cause a halt in a downward trend and turn the trend up. Support levels indicate the price at which most investors feel that prices will move higher.

Technical analysis: The method of predicting future stock price movements based on observation of historical stock price movements.

Theoretical Intermarket Margining System: Also called **TIMS**, provides broker-dealers with a program which is used to compute the baseline margin requirements for Portfolio Margin accounts.

Theoretical Value: The hypothetical value of an option as calculated by a mathematical model such as the *Black-Scholes Option Pricing Model*.

Theta: Theta is an estimate of how much the theoretical value of an option declines when there is a *passage of one day* while there is no change in the stock value or volatility. Theta is expressed as a negative number since the passage of time will decrease time value.

Time decay: A term used to describe how the theoretical value of an option *erodes* or reduces with the passage of time.

Time value: The portion of the option premium that is attributable to the amount of time remaining until the expiration of the option contract. Time value is whatever value the option has in addition to its intrinsic value.

Trading range: The spread between the high and low prices traded during a period of time.

Treasury note (one of the *treasuries*): A marketable, U.S. government debt security with a fixed interest rate and a maturity between one and ten years. T-notes can be bought either directly from the U.S. Government or through a bank.

Trend analysis: An aspect of technical analysis that tries to predict the future movement of a stock based on past data. It is based on the idea that what has happened in the past gives traders an idea of what will happen in the future. The concept is that moving with trends will lead to profits for the investor.

Trigger line / signal: Usually an exponential or simple moving average of a technical indicator which serves as a frame of reference for positive and negative divergences. For example, if the MACD indicator moves above its moving average, a bullish signal is produced.

Upside potential: Additional % of profit, as it relates to the underlying stock cost basis that can be realized if the stock price reaches the strike price at expiration. It applies to out-of-the-money strike prices.

Uptrending Stock: This is a stock increasing in price with higher highs and higher lows.

Vega: Vega is the only "Greek" not represented by a real Greek letter. It is the amount that the price of an option changes compared to a 1% change in volatility.

Velocity (of money): A term used to describe the rate at which money is exchanged from one transaction to another.

Vertical skew: Refers to the situation where individual options on a particular entity have different implied volatilities that form a pattern. The pattern usually takes one of two forms: either the higher strikes have the higher implied volatilities (a forward or positive skew) or the lower strikes have the higher implied volatilities (a reverse or negative skew).

VIX- CBOE Volatility Index: Demonstrates the market's expectation of 30-day volatility. It measures market risk and is often referred to as the *investor fear gauge*.

Volatility: This is the fluctuation, not direction, of a stock price movement. It represents the deviation of day to day price changes. It measures the speed and magnitude at which the underlying equity's price changes.

Volatility skew: The difference in implied volatility (IV) between out-of-the-money, at-the-money and in-the-money options.

Volatility smiles and smirks: Common graphical shapes that results from plotting the strike price and implied volatility of a group of options with the same expiration date.

Volume: The number of trades in a security over a period of time. On a chart, volume is usually represented as a histogram (vertical bars) below the price chart. The NYSE and Nasdaq measure volume differently. For every buyer, there is a seller: 100 shares bought = 100 shares sold. The NYSE would count this as 100 shares of volume. However, the Nasdaq would count each side of the trade and as 200 shares volume.

Volume surge: An increase in the daily trading volume of an equity equal to at least 1.5 times its normal trading volume.

Wash Sale: A wash sale loss is not deductible. A wash sale occurs when you sell a stock for a loss and, within 30 days before or after the trade, buy the same stock, or substantially the same stock. This means that if you sell a stock at $35 for a loss, and buy a $35 call option, you have a wash sale and cannot deduct the loss on the stock.

Wash trading: A wash trade (not to be confused with a wash sale) is a form of stock manipulation in which an investor simultaneously sells and buys the same financial instruments.

Watch list: A list of securities that are in consideration for investment buy/sell decisions.

Weeklys: These are equity and index options (including ETF options) that have series that are approximately one to five weeks to expiration following their initial listing.

What Now Tab of the ESOC: Calculates the returns for a package transaction where an option is bought back and another is sold.

Whisper number: The unofficial and unpublished earnings per share (EPS) forecasts that circulate among professionals on Wall Street. They were generally reserved for the favored (wealthy) clients of a brokerage.

Wilshire 5000 Total Stock Market Index: A market capitalization-weighted index composed of more than 6700 publicly traded companies. These companies must be headquartered in the U.S. and actively traded on an American stock exchange.

Yen carry trade: A strategy in which an investor sells the Japanese currency (yen) with a relatively low interest rate and uses the funds to purchase a different currency (dollar) yielding a higher interest rate. A trader using this strategy attempts to capture the difference between the rates-which can often be substantial, depending on the amount of leverage the investor chooses to use.

About the Author

Dr. Alan Ellman, author of best-selling *Cashing in on Covered Calls, Exit Strategies for Covered call Writing, Complete Encyclopedia for Covered Call Writing, Stock Investing for Students and Selling Cash-Secured Puts* has been devoting more and more of his time to teaching retail investors (Blue Collar Investors) the art and science of selling call and put options in a conservative manner. He is also a retired general Dentist from New York, a certified personal fitness trainer and a licensed Real Estate Salesperson. Dr. Ellman has also successfully completed his Series 65 certification as an Investment Advisor.

As a real estate investor, Alan owns both commercial and residential properties in Texas, Pennsylvania, New York and Florida. He has frequently been invited to speak about his successful investment properties in front of large groups of real estate investors.

In the past eight years, Alan has been increasing the time he spends educating investors in the arena of stock options and specifically covered call options. He writes a weekly journal article that is published on his website and responds to email questions from all over the world. Alan also writes financial columns for blogs and financial publications both in the US and abroad. Alan has also been interviewed on financial radio programs and has hosted dozens of seminars on this investment strategy. His goal is for you to achieve financial independence through education, motivation and due-diligence. To learn how to best accomplish these goals and become CEO of your own money visit his web site at:

www.thebluecollarinvestor.com

Index

Symbols

A

B

C

D

E

F

L

M

N

O

P

Q

R

S

T

V

W